"SILENCE IN HEAVEN

A New Paradigm for Understanding the Book of Revelation
An Appeal to the Church to Prepare for End-Time Persecution.

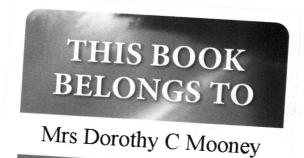

"Silence in Heaven"
A New Paradigm for Understanding the Book of Revelation
An Appeal to the Church to Prepare for End-Time Persecution.

By Gordon Lawrence. **www. silenceinheaven.org**

Order online from: gordon @ silenceinheaven.org
Order by phone: 770-682-8855

Some Scripture quotations are paraphrased by the author for emphasis.

Cover photos by Milo Smotel, Dream Image Photography, Port Huron, MI.

Library of Congress Catalog Pending
Lawrence, J. Gordon (1950 -)
        Silence in Heaven
        A New Paradigm for Understanding the Book of Revelation
        An Appeal to the Church to Prepare for End-Time Persecution
        432 pages

Printed in the United States of America

ISBN - 978-0-9830823-2-3

"SILENCE IN HEAVEN"

A New Paradigm for Understanding the Book of Revelation
An Appeal to the Church to Prepare for End-Time Persecution.

3.5 Years

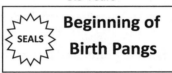

Beginning of Birth Pangs

The Covenant of Peace

3.5 Years

666 — **A Time of Tribulation**

The Mask Comes Off

 The Gathering of the Elect

The Twinkling of an Eye

 The Wrath of God Begins

The Day of the Lord

75 Days

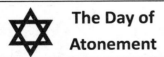 **The Day of Atonement**

The Prodigal Comes Home

1000 Years

 The Millennium

Restoring the Fortunes of Judah

Eternity

 The New Jerusalem

The Return to Eden

Gordon Lawrence
Copyright 2016

Unshaken by the storms that rage,
Over all the earth in every time,
Moves one lone Man through every age
Serene, Invincible, Sublime.

Through countless centuries He goes,
His timeless journey to complete.
Divinely calm as one who knows
The way is sure beneath His feet.

Wild storms of hate beat round His head;
Earth rocks beneath the crash of war.
Yet still, with smooth, unhurried tread,
He moves, untroubled as before

Over the wrecks of fallen states,
Through fair proud nations yet to fall,
Passes the Master of their fates,
The Silent Sovereign of them all.

Unfaltering through the darkest night,
Denied by man, God's loving man,
His face gives back the morning light,
His calm eyes see God's finished plan.

One small troubled life we live,
And then find rest in beds of clay,
But our brief day is glorified,
We have seen Jesus pass this way.

George T. Liddell

Acknowledgements

To my friend Marv Rosenthal,
author of "The Pre-Wrath Rapture of the Church"
who inspired me to write this book.
Thank you.

To my friend and managing editor, Beth Wilson,
author of "Under His Rainbow",
who has faithfully waded through 3 years of editing,
Thank you.

To my new friend and Rapture Consultant, Heidi Walker,
author of "Before God's Wrath",
who has stretched me to keep re-thinking the text,
Thank you.

To my friend Carlos Solera Ph.D (and Mary Kay)
for providing much needed wisdom and counterpoint.
Thank you.

To my Texas friend, Mike Holman,
(Serve India Ministries)
for excellent advice and insight.
Thank you.

To my friends Mel Guinn and Larry Carpenter,
whose publishing expertise
always draws me to a higher standard.
Thank you.

To my friend Doyle McDaniel,
my daily assistant and expediter,
in the never-ending challenge to produce this book.
Thank you.

To my friends in the Cross Pointe Life Group,
who have endured my teaching month after month,
in that wonderful quest to know God's truth.
Thank you.

DEDICATION

MIRACLE LADY

This book is dedicated to my wife Sandra - not just for sentimental reasons, but because her story is much more interesting than my own.

In the fall of 2007, Sandra rose systematically at 5:30 in the morning for a normal day of first grade teaching activities at Lilburn Elementary School. At age 57, she was in good health. In high school, she had been a swimmer and a gymnast, and by nature, she was a disciplined person who maintained healthy habits. On this day, however, when she got out of bed, she noticed that her back seemed weak. When she got dressed, she noticed that she had trouble holding her back erect. *"Strange,"* she thought to herself. *"I slept well and exercised yesterday."* During the day she had twinges of weaknesses that she just couldn't explain. By the next morning, she could NOT stand up without bending forward. Her posture had suddenly become that of an old woman. No, correction. Even a healthy old woman can hold her back erect. Something was terribly wrong.

We immediately went to Emory Hospital in Atlanta. We talked to orthopedics, chiropractors, physical trainers, and finally, neurologists. No one could explain what was happening. There's a term for this malady: idiopathic - meaning there is no explanation. . I was naïve enough to think that the spine was what held your back in place, but it is simply your muscles. We researched back problems and found a lady in Washington state who, while in her 40's, had similar symptoms, leading to a terribly distorted back and neck. They traced her problem to mercury amalgam poisoning in her teeth. She had 14 amalgam fillings removed, and within 2 years, she was, amazingly, back to normal. So Sandra had one amalgam removed through a very technical process of bio-hazardous extraction. We hoped and prayed for some improvement, but nothing happened. We went back to neurologists all over Atlanta. She was fitted for a full body brace, which did no good. She had electric shock treatments from chiropractors and therapeutic patches from neurologists - still, no small sign of improvement. In fact by the third month, her ability to prop herself up after leaning forward was declining. In spite of this, Sandra was a strong, faithful woman. She knew God would help her through this. She just didn't know quite how or when it would happen.

For over a year she walked on crutches, faithfully carrying out her daily duties as a loving, first grade teacher. On one occasion, friends took us to a church that was known for stories of incredible healing. They prayed over us, and then prophesied over us . . . that *when* God healed her - in His time, that God would give to us a ministry of teaching and preaching the Bible, before "crowds" of people. Though I had been a pastor and a teacher, these people knew nothing about us. And at that time, my only ministry was a small group of eight people, and my architectural job kept me busy with another four staff members. Though I appreciated the prophetic word, I had no ambition to speak before crowds of people. Nevertheless, we left that meeting encouraged that God had a plan for Sandra's life.

We then called the renowned Mao Clinic in Rochester, Minnesota, and requested an appointment. They obliged, and we hit the road running. When we arrived at the hospital, we were immediately engaged in a different kind of examination. For four days, they alternated, almost hourly, between doctor interviews and testing, including an EMG test (electromyography), which is a nerve conduction test. This was not the first time she had done an EMG - inserting multiple needles all over your back to determine the levels of sensitivity. At the end of the process, the neurologist gave us the bad news: they had diagnosed a muscle disease. We knew the prognosis: muscle deterioration - maybe isolated - maybe spreading to other muscles in the body. Needless to say, it was a long 15 hour ride home. Though somehow, we didn't quite believe Mao's diagnosis, since she had passed the EMG test previously in Atlanta.

Back to Emory we went. Sure enough, Emory confirmed. The one thing they DID know. She did NOT have a muscle disease. Dr. Glass, the head of the Emory Neurology, promised Sandra that they WOULD find a solution to her problem. About that time, an elderly doctor, the senior neurologist on staff, walked by and took notice of Sandra's case. He said that Sandra had a movement disorder called Truncal Dystonia, which affects the trunk of the body, disabling the back muscles to do their job. Their recommendation: brain surgery - a procedure well known to Parkinson's patients, called DBS, or Deep Brain Stimulation. In this procedure, contacts are implanted into the brain, then stimulated by electrical charges. Sandra was cautioned however, not to be too optimistic. They gave her a 50% chance of getting 50% better.

The day came for surgery. Her head was harnessed in a frame called a "halo" insuring that she could not move during surgery. She laid on a cold slab of metal for 8 hours during surgery. Since the brain does not feel pain, she was awake for the entire procedure. They numbed the skull slightly and then drilled two holes five inches deep into her brain tissue. There they implanted 3 metal contacts in the basil ganglia of the brain, and then connected the wires behind her ear to a battery back in the abdomen. For Parkinson's patients, this is an easier procedure because they can adjust the electrical impulse to immediately affect the tremors. In Sandra's case, there were no tremors, and therefore no means of identifying a positive response. We were told to wait patiently for weeks, or months, until one day the contacts would fire up the weakened muscles. We claimed one verse of scripture, Luke 13:13, as our hope for a normal life: *"And Jesus laid His hands on her; and immediately she was made erect again and began glorifying God. "*

We did wait, faithfully praying that God would one day energize her back and allow her the simple joy of walking. On the "adjustment" trip to Emory, the PA was programming her brain while giving her the instructions to tap her fingers together rapidly. She tapped and they programmed. Her tapping became slower and slower, and finally she said, "I think my arm is going to . . . " and her arms dropped to her side. They were programming the parameters of the electrical charges to the brain. We were encouraged that there was a cause and affect that could be measured.

Eight months after surgery and 3 1/2 years after the initial symptoms, Sandra called me one day from school, and with much emotion in her voice, she said, *"I'm walking! I'm walking! Thank you Jesus, I'm walking!* The long journey was over. Sandra likes to say **"My test became my testimony."** God allowed Sandra to honor him through her faithfulness. And Sandra allowed God to use high tech, 21st century brain surgery to cure what otherwise would have been a lifelong crippling illness. And now, every two days, she charges a Medtronic battery pack implanted into her abdomen. If the charge was somehow drained, we are told that she would go back to a crippling lifestyle. And if the "grid" goes down, you'll find us looking for a car battery or a generator to keep her charged up. Thank you Emory, thank you Medtronic, and thank you, most of all, to Jehovah Jireh, the God who heals. Emory Hospital tells us that Sandra is the "poster child" for Truncal Dystonia, and her case is now a regular part of the curriculum for training tomorrow's neurologists. Today, Sandra enjoys life as a retired school teacher, visiting the grandkids, assisting me in the writing of this book, and . . . working out in the gym! Her healing is truly a miracle of God's grace, and her faith is truly a testimony to me and the world that *"faith is the assurance of things hoped for, and the evidence of things not seen."*

> Luke 13:13, *"And Jesus laid His hands on her;*
> *and she was made erect again and began glorifying God."*

In Memoriam

Marlon Charles Helms
July 1, 1955 - May 4, 2014

On the morning of Saturday, May 3, everything was normal at the Helms household. Marlon and wife Cathy (my sister) went to Home Depot to purchase a new riding lawnmower, and then returned home to prepare for the afternoon birthday party for grand-daughters Alivia and Ava. Marlon had been working for the past month trimming the limbs of a large oak tree in his back-yard. On this particular Saturday, he had been working diligently with a pole saw to cut down one more large limb. An hour before the party, he thought he might be able to finish off the limb and then get dressed. Tragedy came crashing down on the family that day when the big limb twisted at the last moment and struck Marlon on the forehead. He died the next day from severe head injuries.

This beloved father of three will be remembered for his quiet, straight-forward approach to life. He was a builder, a horticulturalist and an inspector for the Housing and Urban Development Authority.

The interesting twist in this story relates to Marlon's kidney.   As a deacon at Idlewild Baptist Church in Mint Hill, NC, he volunteered several months prior to take a church member, Mark Kelly, to his kidney dialysis appointment. Mark's only kidney was failing, and ironically, the weekend of Marlon's accident, Mark's health had taken a turn for the worse. Upon Marlon's death early Sunday morning, Cathy his wife (also a nurse), asked the nurses to try to arrange for a kidney donation for Mark Kelly. The nurses informed her that matches are rare, and especial-ly unlikely for two families who just happened to share the same church.

To everyone's surprise, the match came back 100%. Marlon, whose organs had now been donated to dozens of recipients, was able to save the life of this man whom he had befriended just months ago.

With God, there is no such thing as coincidence. We can only marvel at how a series of events can continue to link together against all odds. Marlon's son Aaron had just been promoted at Textron Inc. as a Sales Director for Cessna Citation Jets. He had been on the job for only 2 weeks and had told his father: *"Dad, one of these days, I'm going to take you on a ride in a Cessna jet."*

The week of Marlon's death, the transplant team packed up Marlon's heart and shipped it to a thankful recipient in New York. The means of transportation . . . was a Cessna jet.

The promise of Romans 8:28 continues to echo through the ages, and give us hope in the midst of devastating heartbreak: *"And God causes all things to work together for good, to those who love Him and are the called according to his purpose. "*

TABLE OF CONTENTS

AUTHOR'S NOTES

The book called Revelation is a cryptic and complex book, full of mystery and symbols and images. Most readers approach this book with a sense of ominous obligation. They say to themselves, *"I must read the book;"* but once they begin, their anticipation turns to confusion, and they conclude *"It's too complicated. I just can't understand"*. Perhaps that is why John begins the book by saying, *"Blessed is he who reads and hears the words of prophecy."* The language and imagery of Revelation are like a foreboding moat that surrounds a beautiful castle. As with most scriptural reading, part of the key to understanding is repetition. Read it over and over, and eventually, the Holy Spirit will enlighten your mind and warm your heart.

There is one image in this book that will pave the way to your understanding. In some ways, the 400 pages of this book are written as a musical overture to guide you to this single image. If you will faithfully commit to understanding this image, the rest of Revelation will begin to fall into place for you.

Imagine . . . that there is a scroll in heaven that only Jesus can open. The scroll is written on both sides and is closed by seven wax seals that line the vertical outside edge of this ragged and ancient document. Systematically, Jesus peels off one seal at a time, revealing a series of events that expose the world to apocalyptic drama. When He peels off the sixth seal, the world is plunged into darkness . . . and then followed . . . by a blinding light which reveals that King Jesus has broken through the skies to rescue His beloved Church. But the drama is not over. Jesus then peals away the seventh seal, and surprisingly, nothing happens. Suddenly, the perfect splendor of heaven's harmonious angelic choir is muted and silent. For the first and only time in eternal history, there is **SILENCE IN HEAVEN**. John waits and nothing happens. For seconds, leading to minutes, the myriads of angels are frozen in formation, silently waiting in some sort of fearful anticipation of the next event. Finally, the suspense of 30 long minutes of deadly silence is ended by seven angels, who step forward holding trumpets that will soon sound the alarm, one by one. As the scroll opens wide, the apostle John looks on in horror as he sees and now understands the meaning of the seventh seal. Jehovah God, the loving and all knowing Creator of heaven and earth, has finally passed judgment on an unrepentant world. Malachi 4:5 calls this "the great and terrible Day of the Lord." **THE WRATH OF GOD IS ABOUT TO BEGIN.** The image is now complete. The scroll is open. Jesus has rescued the Church, and "all heaven breaks loose" as God prepares to destroy the planet. He must first rescue the remnant of Israel, and then refashion earth once more, into the final, perfect image of His love. The clock is winding down, as we approach those final days.

King Solomon was right in Ecclesiastes 12:12, when he said, *"Be warned, my son: the writing of many books is endless, and excessive devotion to books wearies the body."* The study of last things (eschatology) can be a wearisome process. The book of Revelation requires digging deeper, asking harder questions and resolving that some things are speculation, and some other things will never be known. If there is one verse of scripture that has driven my process of enquiry more than any other, it is Ephesians 1:9,10:

He made known to us the mystery of His will,
according to His kind intention which He purposed in Him,
with a view to an administration suitable to the fullness of the times, that is,
the summing up of all things in Christ,
things in the heavens and things on the earth.

Those words fascinate me: "the summing up of all things in Christ". For the unbeliever, this should give a clear WARNING: "that Christ will be the focus of all eternity." For the believer, this should be a great and wonderful PROMISE . . . ."that Christ will be the focus of all eternity!"

The next page provides an outline of this book. This is not your typical book on Revelation. In fact, it probably needs some explanation to help you navigate the pages. My strategy in writing this book has been rather eclectic, and I will suggest to you three forms that the book will take:

1) expositional. Most books are lengthy chapters which expose much commentary and then footnote the scripture. This book is just the opposite. My intent is to expose the full text of scripture (every verse in Revelation) and then provide selective commentary.

2) encyclopedic. This book does not read like a book. Sometimes it reads like an encyclopedia. There are many pages that provide necessary background information that build a foundation for understanding biblical prophecy.

3) editorial. Although I believe this book has much substance, my intent is not to provide the most profound scholarship on the planet. My intent is to provide personal editorial insight that God has made meaningful to me, in the hopes that it will be equally meaningful to you.

Songwriters Phillips, Craig and Dean describe the end-time as follows: **"At the Concert of the Age, the Great I Am Takes Center Stage."** With this as my theme, and using musical metaphor, my outline will simply follow the form of "Prelude" and "Finale." Hopefully, your imagination can hear the harmonic thunder as Heaven prepares to sound the final trumpet.

I. THE **HISTORIC PRELUDE**

The first four chapters of this book are the warm-up act to prepare you for the book of Revelation. **Chapter One** introduces Israel as the grand and glorious vehicle that God would use to interpret salvation to the world. **Chapter Two** introduces a little known character named Amalek, who was the first foreigner to fight against Moses. God promised to battle with the descendants of Amalek throughout human history. **Chapter Three** is a thumbnail tour of the book of Daniel, highlighting the prophetic themes that surface again later in Revelation. **Chapter Four** defines the majestic words of Jesus as He speaks of His own Second Coming.

A. Israel, the Apple of God's Eye.
B. The Spirit of Amalek
C. Daniel, the Prophetic Link
D. Jesus and The Olivet Discourse

II. THE **DRAMATIC FINALE**

The Historic Prelude prepared you for a "study Bible" version of Revelation. Please note this outline is different than any you have seen before. Two things make that true. One, "The Gathering of the Elect", is another way of saying the Rapture. Most interpretations will place the rapture PRIOR to the seventieth week of Daniel. Secondly, "The Day of Atonement" is not typically a chapter designation in the book of Revelation. This author will place much emphasis on the salvation of Israel at the seventh trumpet. The emphasis in this book, over and over again, will be this seven part division, continually reinforced. As the apostle says to us in 2 Peter 1:13, *"I stir you up by way of reminder."* The **First Four Chapters** below will carry you through the mysterious seventieth week of Daniel. **Chapter 5** is the mysterious 30 day75 day period spoken of in Daniel 12:11. **Chapter Six** is the mysterious thousand year period in which the nations of the earth bend a knee to Israel and King Jesus. And finally, **Chapter Seven** reveals the consummation of the ages, which brings God's Church and God's Chosen together as God's Children. The Journey is about to begin.

1. Beginning of Birth Pangs
2. The Great Tribulation
3. The Gathering of the Elect
4. The Wrath of God Begins
5. The Day of Atonement
6. The Millennial Reign of Israel
7. The New Jerusalem

The Bible teaches that Jesus the Messiah came to the earth 2000 years ago. He taught, healed and performed miracles. He died for the sins of the world, He rose from the dead, and He promised to come again in the last days to claim His bride, the Church - and to set in motion the judgment of the unrepentant world.

The dominant theology of the Second Coming of Christ among Western evangelicals is called the Pre-Tribulation Rapture. The implication of this teaching is that Christ will rapture the Church PRIOR to a seven year period of global crisis which ushers in the deceptive rule of the Anti-Christ and climaxes with the Wrath of God and the Battle of Armageddon. PreTrib Rapture teaching believes that the Church will be spared the time of Tribulation. Another word for Tribulation is persecution. Jesus prophesied that believers through the centuries would be persecuted. Why should we believe that the Church will not be purified during a time of persecution that is Satan's final stand against the Kingdom of God?

I grew up in a conservative, evangelical, Bible-believing church that taught Pre-Tribulation theology. All of my heroes in church ministry have believed in the tradition of PreTrib Theology: MacArthur, Walvoord, Pentecost, Ryrie, Jeremiah, LaHaye, Van Impe, Lindsay, Hagee, Ankerburg, etc. My seminary training exposed me to Pre-Trib, Mid-Trib, and Post-Trib theology but my primary influences were still grounded in PreTrib theology. I have taught Pre-trib eschatology for years - though I confess, I struggled to make sense of it. And then I was introduced to an interpretation called "pre-wrath" rapture that got my attention 16 years ago. I studied it, and challenged it, and asked lots of hard questions. Finally, I embraced the "pre-wrath" position as the most scripturally accurate interpretation of end-time eschatology. This book will be my contribution to an attempt at honest, objective Biblical investigation that will provide a clear alternative to the Pre-Tribulation Theology.

TRUTH AND SPECULATION.

It is very important when studying the prophecy of Jesus' Second Coming to acknowledge that there are two categories into which our interpretations fall. One is absolute, rock-solid truth. The other is speculation. There is no doubt that Jesus will return to gather His beloved saints in the end time. There is sanctified speculation, however, in this volume and all others, as to how and when and where that will take place. Our goal is to put the pieces of truth together in such a way that you can clearly separate "what will be" from "what might be". With this acknowledgement, I try to remain true to scripture in my interpretation.

"FOREVER KING"

Newsong, Eddie Carswell, 1988
Word Records, Copyright, 2009

Humor me. As you begin this study of the book of Revelation,
go to the following internet site, and listen to this majestic song:
youtube newsong forever king, say yes album
You'll be blessed.

Before the kingdom, You were the king
And when there was nothing, You were everything
Before foundations stood, Before evil, before good,
You were forever.
Before the night, before the day,
Before the man was formed from clay.
Before life, before death, before the first breath,
You were forever.

Forever King, You're everything
My heart has need to know
My first, my last, my future, my past
The strength of all my hope.
You're the rock of all the ages, eternal timeless Savior
Forever King, You're Everything, Forever.

After the stars desert the sky,
after the rivers all run dry
When the earth is no more, and the heaven's roar,
You'll be forever.
Then we'll gather round Your throne
Of every nation all Your own, and in one accord,
Oh we'll praise You Lord. You are forever.

Forever king, You're everything
My heart has need to know
My first, my last, my future, my past
The strength of all my hope.
You're the rock of all the ages, eternal timeless Savior
Forever King, You're Everything, Forever.
You're the rock of all the ages, eternal timeless Savior
Forever King, You're Everything, Forever King.

Four Goals of this Book

1. To prove that Matthew 24:30,31 is the Second Coming of Christ and the Rapture of the Church.

> The popular end-time theology known as the Pre-Tribulation Rapture identifies this passage of scripture as the <u>END</u> of the seventieth week of Daniel.
> * The Pre-Wrath Position will explain that Matthew 24:30,31 CANNOT be the end of the age, because it clearly follows the sixth seal in Revelation 6.

2. To explain that the opening of the Revelation 5 Scroll unleashes the Wrath of God.

> The popular end-time theology known as the Pre-Tribulation Rapture claims that the seven seals and the seven trumpets are both part of the first half of the Seventieth week of Daniel.
> * The Pre-Wrath position will explain that the scroll has to be completely open before the Trumpet Judgments begin.

3. To prove that the Great Tribulation and the Wrath of God are two separate parts of the seventieth week of Daniel.

> The popular end-time theology known as the Pre-Tribulation Rapture claims that The Great Tribulation and the Wrath of God are the same in the last 3.5 years of The seventieth week of Daniel.
> * Pre-Wrath teaching will prove that the Great Tribulation and the Wrath of God are not synonymous, but rather, are two very separate events.

4. To explain that the Church of the 21st Century will experience the Tribulation of Satan but not the Wrath of God.

> The popular end-time theology known as the Pre-Tribulation Rapture claims that The Church will escape the time known as Tribulation and will be raptured into the heavens before the Tribulation begins.
> * The Pre-Wrath position will prove that the true Church will endure the Tribulation of Satan, and it will emerge as either the Philadelphia church that Perseveres, or the Smyrna Church that faces Persecution, possibly leading to death.

Y'SHUA HA MASHIAH

In a recent trip to Israel, I was an assistant tour host with the partners of Crossfire, a professional basketball ministry that challenges college teams and shares their testimony worldwide. Randy Shepherd and Jamie Johnson are young men of uncompromising faith, and to watch them in action is amazing. Randy wanted to share his faith with the young Jewish and Arab boys of Jerusalem, so he asked me what he could say to them. I suggested he say, "Yshua ha Meshiach", which means "Jesus is the Messiah." Randy practiced for two days trying to untie his tongue as he articulated this Hebrew phrase. The day came when we

walked through the Damascus Gate, weaving our way through the narrow marketplace past the vendors, shoppers and pickpockets. We approached a large open space with an elevated platform. Randy stepped into place and began spinning his basketball on one finger. Within seconds, a hundred little Arab/Jew boys were watching in rapt attention. Randy then pulled a toothbrush out of his pocket and without missing a beat, he began brushing his teeth while balancing the ball on the end of the toothbrush. The crowd continued to grow in a circus-like atmosphere of entertainment and anticipation. Then Randy pulled a razor out of his pocket and began imaginary shaving motions while balancing

the spinning basketball on the end of the razor. The little boys loved it, and Randy had succeeded in welding the crowd together. Now that he had their attention, in one fluid motion he dropped the ball and razor to his side and boldly announced these words - "Yshua ha Meshiach! Yshua ha Meshiach!" In what seemed like a nuclear moment, the crowd of 300 boys from ages 5 to 15 suddenly vanished, like a bomb had dropped into their midst. The very mention of Jesus was enough to scare the crowd into scattering as if a terrorist had just launched a kazam rocket in their midst. The name of Jesus is despised and feared among the pagan nations. But someday, all the world will kneel before King Jesus and understand that He is the Preeminent Personality in all of human history. Every tongue will sing the chorus that Jesus Christ is the Messiah.

Primary New Testament References

FOR THE SECOND COMING

The study of Christ's Second Coming requires constant cross referencing of verses.   At some point, Bible students speak in "code". They refer to a verse by the mere mention of its address, expecting that the listener understands. For this reason, knowing the location of each of the following passages of scripture will become critical to "keeping up" with the discussion. This is the "short list", by no means exhaustive of the many verses, Old Testament and New, that will become the foundation of studying Jesus' return.

Matthew 24 - The Olivet Discourse.

> The Primary Text, Jesus' own words, which introduce us to Beginning of Birth Pangs, Tribulation, The Gathering of the Elect and the Wrath of God.

Luke 17:26 - Until the Day that Noah Entered the Ark

> The passage about deliverance and judgment.

1 Corinthians 15:51,52 - The Twinkling of an Eye

> . . . at the last trumpet, the dead will be raised, we will be changed.

1 Thessalonians 4:16 - The Shout, the Voice, the Trumpet

> The Classic rapture passage. The Lord will descend and we will be caught up with Him.

1 Thessalonians 5:1-9. The Thief in the Night and Not Destined for Wrath

> The primary passage which deals with the imminent return of Christ.

2 Thessalonians 2:1-4. The Apostasy Comes First

> Paul teaches that apostasy and the man of lawlessness must precede the Second Coming.

Revelation 6 - The Sixth Seal: The Sun Moon and Stars

> The cosmic disturbance which precedes the return of Christ.

Revelation 7 - The Saints Arrive in Heaven

> The multitude which no one could count comes out of the Great Tribulation.

THE FIRST TEN CHAPTERS

Mnemonic devices are sometimes necessary to help us remember the sequence of events in a long narrative. The following seven word phrases are intended to playfully give you an overview of the Book of Revelation by introducing you to clues in the first ten chapters. Some pneumonic devices help you memorize a sequence. These ten points are a warmup exercise, rather than a list to memorize. Hey, that rhymes too!. Get ready to start: here's the clue.

Chapter One. God the Father Will Exalt the SON.

Chapter Two. Of the Seven Churches, There are TWO.

Chapter Three. Be Faithful Church, A Crown You'll SEE.

Chapter Four. John Looked Up to See a DOOR.

Chapter Five. The Lion and the Lamb are ALIVE.

Chapter Six. The Scroll is Opened, The Seals UNFIXED.

Chapter Seven. The Raptured Saints Just Arrived in HEAVEN.

Chapter Eight. The Wrath of God at the GATE.

Chapter Nine. Trumpets of Wrath They Are Not MINE.

Chapter Ten. The Mighty Angel, Jesus, Will Soon WIN.

FROM BONDAGE TO DELIVERANCE

The best known story in the Old Testament is a foreshadowing of the seventieth week of Daniel. God has commanded the Jewish people to remember the dark days of Egyptian bondage, and to celebrate their rescue from Pharaoh and their eventual destiny in the Promised Land. The entire Exodus narrative is a glimpse of things to come. Notice carefully that the order of the rescue of the nation of Israel parallels the last seven years.

BIRTH PANGS - The 400 Years of Egyptian Slavery

> Bondage is the only way to describe the oppression that the Children of God experienced. There will come another time when God's children will begin to see a global bondage as we approach the horizon of history.

TRIBULATION - The Ten Plagues

> Though many have made the comparison of the plagues with the trumpet and and bowl judgments, these are merely the foreshadowing of a greater wrath that is yet to come.

THE GATHERING OF THE ELECT - The Blood of the Lamb

> God always has a remnant and He always rescues the remnant. The Children of Israel were rescued because of their faith to believe what Moses had commanded. The Lamb that saved them then will rescue us once again.

THE WRATH OF GOD BEGINS - The Angel of Death

> As with the stories of Noah and Lot, deliverance came just before judgment. Pharaoh had been warned and he refused to repent. The death of every first born is a foreshadowing of the judgment that the defiant world will feel in the last days.

THE DAY OF ATONEMENT - Sinai, The Giving of the Law

> The contract with God began with the Ten Commandments. The clock was reset, and Israel had the opportunity to take the path of obedience. 3000 died that day, and many generations would pass before Israel would truly be saved.

THE MILLENNIUM - The Promised Land

> Jerusalem today is still the center of the global stage. God promised them a land many years ago, and they still live under foreign oppression. But there will come a time when Israel shall rule the nations.

THE NEW JERUSALEM - The Temple of God

> The ark of the covenant and the temple were supposed to be the dwelling place of God during the ancient days of Israel. No longer will there be merely a symbol of His presence, for God will inhabit the praise of His people.

The Outline of Revelation

Revelation 1 - The Triumphant Christ

In the Spirit on the Lord's Day	1-11
One like a Son of Man	12-20

Revelation 2 and 3 - The Seven Churches

Ephesus, the loveless church	2:1-7
Smyrna, the persecuted church	8-11
Pergamum, the compromising church	12-17
Thyatira, the prostituted church	18-29
Sardis, the dead church	3:1-6
Philadelphia, the persevering church	7:13
Laodicea, the moderate church	14-22

Revelation 4 - John Sees the Throne in Heaven

John is invited to Heaven	1
John sees heavenly throne	2-6
The Four Living Creatures	7-11

Revelation 5 - The Scroll

Who is Worthy? No one is worthy	1-4
The Lion is worthy	5-10
Myriad number of Angels	11-14

Revelation 6 - The Six Seals

The First Three Seals - Birth Pangs	1-6
Seals Four and Five, Tribulation	7-11
The Sixth Seal - Cosmic Disturbance	12-17

Revelation 7 - The 144,000 and The Raptured Saints

The Calm Before the Storm,	1-3
The 144,000 godly Men of Israel	4-8
Raptured Saints arrive in Heaven	7-12
The Elder introduces the Great Multitude	13-17

Revelation 8 and 9 - The Seven Trumpets of God's Wrath

Silence in Heaven	8:1-6
The Wrath of God Begins	8:7-13
Angels 1-4	
The Torment of Scorpion	9:1-12
Angels 5	
The River Euphrates	9:13-21
Angel 6	

Revelation 10 - The Little Scroll

The Strong Angel and Little Book	1-7
John eats the Scroll	8-11

Revelation 11 - The Temple, Two Witnesses and Trumpet

Measuring the Temple of God	1-2
The Two Witnesses	3-12
The Seventh Trumpet	13-19

Revelation 12 - The Woman, the Dragon and War in Heaven

Past History: The Woman Israel	1-5
Future History: The War in Heaven	7-17

Revelation 13 - The Dragon, Beast and False Prophet

The Beast of Seven Heads and Ten Horns	1-10
The False Prophet	11-18

Revelation 14 - The Three Angels and the 144,000

The Coronation of King Jesus	1-13
The Battle of Armageddon	14-20

Revelation 15 - The Gathering for War

The Victorious Sing to the Lamb	1-4
The Temple of the Tabernacle is Opened	5-8

Revelation 16 - The Seven Bowls and Armageddon

The Conclusion of God's Wrath	1-21
Bowls 1-7	

THE CHRONOLOGY OF REVELATION

1. The Beginning of Birth Pangs.
    Revelation 1.   The Triumphant Christ
    Revelation 2 and 3.   The Seven Churches
    Revelation 4.   John Sees the Throne in Heaven
    Revelation 5.   Who is Worthy to Open the Scroll
    Revelation 6a.   The First Three Seals - The Beginning of Sorrows

2. The Great Tribulation.
    Revelation 6b.   Seals Four and Five
    Revelation 11a.   The Temple and Two Witnesses
    Revelation 12.   The Woman, The Dragon and War in Heaven
    Revelation 13.   The Dragon, the Beast and the False Prophet
    Revelation 17.   The Harlot and the Eighth King

3. The Gathering of the Elect.
    Revelation 6c.   The Sixth Seal
    Revelation 7.   The 144,000 and the Raptured Saints

4. The Wrath of God Begins.
    Revelation 8 and 9.   The Seventh Seal and the Six Trumpets

5. The Day of Atonement.
    Revelation 10.   The Mighty Angel and the Little Scroll
    Revelation 11b.   Jesus Reclaims the Earth, the Seventh Trumpet
    Revelation 14.   The Three Angels and the 144,000
    Revelation 15.   Before the Bowls
    Revelation 16.   The Seven Bowls of God's Wrath
    Revelation 18.   Babylon the Great City is Fallen
    Revelation 19   The Marriage Supper, Then Armageddon

6. The Millennium.
    Revelation 20.   A Thousand Years

7. The New Jerusalem.
    Revelation 21.   The New Earth
    Revelation 22.   Forever in the Kingdom

A Tribute to Robert Van Kampen

*"Scripture was written for us all,
and scholars have no corner on its truth.
Those who sincerely and diligently
seek God's truth can find it."*

ROBERT VAN KAMPEN

1938 - 1999 (60 years)

Robert Van Kampen was a Chicago stockbroker, known as "the charger", who pioneered a program of insurance coverage for tax-exempt bond funds. He founded Van Kampen Merritt Investments and eventually sold his company to Xerox for 200 million dollars. He then turned his attention to eternal investments. He began a 14 year quest to study scripture and unlock some of the riddles in the book of Revelation. Friends say that he frequently rode the L train in Chicago just to ask Moody Bible Institute professors questions while they were riding to work. He had a large wall in his den dedicated to positioning note cards of scripture that strategically located every verse related to end-time study. With the counsel of many scholars, Van Kampen and friend Marv Rosenthal introduced a new position in theology called the "pre-wrath" rapture. He then wrote a masterful 500 page exposition called *"The Sign,"* as well as a novel called "The Fourth Reich." He died at age 60 awaiting a heart transplant, and his family now oversees his trust and manages the Scriptorium, the largest collection of ancient Bibles in the world, housed at the Holy Land Experience in Orlando, Florida. Van Kampen turned to his friend Marv Rosenthal as a potential ally in this new quest to take on the entire theological establishment. The Pre-trib Rapture, with help from the "Left Behind" series, was firmly embedded in the evangelical movement as the dominant rapture position. Who could imagine that the paradigm was about to shift?

A Tribute to Marvin J. Rosenthal

"Upon the earth and in the heavens, there is a war raging for the souls of men. This war is spiritual and invisible, the results eternal and irreversible. The origin, purpose and consummation of human history form the tapestry of this universal warfare."

Marvin J. Rosenthal

1935 -

Van Kampen turned to his friend Marv Rosenthal, the notable Executive Director of Friends of Israel ministries as a source of counsel. Van Kampen told Rosenthal he had determined the scriptural timing of the Rapture in the book of Revelation. Rosenthal was not interested. As a former Dallas Theological student, he was a staunch Pre-Trib advocate. But after a year of Van Kampen's earnest plea to study his research, Rosenthal finally conceded some time to review Van Kampen's position. As a Jewish Christian, Marv brought a new perspective to the challenge. Marv's scholarly study and his quest for truth forced him to agree with Van Kampen. Marv nobly resigned his position with Friends of Israel because he himself had crafted their doctrinal statement, which embodied a pre-trib position. Marv then rocked the theological world in 1990 with his uniquely Jewish insight into the Second Coming of Christ. His book, *"The Pre-Wrath Rapture of the Church",* along with Van Kampen's work, began to force pastors and scholars to honestly re-evaluate their eschatology. Pastors around the world have thanked Marv for standing firm at the risk of losing his reputation and his ministry. The Pre-Wrath movement now challenges the Church to prepare for the possibility that believers may indeed suffer tribulation. A fresh view of this subject will surprise you.

"When Jesus returns,
it will be to execute judgment on those
who have rejected Him throughout the ages.
At His first coming He was the Lamb,
who came to take away the sins of the world,
but at the Second Coming,
He is "faithful and true"
in carrying out every promise He ever made.
His blazing eyes will pierce the hearts
of those who denied Him,
and His clothing will be stained
with the blood of His enemies."

David Jeremiah
"Escape the Coming Night"

INTRODUCTION

"THOSE WHO HAVE INSIGHT"

Lambert Dolphin is a brilliant astro-physicist who was associated with the Stanford Research Institute in Menlo Park, California for a period of 30 years. Since 1987, he has dedicated his time to aligning the infinite models of time and space with his understanding of Biblical teaching as a follower of Christ. On one occasion, Dolphin was speaking to a distinguished group of international physicists and he made the following declaration:

"Ladies and Gentlemen. I have given my life to the understanding of micro and macro models of the universe. I come before you today to announce that I have found the building block of all material substance. It is not a cell, it is not a molecule, and it is not even an atom. This element has existed since the beginning of time, and without this single element, the universe could not exist! The element that I want to introduce to you is . . . . . ." and he paused. The crowd waited on the edge of their seats, anxious to hear this ground breaking discovery that might well revolutionize the world as we know it today. With high regard for Lambert Dolphin, they leaned forward to capture every syllable of this announcement.

"The building block of the universe is . . . . The WOG."

The scientific world was sure that Dolphin had just introduced them to a new paradigm in quantum physics, or string theorem, or light amplification. They couldn't wait to hear more. In a room full of geniuses that were waiting for deep academic insight, Dolphin simple declared the following:

> *The Bible says, "By faith we understand*
> *that the worlds were prepared by the <u>Word of God,</u>*
> *so that what is seen was not made out of things which are visible."*

"The building block that I am talking about, the WOG, is . . . the Word of God."

Oops. Not exactly what a group of politically correct, erudite intellectuals was wanting to hear. But he's right, of course! Hebrews 11:3 holds the simple, yet profound key to our understanding of molecular biology. Christ is the glue that holds the universe together. Colossians 1:16,17 says: *"For by Him all things were created, both in the heavens and on earth, visible and invisible, whether thrones or dominions or rulers or authorities--all things have been created through Him and for Him. He is before all things . . .* (watch the next seven words)
and in Him all things hold together.

This book is dedicated to the proposition that Jesus is the glue that holds the macro planets and the micro cells together in one unified act of incomparable universal cohesion. I know that it's not popular, nor is it politically correct to exalt Jesus over other religions. After all, we have to level the playing field and keep things neutral for all those folks who just think it's not fair or equitable to lift one religion above another. That is my segue to say that Christianity is NOT a religion. It is a relationship with Jesus - a personal, intimate relationship contingent upon a commitment of faith - faith to believe in the death, burial and resurrection of Christ; and then to believe that if we merely ask, the Holy Spirit of God will take up residence in our lives, and give us fulfillment that defies explanation or understanding in the natural order. This book is based on an ideology that upholds the following orthodox beliefs:

I believe in Jesus' Pre-Existence. Before the foundations of the world, Jesus was there, administering with the Father, the creation of all things.

I believe in Jesus' Incarnation. He emptied himself of divine attributes, and took on human flesh, in order that He who knew no sin could become sin for our righteousness sake.

I believe in Jesus' Ministry. He walked the streets and villages - teaching, ministering, healing and preaching a message of repentance that introduced mankind to the kingdom of God.

I believe in Jesus' Crucifixion. He died a cruel death and took upon himself the sins of the world, in order that He could pay the penalty for our sins.

I believe in Jesus' Resurrection. He cheated death and defied the natural order by rising from the dead to become what scripture calls "the firstfruits of the resurrection."

I believe in Jesus' Ascension. It was necessary for Jesus to return to Heaven so that He could send the Holy Spirit, the Comforter - and indwell each of us with God's presence and power.

I believe in Jesus' Second Coming. He promised to return for His bride the Church. He promised to restore the prodigal nation of Israel and He promised to exact judgment on the unrepentant. We live in anticipation of this future reality.

My wife Sandra grew up in First Baptist Church of Tucker, Georgia - in the vicinity known as the "buckle" on the Bible belt. She was at church 3 times a week growing up, every service, every sermon. And yet, she confesses that she did not know until she went off to college that Jesus was actually going to return to earth to consummate human history. Is that possible? Unfortunately yes. It's not popular to preach on the Second Coming of Christ. To teach the book of Revelation is considered to be abstract and confusing.

The following are two questions that the Church needs to answer.
1) How strong a believer can you possibly be if you don't know **ANYTHING** about the Second Coming of Christ?
2) And second, how much stronger can you be if you are **COMMITTED** to understanding the truth of Jesus' Second Coming?

Perhaps the answer to both questions depends on how clearly and how simply the substance of the Second Coming of Christ is taught. For that reason, I want to suggest a new paradigm for learning about Revelation. Here's an oversimplification of the two stages that I think should be the framework for understanding Revelation:

1) The Good Guys Win.
2) The Bad Guys Lose.

Yeah, maybe that's a little too simplistic. So let's try again. It was ABC sportscaster Jim McKay who popularized the term, "the thrill of victory, the agony of defeat." Here's my suggestion for a two tiered approach to teaching and learning the book of Revelation.

Rule # 1. Read and study FIRST only those chapters in Revelation that apply to the Second Coming of Christ. Chapters 1-11, 14, 20 and 21 introduce you to the seven churches, the scroll, the seven seals, the gathering of the elect, the trumpet judgment, the rescue of the nation of Israel, the Millennium and the New Jerusalem. I would recommend you read these chapters 7 times before you even begin to **THINK** about reading the rest of the chapters. When you fully understand the beauty and simplicity of Christ's return to earth . . . THEN you can learn about the villains of the story. This section we will call "The Thrill of Victory."

Rule #2. After you have learned about Christ's rapture (the gathering) and return for Israel, then you may proceed to read about the following: The Anti-Christ, the beast, the ten nations, ten toes and the Great Harlot Babylon. The typography, complexity and utter darkness of the last chapters (12, 13, 15, 16, 17, 18 and 19) of Revelation should be read only after you have thoroughly understood the first chapters . This section we will call "The Agony of Defeat."

God gave the nation of Israel three feasts that symbolize the summing up of all things. The outline for this book reflects the three Fall Feasts of Israel.

1) The Thrill of Victory

A. Gathering His Church	(which reflects The Feast of Trumpets)
B. Restoring His Chosen	(which reflects The Day of Atonement)
C. Uniting His Children	(which reflects The Feast of Tabernacles)

Rule # 2 introduces the villains in God's story of redemption and revelation in Satan's cosmic quest to usurp the power and position of the God of the universe. When you read Chapters 12,13, 15-19, you get a taste of the origin of evil and Satan's pervasive desire to corrupt and conquer God's crowning act of creation.

2) The Agony of Defeat

   A. **The Spirit of Amalek**
   B. **The Sword of Antiochus**
   C. **The Scourge of Anti-Christ**

These three men represent the worst of all the villains throughout history. But remember Rule #1 and Rule #2. Study the book of Revelation to learn about the Second Coming of Christ: Gathering His Church, Restoring His Chosen and Uniting His Children. Only then should you venture into the dark riddles of the false trinity and their insidious plot to undermine the good things of God.

GOOD BIBLE STUDY MEANS

Asking Hard Questions

If you're going to study the book of Revelation, you MUST be prepared to ask hard questions. Set aside your traditions and your pre-suppositions and be prepared to challenge conventional thinking in order to truly understand the deep things of God. The following are SEVEN HARD QUESTIONS that you must face in your journey into the study of end time events.

1) Are we living now in the period of time Jesus called "birth pangs"?

2) What does it means in Matthew 24 when Jesus says the Tribulation is cut short?

3) Matthew 24:31 appears to be the Rapture. Is that correct?

4) Are the wrath of God and the Great Tribulation the same thing?

5) At what point does the nation of Israel receive salvation?

6) What is the significance of 'silence in heaven' in Revelation 8?

7) In Revelation 6, are there signs that precede the Second Coming?

THE PARADIGM SHIFT.

One of the problems with trying to predict the prophecies of God is the term that we call "progressive revelation." God keeps revealing new "stuff" to us that opens our minds and puts another piece of the puzzle together. Two of the obvious events in the past 100 years that have caused theologians to rethink their paradigms are as follows:

The Rebirth of Israel, 1948. Before this date, the disdain of the Jews throughout the world made it seem a remote chance that they would ever have a homeland. But the Sovereignty of God has not only provided a homeland, but also provided supernatural protection from their enemies to this very day. Before this date, the average evangelical concluded that any mention of Israel in the NT was merely a metaphor for the Church. Today, we understand that Israel fulfilled the prophecy of "dry bones" in Ezekiel 38, and they continue to be a sign to us that helps us interpret end-time events and timetables. **This was a paradigm shift.** It is vitally important to understand that we must be careful which theories we turn into doctrine, for fear that God will change the paradigm and prove our hypotheses to be mistaken.

911 Attack of the World Trade Center, 2001. It is unthinkable that foreign terrorists, operating as Islamic Jihadists, would be able to commandeer 3 commercial passenger jetliners on a suicide attack directed toward our Pentagon, our Capital Building and the World Trade Center in New York. This single event made clear our new understanding that the sons of Esau were still a threat to Jews, as well as to the world community. **This was a paradigm shift.** Much of Revelation should now be reinterpreted to understand that religious wars and nationalistic ideologies will play a major role in the final days. For those who consider religion to be useless, superficial or perhaps irrelevant, you better come to grips with the reality that Satan is setting the stage to assault the children of God.

There is another paradigm shift that the Church must now confront. For the past hundred years, mainline theologians have trained us to believe that the Church would escape the hint of persecution during the dark days that we call "Tribulation." This book will suggest to you that another paradigm shift is about to take place. Paul warned us not to be ignorant and not to be deceived by various rumors about the Second Coming of Jesus. For this reason, I ask you to read the pages of this book and ask yourself and fellow believers around you the hard questions that pertain to Jesus' return. The next paradigm shift that the church will experience is:

The Pre-Wrath Rapture of the Church. Jesus prophesied that persecution was inevitable in this life if we are to identify ourselves with The Crucified Messiah. I don't want to be persecuted. I don't seek to be a martyr, and I pray that my children and grandchildren will be spared the terrible suffering of end-time persecution.

But . . . the Church has become soft and defenseless in a culture that is slowly stealing away the very core of our Christian faith. That core is . . . the understanding that identification with Christ is not merely a trend toward personal reformation or personal development . . . or even the quest toward moral conviction to stand against the evils of society.

No, the core of our Christian faith is standing strong like the biblical heroes, Abraham, Joseph, Moses and Daniel. We must train up our children and our grandchildren to understand that Christ has called us to the ultimate possibility: Paul's words in 2 Timothy 3:12: *"All who desire to live godly in Christ Jesus will be persecuted."* This book will state with conviction that the Church must prepare for the growing assault of Satan before we are gloriously rescued and delivered into the presence of the Lord of Glory. **The paradigm is shifting again.**

THE HISTORIC PRELUDE

A

Israel: The Apple of God's Eye

It is a great privilege to live on planet earth during the 21st Century. We are the fortunate observers of 2000 years of watching God slowly and meticulously paint a picture of His redemption of mankind. The clock is now winding down, and it appears that the "birth pangs" that Jesus spoke of in the Olivet Discourse are finally becoming reality. And yet, we are still slow to embrace the reality of the times we live in. God gave us the tiny nation of Israel thousands of years ago as a sign of His progressive revelation on earth. How little we know about Judaism. How little we seem to understand that Israel is the neon signpost that God is using to point us to the final days, and the consummation of all things eternal.

CONNECTING THE DOTS

What You Will Learn in This Chapter.

Like most Gentile kids, we don't have much contact with Jewish kids. My only point of reference for understanding Jewish people was movie stars and Bible stories. So when I met Richard Shulman, my perspective began to change. Richard and I became friends in middle school, and occasionally we would walk home from school together. It was Richard that introduced me to the term 'goyim' (meaning foreigner). He would playfully call me that name, and I don't think I learned what it meant for another two years. Richard was a likable kid, whose father owned the local scrap yard. Typical of many teenagers, Richard was gently mocked for having a dad who owned a junk yard - until one day the news got back to Richard's ignorant Gentile friends that the Schulman family enjoyed much wealth from Gentile scrap auto parts! The purpose of this opening chapter is to introduce you to the Jewish people. Zechariah 2:8 says: "For thus says the LORD of hosts, 'After glory He has sent me against the nations which plunder you, for he who touches you, touches the apple of His eye." You cannot understand the book of Revelation without first understanding the role that the nation of Israel plays in the drama of God's plan for the redemption of mankind. The average Christian knows little about the history of the Jews or the current status of Israel in the world. This is merely a thumbnail sketch to help you prepare for Israel's salvation in the last days.

1. The Domination of Israel.

> Israel has been under siege for 3500 years. Since the time of Pharaoh, God has allowed the world powers to dominate this tiny nation. Understanding the history of each of these world powers is **ESSENTIAL** to understanding Revelation.

2. The Shema

> The Shema is the Jewish confession of faith. This single passage of scripture invites you to understand "the prime directive" of the Jewish people.

3. The Feasts of Israel

> God called the feasts the "appointed times". You will learn the difference between the spring feasts of the past and the fall feasts of the future.

4. The Feast of Trumpets

> This feast symbolizes the rapture of the Church.

5. The Day of Atonement

This feast symbolizes the salvation of Israel.

6. The Feast of Tabernacles

This feast symbolizes the final union of Israel and The Church as the children of God.

7. God's Calendar for the End-time

When you put the feasts together you begin to see God's perfect pattern for bringing His children together.

8. The Time of the Gentiles.

We live in a day known in scripture as "the time of the Gentiles." It is important To know when this time ends and what happens at that juncture of history.

9. The Map of Israel

If you're going to study about Israel, you must know something of its geographic position in the Middle East, and the location of its ancient boundaries.

10. The Tribes of Israel

The tribes of Israel constitute the 144,000 spoken of in Revelation 7 and 14. This page is merely intended to list the twelve tribes as a point of reference.

11. Famous American Jews

You'll be surprised to find out how many famous people have Jewish DNA. The Jews are a noble people who have always walked a narrow path between being survivors and being achievers.

12. Theodore Herzl

Zionism, the idea of re-populating the land of Israel, began with this man.

13. An Evangelical View of the Middle East Conflict

The key to understanding this age old battle is the terms 'population' and 'migration'.

13. "The Legacy of the Jew" by Mark Twain

You may understand the Jewish people differently when you read this statement.

THE DOMINATION OF ISRAEL

The Jewish people are nothing less than a sociological phenomenon. Having been displaced from their native land for 2500 years, it is incredible to believe that they still exist as a pure ethnic culture. As predicted in scripture, the Jews reclaimed the 'land of milk and honey' on May 14, 1948 as a protected declaration of the United Nations. The Jews always have been and always will be a sign of the movement of God in the world. As we focus our attention on the middle east, watch carefully as scripture continues to unfold, and the nations marvel as God's chosen people point to His plan for the ages.

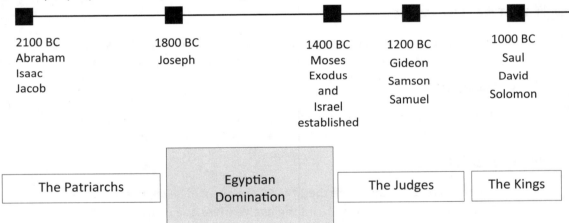

2100 BC	1800 BC	1400 BC	1200 BC	1000 BC
Abraham	Joseph	Moses	Gideon	Saul
Isaac		Exodus	Samson	David
Jacob		and	Samuel	Solomon
		Israel		
		established		

The Patriarchs	Egyptian Domination	The Judges	The Kings

Egyptian Domination - The story of Joseph begins the tale of the Hebrew people's enslavement. For <u>400 years</u>, longer than America has been a nation, the people waited for a leader who would deliver them from Egypt's tyranny.

Assyrian Domination - There are two notable dates during the 1000 years before Christ. In <u>722 bc</u>, the Assyrian Empire captured the <u>northern kingdom of Israel</u>, marrying the women and creating a half breed nation. The <u>Samaritans</u> were the resultant culture, hated by the Jews because of the mixed heritage.

Babylonian Domination - The other notable date. In 586 bc, the country of Iraq, known in those days as the Babylonian Empire, moved into Jerusalem, part of the southern kingdom called Judah, capturing the residents and taking thousands back to Babylon for a period of <u>70 years.</u>

The Divided Kingdom - The Golden Age of Israel was the time of the United Monarchy, under the rule of Saul, David and Solomon. Because of the nation's disobedience, the kingdom divided into North and South. The northern kingdom was now called <u>Israel</u> and the southern kingdom called <u>Judah.</u> Of the 12 tribes of the united kingdom, 10 were part of the northern kingdom and 2 (Benjamin and Judah) were part of the southern kingdom.

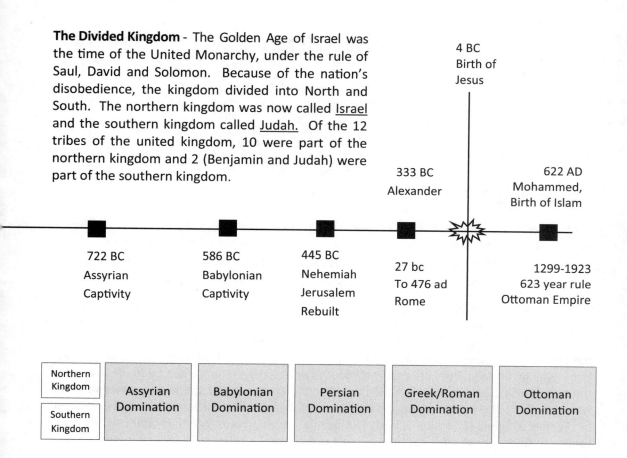

Medo-Persian Domination - The area known today as <u>Iran</u> was the Persian Empire which became the world power in <u>539 bc.</u> The king that was responsible for ending Israel's slavery and returning them to the southern capital of Jerusalem was <u>King Cyrus.</u>

Greek Domination - <u>Alexander the Great</u> defeated the Persians in 331 bc, but died 8 years later. His kingdom was divided into 4 regions, and the last leader, <u>Antiochus Epiphanes</u> terrorized Jerusalem for 3 years until finally conquered by the <u>Macabean Revolt</u>. **Roman Domination** - Israel became a client kingdom of Rome <u>in 63 bc</u> when Pompey took control. Herod the Great was appointed 'king of the Jews' in 40 bc, and in 4 bc, <u>Herod Antipas</u> came to power, attempting to kill all the young Jewish boys.

Ottoman Domination - The Turkish Empire with Islam as its backbone, not only conquers other empires, but seeks to eradicate their culture.

THE SHEMA

Deuteronomy 6:4-5
"Hear, O Israel! The LORD is our God, the LORD is one!
And you shall love the LORD your God with all your heart
and with all your soul and with all your might."

Deuteronomy 6:6-9
"These words, which I am commanding you today, shall be on your heart.
You shall teach them diligently to your sons
and shall talk of them when you sit in your house
and when you walk by the way and when you lie down and when you rise up.
You shall bind them as a sign on your hand and they shall be as frontals on your forehead.
You shall write them on the doorposts of your house and on your gates."

This is the celebrated "Shema" (pronounced sh-ma). It is the confession of faith of the Jewish religion. It is their most important verse because it embraces their theology of monotheism - one God. It is the origin of "The Great Commandment." Jesus quoted this verse in Mark 12:30, but he added one very important word. Can you find the word that Jesus added, and do you know why he added it? (mind) Important Jewish passages were identified by the first word of the text. This passage is literally called the "hear," because that is the Jewish meaning of the word 'shema'. The name Samuel (sh-mu-el) is a derivation of the shema, because God called for Samuel 3 times, (1 Samuel 3:1-10) and Samuel uttered seven very important words in response to God: *"Speak Lord, for your servant is listening."* You would do well to begin to use these seven words in your prayer time with God. ***"Speak, Lord, for your servant is listening."***

4 "Hear, O Israel! The LORD is our God, the LORD is one!"

This Means - **Our God wants us to WORSHIP Him.**

In a time when plural gods were the popular rage of a pagan society, Jehovah God reminded His people that He alone was the Sovereign of the Universe. We call this monotheism.

*5 "And you shall love the LORD your God
with all your heart and with all your soul and with all your might."*

This Means - **Our God wants us to FELLOWSHIP with Him.**

Apart from the holiness of God, perhaps the most important attribute of Jehovah God is that He is a Person. And because He is a Person, He is both personal and a personality - which then implies that He is a relational God. If He is relational, then it follows that He desires fellowship for communication, interaction and response. God created us, He sustains us, He redeems us - and he wants to fellowship with us. Can you grasp the concept that "He loves each one of us as if there were only one of us!"

> 6 "And these words, which I am commanding you today, shall be on your heart;
> 7 and you shall teach them diligently to your sons and shall talk of them
> when you sit in your house and when you walk by the way
> and when you lie down and when you rise up."

This Means - **Our God wants us to LEARN from Him.**

The Jewish system of teaching was a rhetorical 'question and answer' format in which the student and teacher echoed the substance of the lesson. The word 'catechism' is a Greek word meaning "a resounding echo". The father is taught here to reinforce the constant theme of scripture and children are taught here to echo their parents' teaching.

> 8 "And you shall bind them as a sign on your hand
> and they shall be as frontals on your forehead.
> 9 "And you shall write them on the doorposts of your house and on your gates."

This Means - **Our God wants us to REMEMBER Him.**

For 3000 years, the Jews have engaged in the custom of enclosing 4 verses of scripture (primarily the Shema) in a leather pouch on their left arm (close to the heart) and on their forehead (close to their mind). These pouches are held on by leather bands, which the Pharisees in Jesus' day made very wide to attract attention. See Matthew 23:5. The English name for this ornament is **'phylactery',** which means 'to guard' in the Greek language.

The doorpost has been important to the Jews since God told the Israelites to mark their doorposts with the blood of the lamb, thereby exempting the death angel from taking their firstborn. Today the Jews install a **"mezuzah"** (which means doorpost) on their door jamb to symbolize their love for the word of God. Too often, however, this becomes merely an empty tradition or a sign of superstition. Each mezuzah, like the phylactery, contains the Shema (Kosher, by the way) enclosed in the concave back surface of the ornament. In Jerusalem, mezuzahs hang on the doorpost of every hotel room, and they range in variety from simple wood carvings to expensive gold and silver. God gave us these symbols to be reminded of His love for us. Psalm 22: 27 says, *"All the ends of the earth will remember and turn to the LORD, And all the families of the nations will worship before Thee."*

THE SPRING FEASTS OF ISRAEL

1) Passover is a sign which points to

the **Atoning Death** of Christ.

2) Unleavened Bread is a sign which points to

the **Sinless Nature** of Christ.

3) First Fruits is a sign which points to

the **Physical Resurrection** of Christ.

4) Pentecost is a sign which points to

the **Empowering Work** of the Holy Spirit

Ceremonial Events that were Instituted in 1400 bc and were fulfilled as Historic Events in 33 ad.

*God gave Israel seven feasts, or "appointed times", and instructed them to be celebrated as a perpetual ordinance, throughout all their generations. The first four, Passover, Unleavened Bread, First Fruits and Pentecost, have already been fulfilled by the Lord's death, burial, resurrection and manifestation of the Holy Spirit. The first three were celebrated in the first month of the agricultural season of spring. The fourth is celebrated 50 days later. For 3500 years, the Jews have been faithful to observe each of these appointed times. For them, **Passover** is a reminder of the miraculous deliverance they experienced when Moses led the people out of Egyptian bondage. **Unleavened Bread** reminds them of the haste with which they gathered their belongings and headed for the desert. The celebration of **First Fruits** actually began 40 years later, after the nation was in the land. When they gathered the first part of the barley harvest the priest would stand before the people and wave a sheaf, as a sign of the good harvest to come. The first **Pentecost** occurred when Moses came down from Mt. Sinai to give the nation the Ten Commandments. Pentecost has always been a celebration acknowledging the beginning or origination of things. It is very important for the Church to understand that we have been grafted in (Romans 11:17) to "the rich root of the olive tree." There is much that we need to understand from Jewish tradition as we learn to love the people that God has called his "chosen ones."*

THE FALL FEASTS OF ISRAEL

5) Trumpets is a sign which points to

the **Second Coming** of Christ.

6) The Day of Atonement is a sign which points to

the **Prodigal Salvation** of Israel.

7) Tabernacles is a sign which points to

the **Eternal Presence** of God among us.

Ceremonial Events that were instituted in 1400 bc and now prophesy the consummation of Human History

The last three Feasts of Israel are celebrated during the seventh month of the agricultural season. But to further complicate the calendar, the Jews celebrate "Rosh Hashanah", the beginning of the civil new year, concurrent with The Feast of Trumpets. This change or addition to the Jewish calendar occurred due to the destruction of the temple and the feeling that this vacuum in the ceremonial / sacrificial system gave need for an additional celebration. The Feasts of Trumpets, Atonement and Tabernacles is a prophetic foreshadowing of the coming of Israel's Messiah, the salvation of the nation of Israel and the new Jerusalem. There should be little doubt in the mind of the believer that these seven feasts constitute God's "Calendar of the Ages." The Jewish people have a calendar system based on the moon. They have 12 months of 29 and 30 day periods, totaling 354 days. In order to adjust for the solar calendar, every 19 years they add seven leap years and one additional month. According to scripture, the seasons are regulated by the moon. Science tells us that the ocean tides are controlled by the moon's relationship to the earth. Even the female menstrual cycle seems to be regulated by the Earth's little "sister". Psalm 89:37 tells us that God's promise "shall be established forever like the moon, and the witness in the sky is faithful." Isaiah 60:19 tells us there will come a day when "No longer will you have the sun for light by day, nor for brightness will the moon give you light; But you will have the LORD for an everlasting light, and your God for your glory."

TRUMPETS - SYMBOL OF REVELATION

The Fall Feasts - Trumpets, Day of Atonement and Tabernacles - all occur in the seventh month of the year, the latter months, just as the prophetic parallel events occur in the final days of human history. The Feast of Trumpets is now called Rosh Hashanah, which means the head (Rosh) of the year. Rosh Hashanah is the beginning of the civil new year for Israel, and falls on the first day of the month, followed by Atonement on the 10th day, and Tabernacles on the 15th day. Trumpets is the only feast to fall on the first of the month, which means that the moon is dark and only a thin crescent. For that reason, Rosh Hashanah is observed for two days - just in case the clouds veil the moon. There is always a great sense of anticipation and observation attached to watching for the crescent moon's appearance. Trumpets used to be blown during the sacrificial system. Since that system no longer exists, there are only three reasons for the Trumpets to be blown: 1) the call to **Assembly**, 2) the call to **War**. and 3) the **Coronation** of the King.

Leviticus 23:24-25 *"Speak to the sons of Israel, saying, 'In the seventh month on the first of the month you shall have a rest, <u>a reminder by blowing of trumpets</u>, a holy convocation.*

1) The Call to Assembly.

Numbers 10:2-3 *"Make yourself two trumpets of silver, of hammered work you shall make them; and you shall use them <u>for summoning the congregation </u>and for having the camps set out. When both are blown, all the congregation shall gather themselves to you at the doorway of the tent of meeting."*

2) The Call to War.

Numbers 10:9. *"When you go to war in your land against the adversary who attacks you, then <u>you shall sound an alarm with the trumpets</u>, that you may be remembered before the LORD your God, and be saved from your enemies.*

3) The Coronation of a King.

1 Kings 1:34-39. *"Let Zadok the priest and Nathan the prophet anoint him there as king over Israel, <u>and blow the trumpet and say</u>, 'Long live King Solomon!'*

The Meaning of Assembly, War and Coronation.

The Call to Assembly - The Rapture.

> *Matthew 24:31* "And He will send forth His angels with <u>a great trumpet and they will gather together His elect</u> from the four winds, from one end of the sky to the other."

> *1 Thessalonians 4:16* "For the Lord Himself will descend from heaven with a shout, with the voice of the archangel and with the <u>trumpet</u> of God, and the dead in Christ will rise first."

The Call to War - The Wrath of God

> *Revelation 8:13* Then I looked, and I heard an eagle flying in midheaven, saying with a loud voice, "<u>Woe, woe, woe to those who dwell on the earth</u>, because of the remaining blasts of the trumpet of the three angels who are about to sound!"

The Coronation of the King -

> *Revelation 15:3* And they sang the song of Moses, the bond-servant of God, and the song of the Lamb, saying, "Great and marvelous are Your works, O Lord God, the Almighty; Righteous and true are Your ways, <u>King of the nations!</u>

The significance of the Call to Assembly and the Call to War is that the Final Trump (or series of trumpet blasts) signals the sequential events of the Rapture and the Wrath of God. Notice the two passages to follow. Christ Himself compares His second coming to the days of Noah and Lot. In both cases, <u>deliverance came just before judgment.</u> God will rapture His church just prior to pouring out His Wrath on planet earth.

> *Luke 17:26-30* "And just as it happened in the days of Noah, so it will be also in the days of the Son of Man: they were eating, they were drinking, they were marrying, they were being given in marriage, <u>until the day that Noah entered the ark, and the flood came and destroyed them all.</u> It was the same as happened in the days of Lot: they were eating, they were drinking, they were buying, they were selling, they were planting, they were building; <u>but on the day that Lot went out from Sodom it rained fire and brimstone from heaven and destroyed them all.</u> It will be just the same on the day that the Son of Man is revealed."

A final note. Only twice does God blow the trumpet in scripture, and both times it is the shofar, not the silver trumpet. The first time is the giving of the Law on Mt Sinai. (Exodus 19:18-20) "When the sound of the trumpet grew louder and louder, Moses spoke and God answered him with thunder." The second trumpet blast (Zechariah 9:14) signals the return of the Messiah, "and his arrow will go forth like lightning, and the Lord GOD will blow the trumpet . . ."

DAY OF ATONEMENT - SYMBOL OF RESTORATION

Leviticus 23:26-28 The LORD spoke to Moses, saying, "On exactly the tenth day of this seventh month is <u>the day of atonement</u>; it shall be a holy convocation for you, and you shall humble your souls and present an offering by fire to the LORD. "You shall not do any work on this same day, for it is a day of atonement, to make atonement on your behalf before the LORD your God. If there is <u>any person who will not humble himself</u> (fast) on this same day, <u>he shall be cut off from his people.</u>

This day is called **YOM KIPPUR** meaning the day (yom) of **COVERING**. In the past, the priest would enter the Holy of Holies in the Jewish Temple and perform ceremony all day to cover the sins of the people, as prescribed by scripture. In the future, this day represents the national day of salvation (Rom 11:26), when *"all Israel will be saved."* For the Jewish population that are alive at the time of the Wrath of God, there will be great mourning of the sons of Jacob when they finally conclude that the Messiah they have been waiting for was Jesus, whom they rejected.

Exodus 30:10 "Aaron shall make atonement on its horns once a year; he shall make atonement on it <u>with the blood of the sin offering of atonement once a year</u> throughout your generations. It is most holy to the LORD."

The Elaborate Ritual of the High Priest on the Day of Atonement.

All Israel depended upon the High Priest to enter the Holy of Holies on this sacred day and literally cover the sins of the people for the past year. The following is a summary.

1) Five times during the day, the high priest would wash his hands and feet, then bathe in a golden bathtub. Normally he wore golden garments with a purple robe and tiny bells at the hemline. On this day, he wore white linen garments. He would then wash his hands and feet again.

2) The priest began by taking a golden fire pan (filled with hot coals) and sprinkling two handfuls of incense in the pan. He then ascended the stairs of the temple, into the Holy of Holies, behind the veil. He meditated there while the soothing aroma rose before the Lord - and the watchful eyes of the people in the distance. He then left the temple to wash, bathe and put on new garments.

3) A young bull was brought before the High Priest, who pressed his hands into the forehead of the bull, as an act of identification. The bull was then slaughtered, and his blood was poured into a golden bowl. An attendant would stir the blood so that it would not congeal. The priest sprinkled the blood of the bull seven times before the Ark of the Covenant.

50

4) Two young goats were brought before the High Priest. One was for Yahweh, (the Lord), and one was for Azazel, an obsure identification with Satan. One goat was sacrificed to the Lord; the other was called the scapegoat. It was this goat that would bear the sins of the people, be led out into the desert, and eventually pushed off a cliff to its death.

The Modern Observance of Atonement.

Since the destruction of the Temple in 70 ad ended the ceremonial system of animal sacrifice, tradition has followed the suggestion of one rabbi who quoted Hosea 6:6, "I desire mercy not sacrifice." For that reason, good works have now become the legitimate substitute for the blood sacrifice which atones for sin. One tradition which persists, however, is that of Kaparot, which provides for a chicken sacrifice, done under the careful scrutiny of kosher butchers. The difference between the Old Covenant and the New Covenant can be described with a credit card. The card has no value of its own, but merely covers temporarily the purchase until it can be redeemed with the payment which is to follow. In God's economy, Atonement was an acceptable act of covering UNTIL the Messiah came to redeem the payment of personal sin.

The Future Salvation of Israel.

What the Jewish people don't yet understand is that Atonement is merely a covering for their sins. The blood sacrifice of Jesus on the cross was not atonement of sin. It was a complete forgiveness of sins - a removal, an eradication - as far as the east is from the west.
When the Jews finally recognize their Messiah, there will be a great time of mourning.

> *Zechariah 12:9-10 And in that day I will set about to destroy all the nations that come against Jerusalem. I will pour out on the house of David and on the inhabitants of Jerusalem, the Spirit of grace and of supplication, so that they will look on Me whom they have pierced; and they will mourn for Him, as one mourns for an only son, and they will weep bitterly over Him like the bitter weeping over a firstborn.*

> *Romans 11:25-28 For I do not want you, brethren, to be uninformed of this mystery--so that you will not be wise in your own estimation--that a partial hardening has happened to Israel until the fullness of the Gentiles has come in; and so all Israel will be saved;*

> *Revelation 7:4 And I heard the number of those who were sealed, one hundred and forty -four thousand sealed from every tribe of the sons of Israel:*

After the Tribulation, just after the sixth seal, God will seal 144,000 of the sons of Israel to protect them from the Wrath to come. Those who survive the terrible "Day of the Lord" will be allowed to witness King Jesus in all His glory. At that moment, the veil will be lifted from their eyes, and they will see Jesus as their long awaited Messiah.

TABERNACLES - SYMBOL OF CONSUMMATION

Leviticus 23:34-43 *On exactly the fifteenth day of the seventh month, when you have gathered in the crops of the land, you shall celebrate the feast of the LORD <u>for seven days</u>, with a rest on the first day and a rest on the eighth day. 'Now on the first day you shall take for yourselves the foliage of beautiful trees, palm branches and boughs of leafy trees and willows of the brook, and you shall rejoice before the LORD your God for seven days. <u>'You shall live in booths for seven days</u>; all the native-born in Israel shall live in booths, so that your generations may know that I had the sons of Israel live in booths <u>when I brought them out from the land of Egypt</u>. I am the LORD your God."*

Tabernacles was the final feast of the year. It was one of three pilgrimage feasts (with Passover and Pentecost), and it lasted for seven days. It is also referred to as "Ingathering, or Sukkot (sa-coat) or the Feast of Booths." It was a time of celebrating the success of the past year, and praying for a bountiful harvest for the coming year. In the agricultural economy of Israel, rain was everything. Unlike many parts of the world, Israel's rain comes primarily from November to March. Without rain during that critical time, drought and famine could occur. For that reason, the people of Israel prayed both personally and collectively as a nation for what they called "the latter rains."

Think of Tabernacles as a seven day combination of Thanksgiving and Fourth of July. The ancient rabbis were quoted as saying, *"if you haven't experienced the drawing of water ceremony at Tabernacles, you have not experienced joy in your life."* During the day, they celebrated the "drawing of water" ceremonies. At night, they reveled in the spectacular light shows and music accompaniment.

This was called "the Great Feast." More pilgrims came to this feast than any other. For this reason, there was "no room in the inn." Thousands of pilgrims would pitch their tents within 3000 feet (a Sabbath journey) to the city of Jerusalem. But on the occasion of this feast, God chose for them to remember their desert wanderings and celebrate the actual creation of wilderness booths. According to prescription, they cut down the branches of four trees - the willow, date palm, the myrtle and a citrus tree. They created a make-shift hut which would provide shelter for the sevens days of the festival. As the families traveled toward Jerusalem, and upon making the final ascent up the mountain to the city, the people would sing songs from Psalm 120-134, which we now refer to as the Song of Ascent. The following are excerpts from Psalm 121.

> *I will lift up my eyes to the mountains; From where shall my help come?*
> *My help comes from the LORD, Who made heaven and earth.*
> *The LORD will guard your going out and your coming in*
> *From this time forth and forever.*

Each evening of the seven day celebration, a spectacular light show would entertain the crowds of people. Menorahs, oil lamps and torch dances would flood the night sky with a joyful display of light and music that was literally the highlight of the year. In the context of this season, Jesus spoke to his disciples and said. *"I am the Light of the world; he who follows Me will not walk in the darkness, but will have the Light of life."*

The Water Libation Ceremony was the highlight of Tabernacles. Every morning the people would follow the High Priest from the Temple to the Pool of Siloam. He would dip a golden pitcher into the waters and carry it back to the temple to be poured out as a symbol of the rains that God would provide in the coming months. Three kinds of water were available to the people: wells, cisterns and living waters. Wells were dug deep into the ground, cisterns were man made rain collectors, and living waters - the rivers and streams - were deemed the most valuable resource in the land. Into this context, Jesus spoke during the week of Tabernacles.

> *John 7:37 Now on the last day, the great day of the feast, Jesus stood and cried out, saying, "If anyone is thirsty, let him come to Me and drink. He who believes in Me, as the Scripture said, 'From his innermost being will flow rivers of living water.'" But this He spoke of the Spirit, whom those who believed in Him were to receive; for the Spirit was not yet given, because Jesus was not yet glorified.*

As a result of these statements from Christ, scripture says in John 7:43, *"So a division occurred in the crowd because of Him."* Tabernacles is a symbol of the consummation of human history, the climax of God's mercy toward the remnant of mankind that acknowledges their sin and need of a savior. Revelation 21:3 declares the magnificent conclusion of God's plan of redemption. *"And I heard a loud voice from the throne, saying, "Behold, the tabernacle of God is among men, and He will dwell among them, and they shall be His people, and God Himself will be among them."*

God's Calendar for the End-Times

Any discussion about the end-times should focus on these three ancient feasts of Israel. God's desire is to unite His Chosen seed of Israel with His beloved Church.

THE FEAST OF TRUMPETS.   ## Gathering His Church.

In the Old Testament, the trumpets blew for 3 reasons:
call to assembly, call to war or the coronation of a king. In this instance, the assembly of the church is raptured, heaven prepares for judgment during the trumpet and bowl judgments, and preparation is made for the Messiah's coronation at the seventh trumpet.

THE DAY OF ATONEMENT.   ## Restoring His Chosen.

Atonement was the one day a year that the sins of the people were forgiven by the High Priest through the sprinkling of the sacrificial blood. Christ, as the heavenly high priest will now return to earth and reconcile His prodigal children as they mourn, and then later celebrate, their new relationship with the Messiah they once rejected.

THE FEAST OF TABERNACLES.   ## Uniting His Children.

God's ultimate plan has finally become reality. His Church and His Children can now be united in the perfect environment of Paradise and the New Jerusalem. Scripture says that the New Jerusalem descends out of heaven. I believe that the Garden Paradise is intrinsically connected to the New Jerusalem in heaven right now, and at the appointed time, will clothe the barren earth with a new garment.

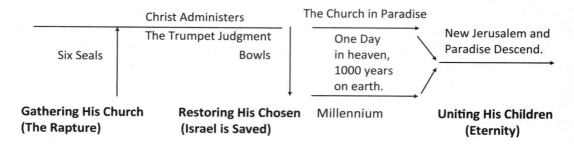

The Times of the Gentiles

There are only two kinds of people in the world: the Jews and the Gentiles. The Greek word for Gentile is 'ethnos', from which we get the word ethnic. The Bible also translates this word as 'nations'. The Hebrew word for Gentile is 'goy', which means a foreigner (pl = goyim). Jerusalem has been under the domination of other nations since 586 bc when Babylon first captured the city and carried the best of Israel off to captivity for 70 years. The time of the Gentiles continues today, even while Israel is a sovereign nation because they are still under siege of the nations. This time of the Gentiles will not be complete until Jesus stands on Mt Zion with the newly saved remnant of Israel, and then days later, He fights the battle of Armageddon against those who defy Him and hate Israel.

Rom 1:16 For I am not ashamed of the gospel, for it is the power of God for salvation to everyone who believes, **to the Jew first and also to the Greek (Gentile).**

———————

Luke 21:23 "Woe to those who are pregnant and to those who are nursing babies in those days; for there will be great distress upon the land and wrath to this people;

Luk 21:24 and they will fall by the edge of the sword, and will be led captive into all the nations; and Jerusalem will be trampled under foot by the Gentiles **until the times of the Gentiles are fulfilled.**

———————

Rom 11:25 For I do not want you, brethren, to be uninformed of this mystery - so that you will not be wise in your own estimation - that a partial hardening has happened to Israel **until the fullness of the Gentiles has come in;**

586 BC	2600 Years of Gentile Domination	2000 AD (21st Century)
The Babylonian Captivity of the Southern Kingdom of Judah	—————————————→	and until The Seven Years and The Seventh trumpet of Victory.

Map of Biblical Israel

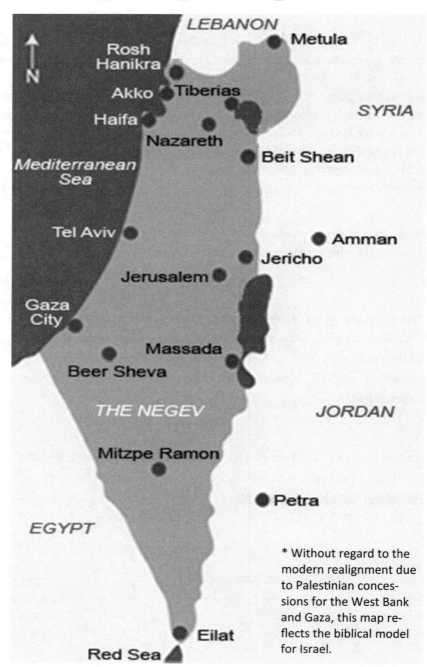

* Without regard to the modern realignment due to Palestinian concessions for the West Bank and Gaza, this map reflects the biblical model for Israel.

"THE TRIBES OF ISRAEL"

Abraham's sons, Ishmael and Isaac
Isaac's sons, Esau and Jacob (later named Israel)

SONS OF JACOB (Genesis 49)

1. Reuben	Leah, first wife of Jacob	
2. Simeon	Leah	
3. Levi	Leah	given no land
4. Judah	Leah	David and Jesus were descendants
5. Issachar	Leah	
6. Zebulun	Leah	
7. Dan	Bilhah, maiden to Rachel	
8. Naphtali	Bilhah	
9. Gad	Zilpah, maiden to Leah	
10. Asher	Zilpah	
11. Joseph	Rachel, second wife of Jacob	
12. Benjamin	Rachel	Southern Kingdom of Judah

THE LIST OF TRIBES IN REVELATION 7.

1. Judah
2. Reuben
3. Gad
4. Asher
5. Naphtali
6. **MANASSEH** (Son of Joseph)
7. Simeon
8. Levi (guardians of the temple in lieu of territory)
9. Issachar
10. Zebulon
11. **JOSEPH** (Ephraim, son of Joseph)
12. Benjamin

A. Judah became the kingdom of the two southern tribes, Judah and Benjamin, which are today considered to be the "true Israel"

B. The other ten tribes are considered the northern kingdom, which was dispersed around the world.

C. Joseph had two sons, Manasseh and Ephraim, who became part of the list of 12 tribes. Joseph's faithfulness allowed him to have a double portion.

D. Dan is not included, possibly because of the condemnation of Genesis 49:17

E. This list is not about territory, therefore Levi is included.

F. These 12 tribes are considered the "firstfruits" of those who enter the Millennium.

FAMOUS JEWS OF AMERICAN CULTURE

The Jewish people are a noble people who have contributed much to the development of civilization. They are also a maligned people, despised by most of the world today. We would do well to remember that they inhabit lofty places of prominence in the world, in spite of their second-class stature. The following list is not exhaustive, but is representative of some of the great names that you will recognize.

SCIENCE: Albert Einstein, William Herschel, Robert Oppenheimer, Edward Teller, Jonas Salk, Carl Sagan, Neils Bohr, Stephen Jay Gould, Robert Jastrow

U.S. SUPREME COURT JUSTICES: Louis Brandeis, Stephen Breyer, Benjamin Cardoza, Abe Fortas, Felix Frankfurter, Arthur Goldberg, Ruth Bader Ginsburg, Elena Kagen

LAWYERS: Gloria Allred, Allen Dershowitz, William Kuntzler, Elliot Spitzer, Marcia Clark, Ed Koch, Scooter Libby, Robert Shapiro

FILM DIRECTORS: Stephen Spielburg, Cecil B. Demille, Jeffrey Katzenburg, Stanley Kubrick, Mel Brooks, Aaron Spelling, Oliver Stone

TELEVISION: Barbara Walters, Connie Chung, Howard Cosell, Ted Koppel, Bill Maher, Jerry Springer, Mike Wallace, Matt Lauer, Howie Mandell, Suze Orman, Norman Lear, Ephrem Zimbalist, Jr. Joan Lunden, Bob Saget

MUSIC: Irving Berlin , Leonard Bernstein, Barbra Streisand, Izaac Perlman, Bob Dylan, George Gershwin, Jerome Kern, Paula Abdul, Art Garfunkel, Paul Simon, Victor Borge, Herb Alpert, Oscar Hammarstein, Adam Lambert, Peter Yarrow, Julio Iglesias, Al Jolson, Max Weinberg, Marvin Hamlisch, Josh Groban, Leonard Bernstein, Steven Sondheim, Ethan Bortnick

LITERATURE/JOURNALISM: Charles Krauthammer, Isaac Assimov, Alfred Edersheim, Carl Bernstein, Matt Drudge, Bernie Goldberg, Gloria Steinham, Mike Wallace, Walter Winchell, Elie Wiesel, Eric Fromm, Ann Landers, Abigail Van Buren

FINANCE: Alan Greenspan, Milton Friedman, Ben Bernanke, Clark Howard

BUSINESS: Milton Hershey, Michael Dell, Steve Ballmer (Microsoft), Larry Ellison (Oracle) George Soros, Bernie Madoff, Calvin Klein, Ralph Lauren, Levi Strauss

COMEDY: Jerry Seinfeld, Jerry Lewis, Jack Benny, Milton Berle, Bob Hope, Rodney Danger-field, Billy Crystal, George Burns, Curly Howard, Moe Howard, Shemp Howard, Groucho Marx and Brothers, Joan Rivers, Jon Stewart, Adam Sandler

ARCHITECTS: Frank Gehry, Louis Kahn

Among the actors, I have linked some of them to show an association which seems to me con-nects them loosely to their Jewish heritage. I'm sure the connections in Hollywood are endless because, unlike American anglos that are usually assimilated into society, the Jews have a si-lent code of sticking together and supporting each other. Cultures do that, don't they? It should also be noted that many of these listed are Jewish by some loose genetic ancestry, not necessarily Jewish in religious faith

ACTING:
  Seinfeld - David Steinberg, Jerry Seinfeld, Julia Louis Dreyfus, Jason Alexander
  The Princess Bride - William Goldman, Peter Falk, Fred Savage, Wallace Shawn, Mandy Patinkin, Christopher Guest, Billy Crystal, Carol Cane
  Indiana Jones - Shia LeBouf, Harrison Ford
  Star Trek - William Shatner, Brent Spiner, Leonard Nimoy
  Married Couples - Sarah Jessica Parker, Matthew Broderick
  A Perfect Murder - Michael Douglas, Gwyneth Paltrow
  Friends - David Schwinner, Lisa Kudrow.
  Happy Days - Tom Bosley, Henry Winkler

Elvis Pressley, Ben Stiller, Adam Sandler, Kate Hudson, Joaquin Phoenix, Wynona Ryder, Tori Spelling, Noah Wylie, Jack Black, Robert Downey, Jr., David Duchovny, Sean Penn, Kyra Sedgewick, Kate Capshaw, Jamie Lee Curtis, Tony Curtis, Carrie Fisher, Jeff Goldblum, Steve Guttenburg, , Jane Seymour, Steven Seagal, Albert Brooks, James Caan, Richard Dreyfus, Scott Glenn, Goldie Hawn, Kevin Kline, Bette Midler, Leslie Ann Warren, Woody Allen, Dyan Cannon, Elliot Gould, Dustin Hoffman, Michael Landon, Elizabeth Taylor, Ed Asner, Lauren Bacall, Mel Brooks, Monty Hall, Walter Matthau, Marilyn Monroe, Paul Newman, Dinah Shore, Mae West, Neil Simon

ART: Joe Schuster, Jerry Siegel (superman) Stan Lee (Marvel Comics) Al Capp (Lil Abner)

PHILOSOPHY: Mortimer Adler, Allen Bloom, Ayn Rand

"The days of the Messiah will occur when the Jews
return to Palestine. This King who arises will have
the seat of his rule in Zion. His fame will be even greater
than that of King Solomon. Because of His consummate justice,
the nations will obey him. God Himself
will destroy anyone who rises up against Him."

THEODOR HERTZL
1860-1904 (44 years)

On May 14, 1948, the United Nations acknowledged the right of the Jews to establish the nation/state of Israel. After 2500 years of domination by foreign nations, they had finally returned home to their "promised land." The catalyst of this dramatic event was Theodor Hertzl, who began The Zionist Movement fifty years earlier. Trained as a lawyer in Austria, he traveled to France and witnessed the brutal execution of a Jewish soldier in the French army, accused of being a German spy. He saw firsthand the bigotry that we call today "anti-Semitism." He turned his attention from the legal profession and became a journalist, a means by which he could gain the attention of the world. He wrote the book, *The Jewish State*, as a call to Jews everywhere to nationalize and secure a homeland. The Zionist movement was born, and Hertzl carried the banner until his death eight years later. He believed that God had ordained Zionism to fulfill scripture: **"God would not have sustained the Jewish people for so long if it had not been designated some destiny in human history. It is true that we aspire to our ancient land. But what we want in that ancient land is a new blossoming of the Jewish spirit."** His best known quote: **"If you will it, it is no dream."**

Oh, that the salvation of Israel
would come out of Zion!
When the LORD restores His captive people,
Jacob will rejoice, Israel will be glad.
King David, PSALM 14:7

The Importance of Israel

For thus says the LORD of hosts,
"After glory He has sent me
against the nations which plunder you,
for he who touches you,
touches the apple of His eye."
Zechariah 2:8

The term "apple of His eye"
is a veiled reference to the cornea of the eye,
which is the outer aperture of the eyeball.
It is the most sensitive, the most delicate
and could easily be considered
the most precious part of the body
because of our total dependence on sight.
Israel is called by God Himself
"the apple of His eye".

The Importance of Jerusalem

Thus says the Lord GOD,
"This is Jerusalem;
I have set her at the center of the nations,
with lands around her."
Ezekiel 5:5

The Hebrew word for center is the word 'tabor.'
This is not a geometric term. This is not a geographic term.
The word "tabor" means "navel."
Jerusalem is the "bellybutton" of the planet.

An Evangelical View of the Middle East Conflict

It is quite amazing that the middle east is occupied by 400 million Arabs and 7.8 million Jews (1.3 percent) and the Arabs live on 2 million square miles of land, while the Jews live on 7,900 square miles (one tenth of one percent) - and YET, the Arabs are unwilling to tolerate the Jewish nation state. Any discussion about the origins of Palestinians and Jews will always degenerate into two sides that seem hopelessly unable to agree on anything. So let's try to begin by stating some indisputable facts. My intent is to provide the average church member with enough objective information to support Israel. The following are four reasons: 1) Israel is the only democracy in the Middle East. 2) Israel is the root of the Christian faith. 3) Israel was established by the United Nations in 1948 as a sovereign nation, and 4) Israel has proven to have the highest standard of living of any country in the Middle East.

1. ORIGIN OF THE PHILLISTINES. In the biblical account of tribal origins, we find that Noah's son Ham, gave birth to Cush, Put, Mizraim and Canaan. Mizraim, who appears to be the founder of Egypt, gave birth to Pathrusim, the name that Genesis 10:14 identifies with the Philistines. Most historical accounts link the Philistines to sea-faring tribes, perhaps as far away as Greece. They journeyed to the land of Canaan (another son of Ham) and by the time of 1200 bc, the Philistines and the Canaanites were determined to destroy the Israelites. The best known Philistine was named Goliath, whose 9 foot frame fell before the young Israelite lad named David. According to the Bible, the Philistines and the Canaanites, along with the Hittites, Hivites, Jebusites, Amorites and Perizzites, were destined to be conquered by Israel. Encyclopedic sources have this to say about the Philistines: *"Nothing is known for certain about the language of the Philistines, and the Philistine culture was almost fully integrated with that of Canaan and the Canaanites."* The reasonable conclusion should be that Israel, by the time of King David, had either eliminated or dispersed these pagan communities that did not honor Jehovah as God. There is no evidence in history to suggest that the Palestinians today (who are Arabs) are in any way descended from Philistines. In fact, the term "Palestine" has been associated with Israel, leading up to the time of Israel's birth in 1948. The Jerusalem Post used to be called the Palestine Post. The Palestine Symphony Orchestra was an "all-Jewish" musical organization.

2) THE DIASPORA. In AD 70, Israel was destroyed by the Romans and many of the Jewish people fled to other parts of the earth, primarily Europe.

3) ORIGIN OF THE TERM 'PALESTINE.' In AD 135, the Emperor Hadrian blotted out the name "Provincia Judea" and renamed it "Provincia Syria Palaestina" because of his hatred for all things Jewish. At this point the name Palestine was associated only with the Jews.

4) THE BIRTH OF ISLAM. Mohammed was an Arab trader who began a pilgrimage which resulted in the writing of the Qur'an. He died in 632 ad, and the religion of Islam became the dominant religion in the Arab world.

5) **THE AL AKSA MOSQUE and DOME OF THE ROCK.** The Mosque, which is located in the Old City of Jerusalem, is the third holiest site in Islam. It was originally built in 705 ad, destroyed twice by earthquakes, and then rebuilt in 1035 to its current state. The Dome of the Rock sits on the Temple Mount, also known as Mt Moriah, above the large stone where Abraham was instructed to offer his son Isaac.

6) THE CRUSADES. Because of the pervasive force and influence of Islam in the region of Israel, Pope Urban II (1096) solicited the allegiance of Frenchmen and Italians to go to Jerusalem and fight to restore access to the holy sites. Their primary war was with the Muslims, but Jews were also evicted from the land.

7) THE OTTOMON EMPIRE. For a period of 623 years, from 1299 to 1922, the former Turkish Empire dominated the Middle East as a major world empire. Sultans served as the governmental body, while Caliphs served as the religious body. The eastern arm of Christianity, headquartered in Constantinople (now Istanbul) was seized and the empire grew in fierce power. The Caliphs were similar to popes in their influence and political power. After World War I, the positions of sultan and caliph were formally abolished in 1922 and 1924 as a result of the Treaty of Lausanne, which dismantled the empire and recognized the new Republic of Turkey.

8) THE ZIONIST MOVEMENT. In the 1880s, Jews began to return to a land that was desolate and almost uninhabited. In his book *"The Innocents Abroad"*, Mark Twain referred to Israel as *"a desolate land, given over wholly to weeds - a silent, mournful expanse."* The Jews began to drain the swamps, till the land and populate the villages. While it is true that Arabs lived among them, there was never an ethnic culture that developed the land other than the Jews. It was, and always has been, the Jews who civilized the land of Israel and the capital of Jerusalem. Archeology today proves the continued existence of a Jewish culture.   After World War I, the British Empire took control of Israel, and the Balfour Declaration of 1917 set in motion the plan to give Israel a homeland.

9) THE NATION-STATE OF ISRAEL. Because the Jewish people had been severely targeted by the Germans during the Holocaust of World War II, the United Nations, on May 14, 1948, officially recognized Israel as a sovereign nation. Immediately the surrounding nations sought to remove Israel by military force, but Israel held its ground. In 1967, in the Six Days War, Israel successfully defeated Egypt, Jordan and Syria as these neighboring enemies attempted once again to destroy little Israel.

10) THE PALESTINIAN LIBERATION AUTHORITY. The PLO was organized in 1964 to formalize the Arabs who lived in Israel and Jordan into an enemy against Israel. The reorganized PA (Palestinian Authority) continues today to provide a resistance movement which ultimately wants to take the land from Israel, rather than live peacefully together. For evangelical Christians, it is important that we support Israel and remain wary of the PA's attempt to compromise the Jewish nation. Despite the world's attempts to paint Israel as an "occupier", believers must stand strong in our support of their nationhood and their sovereign right to govern the land.

11) THE PRINCIPLE OF POPULATION AND MIGRATION. Around the world today, there is one word that is used repeatedly to describe the Jews who reside in Jerusalem. It is the word **'occupiers'.** It is a harsh and undeserving term. The world loves to accuse the Jews of living in a land that they have "taken over." When the Jews from around the world began to populate Israel, the city and the state began to grow and prosper. That is an undisputable fact. Scripture prophesied that the land would blossom when Israel returned to the land. In 1948, that very phenomenon began to happen. When a people group moves into an area, and eventually dominates the population, the culture begins to change in their favor. When Mormons began to populate Salt Lake City, the city became Mormon. When Norwegians populated Minnesota, the region took on some of their personality. When the Chinese population segregated in a particular area of San Francisco, the result was China-town. When the Muslim population around the world moves into an area, their culture eventually "takes over" and other cultures become a minority. Every city in the world is populated by pockets of immigrants. Sometimes one culture grows to the point of domination. This is the principle of migration and population. It's not rocket science, and neither should it be argued that Israel does not have the right to populate an area, and then affect its culture. Another interesting thought is that Israel is the only one of the three major religions (Judaism, Christianity and Islam) that does not even try to evangelize the local citizenry. And yet, the world loves to hate the Jews. It's too bad that the world media has lost the ability to be objective.

> *"Keep in mind that the Arabs control 99.9 percent of the Middle East lands.*
> *Israel represents one-tenth of one percent of the landmass.*
> *But that's too much for the Arabs. They want it all.*
> *And that is ultimately what the fighting in Israel is about today.*
> *No matter how many land concessions the Israelis make,*
> *it will never be enough."*

> *from "Myths of the Middle East"*
> **Joseph Farah, Arab-American editor and journalist,**
> **WorldNetDaily, 11 October 2000**

THE LEGACY OF THE JEW

If the statistics are right,
the Jews constitute but one percent of the human race.
It suggests a nebulous dim puff of star dust
lost in the blaze of the Milky Way.
Properly the Jew ought hardly to be heard of,
but he is heard of, has always been heard of.
He is as prominent on the planet as any other people,
and his commercial importance is extravagantly out of proportion
to the smallness of his bulk. His contributions
to the world's list of great names in literature, science, art, music,
finance, medicine, and abstruse learning
are also way out of proportion to the weakness of his numbers.
He has made a marvelous fight in the world,
in all the ages; and has done it with his hands tied behind him.
He could be vain of himself, and be excused for it.
The Egyptian, the Babylonian, and the Persian rose,
filled the planet with sound and splendor,
then faded to dream-stuff and passed away;
the Greek and the Roman followed, and made a vast noise,
and they are gone; other peoples have sprung up
and held their torch high for a time, but it burned out,
and they sit in twilight now, or have vanished.
The Jew saw them all, beat them all,
and is now what he always was, exhibiting no decadence,
no infirmities of age, no weakening of his parts,
no slowing of his energies, no dulling of his alert and aggressive mind.
All things are mortal but the Jew; all other forces pass, but he remains.
What is the secret of his immortality?
MARK TWAIN
("Innocents Abroad")

There is a demonic spirit

that has passed from generation to generation,

always manifesting itself as a counteragent to the Jewish nation,

always bent on extermination of the global Jewish population.

That spirit, which I refer to as "The Spirit of Amalek",

is responsible for propagating a poisonous disease

around planet earth called

"GENOCIDAL ANTI-SEMITISM".

GL

B

THE SPIRIT OF AMALEK

"The Enemy of the Ages"

"Drive them into the sea" has become the sadistic slogan of the erratic former Iranian president Mahmoud Achmadinejad. It's not enough for 400 million Arabs to inhabit 98.2% of the land of the Middle East. They don't want Israel to live on the other 1.8%. The issue throughout history is not just that Jews don't like Jesus, or that they have funny beards and strange customs. No. The issue for most of the world's nations that hate the Jews is that they are driven by a mad quest which has its origin in a spiritual DNA that dates back to the time of Moses. *"The spirit of Amalek",* unfortunately, is alive and well, fueled by Satan's fury and his desire to discredit and literally exterminate these people who were set apart by God many years ago as "the chosen people."

THE ENEMY OF THE AGES

Every neighborhood has its bully. When I was a third grader, there was an older kid named Wayne who was the terror of the playground. Anytime Wayne was around, all of us younger kids were fearfully in submission because Wayne was the king of the hill. To say that he was rough and crude was an understatement. He used his hygiene, or lack of it, as one of his tools of intimidation. I now understand, however, that language was by far his best weapon. He could swear like a sailor (no disrespect intended for my Navy friends). Somewhere I heard the quote, "Profanity is a crutch for conversational cripples." Bullies often begin their campaign of fear with abusive language. They talk loud and arrogantly, and often succeed in dominating - although we all know they are suffering from insecurity and lack of true social skills. He was two inches taller than me, and I always tried to be a conciliator between Wayne and the other kids. Finally one day, the volcano erupted. To get my attention, Wayne took my baseball glove and tossed it over the fence into a patch of weeds. Uh-oh. You don't go messin' with my glove. Baseball was my first love, and suddenly Wayne made his tough guy game too personal. I challenged him and he pushed me. Normally this was enough to make any third grader back down. On this occasion, fire was in my eyes, and I surprised him by countering his abuse. I went after him with all the force of an eight year old freight train. He hit me. I hit him back. And for the first time in his life, his superficial ego met resistance. Now I had seen enough movies to know that the bad guys usually lose, so I came after him with the confidence of a heavy weight, with full determination to risk my body, or my life, in order to teach Wayne a "once and for all, leave us alone" lesson that he would never forget. With noses bloodied and faces bruised, I won the battle and Wayne never bothered our neighborhood again.

Amalek was the consummate bully in the neighborhood called Arabia. The storyline is much overlooked by New Testament Christians who try to construct their own personal building of faith without establishing an Old Testament foundation.

This chapter of the book will set the stage for three of the great villains in world history. According to Exodus 17:16, *"The LORD has sworn; the LORD will have war against Amalek from generation to generation."* No other enemy in biblical chronology has the lofty reputation of battling with God Himself throughout the generations. Amalek becomes the symbol of anti-Semitism through the ages. But the message that I really want you to see goes beyond the historical person of Amalek. For Amalek is symbolic of all of the enemies of God. And I would suggest to you that there is literally a spiritual DNA that passes through the generations, carrying the demonic bloodline which hates Israel and defies God.

The person and theme of Amalek is so important to a proper understanding of Revelation that I almost named this entire book, *"The Spirit of Amalek."* In this chapter you will find an ancient clue to a modern problem. Why does the world hate the Jews? Yes, it begins with Isaac and Ishmael, and it continues with Jacob and Esau. But the full force of anti-Semitism is found in the battle fought between Moses and Amalek.

"Scientists announce that they have essentially cracked the human genetic code - a decade-long effort by over 1,000 researchers that could revolutionize the diagnosis and treatment of diseases once considered incurable. Decoding the 3 billion chemical "letters" in human DNA is seen as one of history's great scientific milestones - the biological equivalent of the moon landing."

Wouldn't it be refreshing if scientists finally came out with a study called:

"Why did God . . . "

Yes, DNA is a fascinating study of physical genetics. But even more fascinating than the mental exercise of chasing after how and why God created the physical universe is the spiritual exercise of chasing after the very heart of God to understand the amazing spiritual lineage of sin and death throughout every generation, in every tribe and tongue on planet earth. The DNA of Amalek is alive and well, and it continues to breed and re-populate itself through the hatred of the Arab nations who have chosen a foreign god.

You will find in the subsequent pages of this book that Satan is nothing but a counterfeit. Through the ages, he has attempted a poor imitation of everything good and beautiful that God has ever created. One of the great truths of scripture is that salvation is simply the habitation of God's spirit residing in the regenerated, redeemed soul of man. The book of Revelation is a frightening glimpse into the future that reveals Satan's counterfeit of this same process, by demonizing the heart and soul of man. Instead of being filled by "the Spirit of God," Satan is succeeding in filling the soul of man with "the spirit of Amalek." It is this spirit that continues to breed venom upon Israel and America and the Church. The gloves are off. Spiritual warfare is the shadowed reality of Amalek fighting Jehovah God through every generation.

THE ORIGIN OF AMALEK

JACOB AND ESAU STRUGGLE BEFORE BIRTH.

Gen 25:22 But the children struggled together within her; and she said, "If it is so, why then am I this way?" So she went to inquire of the LORD.

Gen 25:23 The LORD said to her, **"Two nations are in your womb**; And two peoples will be separated from your body; And one people shall be stronger than the other; **And the older shall serve the younger."**

Gen 25:24 When her days to be delivered were fulfilled, behold, there were twins in her womb.

Gen 25:25 Now the first came forth red, all over like a hairy garment; and they named him Esau.

Gen 25:26 Afterward his brother came forth with his hand holding on to Esau's heel, so his name was called Jacob; and Isaac was sixty years old when she gave birth to them.

> *Two nations are in your womb.* *Esau became the nation of Edomites. Edom means "reddish", a reference to the red-haired older brother. Jacob's name was changed to Israel after wrestling with an angel, and his ancestors became the Israelites.*
> *The older shall serve the younger. Like the older brothers of Joseph who kneeled before him as a ruler of Egypt, Jacob was destined to be the seed through whom the nation of Israel would be born.*

WHY DOES GOD HATE ESAU?

Mal 1:1 The oracle of the word of the LORD to Israel through Malachi.

Mal 1:2 "I have loved you," says the LORD. But you say, "How have You loved us?" "Was not Esau Jacob's brother?" declares the LORD. "Yet I have loved Jacob;

Mal 1:3 **but I have hated Esau**, and I have made his mountains a desolation and appointed his inheritance for the jackals of the wilderness."

> *I have hated Esau. In Genesis 28:20, Jacob vows to honor God. Nowhere in scripture do we find this attempt on the part of Esau. The birthright and the blessing were God's plan because the heart of Esau did not turn toward Jehovah God. What does it mean that God hated Esau? It can only mean that God knew that the descendants of Esau would be at war with Israel, and would ultimately become Satan's vehicle for trying to exterminate His chosen people.*

THE OLDER WILL SERVE THE YOUNGER.

Rom 9:11 for though the twins were not yet born and had not done anything good or bad, so that God's purpose according to His choice would stand, not because of works but because of Him who calls,
Rom 9:12 it was said to her, **"The older will serve the younger."**
Rom 9:13 Just as it is written, "Jacob I have loved, but Esau I hated."

> *"the older will serve the younger."* *Throughout scripture, there is evidence that God blessed the second born, not the first, who was considered to be the primary heir. Adam was the firstborn, Jesus was "the last Adam." Cain and Abel, Ishmael and Isaac, Esau and Jacob.*

ESAU SELLS HIS BIRTHRIGHT.

Gen 25:29 When Jacob had cooked stew, Esau came in from the field and he was famished;
Gen 25:30 and Esau said to Jacob, "Please let me have a swallow of that red stuff there, for I am famished." Therefore his name was called Edom.
Gen 25:31 But Jacob said, "First sell me your birthright."
Gen 25:32 Esau said, "Behold, I am about to die; so **of what use then is the birthright to me**?"
Gen 25:33 And Jacob said, "First swear to me"; so he swore to him, and sold his birthright to Jacob.

> *"of what use is the birthright to me?"* Esau was considered to be more brawny than his younger, more refined brother. Though Esau was Isaac's favorite, Rebecca favored Jacob and sought to see him gain favor with Isaac. Esau's casual attitude toward his birthright perhaps revealed his lack of good judgment, as revealed again later when he married Canaanite women against his parents' wishes. This injunction was also contrary to the mandate of Grandfather Abraham.

ESAU BRINGS GRIEF TO ISAAC.

Gen 26:34 When Esau was forty years old he married Judith the daughter of Beeri the Hittite, and Basemath the daughter of Elon the Hittite;
Gen 26:35 and they brought grief to Isaac and Rebekah.

> *The Hittites were generally considered to be Canaanites, from the lineage of Ham, and were not on the approved list of brides for Esau. Just as Esau showed poor judgment in selling his birthright, once again, he proved that he should not be the family heir apparent.*

AMALEK, THE GRANDSON OF ESAU

ISRAEL FIGHTS AGAINST AMALEK.

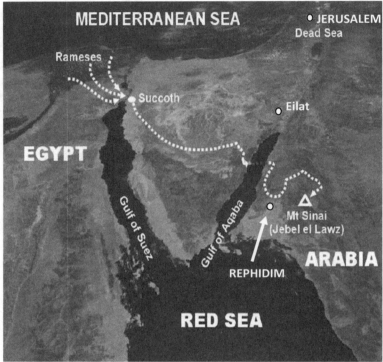

Exo 17:8 Then Amalek came and fought against Israel at Rephidim.

After the children of Israel had successfully crossed the Red Sea in the area of the Gulf of Aqaba, they were immediately confronted by another adversary. Amalek, the grandson of Esau, was their first obstacle before reaching Mount Sinai. Amalek then, became the first and lasting enemy of the Jews.

Psa 83:4 They have said, **_"Come, and let us wipe them out as a nation_**, That the name of Israel be remembered no more."

Psa 83:5 For they have conspired together with one mind; Against You they make a covenant:

Psa 83:6 The tents of Edom and the Ishmaelites, Moab and the Hagrites;

Psa 83:7 Gebal and Ammon and **Amalek**, Philistia with the inhabitants of Tyre;

Psa 83:8 Assyria also has joined with them; They have become a help to the children of Lot.

From Edom (south) to Tyre (north) to Assyria (east). The inference is that all the tribes and nations surrounding Israel were determined to exterminate the chosen people of God. Genocidal anti-semitism has become their burning hatred.

WHEN MOSES HELD HIS HANDS UP.

Exo 17:9 So Moses said to Joshua, "Choose men for us and go out, fight against **Amalek.** Tomorrow I will station myself on the top of the hill with the staff of God in my hand."

Exo 17:10 Joshua did as Moses told him, and fought against **Amalek**; and Moses, Aaron, and Hur went up to the top of the hill.

Exo 17:11 So it came about when Moses held his hand up, that Israel prevailed, and when he let his hand down, Amalek prevailed.

Exo 17:12 But Moses' hands were heavy. Then they took a stone and put it under him, and he sat on it; and Aaron and Hur supported his hands, one on one side and one on the other. Thus his hands were steady until the sun set.

Exo 17:13 So Joshua overwhelmed **Amalek** and his people with the edge of the sword.

Exo 17:14 Then the LORD said to Moses, "Write this in a book as a memorial and recite it to Joshua, that **I will utterly blot out the memory of Amalek** from under heaven."

Exo 17:15 Moses built an altar and named it The LORD is My Banner;

Exo 17:16 and he said, "The LORD has sworn; **the LORD will have war against Amalek** from generation to generation."

This story is another manifestation of God's power. Moses controlled the war simply by holding his hands up. God even allowed human assistance. Notice the important prophecy. Amalek was so grievous that God would blot out the memory of Amalek. Notice the phrase "The Lord will have war with Amalek" implies that Israel will be at war. Notice the passage in Psalms 83 is a manifestation of "genocidal anti-Semitism." There are 10 nations represented in this list. Could this possibly be some clue to the ten horn confederacy that rises against Israel In the last days?

Deu 25:17 "Remember what Amalek did to you along the way when you came out from Egypt,

Deu 25:18 how he met you along the way and attacked among you all the stragglers at your rear when you were faint and weary; and he did not fear God.

Deu 25:19 "Therefore it shall come about when the LORD your God has given you rest from all your surrounding enemies, in the land which the LORD your God gives you as an inheritance to possess, **you shall blot out the memory of Amalek** from under heaven; you must not forget.

THE SPIRIT OF AMALEK

AMALEK - This Canaanite descendent of Esau fought against Israel when they entered the Promised Land. (Exodus 17:8) Amalek was guilty then, and his descendants are guilty now, of genocidal anti-Semitism - the intent to exterminate the Jewish people. *"The LORD has sworn; the LORD will have war against Amalek from generation to generation." Ex 17:16*

AGAG and KING SAUL - God instructed Saul to kill Agag and his kingdom, including livestock. Saul kept the spoils and spared Agag. God took his kingship away and Samuel took the life of King Agag. Ironically Saul died at the hands of a young Amalekite. 2 Sam 1:2

THE YOUNG AMALEKITE AND KING DAVID - The young man came to the camp of David, returning Saul's crown, and admitted helping Saul fall on his sword. In spite of his relative innocence, David knew he had to be killed. 2 Samuel 1:2-15

HAMAN - Promoted to second in the Persian kingdom, this Agagite was jealous of Mordecai, Queen Esther's uncle, so he made an edict to exterminate all the Jews in the kingdom. Esther 3:6

ANTIOCHUS EPIPHANES - One of four eventual successors of Alexander the Great, this Syrian leader came through Jerusalem after losing a battle and desecrated the temple. After three years he was defeated and Hanukkah was born. Antiochus was the archetype of the Anti-Christ.

KING HEROD - Born as an Edomite (the lineage of Amalek), Herod was so jealous at the birth of Jesus that he had all the male children under 2 years of age executed. Matthew 2:16

ADOLPH HITLER - The spirit of Amalek (genocidal anti-semitisim) reached its crescendo in the wicked ideology of Hitler. *"If I can send the flower of the German nation into the hell of war without the smallest pity for the spilling of precious German blood, then surely I have the right to remove millions of an inferior race that breeds like vermin."*

MAHMOUD AHMADINEJAD - *"Anybody who recognizes Israel will burn in the fire of the Islamic nation's fury. Remove Israel before it is too late and save yourself from the fury of regional nations. The skirmishes in the occupied land are part of a war of destiny. The outcome of hundreds of years of war will be defined in Palestinian land. As the Imam said, "Israel must be wiped off the map."*

THE ABOMINATION OF DESOLATION - The evil seed of Amalek, 4000 years later, will be the Anti-Christ. Satan will finally have an emissary to challenge the sovereignty of God. The long battle between Isaac and Ishmael will culminate in the battle of Armageddon.

THE HISTORY OF AMALEK

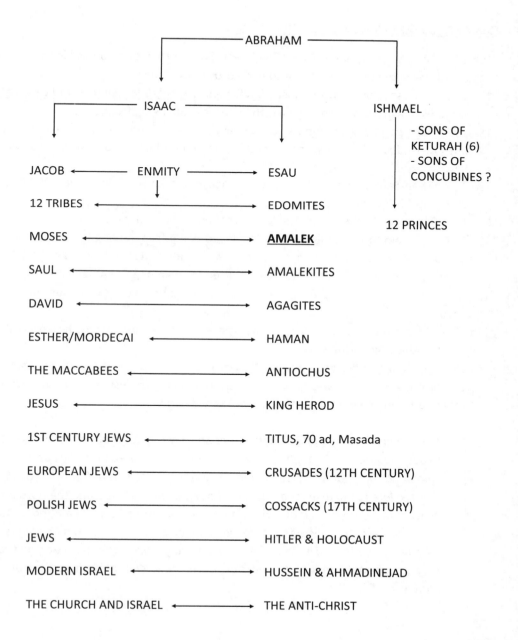

ABRAHAM

ISAAC

ISHMAEL
- SONS OF KETURAH (6)
- SONS OF CONCUBINES ?

12 PRINCES

	ENMITY	
JACOB ←		→ ESAU
12 TRIBES ←		→ EDOMITES
MOSES ←		**AMALEK**
SAUL ←		→ AMALEKITES
DAVID ←		→ AGAGITES
ESTHER/MORDECAI ←		→ HAMAN
THE MACCABEES ←		→ ANTIOCHUS
JESUS ←		→ KING HEROD
1ST CENTURY JEWS ←		→ TITUS, 70 ad, Masada
EUROPEAN JEWS ←		→ CRUSADES (12TH CENTURY)
POLISH JEWS ←		→ COSSACKS (17TH CENTURY)
JEWS ←		→ HITLER & HOLOCAUST
MODERN ISRAEL ←		→ HUSSEIN & AHMADINEJAD
THE CHURCH AND ISRAEL ←		→ THE ANTI-CHRIST

Saul and the Amalekite King

KING SAUL SPARES KING AGAG

1Sa 15:1 Then Samuel said to Saul, "The LORD sent me to anoint you as king over His people, over Israel; now therefore, listen to the words of the LORD.

1Sa 15:2 "Thus says the LORD of hosts, *'I will punish Amalek for what he did to Israel,* how he set himself against him on the way while he was coming up from Egypt.

1Sa 15:3 *'Now go and strike Amalek* and utterly destroy all that he has, and do not spare him; but put to death both man and woman, child and infant, ox and sheep, camel and donkey.'"

1Sa 15:4 Then Saul summoned the people and numbered them in Telaim, 200,000 foot soldiers and 10,000 men of Judah.

1Sa 15:5 Saul came to the city of Amalek and set an ambush in the valley.

1Sa 15:6 Saul said to the Kenites, "Go, depart, go down from among the Amalekites, so that I do not destroy you with them; for you showed kindness to all the sons of Israel when they came up from Egypt." So the Kenites departed from among the Amalekites.

1Sa 15:7 So Saul defeated the Amalekites, from Havilah as you go to Shur, which is east of Egypt.

1Sa 15:8 He captured Agag the king of the Amalekites alive, and utterly destroyed all the people with the edge of the sword.

1Sa 15:9 *But Saul and the people spared Agag* and the best of the sheep, the oxen, the fatlings, the lambs, and all that was good, and were not willing to destroy them utterly; but everything despised and worthless, that they utterly destroyed.

Now go and strike Amalek. Notice that Saul's very first order of business as king was to destroy Amalek. Though he fought and won, he compromised by not fulfilling God's command completely. Verse 22 reminds us that "to obey is better than sacrifice". It was too late to make amends. Notice that King Saul did the same thing we do. When he was confronted about his sin, he repented and asked Samuel and God for forgiveness, and he fully expected that life would go on as usual. Little did he understand the magnitude of his sin. The sins of Amalek were a grievous offense to God and compromise would not be tolerated. Saul's disobedience would cost him his kingdom, and ultimately, his life.

GOD AND SAMUEL CONDEMN KING SAUL

1Sa 15:10 Then the word of the LORD came to Samuel, saying,

1Sa 15:11 **"I regret** that I have made Saul king, for he has turned back from following Me and has not carried out My commands." And Samuel was distressed and cried out to the LORD all night.

1Sa 15:12 Samuel rose early in the morning to meet Saul; and it was told Samuel, saying, "Saul came to Carmel, and behold, he set up a monument for himself, then turned and proceeded on down to Gilgal."

1Sa 15:13 Samuel came to Saul, and Saul said to him, "Blessed are you of the LORD! I have carried out the command of the LORD."

1Sa 15:14 But Samuel said, "What then is this bleating of the sheep in my ears, and the lowing of the oxen which I hear?"

1Sa 15:15 Saul said, "They have brought them from the Amalekites, for the people spared the **best of the sheep and oxen**, to sacrifice to the LORD your God; but the rest we have utterly destroyed."

1Sa 15:16 Then Samuel said to Saul, "Wait, and let me tell you what the LORD said to me last night." And he said to him, "Speak!"

1Sa 15:17 Samuel said, "Is it not true, though you were little in your own eyes, you were made the head of the tribes of Israel? And the LORD anointed you king over Israel,

1Sa 15:18 and the LORD sent you on a mission, and said, 'Go and utterly destroy the sinners, the Amalekites, and fight against them until they are exterminated.'

1Sa 15:19 "Why then did you not obey the voice of the LORD, but rushed upon the spoil and did what was evil in the sight of the LORD?"

I regret. See comment on 1 Samuel 15:35

best of the sheep and oxen. We are as guilty as King Saul of re-interpreting the commands of God to fit our circumstances. Though God spoke clearly through Samuel and told him to destroy ALL the people, ALL the livestock, ALL the possessions of this clan of people - Saul decided that he should re-interpret God's command and spare the King and some of the spoils of war.

People often fit into one of two categories: they are either leaders or followers. The followers are usually those who follow the rules, and live within the boundaries of the laws of the land. For the leader, it's a bit more complicated. They often think outside the box and march to the beat of a different drummer. To be visionary is good, and leaders must often follow their heart. BUT, when God commands, there is no room for interpretation. The leader must always remember to heed the voice of the Shepherd.

OBEY IS BETTER THAN SACRIFICE.

1Sa 15:20 Then Saul said to Samuel, "I did obey the voice of the LORD, and went on the mission on which the LORD sent me, and have brought back Agag the king of Amalek, and have utterly destroyed the Amalekites.

1Sa 15:21 "But the people took some of the spoil, sheep and oxen, the choicest of the things devoted to destruction, to sacrifice to the LORD your God at Gilgal."

1Sa 15:22 Samuel said, "Has the LORD as much delight in burnt offerings and sacrifices As in obeying the voice of the LORD? Behold, **to obey is better than sacrifice**, And to heed than the fat of rams.

1Sa 15:23 "For rebellion is as the sin of divination, And insubordination is as iniquity and idolatry. Because you have rejected the word of the LORD, He has also rejected you from being king."

> ***To obey is better than sacrifice.*** *Seven words. Saul did not understand that even though he said, "I did obey", those words fell empty on the ears of God. Saul obeyed 80% of what God asked, but 80% is not enough. In a court of law, 80% may be seen as good intention, or "he had his heart in the right place." But in the court of God, almost is not good enough. Even if Saul had pure intentions to give the best sacrifices to God, there is no equivalent for obedience.*

KING SAUL BEGS FOR MERCY.

1Sa 15:24 Then Saul said to Samuel, "I have sinned; I have indeed transgressed the command of the LORD and your words, because I feared the people and listened to their voice.

1Sa 15:25 "Now therefore, please pardon my sin and return with me, that I may worship the LORD."

1Sa 15:26 But Samuel said to Saul, "I will not return with you; for you have rejected the word of the LORD, and the LORD has rejected you from being king over Israel."

1Sa 15:27 As Samuel turned to go, Saul seized the edge of his robe, and it tore.

1Sa 15:28 So Samuel said to him, **"The LORD has torn the kingdom of Israel from you** today and has given it to your neighbor, who is better than you.

1Sa 15:29 "Also **the Glory of Israel** will not lie or change His mind; for He is not a man that He should change His mind."

SAMUEL EXECUTES KING AGAG, THE KING OF THE AMALEKITES.

1Sa 15:30 Then he said, "I have sinned; but please honor me now before the elders of my people and before Israel, and go back with me, that I may worship the LORD your God."

1Sa 15:31 So Samuel went back following Saul, and Saul worshiped the LORD.

1Sa 15:32 Then Samuel said, "Bring me Agag, the king of the Amalekites." ***And Agag came to him cheerfully.*** And Agag said, "Surely the bitterness of death is past."

1Sa 15:33 But Samuel said, "As your sword has made women childless, so shall your mother be childless among women." **And Samuel hewed Agag to pieces** before the LORD at Gilgal.

1Sa 15:34 Then Samuel went to Ramah, but Saul went up to his house at Gibeah of Saul.

1Sa 15:35 Samuel did not see Saul again until the day of his death; for Samuel grieved over Saul. **And the LORD regretted** that He had made Saul *king over Israel.*

> ***And Agag came to him cheerfully.*** *Agag was another leader that was out of touch. For him, this was a political game that was being played. He expected that since Saul had spared him, Samuel would do the same. Once again, Israel's disobedience would reap severe consequences for the future. The Amalekites who survived would go on to plague the children of Israel throughout every generation until the end of the age.*

> ***And Samuel hewed Agag.*** *In the modern court system, Agag would have received a delayed and lengthy trial and would have been granted a comfortable asylum in an executive "courtesy" prison. Samuel understood swift justice. This was not the time for mercy or grace or tolerance. Samuel, as a judge, also wore the hat of being a military commander. He had no problem settling this account on the spot. Notice it says he did this "before the Lord."*

> ***And the Lord regretted.*** *Gen 6:6 says "The LORD was sorry that He had made man on the earth, and He was grieved in His heart." We understand that God is sovereign, and He knows in advance all things, for no fact or decision is beyond His control. When it says "the Lord regretted" perhaps it is better translated to say, he lamented. God knows the outcome of all things. When Jesus wept over Jerusalem, this was not an emotion that took Him by surprise. He wept, He lamented, because this was part of the sovereign plan of an omniscient God who allows the free will of man to inter-mingle with the mysterious sovereignty of a loving God.*

DAVID AND THE AMALEKITE SOLDIER

KING DAVID AND THE YOUNG AMALEKITE.

2Sa 1:1 Now it came about after the death of Saul, when David had returned from the slaughter of the Amalekites, that David remained two days in Ziklag.

2Sa 1:2 On the third day, behold, a man came out of the camp from Saul, with his clothes torn and dust on his head. And it came about when he came to David that he fell to the ground and prostrated himself.

2Sa 1:3 Then David said to him, "From where do you come?" And he said to him, "I have escaped from the camp of Israel."

2Sa 1:4 David said to him, "How did things go? Please tell me." And he said, "The people have fled from the battle, and also many of the people have fallen and are dead; and Saul and Jonathan his son are dead also."

2Sa 1:5 So David said to the young man who told him, "How do you know that Saul and his son Jonathan are dead?"

2Sa 1:6 The young man who told him said, "By chance I happened to be on Mount Gilboa, and behold, Saul was leaning on his spear. And behold, the chariots and the horsemen pursued him closely.

2Sa 1:7 "When he looked behind him, he saw me and called to me. And I said, 'Here I am.'

2Sa 1:8 He said to me, 'Who are you?' And I answered him, **'I am an Amalekite.'**

2Sa 1:9 Then he said to me, 'Please stand beside me and kill me, for agony has seized me because my life still lingers in me.'

2Sa 1:10 "So I stood beside him and killed him, because I knew that he could not live after he had fallen. And I took the crown which was on his head and the bracelet which was on his arm, and I have brought them here to my lord."

> *I am an Amalekite. 1 Samuel 31:3 corroborates this story, as follows: "The battle went heavily against Saul, and the archers hit him; and he was badly wounded by the archers. Then Saul said to his armor bearer, "Draw your sword and pierce me through with it, otherwise these uncircumcised will come and pierce me through and make sport of me." But his armor bearer would not, for he was greatly afraid. So Saul took his sword and fell on it." The irony of this story is that the young man acted nobly in honoring Saul's request to die quickly, and also for returning his crown and bracelet. Unfortunately for the young man, David understood there was no mercy and no negotiating with God's original mandate to exterminate ALL the Amalekites.*

2Sa 1:11 Then David took hold of his clothes and tore them, and so also did all the men who were with him.

2Sa 1:12 They mourned and wept and fasted until evening for Saul and his son Jonathan and for the people of the LORD and the house of Israel, because they had fallen by the sword.

2Sa 1:13 David said to the young man who told him, "Where are you from?" And he answered, **"I am the son of an alien, an Amalekite."**

2Sa 1:14 Then David said to him, "How is it you were not afraid to stretch out your hand to destroy the LORD'S anointed?"

2Sa 1:15 And David called one of the young men and said, "Go, cut him down." So he struck him and he died.

2Sa 1:16 David said to him, "Your blood is on your head, for your mouth has testified against you, saying, 'I have killed the LORD'S anointed.'"

*This statue of King David
was sculpted by Nicolas Cordier
around 1600 ad
and now stands in the Borghese Chapel
of the Basilica of Saint Mary in Rome, Italy.
Notice the "horns" on David's crown.
Perhaps this is the proper way
to view the horns
that are later corrupted by the beast.*

QUEEN ESTHER AND HAMAN

Est 3:1 After these events King Ahasuerus promoted **Haman, the son of Hammedatha the Agagite,** and advanced him and established his authority over all the princes who *were* with him.

Est 3:2 All the king's servants who were at the king's gate bowed down and paid homage to Haman; for so the king had commanded concerning him. But Mordecai neither bowed down nor paid homage.

Est 3:3 Then the king's servants who were at the king's gate said to Mordecai, "Why are you transgressing the king's command?"

Est 3:4 Now it was when they had spoken daily to him and he would not listen to them, that they told Haman to see whether Mordecai's reason would stand; for he had told them that he was a Jew.

Est 3:5 When Haman saw that Mordecai neither bowed down nor paid homage to him, Haman was filled with rage.

Est 3:6 But he disdained to lay hands on Mordecai alone, for they had told him who the people of Mordecai were; **therefore Haman sought to destroy all the Jews,** the people of Mordecai, who were throughout the whole kingdom of Ahasuerus.

The Babylonians held Jerusalem captive for 70 years and then the Medo-Persian Empire rose. King Xerxes (otherwise known as Ahashuerus) ruled over Jerusalem from Persia, known today as Iran. The book of Esther describes a significant event in the life of the Jewish people. Because of the Persian Queen's disobedience, Esther (a young Jewish girl) was promoted to Queen. After a threat to the king, Haman was promoted in the kingdom. Haman was an Agagite, a descendent of Agag, the king of the Amalekites, whom Saul refused to kill. Mordecai was the Jewish uncle of Esther, and Mordecai refused to bow down before the pagan gods or the king. This enraged Haman, who then sought to kill all the Jews in the kingdom. In the spirit of Amalek, Haman (who was a descendent) planned an act of extermination (genocide) against the Jewish people. The story ends as Esther boldly exposes Haman's treachery, and Mordecai is promoted to prominence in the kingdom. What we witness in this story is the spirit of Amalek at work to destroy the Jewish nation. The resultant celebration produced a Jewish holiday named Purim.

THE FEAST OF PURIM

Many of the Jewish feasts or holidays originated as a result of Jewish persecution. After Pharaoh persecuted the Israelites in Egypt, Passover was instituted. The attempted genocide of the Jewish people in Persia led to Purim; and the celebration of Hanukkah was the direct result of acknowledging the victory over Antiochus Epiphanes in 165 bc. As a result of Hitler's attempts at genocide, the displaced Jews of the world celebrated nationhood on May 14, 1948. Purim is celebrated on the 14th day of Adar, the last month of the Jewish calendar, which loosely coincides with a time between February and March. The observance includes the following:

1) reading of the book of Esther at the synagogue, which includes mocking Haman. The name Haman is mentioned 54 times in the book of Esther. For each of those times, the congregation makes noise, or hisses and boos at the mention of Haman. Typically they hold a noisemaker called a "grager", which makes a ratcheting sound. The congregation, including the children, enjoy this casual way of acknowledging Haman's sins against the Jewish people. In Deuteronomy 25:19, when it says to blot out the remembrance of Amalek (the ancestor of Haman), some will write Haman's name on two rocks or the bottom of their shoes. They will then bang the rocks together, or scuffle their feet until there is no reference to Haman. Each person will choose a name among the sons of Haman (Esther 9:7) and all ten names will be uttered in one breath, in brief memory of their death by hanging.

2) Preparation of specific foods to remember Esther and Haman. Among the foods are seeds and nuts, which would have been Esther's diet. There are also 3 sided fruit filled pastries called "Haman's ears" and a meat filled dumpling called "kreplach".

3) Giving gifts of food to friends and money to the poor. It is tradition to give 2 different foods to one person and 2 charitable donations to two people in need.

4) Masquerade parties, celebration and drinking to extreme. In some areas of the world, the masquerade is a way of symbolizing that God was in disguise in the background, accomplishing his task to save the Jews. Excessive drinking is accepted during Purim as a way of "blurring" the difference between "the curse of Haman" and "the blessing of Mordecai."

It should be noted that Hitler banned Purim so as not to remember the 75,000 Persians that were killed trying to exterminate the Jews. Joseph Stalin was paralyzed on Purim in 1953, and Julius Streicher, who incited hatred among the Germans, was heard to sarcastically say "Purimfest 1946" as he ascended the scaffold steps at his hanging, after the Nuremburg trials which convicted him of crimes against humanity.

THE SWORD OF ANTIOCHUS

"Then the king will do as he pleases,
and he will exalt and magnify himself above every god
and will speak monstrous things against the God of gods;
and he will prosper until the indignation is finished,
for that which is decreed will be done.
Daniel 11:36

The year was 168 bc. Greece had arrested control of the world empire from the Medo-Persians, and the Greek kingdom had been divided into four parts after the death of the infamous Alexander the Great in 323 bc. Antiochus Epiphanes ruled the Syrian part of the Greek empire and he desired to conquer the Egyptian part of the kingdom for himself. He traveled south to Egypt passing through Israel on his way to wage war. The Roman government was growing in strength and did not want Antiochus to grow stronger, so they "convinced" him (militarily) to go home without a victory. Angered at his failure, Antiochus (whose name Epiphanes means "the shining one") came back through Jerusalem looking to avenge his loss. Tens of thousands were killed, buildings were toppled to the ground, and then Antiochus set his sights on the temple, the crown jewel of Hebrew worship, sitting high above the Western wall of the city on Mount Moriah - an area that is still today called the temple mount. He killed the priests, stole all the golden temple ornamentation, erected a statue in honor of the Greek god Zeus and finally sacrificed a pig on the sacred altar. For three years, Antiochus (whose enemies nicknamed him Epimanes, meaning madman), held Jerusalem in control. Then in 165 bc, Judas ("the Hammer") Macabee began a revolt that ultimately drove Antiochus and his forces off the sacred mountain. Once again, the spirit of Amalek had reared its head to destroy the nation of Israel. The Jews began the painful process of rebuilding and they started with the temple. They needed oil in order to ceremonially cleanse the temple, but there was only enough oil for one day. Miraculously, the oil lasted eight days, and because of this miracle, the resultant celebration produced a Jewish holiday known as Hanukkah, the dedication of lights. Oddly enough, Antiochus had entered Jerusalem on December 25, the birthday of Zeus. He was ejected on December 25, the day of Hanukkuh - and we celebrate the birth of Jesus on December 25. Antiochus' evil deeds are prophesied in Daniel as a symbolic foreshadowing of the end of time, when the Anti-Christ will exalt himself and blaspheme God, in a last-ditch attempt to kill Israel and the Church, and to set himself as ruler of the nations. Satan needs to read the back of the book.

HANUKKAH

"The Festival of Lights"

In John 10:22, Jesus is walking in the temple along the portico of Solomon at a time casually referred only in this passage as the "Feast of Dedication" during the winter months. The Hebrew word for dedication is Hanukkah. What Jesus was actually celebrating was the Jewish victory over the Syrian Greeks in 165. For 2000 years, Hanukkah has been celebrated on Kislev 25, which coincides (approximately) with November and December of our calendar. Because of the popularity of Christmas, the Hanukkah season (eight days) is celebrated much like Christmas - with gifts and food and family activities.

The central theme of Hanukkah is the lighting of the **Hanukkiyah** (han-u-kee-yah). Unlike the traditional seven candlestick menorah, this one has nine candlesticks. Eight of the candles represent the eight days that the oil burned when the Jews were cleansing and rededicating the temple in 165 bc. There was only enough oil for one night, but on this occasion, the oil burned (miraculously) for eight nights. Each night of the Hanukkah season, the parents and children will light an additional light, until all are burning. The ninth candlestick is called the "attendant" candle, and is used to light the other eight.

You can't have a party without food, and this Jewish celebration focuses on **fried foods,** since olive oil was the primary object of the temple rededication. Potato cakes, called "latkes" have been popular through the ages, as well as jelly filled pastries called "sufganiyot".

Besides traditional gift giving, the children are encouraged during this season to play a game which involves spinning a four sided top, called a **"dreidel".** History records that during the dreaded reign of Antiochus, scripture reading was forbidden, so the Jews would pretend to be spinning the top when the guards would pass by. In the current game, the players begin with chocolate coins wrapped in gold foil. The object of the game is to spin the top and win the pot of gold. Players rotate by chipping in a coin or collecting the current pokey. The four letters of the Hebrew alphabet, "nun, gimmel, hey and shin," represent four possible plays: nun means you get nothing, gimmel means you get the current pot, hey means you get half the pot and shin means you chip into the pot.

By the way, the ninth stick on the candelabra is called the "shammish", which means the servant or attendant candle. This candle is sometimes higher, sometimes lower than the other candles, but always used to serve the other candles. Little do the Jews of today understand that Jesus, who is the Servant Messiah (the true shammish). spoke to the Pharisses at Hanukkah, when he said, "I am the light of the world."

EXCERPTS FROM THE BOOK OF MACCABEES

ANTIOCHUS COMES TO TOWN.

¹⁰ And there came out of them a wicked root Antiochus named Epiphanes, son of Antiochus the king, who had been a hostage at Rome, and he reigned in the hundred and thirty and seventh year of the kingdom of the Greeks.

²⁴ And when he had taken all away, he went into his own land, having made a great massacre, and spoken very proudly.

²⁵ Therefore there was a great mourning in Israel, in every place where they were;

³⁰ And he spoke peaceable words to them, but all was deceit: for when they had given him credence, he fell suddenly upon the city, and destroyed many people of Israel.

³⁹ Her sanctuary was laid waste like a wilderness, her feasts were turned into mourning, her sabbaths into reproach and her honor into contempt.

⁴⁰ As had been her glory, so was her dishonor increased, and her excellency was turned into mourning.

⁴¹ Moreover king Antiochus wrote to his whole kingdom, that all should be one people,

⁴² And every one should leave his laws: so all the heathen agreed according to the commandment of the king.

THE APOSTASY

⁴³ Many also of the Israelites consented to his religion, and sacrificed unto idols, and profaned the sabbath.

⁴⁹ To the end they might forget the law, and change all the ordinances.

⁵⁷ And whoever was found with any the book of the testament, or if any committed to the law, the king commanded that they should put him to death.

⁵⁸ Thus they did by their authority to the Israelites every month, to as many as were found in the cities.

⁵⁹ Now the twenty-fifth day of the month they sacrificed upon the idol altar, which was upon the altar of God.

⁶⁰ At which time according to the commandment they put to death certain women that had caused their children to be circumcised.

⁶¹ And they hanged the infants about their necks, and rifled their houses, and slew them those that had been circumcised.

⁶⁴ And there was very great wrath upon Israel.

MATTATHIAS REBELS AGAINST ANTIOCHUS.

[19] Then Mattathias answered and spoke with a loud voice, "Though all the nations that are under the king's dominion obey him, and fall away every one from the religion of their fathers, and give consent to his commandments:

[20] Yet will I and my sons and my brethren walk in the covenant of our fathers."

[38] So they rose up against them in battle on the sabbath, and they slew them, with their wives and children and their cattle, to the number of a thousand people.

[66] As for Judas Maccabeus, he hath been mighty and strong, even from his youth up: let him be your captain, and fight the battle of the people.

[27] Now when king Antiochus heard these things, he was full of indignation: so he sent and gathered together all the forces of his realm, a very strong army.

[28] He opened his treasure, and gave his soldiers pay for a year, commanding them to be ready whenever he should need them.

[39] And with them he sent <u>forty thousand footmen, and seven thousand horsemen</u>, to go into the land of Judea, and to destroy it, as the king commanded.

JUDAS "THE HAMMER" DEFEATS ANTIOCHUS.

[53] How shall we be able to stand against them, except thou, O God, be our help?

[59] For it is better for us to die in battle, than to behold the calamities of our people and our sanctuary.

[60] Nevertheless, as the will of God is in heaven, so let him do.

[8] Then said Judas to the men that were with him, Fear not their multitude, neither be afraid of their assault.

[9] Remember how our fathers were delivered in the Red sea, when Pharaoh pursued them with an army.

[10] Now therefore let us cry unto heaven, if perhaps the Lord will have mercy upon us, and remember the covenant of our fathers, and destroy this host before our face this day:

[11] That so all the heathen may know that there is one who delivers and saves Israel.

[25] Thus Israel had a great deliverance that day.

[38] And when they saw the sanctuary desolate, and the altar profaned, and the gates burned up, and shrubs growing in the courts as in a forest, or in one of the mountains, yea, and the priests' chambers pulled down;

[39] They rent their clothes, and made great lamentation, and cast ashes upon their heads,

[55] Then all the people fell upon their faces, worshipping and praising the God of heaven, who had given them good success.

[56] And so they kept the dedication of the altar eight days and offered burnt offerings with gladness, and sacrificed the sacrifice of deliverance and praise.

THE VICIOUS REIGN OF KING HEROD

*"Go and search carefully for the Child;
and when you have found Him, report to me,
so that I too may come and worship Him."*

Herod the Great lived from 74 bc to 4 bc, and was the client king (from 36 bc to 4 bc) of the area around Jerusalem known as Judea. He is best known for two things: the expansion of the Jewish temple in Jerusalem, and the "massacre of the innocents" at the time of Jesus' birth. Persian astrologers followed the star to Jerusalem in search of the child born "King of the Jews", and Herod appealed to them to reveal His location. Scholars tell us that Herod probably suffered from depression and paranoia. After all, he had three ambitious boys who were in line for his throne. But God warned the magi in a dream to "go home by another way." As the result of their disregard, Herod decreed that there should be wholesale slaughtering of all the baby boys. That's called genocidal anti-Semitism.

> *Matthew 2:16 Then when Herod saw that he had been tricked by the magi, he became very enraged, and sent and slew all the male children who were in Bethlehem and all its vicinity, from two years old and under, according to the time which he had determined from the magi.*

Herod was jealous of baby Jesus. But the Holy Spirit warned father Joseph to retreat to Egypt until Herod's death. Shortly after Jesus' birth, Herod died. Coincidence? Not likely. Herod was an idumean, which means he was an Edomite, which makes him a candidate for the spirit of Amalek. Afraid that no one would attend his funeral, Herod contracted with the wealthiest men in town to attend. His intent was to kill them so that the town would really have something to mourn at the time of his death! How sick is that?

Herod's son Archelaus became king briefly, then was followed by Herod Antipas, who was alive at the time of John the Baptist' ministry. Antipas was married to his brother's wife, Herodius, and because John preached conviction to him, he had John imprisoned. While in jail, Herod had a party, at which Herodius' daughter danced for his pleasure. Because of her performance, he offered her "anything", and she asked for John's head on a platter. Though Herod personally revered John as a righteous man, he showed weakness by conceding to the whims of a drunken crowd. John's death should be viewed as the first Christian martyr.

HOME BY ANOTHER WAY

James Taylor, singer, songwriter
(See Youtube, "Never Die Young" album)

I'm intrigued by the fact that this very popular, secular songwriter
(one of my favorites) would take the time to write this creative song
based on a biblical story. 2,000 years later, Herod is still a villain.

Those magic men the magi, some people call them wise
Or oriental, even kings, well anyway, those guys
They visited with Jesus, they sure enjoyed their stay
Then warned in a dream of king Herod's scheme,
They went home by another way

Yes they went home by another way, home by another way
Maybe me and you can be wise guys too, and go home by another way
We can make it another way, safe home as they used to say
Keep a weather eye to the chart on high, and go home another way

Steer clear of royal welcomes, avoid a big to-do
A king who would slaughter the innocents will not cut a deal for you
He really, really wants those presents, he'll comb your camels fur
Until his boys announce they've found trace amounts
Of your frankincense, gold and myrrh

Well it pleasures me to be here, and to sing this song tonight
They tell me that life is a miracle, and I figured that they're right
But Herod's always out there, he's got our cards on file
Its a lead pipe cinch, if we give an inch, old Herod likes to take a mile

Its best to go home by another way, home by another way
We got this far to a lucky star, but tomorrow is another day
We can make it another way, safe home as they used to say
Keep a weather eye to the chart on high
And go home another way

HITLER AND THE HOLOCAUST

*"If I can send the flower of the German nation
into the hell of war without the smallest pity
for the spilling of precious German blood,
then surely I have the right to remove millions
of an inferior race that breeds like vermin."*
Adolph Hitler

You would think that in this day of multiculturalism and toleration we would have gotten past the absurd notion that Jews are some kind of inferior breed of human. It is true that Christianity has fostered the subliminal notion for centuries that today's Jews are responsible for the death of Jesus. Hopefully we understand the words of scripture when Jesus said that *"scripture must be fulfilled."* The Jews, the Romans, the pagans of all centuries, as well as my own sins, were responsible for nailing Jesus to the cross. Without giving disproportionate attention to the likes of Hitler, this is merely a reminder that the holocaust was a historical event in which the German Third Reich saw itself as the agent of salvation, a once-and-for-all extermination, of the Jewish race. The consequence of Hitler's action resulted in the mass murder of eleven million Europeans, among whom were six million Jews. This is probably a good time to mention that Hitler was a Darwinist, one who believed that the survival of the fittest really meant population control against those who were deemed to be inferior. It should be an affront to every Afro-American, every Jew, and every person who seeks the civil rights of a noble nation, to be righteously incensed at the very notion that Charles Darwin's name should be hallowed in the halls of higher education. It is a primary plot in the agenda of Satan himself to stage evolution as some sort of ethnic cleansing. There is an interesting theory that Adolph Hitler was actually a descendant of the ancient Edomite tribe. Whether this is true or some kind of urban myth doesn't matter. What does matter is that Hitler was definitely an heir to the "spirit of Amalek." Genocide and one-world domination flowed through the veins of this man, whose favorite quote was "ein volk, ein reich, ein fuhrer" (one people, one empire, one leader.) Yes, Hitler wanted to be a one-world leader with a one-world government that reigned for a thousand years. Hitler was a pawn of Satan, a vessel of wrath prepared for destruction (Rom 9:22). It is important that the Church, the Body of Christ, condemn the Holocaust and its agents of genocide. God is not finished with Israel, and we must protect the rights of Israel, while at the same time, seeking for the salvation of every son of Abraham through the redemption of the Messiah.

THE ISLAMIC JIHAD

"Anybody who recognizes Israel will burn in the fire of the Islamic nation's fury. Remove Israel before it is too late, and save yourself from the fury of regional nations. As the Imam said, "Israel must be wiped off the map." **Former Iranian President Mahmoud Ahmadinejad**

The following are excerpts from speeches delivered by Ahmadinejad during his tenure as the political leader of Iran. **IF** this man speaks on behalf of the imams of the Islamic world, and **IF** these words are fuel to ignite the fury of the jihadist movement, then the western world must accept the reality that our sanctions and our threats are impotent to contain the wrath that the Middle East bears against The United States and the Nation of Israel.

"The skirmishes in the occupied land are part of a war of destiny. The outcome of hundreds of years of war will be defined in Palestinian land. The Islamic world will not let its historic enemy live in its heartland. Some European countries insist on saying that Hitler killed millions of innocent Jews in furnaces. We don't accept this claim. They have created a myth in the name of the Holocaust. Unlocking the chest of the Holocaust and re-examining it would be tantamount to cutting the vital arteries of the Zionist regime. The real cure for the conflict is elimination of the Zionist regime. The United States and the Zionist regime of Israel will soon come to the end of their lives. Zionists are the true incarnation of Satan. The Iranian nation seeks peace and security all over the world and wants to have relations with all nations and states except for the Zionist regime. This regime is the flag of Satan, and the continuation of its existence is an insult to human dignity. The world powers should not think that the Iranian nation and other nations in the region will take off their hands from the throat of the Zionists and their supporters. I warn you to abandon the filthy Zionist entity that has reached the end of the line, and accept that the life of Zionists will sooner or later come to an end. World powers have created a black and dirty microbe named the Zionist regime, and today this regime is on its way to annihilation. Those who link their interests to the Zionists will go to hell. Don't be afraid of those Zionists. They are on the verge of death. Their time has passed. Is it possible for us to witness a world without America and Zionism? You should know that this slogan, this goal, can certainly be achieved."

"On the day that the Son of Man is revealed,
Christ says it will be just as it was
In the days of Noah and Lot.
God will deliver His faithful from persecution,
And then, on the same day,
begin His destruction of the wicked who remain."

Robert Van Kampen
"The Rapture Question Answered"

C

DANIEL: THE PROPHETIC LINK

"Man of Integrity. Message of Persecution"

In all the pages of scripture, there is one man that towers above all others as the noblest of God's servants. In Daniel 10:11 and 19, God makes a single reference to Daniel as a "man of high esteem." God honored Daniel by giving him visions that would be "sealed up until the end of time." The book of Daniel is surely about prophecy, but it is also a book about persecution. He and his three friends of furnace fame stand as role models to remind us that we will not likely be exempted from testing during the end-times. Daniel is a book about prophecy. It is a book about persecution. It is also a book about punishment. For those who think they have succeeded in marginalizing God and maximizing self, be assured that the words of the prophet Amos will someday ring true. "Let justice roll down like waters, and righteousness like an ever-flowing stream." Thank you Daniel, for being a man of unparalleled integrity.

THOSE WHO HAVE INSIGHT

Four times in scripture, and only in the book of Daniel do we find four words that describe the wisest of men - "those who have insight." In fact, my favorite phrase in the Bible is seven words, from Daniel 12:7- *"but those who have insight will understand."*

In this context, it is the Christian alone who has been gifted by God with supernatural insight to understand the deep things of God. It is the Christian who has triumphed over sin and death as a result of his confession of faith. Beyond all the intellect, all the sophistication of the world, we find a simple group of people who have learned the ultimate lessons of life:

Dan 11:33 **"Those who have insight** among the people will give understanding to the many; yet they will fall by sword and by flame, by captivity and by plunder for *many* days.

Dan 11:35 "Some of **those who have insight** will fall, in order to refine, purge and make them pure until the end time; because *it is* still *to come* at the appointed time.

Dan 12:3 **"Those who have insight** will shine brightly like the brightness of the expanse of heaven, and those who lead the many to righteousness, like the stars forever and ever.

Dan 12:10 "Many will be purged, purified and refined, but the wicked will act wickedly; and none of the wicked will understand, **but those who have insight will understand.**

In the last days, it will be those who have the insight of scripture and the illumination of the Holy Spirit dwelling in their lives who will be prepared, and who will understand God's plan for the consummation of the ages.

I'm also reminded of Augustine's simple, yet profound theology:

> To Love God is the Greatest Romance.
>
> To Seek God is the Greatest Adventure.
>
> To Find God is the Greatest Achievement.

It is my hope that this book will help you to fulfill Augustine's quest as well.

OUTLINE FOR THE BOOK OF DANIEL

1. Promotion of the <u>Kin.</u>
Young Daniel and his fellow Jews have been captured by the Babylonian Empire, but these boys find favor in the eyes of king Nebuchadnezzar.

2. Prediction of the <u>Win.</u>
Daniel predicts the future kingdoms (Babylon, Medo Persia, Greece and Islam) that will conquer Jerusalem, but someday be ruled by Christ.

3. Persecution to the <u>Men.</u>
Daniel's 3 friends, given Babylonian names of Shadrach, Meshach and Abednego, are persecuted in the fiery furnace for their loyalty to Jehovah God, and they are miraculously delivered.

4. Punishment for the <u>Sin.</u>
God turns King Nebuchadnezzar into a wild animal for seven years before the king finally submits to God's sovereign authority in his life and kingdom.

5. Penalty with a <u>Pen.</u>
King Neb's successor son Belshazar is having a feast when a mysterious finger begins to write a death sentence on the wall. Daniel interprets the dream, and the king dies that very night.

6. Protection in the <u>Den.</u>
Daniel's fellow lieutenants in the king's court trick the new Persian king into sentencing Daniel to death by hungry lions, but God intervenes once again.

7. Pronouncement of the <u>End.</u>
Daniel's vision of the end times reveals the evil of Antiochus, the Tribulation period in the prophetic 70th week, the 10 nation confederacy and the beast known as AntiChrist.

> 7. Prophecy of Four Beasts
>
> 8. Prophecy of the Ram and Goat
>
> 9. Prophecy of the Seventieth Week
>
> 10. Prophecy of Michael the Archangel
>
> 11. Prophecy of The Kings of North and South
>
> 12. Prophecy of 30 and 45 Days

Promotion of the Kin

DANIEL CHAPTER 1

THE BABYLONIAN CAPTIVITY

Dan 1:1 **In the third year of the reign of Jehoiakim king of Judah**, Nebuchadnezzar king of Babylon came to Jerusalem and besieged it.

Dan 1:2 The Lord gave Jehoiakim king of Judah into his hand, along with some of the vessels of the house of God; and he brought them to **the land of Shinar**, to the house of his god, and he brought the vessels into the treasury of his god.

> *the third year.* The date of this siege was 606 b.c.
> *the land of Shinar.* Used 7 times in the Bible to refer to the region called Babylon.

DANIEL AND FRIENDS

Dan 1:3 Then the king ordered Ashpenaz, the chief of his officials, to bring in some of the sons of Israel, including some of the royal family and of the nobles,

Dan 1:4 youths in whom was **no defect**, who were good-looking, showing intelligence in every branch of wisdom, endowed with understanding and discerning knowledge, and who had ability for serving in the king's court; and he ordered him to teach them the literature and language of the Chaldeans.

Dan 1:5 The king appointed for them a daily ration from the king's choice food and from the wine which he drank, and appointed that they should be educated three years, at the end of which they were to enter the king's personal service.

Dan 1:6 Now among them from the sons of Judah were Daniel, Hananiah, Mishael and Azariah.

Dan 1:7 Then the commander of the officials **assigned new names to them**; and to Daniel he assigned the name Belteshazzar, to Hananiah, Shadrach; to Mishael, Meshach; and to Azariah, the name Abed-nego.

> *The process of national indoctrination was not casual or accidental. The government would find the most intelligent men in the land. They would then change their names, teach them a new language, spoil them with fine amenities. and immerse them in the culture, changing them into faithful Babylonians. These men would naturally become role models for the rest of the nation's young men. The pagan culture of today does the same thing. Godly families train up young men to be wise and skilled. Then the culture begins a process of worldly indoctrination.*

Dan 1:8 But **Daniel made up his mind** that he would not defile himself with the king's choice food or with the wine which he drank; so he sought permission from the commander of the officials that he might not defile himself.

Dan 1:9 Now God granted Daniel favor and compassion in the sight of the commander of the officials,

Dan 1:10 and the commander of the officials said to Daniel, "I am afraid of my lord the king, who has appointed your food and your drink; for why should he see your faces looking more haggard than the youths who are your own age? Then you would make me forfeit my head to the king."

Dan 1:11 But Daniel said to the overseer whom the commander of the officials had appointed over Daniel, Hananiah, Mishael and Azariah,

Dan 1:12 "Please test your servants for ten days, and let us be given some vegetables to eat and water to drink.

Dan 1:13 "Then let our appearance be observed in your presence and the appearance of the youths who are eating the king's choice food; and deal with your servants according to what you see."

Dan 1:14 So he listened to them in this matter and tested them for ten days.

Dan 1:15 At the end of ten days their appearance seemed better and they were fatter than all the youths who had been eating the king's choice food.

Dan 1:16 So the overseer continued to withhold their choice food and the wine they were to drink, and kept giving them vegetables.

Dan 1:17 As for these four youths, God gave them knowledge and intelligence **in every branch of literature and wisdom;** Daniel even understood all kinds of visions and dreams.

Dan 1:18 Then at the end of the days which the king had specified for presenting them, the commander of the officials presented them before Nebuchadnezzar.

Dan 1:19 The king talked with them, and out of them all not one was found like Daniel, Hananiah, Mishael and Azariah; so they entered the king's personal service.

Dan 1:20 As for every matter of wisdom and understanding about which the king consulted them, he found them **ten times better** than all the magicians *and* conjurers who *were* in all his realm.

Dan 1:21 And Daniel continued until the first year of **Cyrus the king.**

> *The message here is very simple. Avoiding the distractions of the world and leading a life of discipline to the point of CONVICTION is the criteria that God uses for extra-ordinary service. These men honored God and were then elevated into places of national importance.*

PREDICTION OF THE WIN
DANIEL CHAPTER 2

This statue was the dream of King Nebuchadnezzar, and young Daniel gave the interpretation. The statue represents <u>the Time of the Gentiles</u>, from the Babylonian Captivity until the Jews are delivered in the last days from the nations of the earth who seek to destroy them. The traditional view of the Statue shows the Roman Empire as the fourth kingdom, but we are now at a turning point in history where the revived Islamic Empire is re-emerging as the kingdom which crushes all the others and prepares to unite 10 Arab nations in a final assault on Israel called the Battle of Armageddon.

Dan 2:37 "You, O king, are the king of kings, to whom the God of heaven has given the kingdom, the power, the strength and the glory;

Dan 2:38 and wherever the sons of men dwell, *or* the beasts of the field, or the birds of the sky, He has given *them* into your hand and has caused you to rule over them all. **<u>You are the head of gold.</u>**

Dan 2:39 "After you there will arise **<u>another kingdom</u>** inferior to you, then **<u>another third kingdom</u>** of bronze, which will rule over all the earth.

Dan 2:40 "Then there will be **a <u>fourth kingdom</u>** as strong as iron; inasmuch as iron crushes and shatters all things, so, like iron that breaks in pieces, it will crush and break all these in pieces.

Dan 2:41 "In that you saw the feet and toes, partly of potter's clay and partly of iron, it will be **<u>a divided kingdom</u>**; but it will have in it the toughness of iron, inasmuch as you saw the iron mixed with common clay.

Dan 2:42 "As the toes of the feet were partly of iron and partly of pottery, so some of the kingdom will be strong and part of it will be brittle.

Dan 2:43 "And in that you saw the iron mixed with common clay, they will combine with one another in the seed of men; but they will not adhere to one another, even as iron does not combine with pottery.

Dan 2:44 "In the days of those kings the God of heaven will set up **<u>a kingdom which will never be destroyed,</u>** and *that* kingdom will not be left for another people; it will crush and put an end to all these kingdoms, but it will itself endure forever.

Dan 2:45 "Inasmuch as you saw that a stone was cut out of the mountain without hands and that it crushed the iron, the bronze, the clay, the silver and the gold, the great God has made known to the king what will take place in the future; so the dream is true and its interpretation is trustworthy."

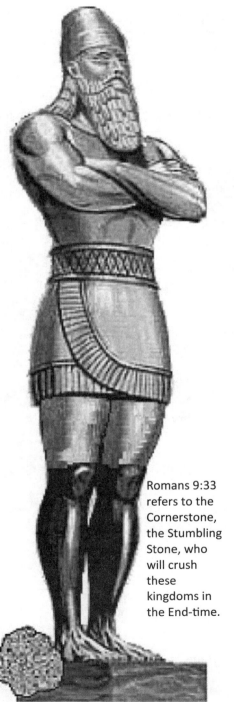

Head of Gold
The First
Kingdom

Babylon, 586-616 BC
Nebuchadnezzar
Captured the Southern
kingdom of Judah

Arms of Silver
The Second
Kingdom

Medo Persia
539-331 BC
The two kingdoms
are represented
by two arms.

Thighs of Brass
The Third Kingdom

Greece, 331-168 BC
The Persian Empire
was conquered by
Alexander. After his
death, 4 kings divided
the kingdom. Rome ruled
From 168 BC - 476 AD,
and two capitols emerged
Rome and
Constantinople.

Romans 9:33
refers to the
Cornerstone,
the Stumbling
Stone, who
will crush
these
kingdoms in
the End-time.

Legs of Iron
The Fourth Kingdom

The Islamic Empire,
began with Mohammed
in 633 ad (a little while)
and the Ottoman Empire
crushed all of the prior
Kingdoms from 1299 to
1924, changing culture
and language. It has long
been divided by Sunni
and Shi'ite.

Toes of Iron/Clay
The Fifth Kingdom

Ten Future Kings and ten
Nations will rise against
Israel in the last days.

Persecution to the Men

DANIEL CHAPTER THREE

THE KING BUILDS AN IDOL.

Dan 3:1 Nebuchadnezzar the king made an image of gold, **the height of which was sixty cubits and its width six cubits**; he set it up on the plain of Dura in the province of Babylon.

Dan 3:2 Then Nebuchadnezzar the king sent word to assemble the satraps, the prefects and the governors, the counselors, the treasurers, the judges, the magistrates and **all the rulers of the provinces** to come to the dedication of the image that Nebuchadnezzar the king had set up.

Note: The size of the statue : 90 feet tall x 9 feet wide.

THE KING ORDERS LOYALTY OR DEATH.

Dan 3:6 "But whoever does not **fall down and worship** shall immediately be cast into the midst of a furnace of blazing fire."

Dan 3:7 Therefore at that time, when all the peoples heard the sound of the horn, flute, lyre, trigon, psaltery, bagpipe and all kinds of music, **all the peoples, nations and men of every language** fell down and worshiped the golden image that Nebuchadnezzar the king had set up.

Dan 3:8 For this reason at that time certain Chaldeans came forward and brought charges against the Jews.

Dan 3:15 But if you do not worship, you will immediately be cast into the midst of **a furnace** of blazing fire; **and what god is there** who can deliver you out of my hands?"

Pagan ritual required falling down to worship because it was works-oriented. The Jews had experience at worshipping golden objects. (the calf of exodus). They knew there were greater things to fear than the king. Like a great movie scene where the hero has no chance of survival, God had set the stage for one of the greatest rescues of all time.

THE YOUNG MEN DEFY THE KING

Dan 3:16 Shadrach, Meshach and Abed-nego replied to the king, "O Nebuchadnez-zar, we do not need to give you an answer concerning this matter.

Dan 3:17 "If it be *so,* our God whom we serve is able to deliver us from the furnace of blazing fire; and **He will deliver us** out of your hand, O king.

Dan 3:18 "**But even if He does not,** let it be known to you, O king, that we are not going to serve your gods or worship the golden image that you have set up."

Isaiah prophesied (Is 43:2) 200 years earlier that God would protect Shadrach, Meshach and Abed-nego. "When you walk through the fire, you will not be scorched, Nor will the flame burn you." Famous words from Esther 4:16: "If I perish, I perish."

A MIRACLE HAPPENED

Dan 3:25 He said, "Look! **I see four men loosed and walking** about in the midst of the fire without harm, and the appearance of the fourth is like a son of the gods!"

Dan 3:26 Then Nebuchadnezzar came near to the door of the furnace of blazing fire; he responded and said, "Shadrach, Meshach and Abed-nego, come out, you servants of **the Most High God**, and come here!" Then Shadrach, Meshach and Abed-nego came out of the midst of the fire.

The fourth man in the furnace was a theophany, a vision of God. More precisely, this was a Christophany, a vision of Jesus. The term "Most High God" was a correct way to describe the God of Israel. The Hebrew translation is "El Elyon". God (who is omnipotent; High (meaning worthy to be worshipped); and Most (meaning higher than all the other gods.) We need to be reminded to call Him "Most High God" today.

NEBUCHADNEZZAR BLESSES GOD.

Dan 3:28 Nebuchadnezzar responded and said, "Blessed be the God of Shadrach, Meshach and Abed-nego, who has sent His angel and delivered His servants who put their trust in Him, **violating the king's command**, and yielded up their bodies so as not to serve or worship any god except their own God.

Dan 3:29 "Therefore I make a decree that any people, nation or tongue that speaks anything offensive against the God of Shadrach, Meshach and Abed-nego shall be torn limb from limb and their houses reduced to a rubbish heap, inasmuch as there is no other god who is able to deliver in this way."

Dan 3:30 Then the king caused Shadrach, Meshach and Abed-nego to prosper in the province of Babylon.

Civil disobedience is allowed when man's law clearly violates God's law. In the words of Jesus: "Render unto Caesar the things of Caesar and unto God the things of God."

PUNISHMENT FOR THE SIN

DANIEL CHAPTER 4

Dan 4:1 Nebuchadnezzar the king to all the peoples, nations, and men of every language that live in all the earth: "May your peace abound!

Dan 4:2 "It has seemed good to me to declare the signs and wonders which **the Most High God has done for me.**

Dan 4:3 "How great are His signs And how mighty are His wonders! His kingdom is an everlasting kingdom And His dominion is from generation to generation.

Dan 4:4 "I, Nebuchadnezzar, **was at ease in my house** and flourishing in my palace

Dan 4:9 'O Belteshazzar, chief of the magicians, since I know that a spirit of the holy gods is in you and no mystery baffles you, tell me the visions of my dream which I have seen, along with its interpretation.

Dan 4:18 'This is the dream which I, King Nebuchadnezzar, have seen. Now you, Belteshazzar, tell me its interpretation, inasmuch as none of the wise men of my kingdom is able to make known to me the interpretation; but you are able, for **a spirit of the holy gods is in you.'**

DANIEL INTERPRETS THE KING'S DREAM.

Dan 4:19 **"Then Daniel, whose name is Belteshazzar, was appalled** for a while as his thoughts alarmed him. The king responded and said, 'Belteshazzar, do not let the dream or its interpretation alarm you.' Belteshazzar replied, 'My lord, if only the dream applied to those who hate you and its interpretation to your adversaries!

Dan 4:20 'The tree that you saw, which became large and grew strong, whose height reached to the sky and was visible to all the earth

Dan 4:21 and whose foliage was beautiful and its fruit abundant, and in which was food for all, under which the beasts of the field dwelt and in whose branches the birds of the sky lodged,

Dan 4:22 it is you, O king; for you have become great and grown strong, and your majesty has become great and reached to the sky and **your dominion to the end of the earth.**

Dan 4:23 'In that the king saw an angelic watcher, a holy one, descending from heaven and saying, "Chop down the tree and destroy it; yet leave the stump with its roots in the ground, but with a band of iron and bronze around it in the new grass of the field, and let him be drenched with the dew of heaven, and let him share with the beasts of the field until **seven periods of time** pass over him,"

Dan 4:24 this is the interpretation, O king, and this is the decree of the Most High, which has

come upon my lord the king:

Dan 4:25 that you be **driven away from mankind** and your dwelling place be with the beasts of the field, and you be given grass to eat like cattle and be drenched with the dew of heaven; and seven periods of time will pass over you, until you recognize that the Most High is ruler over the realm of mankind and bestows it on whomever He wishes. Dan 4:26 'And in that it was commanded to leave the stump with the

roots of the tree, your kingdom will be assured to you **after you recognize that it is Heaven that rules.**

Dan 4:27 'Therefore, O king, may my advice be pleasing to you: **break away now from your sins** by doing righteousness and from your iniquities by showing mercy to the poor, in case there may be a prolonging of your prosperity.'

Dan 4:28 "All this happened to Nebuchadnezzar the king.

Painting of this story by William Blake, 1795

THE FULFILLMENT OF THE DREAM.

Dan 4:29 "Twelve months later he was walking on the roof of the royal palace of Babylon.

Dan 4:30 "The king reflected and said, **'Is this not Babylon the great, which I myself have built** as a royal residence by the might of my power and for the glory of my majesty?'

Dan 4:31 "While the word was in the king's mouth, a voice came from heaven, saying, 'King Nebuchadnezzar, to you it is declared: **sovereignty has been removed from you,**

Dan 4:34 "But at the end of that period, I, Nebuchadnezzar, raised my eyes toward heaven and **my reason returned to me,** and I blessed the Most High and praised and honored Him who lives forever; For His dominion is an everlasting dominion, And His kingdom endures from generation to generation.

Dan 4:35 **"All the inhabitants of the earth are accounted as nothing,** But He does according to His will in the host of heaven and among the inhabitants of earth; And no one can ward off His hand or say to Him, 'What have You done?'

Dan 4:36 "At that time my reason returned to me. And my majesty and splendor were restored to me for the glory of my kingdom, and my counselors and my nobles began seeking me out; **so I was reestablished in my sovereignty, and surpassing greatness was added** to me.

Dan 4:37 "Now I, Nebuchadnezzar, praise, exalt and honor the King of heaven, for all His works are true and His ways just, and He is able to humble those who walk in pride."

Galatians 6:7 says, "Be not deceived. God is not mocked. Whatsoever a man sows, that shall he also reap." What applied to him applies to us as well.

PENALTY WITH A PEN

DANIEL CHAPTER 5

KING BELSHAZZAR'S PAGAN FEAST

Dan 5:1 Belshazzar the king held a great feast for a thousand of his nobles, and he was drinking wine in the presence of the thousand.

Dan 5:2 When Belshazzar tasted the wine, he gave orders to bring the gold and silver vessels which **Nebuchadnezzar his father** had taken out of the temple which *was* in Jerusalem, so that the king and his nobles, his wives and his concubines might drink from them.

Dan 5:3 Then they brought **the gold vessels that had been taken out of the temple**, the house of God which *was* in Jerusalem; and the king and his nobles, his wives and his concubines drank from them.

Dan 5:4 They drank the wine and praised the gods of gold and silver, of bronze, iron, wood and stone.

Belshazzar was the son of Nabonidus, a successor to Nebuchadnezzar.

THE HANDWRITING ON THE WALL

Dan 5:5 Suddenly **the fingers of a man's hand** emerged and began writing opposite the lampstand on the plaster of the wall of the king's palace, and the king saw the back of the hand that did the writing.

Dan 5:6 Then the king's face grew pale and his thoughts alarmed him, and his hip joints went slack and **his knees began knocking together.**

Dan 5:7 The king called aloud to bring in the conjurers, the Chaldeans and the diviners. The king spoke and said to the wise men of Babylon, "Any man who can read this inscription and explain its interpretation to me shall be clothed with purple and have a necklace of gold around his neck, and have **authority as third ruler in the kingdom."**

Dan 5:8 Then all the king's wise men came in, but they could not read the inscription or make known its interpretation to the king.

DANIEL PROPHESIES THE KING'S DOOM

Dan 5:17 Then Daniel answered and said before the king, "Keep your gifts for yourself or give your rewards to someone else; however, I will read the inscription to the king and make the interpretation known to him.

Dan 5:22 "Yet you, his son, Belshazzar, have not humbled your heart, even though you knew all this,

Dan 5:23 but **you have exalted yourself against the Lord of heaven**; and they have brought the vessels of His house before you, and you and your nobles, your wives and your concubines have been drinking wine from them; and you have praised the gods of silver and gold, of bronze, iron, wood and stone, which do not see, hear or understand. **But the God in whose hand are your life-breath and all your ways, you have not glorified.**

Dan 5:24 "Then the hand was sent from Him and this inscription was written out.

Dan 5:25 "Now this is the inscription that was written out: 'MENE, MENE, TEKEL, UPHARSIN.'

Dan 5:26 "This is the interpretation of the message: 'MENE'- **God has numbered your kingdom and put an end to it.**

Dan 5:27 " 'TEKEL'--you have been weighed on the scales and found deficient.

Dan 5:28 " 'PERES'--your kingdom has been divided and given over to the Medes and Persians."

Dan 5:29 Then Belshazzar gave orders, and they clothed Daniel with purple and put a necklace of gold around his neck, and issued a proclamation concerning him that he now had authority as the third ruler in the kingdom.

Dan 5:30 That same night Belshazzar the Chaldean king was slain.

Dan 5:31 So Darius the Mede received the kingdom at about the age of sixty-two.

> Though historical data on *Darius is sketchy, he was likely the uncle or father-in-law of Cyrus the Great. The important thing to remember is that one empire has just fallen (Babylon) and another, Medo-Persia, has just taken its place. The dream and Interpretation of Daniel had proven to be true.*
>
> *Daniel's message was simple:*
>
> > *1) You have exalted yourself against the God of heaven.*
>
> *Daniel's prophetic judgment was also simple:*
>
> > *1) Your kingdom is done.*
> > *2) Your legacy is none.*
> > *3) The Persians have won.*
>
> *The amazing fact about this story is that Daniel, who was now third man of power In the country, was miraculously protected by God, and eventually elevated to power once again in the new kingdom, the Persian Empire.*

PROTECTION IN THE DEN
DANIEL CHAPTER 6

DANIEL RISES IN THE KINGDOM

Dan 6:3 Then this Daniel began distinguishing himself among the commissioners and satraps because _he possessed an extraordinary spirit,_ and the king planned to appoint him over the entire kingdom.

THE COMMISSIONERS PLOT AGAINST DANIEL.

Dan 6:4 Then the commissioners and satraps began trying to find a ground of accusation against Daniel in regard to government affairs; but they could find no ground of accusation or evidence of corruption, inasmuch as _he was faithful, and no negligence or corruption was to be found in him._

Dan 6:7 "All the commissioners of the kingdom, the prefects and the satraps, the high officials and the governors have consulted together that the king should establish a statute and enforce an injunction that anyone who makes a petition to _any god or man besides you, O king,_ for thirty days, shall be cast into the lions' den.

DANIEL PRAYS TO HIS GOD.

Dan 6:10 Now when Daniel knew that the document was signed, he entered his house (now in his roof chamber he had windows open toward Jerusalem); _and he continued kneeling on his knees three times a day,_ praying and giving thanks before his God, as he had been doing previously.

THE COMMISSIONERS SABOTAGE DANIEL.

Dan 6:11 Then these men came by agreement and found Daniel making petition and supplication before his God.

Dan 6:12 Then they approached and spoke before the king about the king's injunction, "Did you not sign an injunction that any man who makes a petition to any god or man besides you, O king, for thirty days, is to be cast into the lions' den?" _The king replied, "The statement is true, according to the law of the Medes and Persians, which may not be revoked."_

Dan 6:13 Then they answered and spoke before the king, "Daniel, who is one of the exiles from Judah, pays no attention to you, O king, or to the injunction which you signed, but keeps making his petition three times a day."

THE KING RELUCTANTLY CONDEMNS DANIEL.

Dan 6:14 Then, as soon as the king heard this statement, _he was deeply distressed_ and set _his_ mind on delivering Daniel; and even until sunset he kept exerting himself to rescue him.

Dan 6:15 Then these men came by agreement to the king and said to the king,
"Recognize, O king, that it is a law of the Medes and Persians that no injunction or statute which the king establishes may be changed."

Dan 6:16 Then the king gave orders, and Daniel was brought in and cast into the lions' den. *The king spoke and said to Daniel, "Your God whom you constantly serve will Himself deliver you."*

Dan 6:17 A stone was brought and laid over the mouth of the den; and the king sealed it with his own signet ring and with the signet rings of his nobles, so that nothing would be changed in regard to Daniel.

Dan 6:18 Then the king went off to his palace and spent the night fasting, and no entertainment was brought before him; and his sleep fled from him.

GOD SPARES DANIEL AND THE KING REJOICES.

Dan 6:19 Then the king arose at dawn, at the break of day, and went in haste to the lions' den.

Dan 6:20 When he had come near the den to Daniel, he cried out with a troubled voice. The king spoke and said to Daniel, *"Daniel, servant of the living God, has your God, whom you constantly serve, been able to deliver you from the lions?"*

Dan 6:21 Then Daniel spoke to the king, "O king, live forever! Dan 6:22 "My God sent His angel and shut the lions' mouths and they have not harmed me, inasmuch as I was found innocent before Him; and also toward you, O king, I have committed no crime."

Dan 6:23 Then the king was very pleased and gave orders for Daniel to be taken up out of the den. So Daniel was taken up out of the den and no injury whatever was found on him, because he had trusted in his God.

Dan 6:24 The king then gave orders, and they brought those men who had maliciously accused Daniel, and they cast them, their children and their wives into the lions' den; and they had not reached the bottom of the den before the lions overpowered them and crushed all their bones.

Dan 6:25 Then Darius the king wrote to all the peoples, nations and men of every language who were living in all the land: "May your peace abound! Dan 6:26 *"I make a decree* that in all the dominion of my kingdom men are to fear and tremble before the God of Daniel; For He is the living God and enduring forever, And His kingdom is one which will not be destroyed, And His dominion will be forever. Dan 6:27 "He delivers and rescues and performs signs and wonders In heaven and on earth, Who has also delivered Daniel from the power of the lions." Dan 6:28 So this Daniel enjoyed success in the reign of Darius and in the reign of Cyrus the Persian.

PRONOUNCEMENT OF THE END

PROPHECY OF FOUR BEASTS - Daniel 7

Daniel Chapter 7 is a summary of the kingdoms during the Time of the Gentiles (Luke 21:24). The Times of the Gentiles begins with Babylon and ends with the seventh trumpet and ultimately the battle of Armageddon. The way to view chapter 7 then is to see three kingdoms: Babylon, Medo-Persia and Greece - and then fast forward. . . until we reach the final, the eighth kingdom, who is a future beast, different and more deadly than the other three.

THE PAST KINGDOMS OF BABYLON, MEDO-PERSIA AND GREECE

Dan 7:2 Daniel said, "I was looking in my vision by night, and behold, the four winds of heaven were stirring up the great sea.

Dan 7:3 "And four great beasts were coming up from the sea, different from one another.

Dan 7:4 "**The first was like a lion** and had the wings of an eagle. I kept looking until its wings were plucked, and it was lifted up from the ground and made to stand on two feet like a man; a human mind also was given to it.

Dan 7:5 "And behold, another beast, **a second one, resembling a bear**. And it was raised up on one side, and three ribs were in its mouth between its teeth; and thus they said to it, 'Arise, devour much meat!'

Dan 7:6 "After this I kept looking, and behold, **another one, like a leopard**, which had on its back four wings of a bird; the beast also had four heads, and dominion was given to it.

> *The first three beasts represent the kingdoms that dominated Israel during the first part of the Times of the Gentiles. The lion with eagle's wings was the actual symbol of ancient Babylon, which conquered Judah in 586 bc. See Jeremiah 4:7 and 13. The bear is the Medo-Persian empire. 'Raised up on one side' refers to Persia, which was stronger than the earlier empire of the Medes. 'Three ribs' refer to the kingdoms of Lydia, (Turkey) Babylon (Iraq) and Egypt, all subdued during this reign of Persian power. The 'leopard' was known for its swiftness, as was Greece under Alexander the Great, who originated the fast war maneuver later used by the Germans, known as 'blitzkreig'. When Rome conquered Greece, Alexander's kingdom was divided into four political powers: Greece, Turkey, Syria and Egypt.*

Lion, Babylon	Bear, Medo-Persia	Leopard, Greece	INTERIM	Dreadful Beast

THE PAST				THE FUTURE

Dan 7:7 "After this I kept looking in the night visions, and behold, a fourth beast, **dreadful and terrifying** and extremely strong; and it had large iron teeth. It devoured and crushed and trampled down the remainder with its feet; **and it was different** from all the beasts that were before it, and it had ten horns.

Dan 7:8 "While I was contemplating the horns, behold, **another horn**, a little one, came up among them, and **three of the first horns** were pulled out by the roots before it; and behold, this horn possessed eyes like the eyes of a man and a mouth uttering great *boasts*.

> ***dreadful and terrifying.*** *The traditional view of this fourth beast refers to The Roman Empire, because of its well-armored military, which did indeed use force to conquer neighboring city-states. But the primary image that emerges from the Roman Empire was the "Pax Romano", a period of approximately 200 years (27bc to 180 ad) in which there were few wars and those who had Roman citizenship experienced protection through the laws of the Roman Senate. The concept of the revived Roman Empire has been the prevailing end-time theology for the past 100 years, but the advent of Islam extremism may well disprove this theory. Compared to Islam's dreadful and terrifying acts of forced assimilation, the Roman period of law and order looks rather calm.*
>
> ***and it was different.*** *The key to understanding this passage is found in the phrase, "and it had ten horns." The lion, the bear and leopard were conventional creatures, but the fourth beast has ten horns, implying that it is not a conventional creature, nor is it from the time period of ancient Israel. Therefore, this fourth beast is actually the eighth kingdom. This beast is dreadful and terrifying and extremely strong. This beast devoured and crushed and trampled (meaning assimilated) the other kingdoms.*
>
> ***another horn.*** *This horn is referring to the prophetic foreshadowing of a future global leader who will negotiate peace with Israel's enemies, allowing the construction of a new temple. At the midpoint of seven years, the Global Leader will utter great and arrogant boasts which will reveal to the world that he is the much feared Man of Lawlessness.*
>
> ***three of the first horns.*** *Scholars agree that the three horns represent three kingdoms that will either be conquered or coerced into following the Anti-Christ in the last days.*

PROPHECY OF THE RAM AND GOAT

PRONOUNCEMENT OF THE END- Daniel Chapter 8

THE SMALL HORN BECOMES MIGHTY.

Dan 8:1 In the third year of the reign of Belshazzar the king a vision appeared to me, Daniel, subsequent to the one which appeared to me previously.

Dan 8:2 I looked in the vision, and while I was looking I was in the citadel of Susa, which is in the province of Elam; and I looked in the vision and I myself was beside the Ulai Canal.

Dan 8:3 Then I lifted my eyes and looked, and behold, **a ram which had two horns** was standing in front of the canal. Now the two horns were long, but one was longer than the other, with the longer one coming up last.

Dan 8:4 I saw the ram butting westward, northward, and southward, and no other beasts could stand before him nor was there anyone to rescue from his power, but he did as he pleased and magnified himself.

Dan 8:5 While I was observing, behold, **a male goat was coming from the west** over the surface of the whole earth without touching the ground; and the goat had a conspicuous horn between his eyes.

Dan 8:6 He came up to the ram that had the two horns, which I had seen standing in front of the canal, and rushed at him in his mighty wrath.

Dan 8:7 I saw him come beside the ram, and he was enraged at him; and he struck the ram and shattered his two horns, and the ram had no strength to withstand him. So he hurled him to the ground and trampled on him, and there was none to rescue the ram from his power.

Dan 8:8 Then **the male goat magnified himself exceedingly**. But as soon as he was mighty, the large horn was broken; and in its place there came up four conspicuous horns toward the four winds of heaven.

Dan 8:9 Out of one of them came forth **a rather small horn** which grew exceedingly great toward the south, toward the east, and toward the Beautiful Land.

Dan 8:10 It grew up to the host of heaven and caused some of the host and some of the stars to fall to the earth, and it trampled them down.

Dan 8:11 It even magnified itself to be equal with the Commander of the host; and it removed the regular sacrifice from Him, and the place of His sanctuary was thrown down.

Dan 8:12 And on account of transgression the host will be given over to the horn along with the regular sacrifice; and **it will fling truth to the ground** and perform its will and prosper.

It will fling truth to the ground. *These seven words personify the time of Anti-Christ. Truth will be mangled during this time. The world will be thoroughly deceived.*

THE MYSTERY OF 2300 DAYS.

Dan 8:13 Then I heard a holy one speaking, and another holy one said to that particular one who was speaking, "How long will the vision about the regular sacrifice apply,
while the transgression causes horror, so as to allow both the holy place and the host to be
trampled?"

Dan 8:14 He said to me, "For 2,300 evenings and mornings; then the holy place will be properly
restored."

Dan 8:15 When I, Daniel, had seen the vision, I sought to understand it; and behold, standing
before me was one who looked like a man.

Dan 8:16 And I heard the voice of a man between the banks of Ulai, and he called out and said,
"Gabriel, give this man an understanding of the vision."

Dan 8:17 So he came near to where I was standing, and when he came I was frightened and
fell on my face; but he said to me, "Son of man, understand that the vision pertains to the
time of the end."

*This is one of the most amazing prophetic mysteries in scripture - and it will continue
to be a mystery. Verse 11 and 12 say: "It will remove the regular sacrifice . . . and fling
truth to the ground." In verse 13, Daniel says; "How long will the vision apply? If the
question is: How long will Tribulation be, then the prophetic puzzle appears to be
reasoning as follows: how long is the time from the end of Tribulation until the holy
place is restored? The holy place restored could mean the following: the end of the
seventh trumpet, the day of atonement (salvation of Israel) or the end of the 75 day
period and the beginning of the Millennium.*

*The following is merely hypothetical calculation. If 2300 evenings and mornings is
actually 1150 days, then we have the following possibilities:*
1) 1260 days (end of 7th trumpet) minus 1150 days = 110 days of tribulation. Or . . .
2) 1335 days (end of 75 days of restoration) minus 1150 days = 185 days of tribulation.

*The big question for believers is: how long is the tribulation period, if we are really
going to have to endure it? No one knows. Since the end of tribulation is connected to
the Second Coming and Rapture, then we understand the following: No one knows.*

An interesting footnote: *Seventh Day Adventists teach that the 2300 days are
actually 2300 years, from 457 bc to 1844 ad, when William Miller set in motion his
theology that Jesus would return on Oct 22, 1844.   The SDA grew from this movement,
despite its false prophecy, which was later declared to be "a heavenly event" that
merely began in 1844. The prophecy of 2300 days is still very much a mystery, even to
those who strive to know its truth. Jesus doesn't know when He will return. . . . .
Neither do we.*

THE PROPHECY OF ANTIOCHUS EPIPHANIES.

Dan 8:18 Now while he was talking with me, I sank into a deep sleep with my face to the ground; but he touched me and made me stand upright.

Dan 8:19 He said, "Behold, I am going to let you know what will occur at the final period of the indignation, for it pertains to the appointed time of the end.

Dan 8:20 "The ram which you saw with the two horns represents the kings of Media and Persia.

Dan 8:21 "The shaggy goat represents the kingdom of Greece, and the large horn that is between his eyes is the first king. Dan 8:22 "The broken horn and the four horns that arose in its place represent four kingdoms which will arise from his nation, **although not with his power.**

Dan 8:23 "In the latter period of their rule, When the transgressors have run their course, A king will arise, Insolent and skilled in intrigue.

Dan 8:24 "His power will be mighty, **but not by his own power**, And he will destroy to an extraordinary degree and prosper and perform his will; He will destroy mighty men and the holy people.

Dan 8:25 "And through his shrewdness He will cause deceit to succeed by his influence; And he will magnify himself in his heart, And he will destroy many while they are at ease. He will even oppose the Prince of princes, **But he will be broken without human agency.**

Dan 8:26 "The vision of the evenings and mornings which has been told is true; But keep the vision secret, For it pertains to many days in the future."

Dan 8:27 Then I, Daniel, was exhausted and sick for days. Then I got up again and carried on the king's business; but I was astounded at the vision, and there was none to explain *it*.

> *Verse 19 is an important connecting point between the prophecy of Antiochus and its future reference to the Anti-Christ himself. Verses 24 and 25 speak of the historic time of Antiochus, but they also speak, word for word, to describe the diabolical plot by the Anti-Christ to destroy Israel and the Church.*
>
> ***Not with his power. . . and, broken without human agency.*** *These refer to Satan-inspired demonic activity that empowered Antiochus Epiphanes in 168 bc to try to destroy both Jews and Judaism. "Broken" refers to the angelic victory over Satan, his demons and Antiochus, when God delivered the Jews and restored them in 165 bc. 'Without human agency' is another way of saying that God intervened, once again, as in times past, to supernaturally overcome inevitable defeat, and cause the children of God to rise victorious - not through their own power, but through God's power and . . . maybe a little bit of our own faith.*

ANALOGY OF NEBUCHADNEZZAR AND ISRAEL

*From beginning to end, the book of Daniel is prophetic.
It is reasonable, therefore, to question the time period of "seven years"
with Nebuchadnezzar, as compared to the "seven years"
of the seventieth week of Daniel.*

1) King Nebuchadnezzar received the favor of God (through Daniel)
because He acknowledged the Most High God.

2) King Nebuchadnezzar rejected Jehovah God,
became independent and worshipped pagan gods.

3) Sovereignty was taken from King Nebuchadnezzar.
The tree (his power) was chopped down, the branches were stripped,
but the stump of the roots were left in the ground.

4) He was caused to endure a time of suffering for a period of seven years.

5) At the end of the seven years
God restored sovereignty to King Nebuchadnezzar.

---

1) The nation of Israel received the favor of God
because they acknowledged the Most High God.

2) The nation of Israel rejected Jehovah God,
and they became independent of God, worshipping pagan gods.

3) Sovereignty was taken from the nation of Israel
The tree was chopped down (the dispersion) the branches were stripped
but the stump of the roots were left in the ground. (a remnant)

4) The nation of Israel will endure a time of suffering for a period of seven years.

5) At the end of the seven years
God will restore sovereignty to the nation of Israel.

PROPHECY OF THE 70TH WEEK
PRONOUNCEMENT OF THE END - DANIEL CHAPTER 9

The Seventy Weeks is a mysterious code that was written into the Bible to give us veiled insight into the Second Coming of Christ. 69 of the 70 weeks took place from the time of Daniel's vision until the crucifixion of Christ. The last week, the 70th, comes to life at the end of time. A "week" in this code is actually a seven year period. We live in the interlude between the 69th and 70th week. But at some appointed time in the future, the 70th week will begin with a "Global Leader" establishing a covenant of peace with Israel and her enemies. At the middle of the 70th week, the Anti-Christ will reveal his satanic nature and openly persecute the Jews and the Christians.

Dan 9:24 "**Seventy weeks** have been decreed **for your people and your holy city**, to finish the transgression, to make an end of sin, to make atonement for iniquity, to bring in everlasting righteousness, to seal up vision and prophecy and to anoint the most holy place.

Dan 9:25 "So you are to know and discern that **from the issuing of a decree** to restore and rebuild Jerusalem **until Messiah the Prince** there will be seven weeks and sixty-two weeks; it will be built again, with plaza and moat, even in times of distress.

Dan 9:26 "Then after the sixty-two weeks **the Messiah will be cut off** and have nothing, and **the people of the prince who is to come** will destroy the city and the sanctuary. And its end will come with a flood; even to the end there will be war; desolations are determined.

Dan 9:27 "**And he will make a firm covenant** with the many for one week, but in the middle of the week **he will put a stop to sacrifice and grain offering**; and **on the wing of abominations** will come **one who makes desolate**, even until a complete destruction, one that is decreed, is poured out on the one who makes desolate."

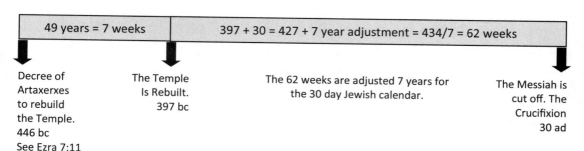

49 years = 7 weeks	397 + 30 = 427 + 7 year adjustment = 434/7 = 62 weeks

Decree of Artaxerxes to rebuild the Temple. 446 bc See Ezra 7:11

The Temple Is Rebuilt. 397 bc

The 62 weeks are adjusted 7 years for the 30 day Jewish calendar.

The Messiah is cut off. The Crucifixion 30 ad

70 years x 7 = 490 years - 7 future = 483 x 360 / 365 = 476 – 446 = 30 ad

Seventy weeks. It was Sir Robert Anderson, the author of "The Coming Prince" who concluded   that a week was seven years and 69 weeks equaled 483 years of time.

For your people and your holy city. It is a curious thing that the bride of Christ is considered to be both the Church and the City of Jerusalem.   See Revelation 19:7,8; 21:2; 21:9,10; and 2 Corinthians 11:2;

From the issuing of a decree. According to history, King Artaxerxes did issue a decree in 446 bc. to rebuild the temple which was captured and destroyed by Babylon in 586 bc.

Until Messiah the Prince. Isn't it interesting that the prophecies of Daniel were known to the Jewish people for hundreds of years in anticipation of the coming Messiah.   They could have calculated the very year that Messiah would come, had they only softened their hearts and asked God for wisdom.

The Messiah will be cut off. As ordained by God, Christ would be crucified, cut off, discredited by the adoring crowds, and second guessed by even his own disciples.

The people of the prince who is to come will destroy the city and the sanctuary. The general assumption is made that this refers to General Titus and the Roman army of 70 a.d. It is very likely, however, that this refers to the Syrian and Arab forces within the Roman army - making the prince who is to come a Mid-Eastern enemy of Israel.

And he will make a firm covenant with the many for one week. It is understood that the Anti-Christ will arise for seven years. Early in his tenure, he will protect the Jewish people by drafting a strong resolution of peace between Israel and her enemies - most likely the united forces of the Islamic world.

He will put a stop to sacrifice and grain offering. Because the sacrificial system ended with the fall of Jerusalem, it will be re-instituted among the orthodox Jews as part of the newly founded temple.

On the wing of abominations. The word abomination means detestable or something that stinks. The Latin root ab hominen means "away from man" or beastly.

One who makes desolate. It is God who creates and it is Satan who seeks to destroy the good things that God has created. To make desolate is to ravage the good things of God.

* The Diaspora was the "dispersion" of the Jews throughout the world in 70 ad.

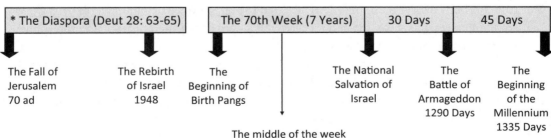

* The Diaspora (Deut 28: 63-65)		The 70th Week (7 Years)		30 Days	45 Days

The Fall of Jerusalem 70 ad

The Rebirth of Israel 1948

The Beginning of Birth Pangs

The middle of the week
A stop to sacrifices and offering,
one who makes Desolate

The National Salvation of Israel

The Battle of Armageddon 1290 Days

The Beginning of the Millennium 1335 Days

Prophecy of Michael the Archangel

PRONOUNCEMENT OF THE END - DANIEL CHAPTER 10

For our struggle is not against flesh and blood, but against the rulers,
against the powers, against the world forces of this darkness,
against the spiritual forces of wickedness in the heavenly places.
Ephesians 6:12

Dan 10:1 In the third year of Cyrus king of Persia a message was revealed to Daniel, who was named Belteshazzar; and the message was true and one of great conflict, but he understood the message and had an understanding of the vision.

> **The year was 535 bc**. *Israel had been captive in Babylon for almost 70 years.*

A. DANIEL'S FASTING PREPARES HIM FOR THE VISION.

Dan 10:2 In those days, I, Daniel, had been **mourning for three entire weeks**.

Dan 10:3 I did not eat any tasty food, nor did meat or wine enter my mouth, nor did I use any ointment at all until the entire three weeks were completed.

B. THE ANGELIC MESSENGER PREPARES HIM FOR THE VISION.

Dan 10:4 On the twenty-fourth day of the first month, while I was by the bank of the great river, that is, the Tigris,

Dan 10:5 I lifted my eyes and looked, and behold, there was **a certain man** dressed in linen, whose waist was girded with a belt of pure gold of Uphaz.

> **Certain man.** *the word for certain is the Hebrew word "echad" which literally means one, and is used In the Shema to describe the oneness of God. Certain is a weak use of this term. Some use the term "glorious". Is this a Christophany? Probably not.*

Dan 10:6 His body also was like beryl, **his face had the appearance of lightning, his eyes were like flaming torches,** his arms and feet like the gleam of polished bronze, and the sound of his words like the sound of a tumult.

Dan 10:7 Now I, Daniel, alone saw the vision, while the men who were with me did not see the vision; nevertheless, a great dread fell on them, and they ran away to hide themselves.

Dan 10:8 So I was left alone and saw this great vision; yet no strength was left in me, for my natural color turned to a deathly pallor, and I retained no strength.

Dan 10:9 But I heard the sound of his words; and as soon as I heard the sound of his words, I fell into a deep sleep on my face, with my face to the ground.

Dan 10:10 Then behold, a hand touched me and set me trembling on my hands and knees.

Dan 10:11 He said to me, "**O Daniel, man of high esteem**, understand the words that I am about to tell you and stand upright, for I have now been sent to you." And when he had spoken this word to me, I stood up trembling.

Dan 10:12 Then he said to me, "Do not be afraid, Daniel, for **from the first day** that you set your heart on understanding this and on humbling yourself before your God, your words were heard, and I have come in response to your words.

Dan 10:13 "But **the prince of the kingdom of Persia** was withstanding me **for twenty-one days**; then behold, **Michael, one of the chief princes**, came to help me, for I had been left there with the kings of Persia.

> **The prince of Persia.** *This is a demon angel that is warring with the heavenly host.*

Dan 10:14 "Now I have come to give you an understanding of what will happen to your people in the latter days, for the vision pertains to the days yet future."

Dan 10:15 When he had spoken to me according to these words, I turned my face toward the ground and became speechless.

Dan 10:16 And behold, one who resembled a human being was touching my lips; then I opened my mouth and spoke and said to him who was standing before me, "O my lord, as a result of the vision anguish has come upon me, and I have retained no strength.

Dan 10:17 "For how can such a servant of my lord talk with such as my lord? As for me, there remains just now no strength in me, nor has any breath been left in me."

Dan 10:18 Then this one with human appearance touched me again and strengthened me.

Dan 10:19 He said, **"O man of high esteem**, do not be afraid. Peace be with you; take courage and be courageous!" Now as soon as he spoke to me, I received strength and said, "May my lord speak, for you have strengthened me."

Dan 10:20 Then he said, "Do you understand why I came to you? But I shall now return to fight against **the prince of Persia**; so I am going forth, and behold, **the prince of Greece** is about to come.

Dan 10:21 "However, **I will tell you** what is inscribed in the writing of truth. Yet there is no one who stands firmly with me against these forces except **Michael your prince.**

> **See Daniel 12:1.** *Michael is described as "the great prince" . . . (of Israel)*
> **See Jude 1:9.** *Michael is described as the archangel. See page 194.*

PROPHECY OF THE KINGS OF NORTH & SOUTH

PRONOUNCEMENT OF THE END - DANIEL CHAPTER 11

THE PERSIAN EMPIRE.

Dan 11:1 "In the first year of **Darius the Mede**, I arose to be an encouragement and a protection for him.

Dan 11:2 "And now I will tell you the truth. Behold, three more kings are going to arise in Persia. Then a fourth will gain far more riches than all of them; as soon as he becomes strong through his riches, he will arouse the whole empire against the realm of Greece.

> **Darius the Mede** was a transitional king until Cyrus the Persian took control in 539 BC. The other four kings were: 1. Cambyses II (530-523 BC) 2. Bardiya or Smerdis (523-522 BC) 3. Darius Hystapses (522-486 BC) 4. Xerxes I (Ahasuerus of Esther) became the dominant king in the Persian Empire. (486-465 BC.

THE GRECIAN EMPIRE.

Dan 11:3 "And **a mighty king** will arise, and he will rule with great authority and do as he pleases.

Dan 11:4 "But as soon as he has arisen, his kingdom will be broken up and parceled out toward the four points of the compass, though not to his own descendants, nor according to his authority which he wielded, for his sovereignty will be uprooted and given to others besides them.

> **a mighty king.** Alexander the Great (332-323 BC) arose from Greece and conquered the entire Persian Empire in about 4 years. Alexander died at an early age and left no heir. Four of his generals succeeded him, parceling the kingdom into the Ptolemaic region (South), the Seleucid region (North) 323 - 130 BC3. the Byzantine (West) and the Parthian / Sassanid region(East).

Dan 11:5 "Then the king of the South will grow strong, along with one of his princes who will gain ascendancy over him and obtain dominion; his domain will be a great dominion indeed.

Dan 11:6 "After some years they will form an alliance, and **the daughter of the king** of the South will come to the king of the North to carry out a peaceful arrangement. But she will not retain her position of power, nor will he remain with his power, but she will be given up, along with those who brought her in and the one who sired her as well as he who supported her in *those* times.

> **the daughter of the king.** Ptolemy of Egypt offered his daughter Berenice to the Syrian King of the North, Antiochus II, who divorced his own wife Laodice. When Ptolemy died, Laodice had Antiochus and Berenice put to death.

Dan 11:7 "But one of the descendants of her line will arise in his place, and he will come against their army and enter the fortress of the king of the North, and he will deal with them and display great strength.

Dan 11:8 "Also their gods with their metal images and their precious vessels of silver and gold **he will take into captivity to Egypt**, and he on his part will refrain from attacking the king of the North for some years.

Dan 11:9 "Then the latter will enter the realm of the king of the South, but will return to his own land.

Dan 11:10 "His sons will mobilize and assemble a multitude of great forces; and one of them will keep on coming and overflow and pass through, that he may again wage war up to his very fortress.

Dan 11:11 "The king of the South will be enraged and go forth and fight with the king of the North. Then the latter will raise a great multitude, but that multitude will be given into the hand of the former.

Dan 11:12 "When the multitude is carried away, his heart will be lifted up, and he will cause tens of thousands to fall; yet he will not prevail.

Dan 11:13 **"For the king of the North** will again raise a greater multitude than the former, and after an interval of some years he will press on with a great army and much equipment.

Dan 11:14 "Now in those times many will rise up against **the king of the South**; the violent ones among your people will also lift themselves up in order to fulfill the vision, but they will fall down.

Dan 11:15 **"Then the king of the North will come**, cast up a siege ramp and capture a well-fortified city; **and the forces of the South** will not stand their ground, not even their choicest troops, for there will be no strength to make a stand.

Dan 11:16 "But he who comes against him will do as he pleases, and no one will be able to withstand him; he will also stay for a time in the Beautiful Land, with destruction in his hand.

Dan 11:17 "He will set his face to come with the power of his whole kingdom, bringing with him a proposal of peace which he will put into effect; he will also give him the daughter of women to ruin it. But she will not take a stand for him or be on his side.

Dan 11:18 "Then he will turn his face to the coastlands and capture many. But a commander will put a stop to his scorn against him; moreover, he will repay him for his scorn.

Dan 11:19 "So he will turn his face toward the fortresses of his own land, but he will stumble and fall and be found no more.

Dan 11:20 "Then in his place one will arise who will send an oppressor through the Jewel of his kingdom; yet within a few days he will be shattered, though not in anger nor in battle.

He will take into captivity in Egypt. This passage of scripture is a ping pong match between Ptolemy II and III and IV of Egypt against the forces of Antiochus II and III of Syria. This difficult historical interpretation is well documented in www.herealittletherealittle.net by Bryan Huie.

C. THE SYRIAN/GREEK LEADER, ANTIOCHUS EPIPHANIES IV

Dan 11:21 "In his place a despicable person will arise, on whom the honor of kingship has not been conferred, but he will come in a time of tranquility and seize the kingdom by intrigue.

Dan 11:22 "The overflowing forces will be flooded away before him and shattered, and also the prince of the covenant.

Dan 11:23 "After an alliance is made with him he will practice deception, and he will go up and gain power with a small force of people.

Dan 11:24 "In a time of tranquility he will enter the richest parts of the realm, and he will accomplish what his fathers never did, nor his ancestors; he will distribute plunder, booty and possessions among them, and he will devise his schemes against strongholds, but only for a time.

Dan 11:25 "He will stir up his strength and courage against **the king of the South** with a large army; so the king of the South will mobilize an extremely large and mighty army for war; but he will not stand, for schemes will be devised against him.

Dan 11:26 "Those who eat his choice food will destroy him, and his army will overflow, but many will fall down slain.

Dan 11:27 "**As for both kings,** their hearts will be intent on evil, and they will speak lies to each other at the same table; but it will not succeed, for the end is still to come at the appointed time. Dan 11:28 "Then he will return to his land with much plunder; but his heart will be set against the holy covenant, and he will take action and then return to his own land.

Dan 11:29 "At the appointed time he will return and come into the South, but this last time it will not turn out the way it did before.

Dan 11:30 "For ships of Kittim will come against him; therefore he will be disheartened and will return and become enraged at the holy covenant and take action; so he will come back and show regard for those who forsake the holy covenant.

Dan 11:31 "Forces from him will arise, desecrate the sanctuary fortress, and do away with the regular sacrifice. And they will set up **the abomination of desolation.**

Dan 11:32 "By smooth words he will turn to godlessness those who act wickedly toward the covenant, but the people who know their God will display strength and take action.

Dan 11:33 "Those who have insight among the people will give understanding to the many; yet they will fall by sword and by flame, by captivity and by plunder for many days.

> **On Kislev 15** in December 168 bc, Antiochus IV desecrated the temple and erected a statue to Zeus. On Kislev 25 (December 25), Zeus' birthday, a pig was sacrificed on the altar in his honor.
> **Antiochus IV** forbid Sabbath worship, as well as sacrifices, feasts and circumcision. His intention, consistent with Greek assimilation, was to eradicate the old culture and create a new culture of language, government and religion. The Hellenistic Jews were willing to compromise, but there is always a faithful remnant.

Dan 11:34 "Now when they fall they will be granted a little help, and many will join with them in hypocrisy.

Dan 11:35 "Some of those who have insight will fall, in order to refine, purge and make them pure **until the end time**; because it is still to come **at the appointed time**.

> Use of the phrase "until the end time" and "at the appointed time" seem to set the stage for end-time events.

THE PROPHETIC FUTURE RULE OF THE ANTI-CHRIST.

Dan 11:36 "Then **the king will do as he pleases**, and he will exalt and magnify himself above every god and will speak monstrous things against the God of gods; and he will prosper until the indignation is finished, for that which is decreed will be done.

Dan 11:37 "He will show no regard for **the gods of his fathers** or for **the desire of women**, nor will he show regard for any other god; for he will magnify himself above them all.

Dan 11:38 "But instead he will honor a god of fortresses, a god whom his fathers did not know; he will honor him with gold, silver, costly stones and treasures.

Dan 11:39 "He will take action against the strongest of fortresses with the help of **a foreign god;** he will give great honor to those who acknowledge him and will cause them to rule over the many, and will parcel out land for a price.

Dan 11:40 **"At the end time** the king of the South will collide with him, and the king of the North will storm against him with chariots, with horsemen and with many ships; and he will enter countries, overflow them and pass through.

Dan 11:41 "He will also enter the Beautiful Land, and many countries will fall; but these will be rescued out of his hand: Edom, Moab and the foremost of the sons of Ammon.

Dan 11:42 "Then he will stretch out his hand against other countries, and the land of Egypt will not escape.

Dan 11:43 "But he will gain control over the hidden treasures of gold and silver and over all the precious things of Egypt; and Libyans and Ethiopians will follow at his heels.

Dan 11:44 "But rumors from the East and from the North will disturb him, and he will go forth with great wrath to destroy and annihilate many.

Dan 11:45 "He will pitch the tents of his royal pavilion between the seas and the beautiful Holy Mountain; yet he will come to his end, and no one will help him.

> ***The king will do as he pleases.*** *Traditional theology identifies this passage as a continuation of the wicked rule of Antiochus Epiphanes. But the use of the term "at the end time" seems to project this passage into the future. This "king", the AntiChrist, will use the governmental system to abuse power like no one in history. He will likely manipulate the adherents of Islam to be his tool for 1) establishing rigid law and ideology and 2) terrorizing the masses by persecution and death. "The desire of women" has two interpretations: 1) this is a term used of Christ to describe the desire that women had to be the Messiah's mother; 2) more likely, that this man would join the ranks of the gay community, who already defies all things natural and traditional.*

PROPHECY OF THE 30 AND 45 DAYS

Pronouncement of the End - Daniel 12

Daniel 12:1 "Now at that time **Michael, the great prince** who stands guard over the sons of your people, will arise. And there will be **a time of distress** such as never occurred since there was a nation until that time; and at that time your people, everyone who is found written in the book, will be rescued. 2 "Many of those **who sleep in the dust of the ground** will awake, these to everlasting life, but the others to disgrace and everlasting contempt. 3 "Those who have insight will shine brightly like the brightness of the expanse of heaven, and those who lead the many to righteousness, like the stars forever and ever. 4 "But as for you, Daniel, conceal these words and seal up the book until the end of time; many will go back and forth, and **knowledge will increase."**

> *Michael, the great prince. This is Michael the archangel, who appears to be the warrior general among the armies of heaven. (Dan 10:13, 10:21, 12:1, Jude 1:9, Rev 12:7). Though traditional Pre-Trib theology believes that the Holy Spirit is the restrainer of 2 Thessalonians 2:6,7 who is taken out of the way, it is more likely that it is Michael who is referred to as the guardian of the Jewish people. The Holy Spirit will continue to give salvation to those who repent, even during the Tribulation and days of wrath.*
>
> *A time of distress. Jeremiah 30:7 refers to this as a time of Jacob's trouble.*
>
> *who sleep in the dust of the ground. This verse affirms the idea that the Old Testament saints and the dead in Christ will sleep until the "gathering of the elect."*
>
> *knowledge will increase. Technology used to be a tool of the government or a large corporation. Today every individual expects to use technology as a personal tool for social development, business, or entertainment. Of the six billion people on the planet, there are 2 billion internet users and 4.6 billion cell phone users. When the time comes, the Anti-Christ will have a perfect platform to communicate his message of manipulation. While the Holy Spirit can communicate directly to the heart of the believer, the Anti-Christ and his false prophet will use technology to convey his message.*

Dan 12:5 Then I, Daniel, looked and behold, two others were standing, one on this bank of the river and the other on that bank of the river. 6 And one said to the man dressed in linen, who was above the waters of the river, "How long will it be until the end of these wonders?" 7 I heard **the man dressed in linen**, who was above the waters of the river, as he raised his right hand and his left toward heaven, and swore by Him who lives forever that

it would be for **a time, times, and half a time**; and as soon as they finish **shatter-**
ing the power of the holy people, all these events will be completed. 8 As for
me, I heard but could not understand; so I said, "My lord, what will be the outcome of
these events?" 9 He said, "Go your way, Daniel, for these words are concealed and sealed
up until the end time. 10 "Many will be purged, purified and refined, but the wicked will
act wickedly; and none of the wicked will understand, **but those who have insight will un-**
derstand.

11 "From the time that the regular sacrifice is abolished and the abomination of desolation
is set up, **there will be 1,290 days**. 12 "How blessed is he who keeps waiting and attains **to**
the 1,335 days! 13 "But as for you, go your way to the end; then you will enter into rest
and rise again for your allotted portion at the end of the age."

*The man dressed in linen. Daniel saw the man in linen (10:5) with a face like the
appearance of lightning, and his eyes were like flaming torches. The only person
allowed to swear by God the Father (who lives forever), is Jesus, the Son.*

*A time, times and half a time. See Daniel 7:25 and Revelation 12:14. When coupled
with Daniel 9:27 (the middle of the week), Sir Robert Anderson, the author of "The
Coming Prince", identified this obscure formula for us. Using a time as one year, and
times as two years, he concluded this to be one-half of the mysterious seventieth week.*

*Shattering the power of the holy people. The time of the Gentiles began in 586 bc,
and will continue until the seventh trumpet and the end of the 7 years when Christ
takes back the title deed from Planet Earth.*

*But those who have insight will understand. I love these seven words. This may
sound like a redundancy to the world, but the reality is that insight is a metaphor for
those of us believers who seek after the truth of God, as found only in the sacred pages
of scripture.*

*There will be 1,290 days. This is the mysterious 30 days after the 7 year period. This
30 day period begins what I like to call "the Day of Atonement", because it is this
time period that marks the salvation of the prodigal nation of Israel.*

*To the 1,335 days. This 45 day period of time after the 30 day period is also
mysterious. There appears to be a special blessing attached to this tenure of time,
probably signifying the soon-coming transition into the Millennial kingdom. The 45 day
time appears to be a time of restoration, possibly including God's redesign and
construction of Ezekiel's Millennial temple.*

"In the Last Days" (Old Testament)

The term 'last days' in the Old Testament is a prophetic word to the nation of Israel that their age-old position as the chosen people of God will be restored. The process is two-fold. First, the nations of the earth will be punished during a cataclysmic time of global warfare, and secondly, Israel will be vindicated and honored once more as the children of God. From an evangelical perspective, the nation has been blinded for centuries, while God prepares for the consummation of the ages. At the appointed time, a remnant of the nation will be saved as Christ ushers them into the millennial kingdom.

ISAIAH
Isa 2:2 Now it will come about that In **the last days** the mountain of the house of the LORD will be established as the chief of the mountains, and will be raised above the hills; and all the nations will stream to it.

JEREMIAH
Jer 23:20 "The anger of the LORD will not turn back until He has performed and carried out the purposes of His heart; In **the last days** you will clearly understand it.

EZEKIEL
Eze 38:16 and you will come up against My people Israel like a cloud to cover the land. It shall come about in **the last days** that I will bring you against My land, so that the nations may know Me when I am sanctified through you before their eyes, O Gog."

HOSEA
Hos 3:5 Afterward the sons of Israel will return and seek the LORD their God and David their king; and they will come trembling to the LORD and to His goodness in **the last days**.

MICAH
Mic 4:1 And it will come about in **the last days** that the mountain of the house of the LORD will be established as the chief of the mountains. It will be raised above the hills, And the peoples will stream to it.

"IN THE LAST DAYS" (NEW TESTAMENT)

The New Testament word for 'last' is the word 'eschatos', from which we get the term 'eschatology'. The study of last things deals broadly with the theological terms heaven, hell, death, judgment, second coming, etc. The term apo-ka-lup-sis' (which means 'revelation') is often confused with the word 'eschatos." It is the revealing of Christ's second coming that ushers in the last days. The Old Testament concept of 'last days' usually relates to the millennium, unlike the New Testament reference, which often refers to any time during the period that we call "the time of the Gentiles."

ACTS
Act 2:17 'AND IT SHALL BE IN **THE LAST DAYS**,' God says, that I will pour forth of my spirit on all mankind; and your sons and your daughters shall prophesy, and your young men shall see visions, and your old men shall dream dreams.

2 TIMOTHY
2Ti 3:1 But realize this, that in **the last days** difficult times will come.
2Ti 3:2 For men will be lovers of self, lovers of money, boastful, arrogant, revilers, disobedient to parents, ungrateful, unholy,
2Ti 3:3 unloving, irreconcilable, malicious gossips, without self-control, brutal, haters of good,
2Ti 3:4 treacherous, reckless, conceited, lovers of pleasure rather than lovers of God,
2Ti 3:5 holding to a form of godliness, although they have denied its power; Avoid such men as these.

HEBREWS
Heb 1:2 in **these last days** God has spoken to us in His Son, whom He appointed heir of all things, through whom also He made the world.

JAMES.
Jas 5:3 Your gold and your silver have rusted; and their rust will be a witness against you and will consume your flesh like fire. It is in **the last days** that you have stored up your treasure!

2 PETER
2Pe 3:3 Know this first of all, that **in the last days** mockers will come with their mocking, following after their own lusts,

JUDE
Jud 1:18 that they were saying to you, "**In the last time** there will be mockers, following after their own ungodly lusts."

THE ESCHATALOGICAL TIMELINE

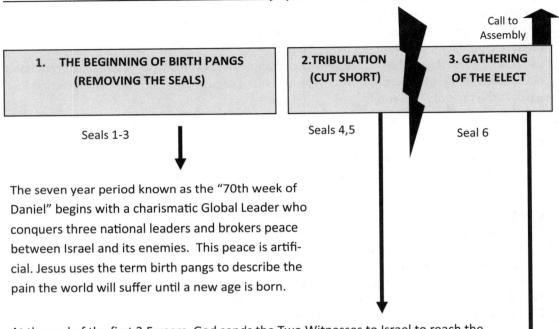

3.5 YEARS

3.5 YEARS

Call to Assembly

| 1. THE BEGINNING OF BIRTH PANGS (REMOVING THE SEALS) | 2.TRIBULATION (CUT SHORT) | 3. GATHERING OF THE ELECT |

Seals 1-3

Seals 4,5

Seal 6

The seven year period known as the "70th week of Daniel" begins with a charismatic Global Leader who conquers three national leaders and brokers peace between Israel and its enemies. This peace is artificial. Jesus uses the term birth pangs to describe the pain the world will suffer until a new age is born.

At the end of the first 3.5 years, God sends the Two Witnesses to Israel to reach the Jewish people with the gospel. The Global Leader reveals himself to be The Anti-Christ, the true Abomination of Desolation spoken of in scripture. He begins a crusade to kill the Jews and the Christians, and offers the mark 666 to all who will bow down to worship him. Everything the Anti-Christ does is counterfeit. He is part of a false trinity, and the Anti-Christ performs miracles in order to produce worshippers. God mercifully cuts short the Tribulation for the sake of faithful believers.

Jesus refers to His second coming as the "gathering of the elect". The timing of this "rapture" is disputed within the Body of Christ. Traditional dispensational theology says the rapture will occur prior to the tribulation period. The position known as "pre-wrath rapture" contends that the church will go through the tribulation period and be snatched away just before God executes judgment on the rest of mankind.

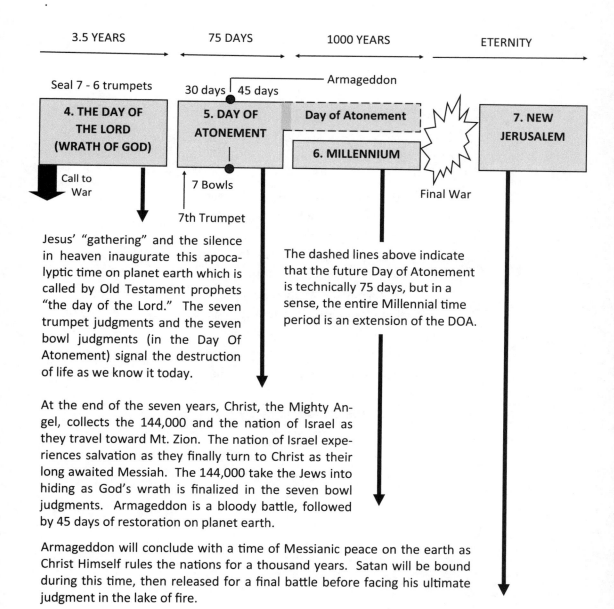

| 3.5 YEARS | 75 DAYS | 1000 YEARS | ETERNITY |

Seal 7 - 6 trumpets

30 days | 45 days — Armageddon

4. THE DAY OF THE LORD (WRATH OF GOD)

5. DAY OF ATONEMENT

Day of Atonement

6. MILLENNIUM

7. NEW JERUSALEM

Call to War

7 Bowls

Final War

7th Trumpet

Jesus' "gathering" and the silence in heaven inaugurate this apocalyptic time on planet earth which is called by Old Testament prophets "the day of the Lord." The seven trumpet judgments and the seven bowl judgments (in the Day Of Atonement) signal the destruction of life as we know it today.

The dashed lines above indicate that the future Day of Atonement is technically 75 days, but in a sense, the entire Millennial time period is an extension of the DOA.

At the end of the seven years, Christ, the Mighty Angel, collects the 144,000 and the nation of Israel as they travel toward Mt. Zion. The nation of Israel experiences salvation as they finally turn to Christ as their long awaited Messiah. The 144,000 take the Jews into hiding as God's wrath is finalized in the seven bowl judgments. Armageddon is a bloody battle, followed by 45 days of restoration on planet earth.

Armageddon will conclude with a time of Messianic peace on the earth as Christ Himself rules the nations for a thousand years. Satan will be bound during this time, then released for a final battle before facing his ultimate judgment in the lake of fire.

The new Jerusalem will likely be a magnificent city of Jewish habitation. The nations of the earth will enjoy Eden on the newly re-created planet earth, and they will worship God with the Jews as they visit Jerusalem to celebrate God's eternal presence in their midst.

"If the return of Israel to her homeland
cocked the prophetic 'hammer'
in preparation for the end-times,
then her gaining control over the entire
city of Jerusalem took off the 'safety',
preparing the weapon for firing -
in other words, preparing for the initiation
of the seventieth week of Daniel
when the final conflict between
God and Satan will be played out on planet earth."

ROBERT VAN KAMPEN
"The Sign"

D
THE OLIVET DISCOURSE

"Jesus Prophesies His Second Coming"

When you begin to study the subject of end-times, or eschatology, you must not begin in Revelation, but rather at Matthew 24 with Jesus' famous Olivet Discourse. It is no doubt ironic that Jesus was sitting on the Mount of Olives while his mind was drawn back to the prophetic words of Zechariah 14:4 which say: *"In that day His feet will stand on the Mount of Olives, which is in front of Jerusalem on the east; and the Mount of Olives will be split in its middle from east to west by a very large valley, so that half of the mountain will move toward the north and the other half toward the south."* Not only does King Jesus create a path to understanding the future, but He also creates a path of safety for the future generation of Israel that will honor Him as Messiah and King.

THE OLIVET DISCOURSE

Matthew Chapter 24

Mat 24:1 Jesus came out from the temple and was going away when His disciples came up to point out the temple buildings to Him.

Mat 24:2 And He said to them, "Do you not see all these things? Truly I say to you, **not one stone** here will be left upon another, which will not be torn down."

Mat 24:3 As He was sitting on the Mount of Olives, the disciples came to Him privately, saying, "Tell us, when will these things happen, and what will be **the sign of Your coming**, and of **the end of the age?"**

Matthew 24 clearly defines four events that are replicated in Revelation Chapter 6. Those events are: The Beginning of Birth Pangs, The Great Tribulation, The Gathering of the Elect, and The Wrath of God. Pre-Tribulation rapture theology teaches that Christ will rescue the Church before the Tribulation begins. However, a careful reading of this passage of scripture clearly places the timing of the rapture AFTER THE TRIBULATON, and just before THE WRATH OF GOD. Why is this important? The Church must prepare itself to stand strong against the inevitable persecution of believers by the Anti-Christ. The rapture is the great reward.

Not one stone. *This prophecy came true in 70 ad, when the Roman forces of General Titus marched on Jerusalem, destroying the temple and much of the city.*

The sign of your coming. *1 Corinthians 1:22 says "Jews ask for signs and Greeks search for wisdom." The Jews expected God to give them signs of significant events, and Jesus promised that He would give them some insight into His return. We also should expect from this verse that there would be certain clues that will prepare us for the most spectacular event the world has ever witnessed.*

The end of the age. *When is the end of the age? Is it the rapture, the end of the seven years, the end of the millennium? What does Jesus say about this? Based on the following verses, It would appear that the end of the age is the end of the millennium, in which death and Hades are finally cast into the lake of fire.*

*Mat 13:49 So it will be at **the end of the age;** the angels will come forth and take out the wicked from among the righteous. 1 Corinthians 15:24 "then comes **the end,** when He hands over the kingdom to the God and Father, when He has abolished all rule and all authority and power. 25 For He must reign until He has put all His enemies under His feet. 26 The last enemy that will be abolished is death."*

Rev 20:14 Then death and Hades were thrown into the lake of fire. This is the second death, the lake of fire.

THE BEGINNING OF BIRTH PANGS

Mat 24:4 And Jesus answered and said to them, "See to it that no one misleads you.

Mat 24:5 "For many will come in My name, saying, 'I am the Christ,' and will mislead many.

Mat 24:6 "You will be hearing of wars and rumors of wars. See that you are not frightened, for those things must take place, but that is not yet the end.

Mat 24:7 "For nation will rise against nation, and kingdom against kingdom, and in various places there will be famines and earthquakes.

Mat 24:8 "But all these things are merely the beginning of **birth pangs.**

***Birth pangs.** The imagery of a woman giving birth is very important for understanding the end of the age. Birth pangs are the first stage symbolized in Revelation 6 by the first three seals. Next comes the regular contractions symbolized by the Tribulation period. The wrath of God is the hard labor that must happen before the earth is purged of its impurities. After hard labor comes the joy of birth. This fourth stage, the delivery, is the Millennium, which finally sees Israel enjoy its privileged status as God's children*

This period marks the first 3.5 years of the seven year period known as the seventieth week of Daniel. During this time a charismatic global leader will unify three nations in order to create the illusion of peace between Israel and its Arab enemies. This global leader will likely mesmerize the world with miracles and signs and wonders.

Revelation 6:1-6 is a necessary cross reference to understand what Jesus means when He says "birth pangs." Jesus is the only person in the universe worthy of opening the scroll. There are seven seals that have to be removed before the scroll can be opened. See page 138 for an amazing parallel between Matthew 24 and Revelation 6.

*Jesus says many will come saying. I am the Christ. **Seal One** in Revelation 6 is a man riding a white horse, and he goes out conquering. This is a clear picture of the Global Leader, later to become the "man of lawlessness."*

*Jesus says there will be wars and rumors of wars. **Seal Two** in Revelation 6 says the rider of the red horse will "take peace from the earth, slaying one another." This clearly personifies war on a global scale.*

*Jesus says that there will be famine and earthquakes. (Parallel in Luke 21:11 adds plagues.) **Seal Three** in Revelation 6 uses the imagery of wheat and barley, oil and wine, and compares it to a days wages. In those days, you will work all day to earn a day's worth of food.*

B. THE PERIOD OF TRIBULATION.

Mat 24:9 "Then they will deliver you to **tribulation**, and will kill you, and **you will be hated by all nations because of My name.**

Mat 24:10 "At that time many will fall away and will betray one another and hate one another.

Mat 24:11 "Many false prophets will arise and will mislead many.

Mat 24:12 "Because lawlessness is increased, most people's love will grow cold.

Mat 24:13 "But the one **who endures to the end**, he will be saved.

> *the Tribulation period begins at the midpoint of the seven years, when the global leader takes off his mask and reveals himself to be the dreaded Abomination of Desolation, otherwise known as the man of lawlessness or the Anti-Christ. The Jews refer to him as Armilus. This time should be referred to as the wrath of Satan, and is symbolized by the governmental demand to take the mark of the beast or suffer persecution leading to death. This period is so intense that God mercifully cuts those days short (v22) before Satan is able to destroy the entire nation of Israel and the Church.*

> *You will be hated. . . because of my name.* Pre-Tribulation theology teaches that the Olivet Discourse is exclusively directed toward the Jewish nation. This verse is very important because it clearly connects tribulation with Christian believers. *This cannot be talking about the Jewish remnant because v9 says they will be hated because of My name.*

> *who endures to the end.* The context of "the end" in this passage clearly refers to the tribulation. If that is true, the rapture must occur at the end of tribulation just prior to the wrath of God. *V14. then the end will come.* See Revelation 14:6. This refers to the angel in mid-heaven who delivers a final gospel appeal to the rebellious world.

Mat 24:14 "This gospel of the kingdom shall be preached in the whole world as a testimony to all the nations, and **then the end will come.**

Mat 24:15 "Therefore when you see the Abomination of Desolation which was spoken of through Daniel the prophet, standing in the holy place (let the reader understand),

Mat 24:16 then those who are in Judea must flee to the mountains.

Mat 24:17 "Whoever is on **the housetop** must not go down to get the things out that are in his house.

Mat 24:18 "Whoever is in the field must not turn back to get his cloak.

Mat 24:19 "But woe to those who are pregnant and to those who are nursing babies in those days!

Mat 24:20 "But pray that your flight will not be in the winter, **or on a Sabbath**.

Mat 24:21 "For then there will be a great tribulation, such as has not occurred since the beginning of the world until now, nor ever will.

Mat 24:22 "**Unless those days had been cut short**, no life would have been saved; but for the sake of the elect those days will be cut short.

Mat 24:23 "Then if anyone says to you, 'Behold, here is the Christ,' or 'There *He is*,' do not believe *him*.

Mat 24:24 "For false Christs and false prophets will arise and will show great signs and wonders, so as to mislead, if possible, even the elect.

Mat 24:25 **"Behold, I have told you in advance.**

Mat 24:26 "So if they say to you, 'Behold, He is in the wilderness,' do not go out, or, 'Behold, He is in the inner rooms,' do not believe them.

Mat 24:27 "For just **as the lightning comes** from the east and flashes even to the west, so will the coming of the Son of Man be.

Mat 24:28 "Wherever the corpse is, **there the vultures will gather.**

the housetop. This verse was taken out of context by a group in North Carolina who prophesied the second coming of Christ at a certain time. As the time approached, each family climbed onto the rooftops, awaiting the return of Jesus. When the time passed, they were embarrassed to join the ranks of those foolish individuals who tried to predict the time of His coming.

or on a Sabbath. The Pre-Tribulation rapture movement would have us believe that this entire passage is directed to the nation of Israel, and not the Church, because it, the Church, has already been raptured out prior to the beginning of birth pangs. Verse 9 says, "You will be hated by all because of My name." Yes, these were Jews who held to the strictness of rabbinical standards, but they were more importantly disciples of Jesus who were hearing this message. Jews could not be the object of this statement . Yes, they would flinch at the idea of breaking the Sabbath, but Jesus reminded them in Matthew 12:8 that He was the Lord of the Sabbath.

unless those days had been cut short. When you put the word 'tribulation' (v21) with the words 'cut short for the sake of the elect" (v22), you cannot interpret the tribulation to be a seven year period. Unless, of course, you believe the words of Jesus here are so cryptic that they cannot be understood.

Behold, I have told you in advance. Just as the Pharisees looked into the face of Jesus and called him a devil (Matthew 12:24), so Satan will succeed in luring the end-time believers into accepting the ultimate lie. Jesus is warning us to prepare.

As the lighting comes. See Revelation 6:12-14. When the sun turns dark and the world is immersed in the total absence of light, then suddenly Jesus will split the skies with light, reminding us of the light that Paul experienced on the road to Damascus.

the vultures will gather. The corpse is the false prophet and the vultures are those who are being mislead. They will be attracted to the sensational, but ignore the truth.

133

THE GATHERING OF THE ELECT.

Mat 24:29 "But immediately **after the tribulation** of those days the sun will be darkened, and the moon will not give its light, and the stars will fall from the sky, and the powers of the heavens will be shaken.

Mat 24:30 "And then the sign of the Son of Man will appear in the sky, and then all the tribes of the earth will mourn, and they will see the Son of Man coming on the clouds of the sky with power and great glory.

Mat 24:31 "And He will send forth His angels with a great trumpet **and they will gather together His elect** from the four winds, from one end of the sky to the other.

> **After the tribulation.** The interpreters of the Pre-Tribulation rapture claim that this event is the second coming of Christ - not the rapture - based on the fact that their tribulation is a seven year period. This is very difficult to reconcile if you compare Revelation 6, the sixth seal, with the timing of the trumpet and bowl judgments.
>
> **And they will gather together His elect.** The interpreters of the Pre-Tribulation rapture claim that Christ is gathering up the nation of Israel, in preparation for Armageddon and the millennium. It seems to me this interpretation is highly inconsistent and deserves an objective answer from the Pre-Tribulation movement.
>
> It is amazing that we have chosen a Latin word, "rapture," over Jesus' own words to describe the snatching up of the believers into the heavens. "The Gathering of the Elect" is a beautiful term which culminates three of the most important events the world has ever witnessed: 1) the prophetic cosmic disturbance 2) the great trumpet, and 3) the coming of Christ "on the clouds" with power and great glory. Is this not the rapture? Is this not preceded by the terrible days of tribulation which was cut short in verse 22? How long will we ignore Jesus' own words to describe the end of the age?

Mat 24:32 "Now learn **the parable from the fig tree:** when its branch has already become tender and puts forth its leaves, you know that summer is near;

Mat 24:33 so, you too, when you see all these things, recognize that He is near, *right* at the door.

Mat 24:34 "Truly I say to you, **this generation** will not pass away until all these things take place.

Mat 24:35 "Heaven and earth will pass away, but My words will not pass away.

Mat 24:36 **"But of that day and hour no one knows**, not even the angels of heaven, nor the Son, but the Father alone.

The parable from the fig tree. *Some interpreters see this analogy as Israel, and some simply see it as a reference to the maturing of time as the end approaches. More important is the term 'all these things' in v33, (the signs - tribulation, sun, moon and stars) which seems to imply that "He is at the door" when these things take place.*

This generation. *Commentators have many views on this phrase. Some think it is a preterist statement of 1st century Judea; some think it means Jews as a race of people. It would seem that the "fig tree" began to blossom in 1948 when Israel became a nation after 2500 years of wandering. A generation in scripture could be 70 or 80 or even 100 years. One could speculate that the generation born after 70 years (2018) could be the generation alive to experience the return of Christ.*

But of that day and hour no one knows. *It is possible that "those who have insight" will know the seasons that precede Christ's return.*

Mat 24:37 "For the coming of the Son of Man will be just like the days of Noah."

Mat 24:38 "For as in those days before the flood they were eating and drinking, marrying and giving in marriage, **until the day that Noah** entered the ark,

Mat 24:39 and they did not understand until the flood came and took them all away; so will the coming of the Son of Man be.

Mat 24:40 "Then there will be two men in the field; one will be taken and one will be left.

Mat 24:41 "Two women will be grinding at the mill; one will be taken and one will be left.

Mat 24:42 "Therefore be on the alert, for you do not know which day your Lord is coming.

Mat 24:43 "But be sure of this, that if the head of the house had known at what time of the night the thief was coming, he would have been on the alert and would not have allowed his house to be broken into.

Mat 24:44 "For this reason you also must be ready; for the Son of Man is coming at an hour when you do not think He will.

Mat 24:45 "Who then is the faithful and sensible slave whom his master put in charge of his household to give them their food at the proper time?

Mat 24:46 "Blessed is that slave whom his master finds so doing when he comes.

Mat 24:47 "Truly I say to you that he will put him in charge of all his possessions.

Until the day that Noah. *See Luke 17:26. This parallel passage uses the terms "on the day" that Noah entered and the flood came; and "on the day" that Lot went out from Sodom, the brimstone came. The idea here is deliverance and judgment, in back to back events.*

D. THE WRATH OF GOD, THE DAY OF THE LORD

Mat 24:48 "But if **that evil slave** says in his heart, 'My master is not coming for a long time,'

Mat 24:49 and begins to beat his fellow slaves and eat and drink with drunkards;

Mat 24:50 the master of that slave will come on a day when he does not expect him and at an hour which he does not know,

Mat 24:51 and will cut him in pieces and assign him a place with the hypocrites; in that place there will be **weeping and gnashing of teeth.**

> *that evil slave. The implication of this phrase is to describe the unrighteous, unrepentant person who rejects God and the deity of Christ. The term 'my master' should probably not be confused with a believer who identified Jesus as master. More accurately, this phrase refers to a man who knows in his heart that God is the master creator, and he still rejects identity or authority in his life.*
>
> *weeping and gnashing of teeth is symbolic of those terrible days that the prophets titled "the Day of the Lord". The wrath of God does not begin until Revelation 8, signaled by the deafening silence in heaven. This is followed by six trumpet alarms which ravage the earth and torment the remnant of rebellious humans. The term "weeping and gnashing of teeth" is used 7 times in the Bible - only by Jesus, 6 times in Matthew and once in Luke.*

CROSS REFERENCE.

Mat 8:12 but the sons of the kingdom will be cast out into the outer darkness; in that place there will be weeping and gnashing of teeth."

Mat 13:42 and will throw them into the furnace of fire; in that place there will be weeping and gnashing of teeth.

Luke 13:28 "In that place there will be weeping and gnashing of teeth when you see Abraham and Isaac and Jacob and all the prophets in the kingdom of God, but yourselves being thrown out.

OLIVET INTERPRETATIONS

When you begin to graphically indicate the chronology of the Pre-Tribulation position, it becomes difficult to reconcile the chart with scripture. The point of this visual is to contrast the location of the Matthew 24:31 narrative of cosmic disturbance and the gathering of the elect. How in the world do you locate the trumpet and bowl judgments BEFORE the Matthew 24 narrative of Christ coming in power and glory, when Matthew 24:29-31 seems clearly to be the sixth seal?

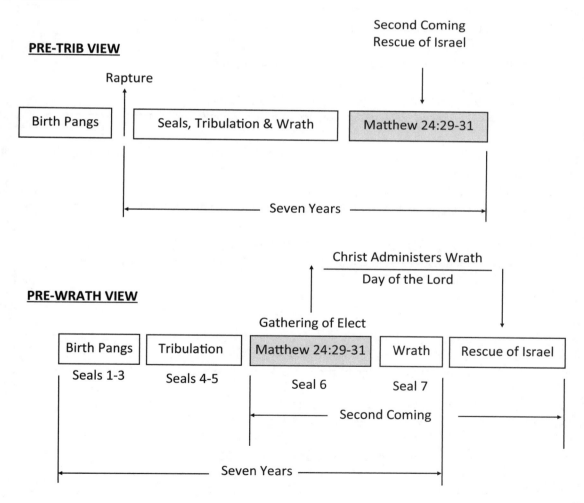

Matthew 24:3 And as He was sitting on the Mount of Olives, the disciples came to Him privately, saying, "Tell us, when will these things be, and what will be the sign of Your coming, and of the end of the age?"

4 And Jesus answered and said to them, "See to it that no one misleads you.

5 "For many will come in My name, saying, **'I am the Christ,' and will mislead many.**

A

6 "And you will be hearing of **wars and rumors of wars**; see that you are not frightened, for those things must take place, but that is not yet the end.

B

7 "For nation will rise against nation, and kingdom against kingdom, and in various places there will be **famines** _____ (and **plagues,** Luke 27:11) and earthquakes.

C

8 "But all these things are merely the beginning of birth pangs.

9 "Then they will deliver you to tribulation, and **will kill you,**
10 and you will be hated by all nations on account of My name. _____

D

21 And there will be a great tribulation, such as has not occurred since the beginning of the world until now, nor ever shall .
22 And unless those days had been cut short, no life would have been saved; but for the sake of the elect, those days will be cut short. _____

E

29 "But immediately after the tribulation of those days **the sun will be darkened**, and the moon will not give its light, and the stars will fall from the sky, and the powers of the heavens will be shaken,

F

Matthew 24:30-31
and then the sign of the Son of Man will appear in the sky,
and then all the tribes of the earth will mourn,
and they will see the **SON OF MAN COMING ON THE CLOUDS OF THE SKY**
with power and great glory.
And He will send forth His angels with A GREAT TRUMPET,
and **THEY WILL GATHER TOGETHER HIS ELECT**
from the four winds, from one end of the sky to the other.

Revelation 6:1 And I saw when the Lamb broke <u>**one of the seven seals**</u>, and I heard one of the four living creatures saying as with a voice of thunder, "Come."

A 2 And I looked, and behold, a white horse, and he who sat on it had a bow; and a crown was given to him; <u>**and he went out conquering**</u>, and to conquer.

B 3 And when He broke the <u>**second seal**</u>, I heard the second living creature saying, "Come."
4 And another, a red horse, went out; and to him who sat on it, it was granted to take peace from the earth, and <u>**that men should slay one another**</u>; and a great sword was given to him.

5 And when He broke <u>**the third seal**</u>, I heard the third living creature saying, "Come." And I looked, and behold, a black horse; and he who sat on it had a pair of scales in his hand.
C 6 And I heard as it were a voice in the center of the four living creatures saying, "A quart of wheat for a denarius, and three quarts of barley for a denarius; and do not harm the oil and the wine."

7 And when He broke <u>**the fourth seal**</u>, I heard the voice of the fourth living creature saying, "Come."
D And I looked, and behold, an ashen horse; and he who sat on it had the name Death; and Hades was following with him. And authority was given to them over a fourth of the earth, to kill with sword and with famine and with pestilence and by the wild beasts of the earth.

E 9 And when He broke the <u>**fifth seal**</u>, I saw underneath the altar the souls of those who had been slain because of the word of God, and because of the testimony which they had maintained;

F 12 And I looked when He broke the <u>**sixth seal**</u>, and there was a great earthquake; and the sun became black as sackcloth made of hair, and the whole moon became like blood
13 and the stars of the sky fell to the earth, as a fig tree casts its unripe figs when shaken by a great wind.

<u>**Notice the amazing parallel between Matthew 24 and Revelation 6.**</u>

The First Seal	The White Horse and The Anti-Christ
The Second Seal	The Red Horse and War
The Third Seal	The Black Horse and Famine
The Fourth Seal	The Pale Horse and Death
The Fifth Seal	Martyrdom
The Sixth Seal	Cosmic Disturbance

Basic Timelines of Eschatology

The following two diagrams provide the simplest of timelines for a basic understanding of the final stages of human history. Notice that both diagrams have four parts. In Diagram One, the 7 years is the "seventieth week" spoken of in Daniel 9:27. The 75 days is the Day of Atonement for the remnant nation of Israel. The Millennium is the thousand year reign of Christ on the earth. The New Jerusalem is the climax of human history in which the heavens and earth are recreated and God's Chosen (Israel) and God's Church are united together to form God's Children.

Diagram Two is a four part summary of the 7 year period. Jesus called the first part "birth pangs", in which the Global Leader makes a covenant with Israel and her enemies. Daniel 9:24 refers to the midpoint of the 7 year period which begins the time known as Tribulation. At this time, the Anti-Christ begins a campaign to destroy Israel and the Church. In Matthew 24:22, Jesus says the tribulation will be cut short, and He will rescue the Church in a blaze of glory, before the dreaded judgment of mankind, called the Wrath of God, or the Day of the Lord.

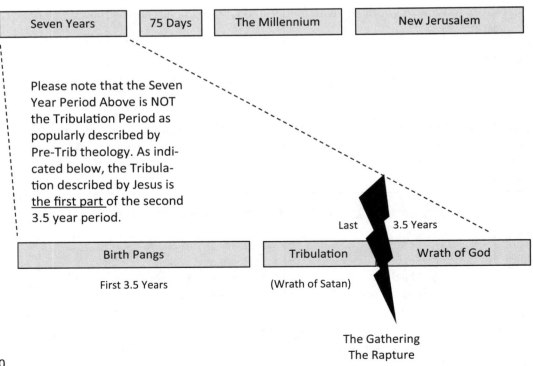

| Seven Years | 75 Days | The Millennium | New Jerusalem |

Please note that the Seven Year Period Above is NOT the Tribulation Period as popularly described by Pre-Trib theology. As indicated below, the Tribulation described by Jesus is the first part of the second 3.5 year period.

Last 3.5 Years

| Birth Pangs | | Tribulation | Wrath of God |

First 3.5 Years

(Wrath of Satan)

The Gathering
The Rapture

THE BIRTH OF THE NEW AGE

In Matthew 24:8, Jesus used the term 'birth pangs' when asked by His disciples to describe *"the sign of your coming and the end of the age."* Notice closely that these two phrases are coupled together - creating, not a single event but a period of time. If Jesus used the term birth pangs, then there must be a birth. When would that be? It seems reasonable to conclude that "the end of the age" would have to be after all of the wrath is ended. Therefore, the beginning of the Millennium must be the beginning of the new age.

It is very important to note the location of the lighting bolt. This is the symbol for the rapture. Jesus refers to this time in Matthew 24:30 as "the Son of Man coming on the clouds in great glory." This occurs just after the tribulation. He then says that the great trumpet will be the signal for "the gathering of His elect." Pre-Tribulation theology incorrectly places the rapture at the beginning of the seven years. Does it not make sense that the Day of the Lord would be initiated by the Lord's return?

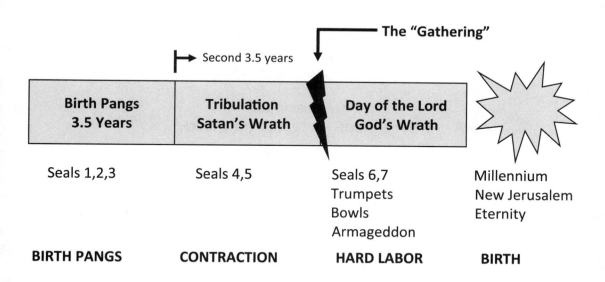

At the present moment in history,
the planet earth is in grave crisis.
This celestial ball
is on a collision course with its creator.
Man has pushed the self destruct button.
Foundations of godliness have crumbled,
things sacred have come unzipped.
We have reached the day
which the prophet had in mind
when he wrote, "Woe unto those
who call evil good and good evil."

MARV ROSENTHAL
"THE PRE-WRATH RAPTURE OF THE CHURCH"

1
BEGINNING OF BIRTH PANGS

"The Covenant of Peace"

The seven year period known as "The Seventieth Week of Daniel" begins with a 3 and a half year period in which heaven introduces a scroll with seven seals. A global leader (seal one) creates a 3 nation confederacy and then brokers peace between Israel and its enemies. Seals two and three are opened, and the world is thrust into unprecedented war and famine. The four seals are symbolized by the "four horsemen of the apocalypse", described in Revelation 6 as the colors of white, red, black and pale. The global leader will likely perform miracles, signs and wonders to counterfeit Christ, and to convince the world that he alone is worthy to be followed.

The Covenant of Peace

Meteorologists occasionally use the phrase, "the calm before the storm," to identify that eerie silence that precedes an ominous weather event. Those who have experienced the phenomenon say that you can literally hear your heart beat just before a tornado. It is that still and that quiet. Historians tell us that the world has experienced only several days per century in which there is not a war raging somewhere on the planet. We talk about peace. We pray for peace. But there is relatively little of it. Jesus refers to this period of time as "birth pangs." Yes, there are still wars and rumors of wars. Then comes the climactic showdown. The nations of Ishmael and Esau rise up to destroy Israel. This hardly seems like a time of peace. Enter the Global Leader. He rises mysteriously out of the sea of humanity to become a calming presence to the masses. He merges his political powers with a religious leader of world renown who will assist the Global Leader in his ascendency to unparalleled fame and power. He suppresses the impending doom of Israel. He negotiates with the warring factions and defers their anger for another time. In typical peace treaty fashion, he orchestrates photo ops to satisfy both Israel and their enemies. He, among all the leaders that have ever tried, is finally able to achieve this elusive dream of brothers in harmony. The world watches with a sigh of relief. Finally a leader emerges who can calm the storm and promise world peace. For three years, the world will bask in his success. And in three short years, he will rise to a prominence that can only be described as messianic in nature. Satan will equip him with charisma and power, and signs and wonders to lull the masses into a mesmerizing confidence. It is likely that he will walk the corridors of hospitals, selectively praying for the sick, and watching them heal before the world's camera. Scripture says that even the elect are precariously close to being deceived by this compassionate broker of world power. But unlike the calm which precedes a visible storm, this calm will catch the world community off guard. They are not prepared for what is about to happen. They have been lured off balance by a master manipulator. The word 'apostasy' becomes the operative term to describe a culture of Jews and Christians who will be convinced that they are looking into the face of the Messiah. Though Jesus said many would come in His name saying, "I am the Anointed One", this one will succeed in echoing the very words of Lucifer in Isaiah 14:13,14:

I will ascend to heaven;
I will raise my throne above the stars of God.
I will sit on the mount of assembly In the recesses of the north.
I will ascend above the heights of the clouds;
I will make myself like the Most High.

Outline of Birth Pangs

A. SIGNS OF THE LAST DAYS.

Difficult Times Will Come

The Conscience that is Seared

The Watershed Concept

The Four Blood Moons

The Shemitah, The Sabbatical Year

Trouble at the Temple Mount

B. THE SCROLL AND THE FIRST THREE SEALS

Panorama of Revelation 1-8

The Triumphant Christ, **Revelation 1**

The Seven Churches, **Revelation 2,3**

Ten Worst Plagues in Global History

The Seven Churches in the Last Days

The Two Crowns and the Two Churches

John is Invited to Heaven, **Revelation 4**

Who is Worthy? **Revelation 5**

The Seals are Opened. **Revelation 6**

Difficult Times Will Come

2 Timothy 3:1-5
But realize this, that **in the last days difficult times will come**.
For men will be lovers of self, lovers of money, boastful, arrogant, revilers,
disobedient to parents, ungrateful, unholy, unloving, irreconcilable, malicious gossips,
without self-control, brutal, haters of good, treacherous, reckless,
conceited, lovers of pleasure rather than lovers of God,
holding to a form of godliness, although they have denied its power;
Avoid such men as these.

On the one hand . . . You can make a case to say that the description above has fit the human race for generations; and you would be right. Yes, we are in the last days. And yes, the times are getting more difficult. This description does fit every generation and every sinful nation on the planet. ***On the other hand*** *. . . The moral compass of our civilization is in a nosedive, and shows no signs of reversal. Mankind will continue to decline - morally and ethically and spiritually - until finally God says, "Enough."*

Psalm 36:1
Transgression speaks to the ungodly within his heart;
There is no fear of God before his eyes.

When scripture says, "The fear of the Lord is the beginning of wisdom," it means that the lack of reverent fear before our Creator is an act of willful defiance that eventually leads to a seared conscience, which in turn leads to a hardened heart that can no longer hear the voice of the Spirit calling for salvation.

Isaiah 5:20
Woe to those who call evil good, and good evil;
who substitute darkness for light and light for darkness;
who substitute bitter for sweet and sweet for bitter!

We are living in the times when one group of people will point to a piece of white paper and call it white, while another group of people will look at the same piece of white paper and call it black. There is an adversarial spirit in the world today. There is a lack of objectivity in our world today that restricts our ability to sit down with some people and get them to agree on anything. To call evil 'good', and to call good 'evil' should remind us of Jesus' confrontation with the Pharisees, when they looked into His very eyes and called Him the devil. Daniel's prophecy says that the Anti-Christ will "fling truth to the ground." We are approaching that low level in human depravity.

THE CONSCIENCE THAT IS SEARED

1Ti 4:1 But the Spirit explicitly says that in later times some will fall away from the faith, paying attention to deceitful spirits and doctrines of demons,

1Ti 4:2 by means of the hypocrisy of liars **seared in their own conscience** as with a branding iron,

> *These are the later times that the spirit speaks of. It is a fearful thing to discuss the falling away from the faith. The implication here is that Satan has succeeded in taking this person out of the race, out of the battle and has neutralized them as both worshippers or warriors for the cause of Christ. Thus we are faced with several possibilities:*
>
> *1) This verse could mean that you can lose your salvation. This sets in motion many doctrinal problems related to the assurance of salvation and eternal security. I do not believe that this verse is making that declaration.*
>
> *2) This verse could mean that many were never saved in the first place, but only in the later times did they finally forsake their faith and prove that they would not endure to the end because there was no meaningful salvation experience in the first place.* It points to those who have given evidence of salvation early in life - due to tradition or sentimentality - only to prove later in life that it was a passing fancy. Jesus spoke of these people in the parable of the soils. The seed was planted and sprouted and then withered away. Scripture says those who endure to the end will be saved. There must be evidence of your faith later in life to prove that early signs of salvation were not just a reaction to a momentary season. *Perhaps these people fall into the category of Matthew 7:21: "Not everyone who says to me Lord, Lord, shall enter the kingdom of heaven. But he who does the will of my Father who is n heaven."*
>
> *3) This verse could mean that the "falling away from the faith" means that you have severely compromised yourself in later life by careless attention to worldly distractions, and you have been rendered completely useless as a believer. The searing of the conscience is a fearful thing. When confronted with the temptation of sin, which we all are, it is not uncommon to fall into sin for a season. Yes, the Holy Spirit is grieved. The Holy Spirit is wounded that we would fall into temptation, and He grieves like a brother, or like one who has just been violated by a best friend. I am reminded of the verse that says, "No temptation has overtaken you but such is common to man; but God is faithful who will not allow you to be tempted beyond that which you are able, but will, with the temptation, provide you the way of escape that you will be able to endure it."*

THE WATERSHED CONCEPT

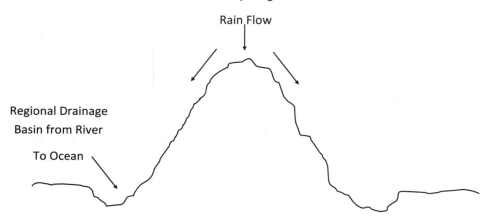

Mountaintop Ridge Divide

Rain Flow

Regional Drainage
Basin from River

To Ocean

By definition, a watershed is an area of land that forms a bounded hydrologic system which links all living things together by a common water source. The ridge of the mountaintop divide requires that the water flows from the ridge in one of two directions. In the continental United States there are 2100 watersheds. One example of a major US "drainage basin" is the Chattahoochee Watershed in the Atlanta, Georgia area. The "Hooch," as people affectionately refer to the river that runs through it, is an area encompassing 3.8 million acres and 10% of the area of Georgia - providing drinking water and recreation for 30% of the state's population.

Watershed as a Social Issue.

The watershed system is not only a means of determining the necessary flow of water between mountain ranges and communities, it is also a concept. The watershed concept, by definition, is a subject (person or issue) that becomes so important and so controversial to the majority of the population that the average person cannot be neutral when faced with a decision to either favor or reject this subject. An example: the social issue of voting age is not a major issue to the general population. Most people don't care, they accept the status quo. They are not likely to become passionate or adversarial about the issue. Abortion, on the other hand, has become a divided issue. People on both sides of the issue are willing to "climb the mountain" in order to defend their position. This constitutes a watershed topic.

The following issues are already being galvanized into a single platform that is so polarizing, and so volatile, that they must be considered "watershed issues." Here's a thought: We are much more liberal and tolerant today than we were 20 years ago. 20 years from now, we will be even more liberal and tolerant than we are today. The "progressive" movement will continue to push forward to force an agenda, not just of fairness, but rather an agenda of control. We must continue to fight the battle for each of these monumental watershed issues.

1. The Watershed Issue: **GOD vs. ATHEISM.**

   The Humanist Manifesto is nothing more than another form of religion. Their primary belief is that we can have good without God. They want to be the only religion.

2. The Watershed Issue: **THE BIBLE vs. RATIONALISM.**

   Modernism seeks to ignore the prophetic and authoritative nature of the Bible. We have had 2000 years to prove the Bible wrong, and liberals still come up short.

3. The Watershed Issue: **CREATION vs. EVOLUTION.**

   The evolutionists' position can be incorrectly summarized as saying: "Nothing becomes something, something becomes life, and life becomes human."

4. The Watershed Issue: **FAMILY VALUES vs. ABORTION**.

   Child sacrifice has been practiced by pagans for thousands of years. The issue of abortion is not a woman's choice. The issue of abortion is sex without consequence.

5. The Watershed Issue: **FAMILY VALUES vs. HOMOSEXUALITY.**

   The center of God's intention for human sexuality was the propagation of the race through the nuclear family. Homosexuality is nothing more than a political agenda.

6. The Watershed Issue: **ISRAEL vs. TOTALITARIANISM**

   The global community is dedicated to protecting nations' rights around the world, except, of course, when it comes to the rights of the Middle East's only democracy.

7. The Watershed Issue: **CHRIST vs. ISLAM.**

   Leveling the playing field is not an option for the Christian Church. Christianity is not just an exclusive religion. Christ is the Pre-eminent Personality in all human history.

THE FOUR BLOOD MOONS

Report from NASA

*The Bible prophesies that in the last days the sun will be darkened and the moon will become like blood. This phenomenon is called a lunar eclipse. The frequency of a lunar eclipse by itself is not unusual, but when a series of lunar eclipses (blood moons) occur within a year's time (called a tetrad), it is especially phenomenal. Even more phenomenal, however, is the occurrence of a tetrad (four) of blood moons on the exact days of the Jewish feast days of Passover and Tabernacles. This is a phenomenon that occurs rarely in human history. The question is this. What is the significance of this event as it relates to Israel? And secondly, what is the implication for those of us who understand that Israel and the heavens (the sun, moon and stars) are both signs pointing to the future coming of Christ? My conclusion, written in 2014, is **NOT** to say that the upcoming tetrad of 2015 is the blood moon of Revelation 6:12. But it is a sign to all believers, that there will come a time, when sun, moon and stars will bow down, and the sky will roll back like a scroll, and suddenly King Jesus will break through the skies to usher in the dawn of a new day. Watch and pray. The signs are all around you.*

Joel 2:31 <u>**"The sun will be turned into darkness and the moon into blood**</u> before the great and awesome day of the LORD comes.

Mat 24:29 "But immediately after the tribulation of those days <u>the sun will be darkened</u>, and the moon will not give its light, and the stars will fall from the sky, and the powers of the heavens will be shaken.

Acts 2:20 "The <u>sun will be turned into darkness</u> and the moon into blood, before the great and glorious day of the Lord shall come."

A total solar eclipse

Revelation 6:12 I looked when He broke the sixth seal, and there was a great earthquake; and the sun became black as sackcloth made of hair, and the whole moon became like blood;

Lunar eclipse (blood moon) This occurs when the earth comes between the sun and a full moon in perfect alignment. The "blood" red color of the moon happens for the same reason that sunrise and sunset appear red. The earth's atmosphere bends light around its edge, and scatters out shorter-wavelength light (green through violet), leaving longer-wavelength light (red, orange, and yellow) in the Earth's shadow. The sun is rising or setting behind the earth from the view of the moon. Unlike a solar eclipse which lasts only minutes, the lunar eclipse can remain for up to 4 hours.

A blood moon, imagine a reddish glow

Four Blood Moons in 1493 and '94, the Great Expulsion of Jews

It is significant to note that the first tetrad recorded in history happened to coincide with the time period of the Spanish Inquisition, a time in which Jews were forced by the Catholics to convert or leave Spain. King Ferdinand and Queen Isabella began this campaign in 1478 and it climaxed on March 30, 1492 with the Edict of Expulsion*. The Jews were either expelled or taxed. Those who were taxed filled the coffers of the Spanish monarchy, which then, surprisingly funded the voyage of Christopher Columbus, leading to a place of refuge and freedom (America) for the Jewish people of the future. Notice that the following tetrad is not only four lunar eclipses from one year to the next, but it also coincides on the very day that two of the Jewish annual Feasts occur.

4/2/1493	Passover
9/24/1493	Total Solar Eclipse
9/25/1493	Feast of Tabernacles
3/22/1494	Passover
9/15/1494	Feast of Tabernacles

Four Blood Moons in 1948, The Rebirth of the Nation of Israel.

Since 586 bc, the nation of Israel has been under the domination of Gentile oppressors. In 70 ad, General Titus of the Roman army destroyed Jerusalem and the Jews were dispersed around the world. Since that time, theologians have erroneously theorized "replacement theology," meaning that the church has taken the place of Israel. As a result of the Holocaust, the United Nations agreed to allow nationhood to Jews returning to their homeland*. In the following years, the first of two tetrads occurred in the 20th century.

4/13/1949	Passover
10/7/1949	Feast of Tabernacles
4/2/1950	Passover
9/12/1950	Total Solar Eclipse
9/26/1950	Feast of Tabernacles

* Note that the blood moons occurred on the Passover after the event. The blood moon of 1949 occurred after the rebirth of the nation of Israel.

Four Blood Moons in 1967, the Six Day War of Israel.

The Jews of the newly founded state of Israel fought back the Arab population in 1948, and then again in 1956. The third attempt to decimate Israel came in 1967 when Egypt, Jordan and Syria all moved their tanks into position on the Israeli border. The Jewish army, known today as the Israeli Defense Force, surprised the enemy and took control of the following strategic areas: Gaza and Sinai Peninsula from Egypt; the West Bank from Jordon; and the Golan Heights from Syria. For those who are unfamiliar with the seven Jewish feasts (which have existed since the time of Moses, circa 1400 bc.) the feasts follow a lunar calendar, therefore occurring on different days in different years. Only two times during the 20th Century did we experience a tetrad of blood moons: the first, around 1948 and the second around 1967. Is this coincidence, or is this the subtle hand of God, preparing us for more cosmic signs in the prophetic future?

4/24/1967	Passover
10/18/1967	Feast of Tabernacles
11/12/1967	Total Solar Eclipse
4/13/1968	Passover
10/6/1968	Feast of Tabernacles.

Four Blood Moons in 2015, the Year of Shemitah.

This page was written on November 17, 2014. At this writing, we don't know what to expect in the year 2015. In the last three tetrads described, the children of Israel were intimately involved in persecution as well as potential genocide. The last tetrad was almost 50 years ago. How significant should we expect this tetrad to be? Unlike the tetrads of the past, Israel today faces organized terrorism around the globe - all aimed at "pushing the Jews into the sea." It is frightening to enumerate the terrorist networks that all have in common the destruction of Israel and the United States: **Al Qaeda**, today based in Egypt; **Isis**, based in Iraq; **Hamas**, based in the Gaza Strip; **Hezbollah**, based in Lebanon; **Boko Haram**, based in Nigeria; **Al Shabaab**, based in Somalia; **Al Nusra Front**, based in Syria; **Ansar Al Sharia**, based in Tunisia and Libya; Not only is this a year (2014-2015) of four blood moons, but it is also a year of Shemitah, the sabbatical year every seven years that prescribed amnesty to debtors and re-organized the Jewish economy. Does that have implications for Israel today? Or are there wider implications for America, even the global community?

April 15, 2014	Passover
April 29, 2014	Total Solar Eclipse
October 8, 2014	Feast of Tabernacles
April 4, 2015	Passover
September 28, 2015	Feast of Tabernacles

"The tetrad of blood moons should be viewed as only a clue, a foreshadowing, of ominous days to come. The general range of time for each tetrad should only be interpreted as a reminder of things to come."

THE SHEMITAH, THE SABBATICAL YEAR

Exo 23:10 "You shall sow your land for six years and gather in its yield,

Exo 23:11 but **on the seventh year** you shall let it rest and lie fallow, so that the needy of your people may eat; and whatever they leave the beast of the field may eat. You are to do the same with your vineyard and your olive grove.

> *Even today, the Jewish practice of allowing the cultivated ground to lie "fallow" in the seventh year allows the farmer to restore the nutrients in the soil through crop rotation. Any crops that produced a bounty during this period of time were considered common property, allowing the poor to enjoy the produce.*

Deu 15:1 "**At the end of every seven years** you shall grant a remission of debts.

Deu 15:2 "This is the manner of remission: every creditor shall **release** what he has loaned to his neighbor; he shall not exact it of his neighbor and his brother, because the LORD'S remission has been proclaimed.

Deu 15:3 "From a foreigner you may exact it, but your hand shall release whatever of yours is with your brother.

Deu 15:4 "However, **there will be no poor among you**, since the LORD will surely bless you in the land which the LORD your God is giving you as an inheritance to possess,

Deu 15:5 if only you listen obediently to the voice of the LORD your God, to observe carefully all this commandment which I am commanding you today.

Deu 15:6 "For the LORD your God will bless you as He has promised you, and you will lend to many nations, but you will not borrow; and you will rule over many nations, but they will not rule over you.

> **every seven years.** *This principle in scripture is called the Shu-mee'-tah, and is taken from the Hebrew word 'shamaw', which means 'to release.' Notice in verse 2 this is called "the Lord's remission." Though we cannot imagine this kind of economic system, the principle, when applied on a small community scale, meant that the poor and the disadvantaged were granted amnesty from their debts every seven years. This functioned as an insurance industry for those who had faced calamity, or attempted a financial risk, or suffered the death of a wage-earner in the family.*

> **there will be no poor among you.** *This is an amazing statement. The Bible speaks of the poor 138 times. Jesus said, "The poor will always be with you." If the Jews had faithfully practiced shemitah, there would have been no poor in Jerusalem because this radical economic system would transform society. Jesus said we would always have the poor because he understood man's failure to properly apply scripture to their lives.*

ELUL 29

Deuteronomy 15:1 says "at the end of every seven years." The practical meaning of this phrase is "the last day of the seven year period." This means the last day of the last month of the civil year. That would be the 29th day of the month of Elul. This 29th day of Elul is called "the Lord's day of Remission" or "Shemitah". Although Shemitah can be viewed as a range of time up to a year in length, technically, it begins on sundown of Elul 29.

Jonathan Cahn, a messianic rabbi and the leader of Hope of the World ministries in New Jersey, details the significance of Shemitah in his two books, "The Harbinger" and "The Mystery of Shemitah."

Below are listed the months of the Jewish calendar. The biblical new year begins with Nissan in the spring at the time of Passover. The civil new year ends with Elul and begins with Tishrei in September/October at the time of Rosh Hashanah.

Nissan
Iyar
Sivan
Tammuz
Av
Elul
Tishrei
Cheshvan
Kislev
Tevet
Shevat
Adar

The seven year cycle of Shemitah is intended to be a time of forgiveness and remission of debt for the Jewish people; but, the reality is - what affects Israel today affects the rest of the world. Matthew 24:32 says: "Now learn the parable from the fig tree: when its branch has already become tender and puts forth its leaves, you know that summer is near;" Believers must watch "the fig tree" (Israel) and prepare for difficult times. Perhaps September 13, 2015 is just another day. Or will it be the next dark day in history?

2001	2008	2015
The Day of Shemitah	**The Day of Shemitah**	**The Shemitah Year**
September 11, 2001 Islamic Attack on the World Trade Center Towers. Jewish Month of Elul 29. September 17, Historic Stock Market Crash	The Great Recession September 29, 2008 Historic Stock Market Crash The Day of Nullification Jewish Month of Elul 29.	September 25, 2014 through September 13, 2015 coincides with the Blood Moons of April 4 and September 28, 2015.

1973 **Shemitah,** January 13, US Supreme Court Decision Legalizing Abortion, Arab Oil Embargo
1974
1975
1976
1977
1978
1979

> Muslims refer to the Arab Oil Embargo as "the Islamic Revival" which empowered the OPEC nations to use oil as a weapon against the United States and western culture. Roe v Wade, legalizing abortion, has sanctioned the murder of 50 million babies in the US, setting in motion national and eternal consequences.

1980 **Shemitah,** Iran Hostage Crisis, Reagan vows to Release Hostages
1981
1982
1983
1984
1985
1986

> 52 diplomats were held for 444 days when students stormed the American Embassy in Tehran. The theocracy of Iran, led by the Ayotollah, became a symbol of defiance to the west and the U.S. Due to candidate Ronald Reagan's tough talk to Iran, the hostages were released on his first day in office as President.

1987 **Shemitah,** Black Monday, October 19th, Historic U.S. Stock Market Crash
1988
1989
1990
1991
1992
1993

> On October 19th, $500 billion in market capitalization evaporated from the Dow Jones stock index. When that happened, investors rushed to sell their stocks, setting up a trading frenzy throughout the world. Black Monday is referred to as the single largest one day market crash in U.S. history.

1994 **Shemitah,** the US Bond Market Massacre
1995
1996
1997
1998
1999
2000

> Following a recession in 1991, the U.S. Federal Reserve created a rate hike that caused panic in the 30 year U.S. bond market. This artificial surge and selloff in the U.S. market spread to the Japan market, and then throughout the financial world market. It just happened to be in the year of Shemitah.

2001 **Shemitah,** September 11, Islamic Attack on World Trade Center Twin Towers, Elul 29
2002
2003
2004
2005
2006
2007

> Coupled with the catastrophic destruction of the twin towers and the Pentagon, leading to 3,120 deaths, the United States was introduced to Islamic terrorists on a global scale. 6 days later, the stock market plunged on September 17, the Jewish month of Elul, the 29th day, which is officially the Day of Remission.

2008 **Shemitah,** September 29, Historic Stock Market Crash, Day of Elul 29
2009
2010
2011
2012
2013
2014

> The fall of financial investment giants Bear Stearns and Lehman Brothers, coupled with years of liberal lending by the mortgage industry (Fannie Mae and Freddie Mac) created a stock market collapse which was "coincidentally" only two months before a very controversial national Presidential election.

2015 **Shemitah,** September 13, the year of Blood Moons. What looms in our future?

TROUBLE AT THE TEMPLE MOUNT

I was standing at The Western Wall, otherwise known as "The Wailing Wall" by the Jewish world, amazed at the drama that was playing out before my eyes. Women were standing at a distance, watching the menfolk approach the Wall with great reverence and respect. Every head was covered - most with the traditional 'kippah' (or yarmulke), some with the broad-rimmed black hat which is the signature of the Orthodox community of men. I had previously written my prayer on a small strip of a paper, as instructed, and had just placed it into a mortar crack on this monumental wall. I then began to inch my way over to "the tunnel" on the left. While curiosity and dignity seemed to overwhelm the first-time visitors at the Wall, the men in "the tunnel" seemed more confident, more casual, more at home - as if this was part of their daily regimen. I quietly observed a large shelf of books lining one of the walls of the tunnel. Most of the men were reading, some were talking. Suddenly, I was approached by a younger man with an inviting smile. *"Would you like to see the tunnel?"* he asked. I cautiously approached the edge of the tunnel, amazed at the sheer volume of beautiful leather bound books. I stood right at the edge of the tunnel, aware that others began watching me. I asked the young man what he was reading. He responded, *"the Torah portion, the weekly reading that is suggested to us as we study the Tanakh. Today we are studying from Ex-o-dus."* I had learned earlier that the Tanakh was an acronym which abbreviated the Torah, the Navaim and the Kethuvim - in other words, the Law, the Prophets and the Writings. These are the three broad categories of the Jewish Bible. The young man surprised me with his next action. He held out a beautiful leather copy of Exodus and invited me to take it. *"Here, this is for you"*. I

was reluctant and mildly dazed at his suggestion. *"Me?" "Take that book?"* *"Sure"* he said. *"You can have this copy."* I graciously accepted and walked away, holding a treasure with untold wealth under my arm. I have just been give a Jewish book at the Wailing Wall. Awesome! I was practically speechless. I hurried back across the large courtyard facing the wall and finally caught up with my tour group, who were about to climb the steps leading up to the temple mount where the Dome of the Rock dominates your vision. I got in line and began the ascent when two Arab guards approached me. *"You can't go up there."* they voiced with authority. *"But I'm part of this tour group!"* With firmness in their voices, they convinced me to quickly turn around. *"No"* they said. *"You must not climb another step!"* I suddenly noticed the pistols and rifles these two men were toting. Confused but much convinced, I turned around and descended the steps. And then it occurred to me. Aha! It must be the book! They think I stole the book! I turned around and approached the guards again. *"The book - they gave me the book."* They looked puzzled but quickly responded with a defiant shout that convinced me not to proceed any further. I turned around again, this time noticing a large crowd of German tourists about to climb the steps. I'll put the book under my arm and hide in the midst of this crowd. I was almost amused at my willingness to plant myself in the midst of this foreign crowd. I may be even more conspicuous now!. Oh well, here goes. Somehow, without an incident, I made it to the top step of the temple mount. My tour group was waiting for me, and since I was actually an assistant tour host, my absence was conspicuous. The tour guide, an Arab Christian named Abed, approached me with an urgency that alarmed me once again. *"Gordon, get that thing off your head! You trying to get arrested?"* What thing? I quickly pondered. Oh, the yarmulke, the kippah! You mean this was the problem? Somehow I had missed the group's instruction NOT to EVER wear a kippah on the temple mount. After all, this is Muslim territory up here. Jews are not allowed to be here. The light finally came on. It had nothing to do with the precious book I had been given. Now I understood the nature of the confrontation with the guards.

I proceeded with my group to visit the Dome of the Rock, the mosque which surrounds the sacred rock upon which Isaac was almost sacrificed by father Abraham. I left the temple mount, smiling at the guards on my way down, with the precious book nestled safely under my arms. I had learned a hard lesson. I had personally experienced the animosity that the sons of Esau harbor for the sons of Jacob. But I shall leave Israel with a sacred token from the Wailing Wall - that silent symbol of Jerusalem's ancient glory.

THE TRIUMPHANT CHRIST
REVELATION CHAPTER 1

IN THE SPIRIT ON THE LORD'S DAY

Rev 1:1 The Revelation of Jesus Christ, which God gave Him to show to His bond-servants, the things which must soon take place; and He sent and communicated *it* by His angel to His bond-servant John,

Rev 1:2 who testified to the word of God and to the testimony of Jesus Christ, even to all that he saw.

Rev 1:3 **Blessed is he who reads** and those who hear the words of the prophecy, and heed the things which are written in it; for the time is near.

Rev 1:4 John to the seven churches that are in Asia: Grace to you and peace, from Him who is and who was and who is to come, and from the seven Spirits who are before His throne,

Rev 1:5 and from Jesus Christ, the faithful witness, **the firstborn of the dead**, and the ruler of the kings of the earth. To Him who loves us and released us from our sins by His blood--

Rev 1:6 and He has made us *to be* a kingdom, priests to His God and Father--to Him *be* the glory and the dominion forever and ever. Amen.

Rev 1:7 BEHOLD, HE IS COMING WITH THE CLOUDS, **and every eye will see Him,** even those who pierced Him; and all the tribes of the earth will mourn over Him. So it is to be. Amen.

Rev 1:8 "I am the Alpha and the Omega," says the Lord God, "who is and who was and who is to come, the Almighty."

Rev 1:9 I, John, your brother and fellow partaker in the tribulation and kingdom and perseverance which are in Jesus, was on the island called Patmos because of the word of God and the testimony of Jesus.

Rev 1:10 I was in the Spirit on the Lord's day, and I heard behind me a loud voice like the sound of a trumpet,

Rev 1:11 saying, "Write in a book what you see, and send it to the seven churches: to Ephesus and to Smyrna and to Pergamum and to Thyatira and to Sardis and to Philadelphia and to Laodicea."

> *Blessed is he who reads.* We are promised a blessing if we "persevere" to understand the prophetic riddles contained in this book, "the summation of all things."

> *The firstborn of the dead.* Our testimony is always wrapped in the resurrection, because it stands as "the hinge of human history,"

> *every eye will see Him.* The idea that Christ will return to the earth and snatch up his beloved Church without being detected . . . is not true to scripture. The cosmic signs of absolute darkness will cover the earth. Then, the illumination of Christ the Son of God, will pierce the darkness, and light will flood the earth, and every eye will see Him. And then, in the twinkling of an eye, Christ will rescue his Church, before the prophetic Day of the Lord passes judgment on the nations.

Rev 1:12 Then I turned to see the voice that was speaking with me. And having turned I saw seven golden lampstands;

Rev 1:13 and in the middle of the lampstands I saw one like a son of man, clothed in a robe reaching to the feet, and girded across His chest with a golden sash.

Rev 1:14 His head and His hair were white like white wool, like snow; and His eyes were like a flame of fire.

Rev 1:15 His feet were like burnished bronze, when it has been made to glow in a furnace, and His voice was like the sound of many waters.

Rev 1:16 In His right hand He held seven stars, and out of His mouth came a sharp two-edged sword; **and His face was like the sun shining in its strength.**

Rev 1:17 When I saw Him, I fell at His feet like a dead man. And He placed His right hand on me, saying, "Do not be afraid; I am the first and the last,

Rev 1:18 and the living One; and I was dead, and behold, I am alive forevermore, and I have the keys of death and of Hades.

Rev 1:19 "Therefore write the things which you have seen, and the things which are, and the things which will take place after these things.

Rev 1:20 "As for the mystery of the seven stars which you saw in My right hand, and the seven golden lampstands: the seven stars are the angels of the seven churches, and the seven lampstands are the seven churches.

> **and His face was like the sun shining in its strength.** *Revelation Chapter One begins with the most majestic description of Christ ever written in scripture. Throughout the Bible, the theme is repeated: Face like the sun, eyes like fire, hair like wool, feet like bronze. Though the book of Revelation is a narrative about the dragon and the beast and the false prophet and the harlot - we must not be distracted from the reality that this book is about only one thing: the return of Christ to reclaim planet earth, to re-claim His bride the Church, to reclaim His chosen people, Israel - and to finalize His judgment against the age-old assault of Satan.*
>
> ***Dan 7:9*** *And the hair of His head like pure wool. His throne was ablaze with flames, Its wheels were a burning fire.*
>
> ***Mat 17:2*** *And He was transfigured before them; and His face shone like the sun, and His garments became as white as light.*
>
> ***Rev 2:18*** *The Son of God, who has eyes like a flame of fire, and His feet are like burnished bronze, says this:*
>
> ***Rev 10:1*** *clothed with a cloud; and the rainbow was upon his head, and his face was like the sun, and his feet like pillars of fire;*
>
> ***Rev 19:12*** *His eyes are a flame of fire, and on His head are many diadems; and He has a name written on Him which no one knows except Himself.*

THE SEVEN CHURCHES
REVELATION CHAPTER 2

The Seven Churches were all located in the country of Turkey. They were literal churches that probably symbolized the scope of both faithfulness and sinfulness found in the church today. Of the Seven, only Smyrna and Philadelphia were found faithful and not declared guilty. Each of the churches that were guilty symbolized a specific kind of sinfulness. God is merciful enough to them that he enumerated their sins, told them to repent, and gave them an opportunity to overcome. Unfortunately, for those churches, and for those of us today, we are blinded by these five basic forms of sin. Perhaps these five sins are represented by denominations within the faith. The five sins are: (from liberal to conservative) Idolatry, Heresy, Materialism, Traditionalism, Nominalism.

THE CHURCH IN EPHESUS

Rev 2:1 "To the angel of **the church in Ephesus** write: The One who holds the seven stars in His right hand, the One who walks among the seven golden lampstands, says this:

Rev 2:2 'I know your deeds and your toil and perseverance, and that you cannot tolerate evil men, and you put to the test those who call themselves apostles, and they are not, and you found them to be false;

Rev 2:3 and you have perseverance and have endured for My name's sake, and have not grown weary.

Rev 2:4 'But I have this against you, that you have left **your first love.**

Rev 2:5 'Therefore remember from where you have fallen, and repent and do the deeds you did at first; or else I am coming to you and will remove your lampstand out of its place-- unless you repent.

Rev 2:6 'Yet this you do have, that you hate **the deeds of the Nicolaitans**, which I also hate.

Rev 2:7 'He who has an ear, let him hear what the Spirit says to the churches. **To him who overcomes,** I will grant to eat of the tree of life which is in the Paradise of God.'

> *your first love. It is possible this passage is referring to their diminishing love for their fellow believers, since Jesus commends them for enduring for His name's sake.*
>
> *The Loveless Church of Ephesus favored the traditions of men over the commandments of God. They took their eyes off the ball, and they were guilty of rituals and ceremonies leading to empty formalities. The traditionalist might say, "We must continue to have preaching service on Sunday night, even if no one comes anymore." We must be able to distinguish the changing traditions of men from the prime directive of the gospel message.*
>
> *The Nicolaitans. See note on Rev. 2:15. Nicholas was likely an errant spiritual leader, or this was a pagan group who sought to compromise the believers. Verdict: Guilty.*

Rev 2:8 "And to the angel of **the church in Smyrna** write: The first and the last, who was dead, and has come to life, says this:

Rev 2:9 'I know your tribulation and your poverty (but you are rich), and the blasphemy by those who say they are Jews and are not, but are **a synagogue of Satan.**

Rev 2:10 'Do not fear what you are about to suffer. Behold, the devil is about to cast some of you into prison, so that you will be tested, and you will have **tribulation for ten days**. Be faithful until death, and I will give you **the crown of life.**

Rev 2:11 'He who has an ear, let him hear what the Spirit says to the churches. He who over-comes will not be hurt by the second death.'

> *The Church in Smyrna will face persecution and will remain true to the gospel mes-sage. The early Gentile church was tempted to hide under the disguise of Jews (the synagogue of Satan) to avoid persecution. There will come a time that end-time believers will stand at their front door and be asked to give loyalty to a subversive ideology. Their choice will be allegiance to Anti-Christ and live or allegiance to Jesus and die. They will choose death because they understand that to hold onto this life means you forfeit attaining the real life, which is eternal. We all have to die. These believers will be some of the boldest among us. Their courage must convince us that dying for the gospel is more important that living a lie.*
>
> *a synagogue of Satan.* To be a religious leader is a fearful responsibility because the masses trust their salvation into the hands of the interpreters of religion in all its forms of worship. Many synagogues in that day were steeped in meaningless ceremony, and not only ignored the truth of the gospel, but also persecuted the church - as was the indictment against the apostle Paul prior to his ministry.
>
> *Tribulation for ten days.* What clue is there in the phrase "ten days"? Will the time of tribulation be weeks or months or years? We do not know. All we know is that the time was cut short because God deemed it too severe for His children.
>
> **the crown of life.** James 1:12 speaks of the crown of life. 2 Timothy 4:8 speaks of the crown of righteousness; 1 Peter 5:4 refers to the unfading crown of glory. Entire books have been written to describe the rewards in heaven, and it may be that some of the saints will be granted various crowns for their service to King Jesus. It's also pos-sible that the crowns of glory, righteousness and life are different ways of referring to the same crown which is awarded to every believer as a symbol that signifies we will reign with him (2 Tim 2;12). A popular gospel music group is called "Casting Crowns". Rev 4:10 says the twenty four elders will cast their crowns before the King, in an act of humility. Perhaps the only significance to our briefly worn crowns is that we will cast them before the King of Life, the King of Righteousness, the King of Glory, as we honor him for granting the eternal gift of salvation.

THE CHURCH IN PERGAMUM

Rev 2:12 "And to the angel of **the church in Pergamum** write: The One who has the sharp two-edged sword says this:

Rev 2:13 'I know where you dwell, where Satan's throne is; and you hold fast My name, and did not deny My faith even in the days of Antipas, My witness, My faithful one, who was killed among you, **where Satan dwells.**

Rev 2:14 'But I have a few things against you, because you have there some who hold the **teaching of Balaam,** who kept teaching Balak to put a stumbling block before the sons of Israel, to eat things sacrificed to idols and to commit acts of immorality.

Rev 2:15 'So you also have some who in the same way hold **the teaching of the Nicolaitans.**

Rev 2:16 'Therefore repent; or else I am coming to you quickly, and I will make war against them with the sword of My mouth.

Rev 2:17 'He who has an ear, let him hear what the Spirit says to the churches. To him who overcomes, to him I will give some of the **hidden manna**, and I will give him a **white stone**, and a new name written on the stone which no one knows but he who receives it.'

> ***Pergamum was the Compromising church.*** *They were faithful to hold fast the name of Jesus, and Antipas was possibly the first Christian martyred in Asia. In spite of these good things, the church was guilty of heresy, being identified with the Nicolaitans (which might mean "victory over the people") and also Balaam, who was the subject of the entire chapter of 2 Peter 2. Verse 15 says: forsaking the right way, they have gone astray, having followed the way of Balaam, the son of Beor, who loved the wages of unrighteousness; The hidden manna and white stone are used only here in scripture, and probably reference blessings in the Millennium.*

> ***where Satan's throne is . . . where Satan dwells.*** *Pergamum was a center for cultic worship. The Nicetorium was a park-like grove of trees that were the collective site for temples dedicated to Zeus, Apollo, Athena, Dionysus and Aphrodite. For this reason, it is speculated that the Anti-Christ may someday be born in the region of Pergamum.*

> ***teaching of Balaam.*** *Numbers 22:22 tells the classic story of Balaam's donkey, who diverted Balaam while traveling, in order to avoid an angel. The donkey, in his defense spoke to Balaam, and Balaam spoke back. Balaam is a symbol of compromise.*

> ***teaching of the Nicolaitans.*** *Jesus hated the Nicolaitans (Rev. 2:5). These were either followers of a leader name Nicholas, or they were a group identified (nike means victory; laos means people) as those who led the people astray.*

> ***hidden manna, white stone.*** *Hebrews 9:24 reminds us that the ark of the covenant will house a golden jar of manna, the mystical food of the Exodus. Jesus prays in Matthew 6:11, "give us this day our daily bread" a reference to manna, a symbol for trusting God's provision. The white stone perhaps references the stone used during a trial: the white stone was used to acquit or the black stone to convict.*

Rev 2:18 "And to the angel of **the church in Thyatira** write: The Son of God, who has eyes like a flame of fire, and His feet are like burnished bronze, says this:

Rev 2:19 'I know your deeds, and your love and faith and service and perseverance, and that your deeds of late are greater than at first.

Rev 2:20 'But I have this against you, that you tolerate **the woman Jezebel**, who calls herself a prophetess, and she teaches and leads My bond-servants astray so that they commit acts of immorality and eat things sacrificed to idols.

Rev 2:21 'I gave her time to repent, and she does not want to repent of her immorality.

Rev 2:22 'Behold, I will throw her on a bed of sickness, and those who commit adultery with her into great tribulation, unless they repent of her deeds.

Rev 2:23 'And I will kill her children with pestilence, and all the churches will know that I am He who searches the minds and hearts; and I will give to each one of you according to your deeds.

Rev 2:24 'But I say to you, the rest who are in Thyatira, who do not hold this teaching, who have not known **the deep things of Satan**, as they call them--I place no other burden on you.

Rev 2:25 'Nevertheless what you have, hold fast until I come.

Rev 2:26 'He who overcomes, and he who keeps My deeds until the end, To Him I will give authority over the nations.

Rev 2:27 And He shall rule them with a rod of iron, as the vessels of the potter are broken to pieces, as I also have received authority from My Father;

Rev 2:28 and I will give him **the morning star.**

Rev 2:29 'He who has an ear, let him hear what the Spirit says to the churches.'

> *Thyatira was the Prostituted Church.* *Though they were commended by Jesus for being a serving church, they were led astray by Jezebel, and the harsh words idolatry and immorality were used to describe the depth (to Satan) of their rebellion. The words sickness and pestilence were used to describe the consequences of their unfaithfulness. For those who overcome, they are promised that they will rule with authority over the nations, and they will have the 'morning star.' Perhaps this means that those who sin the most, and repent the most, will be those who enjoy Jesus the most.*
>
> *The Morning Star.* *See note on Revelation 22:16, see page 387.*

THE CHURCH IN SARDIS

Rev 3:1 "To the angel of **the church in Sardis** write: He who has the seven Spirits of God and the seven stars, says this: 'I know your deeds, that you have a name that you are alive, **but you are dead.**

Rev 3:2 'Wake up, and strengthen the things that remain, which were about to die; for I have not found your deeds completed in the sight of My God.

Rev 3:3 'So remember what you have received and heard; and keep it, and repent. Therefore if you do not wake up, I will come like a thief, and you will not know at what hour I will come to you.

Rev 3:4 'But you have a few people in Sardis who have not soiled their garments; and they will walk with Me in white, for they are worthy.

Rev 3:5 'He who overcomes will thus be clothed in **white garments;** and I will not erase his name from the book of life, and I will confess his name before My Father and before His angels.

Rev 3:6 'He who has an ear, let him hear what the Spirit says to the churches.'

> *the Church in Sardis . . . but you are dead.* The Church in Sardis was guilty of being a church "in name only". In politics, we call nominal republicans "RINO" and nominal democrats "DINO". They are a part of the system, but only by their identification - not by their conviction. This church considered fellowship to be more important than truth. They worshipped the creature rather than the Creator and were no longer aware of their lifelessness. They were what we call the "country club church". They assembled together for social functions and social identity, but not in the spirit of Christ.
>
> *white garments.* It does sound like white robes will be the garment of choice in our eternal future. It is interesting to note that even the angelic hosts of heaven at the time of Armageddon will be robed in white and riding on pure white horses. The only one not wearing white at that time was Christ, whose robe is dipped in the blood of the martyred saints.

Rev 3:7 "And to the angel of **the church in Philadelphia** write: He who is holy, who is true, who has the key of David, who opens and no one will shut, and who shuts and no one opens, says this:

Rev 3:8 'I know your deeds. Behold, I have put before you an open door which no one can shut, because you have a little power, and have kept My word, and have not denied My name.

Rev 3:9 'Behold, I will cause those of the synagogue of Satan, who say that they are Jews and are not, but lie--I will make them come and bow down at your feet, and make them know that I have loved you.

Rev 3:10 'Because you have kept the word of My perseverance, I also will keep you from **the hour of testing,** that hour which is about to come upon the whole world, to test those who dwell on the earth.

Rev 3:11 'I am coming quickly; hold fast what you have, so that no one will take your crown.

Rev 3:12 'He who overcomes, I will make him a pillar in the temple of My God, and he will not go out from it anymore; and I will write on him the name of My God, and the name of the city of My God, the new Jerusalem, which comes down out of heaven from My God, and **My new name.**

Rev 3:13 'He who has an ear, let him hear what the Spirit says to the churches.'

> ***Philadelphia is the Persevering Church.*** *Only Smyrna and Philadelphia qualified to be churches which were not indicted by Christ for their sinfulness. Smyrna was the perse-cuted church and Philadelphia was the church that would remain true and faithful with-out consequence.* ***The hour of testing.*** *This is the highly contested phrase used by Pre-Trib rapture to prove that believers will not go through the Tribulation. The phrase "keep you from" can also be translated "keep you through" the hour of testing. It is very possible that this verse does protect a segment of the church during the Tribula-tion. See Rev 13:10. If anyone is destined for captivity, to captivity he goes; if anyone kills with the sword, with the sword he must be killed. Here is the perseverance and the faith of the saints. Captivity and death are implied to be a necessary prerequisite for those who trust the Lord and do not capitulate to the demands of the new world system.* ***My new name.*** *Revelation 22:4 says that we will have His name written on our foreheads. My sister-in-law Susan Crayton was a missionary in Haiti. During her language training she met a Haitian pastor's son who had been introduced to a now-converted Christian - who was a former voodoo priest. The former pagan priest said that during his days as a witch doctor, he could always identify born again Christians at night because a light was shining from their foreheads.*

THE CHURCH IN LAODICEA.

Rev 3:14 "To the angel of **the church in Laodicea** write: The Amen, the faithful and true Witness, the Beginning of the creation of God, says this:

Rev 3:15 'I know your deeds, that you are neither cold nor hot; I wish that you were cold or hot.

Rev 3:16 **'So because you are lukewarm, and neither hot nor cold,** I will spit you out of My mouth.

Rev 3:17 'Because you say, "I am rich, and have become wealthy, and have need of nothing," and you do not know that you are wretched and miserable and poor and blind and naked,

Rev 3:18 I advise you to buy from Me gold refined by fire so that you may become rich, and white garments so that you may clothe yourself, and *that* the shame of your nakedness will not be revealed; and eye salve to anoint your eyes so that you may see.

Rev 3:19 'Those whom I love, I reprove and discipline; therefore be zealous and repent.

Rev 3:20 **'Behold, I stand at the door and knock;** if anyone hears My voice and opens the door, I will come in to him and will dine with him, and he with Me.

Rev 3:21 'He who overcomes, I will grant to him to sit down with Me on My throne, as I also overcame and sat down with My Father on His throne.

Rev 3:22 'He who has an ear, let him hear what the Spirit says to the churches.'"

Laodicea, the Moderate Church may well be where many Christians are today. Materialism and prosperity have such a strong grip on our lives that we are guilty of the sins of the rich young ruler. The Christian faith is about sacrifice, and the materialistic believer is one who is dangerously close to favoring his toys and pleasures over a life of discipline, choosing to be a consumer rather than a giver. Matthew 19:3 says "it is hard for a rich man to enter the kingdom of heaven." Jesus said "Where your treasure is, there will your heart be also."

Words and Music by Steve Camp
For I've been living in Laodicea
And the fire that once burned bright, I've let it grow dim
And the very Word I swore that I would die for all has been forgotten
As the world's become my friend.

It was the Jewish Christians
that brought the gospel to the world.
If I seem emphatic about the Jewish people,
it's not because I'm Jewish.
It's because I'm God-ish.
You can't divide Israel.
There is no two-state solution.
When Y'shua comes back,
HE will be the solution,
And He will say:
"I will be one state.
Y'shua is not coming back
to an Islamic state of Palestine.
He is coming back to a restored Israel,
as King - their King - the King of all kings.

Rabbi Greg Hershberg
Beth Y'shua International
Macon, Ga

THE SEVEN CHURCHES IN THE LAST DAYS

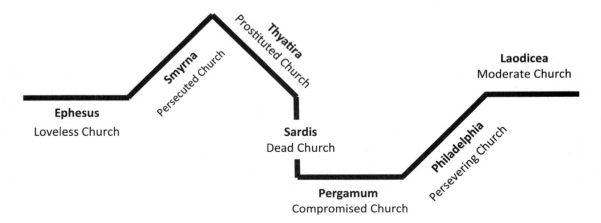

Chapters Two and Three of Revelation identify the seven churches of Asia Minor, as spoken of by John. Referring to seven historical churches, they also imply the variety of churches in "The Time of the Gentiles". Or better, they symbolize the status of the churches at the beginning of birth pangs. The Church Growth Movement of the latter twentieth century has categorized churches into plateaued, growing or declining churches. Typically, American churches are considered to be 70% plateaued, 25% declining and 5% growing.

The plateaued churches are: Ephesus, Pergamum and Laodicea. They represent the loveless church, the moderate church and the compromised church. Ephesus is guilty of traditionalism, Pergamum is guilty of heresy and Laodicea is guilty of materialism.

The declining churches are: Thyatira and Sardis. They represent the prostituted church and the dead church. The church in Thyatira is guilty of immorality while the Sardis church is guilty of being a church in name only.

The growing churches are: Smyrna and Philadelphia. They represent the persecuted church and the persevering church. Both of these churches were deemed to be: NOT GUILTY. They alone of the seven churches were found faithful. They alone of the seven churches would be spared the penalty of death and judgment during the tribulation. They are our models for living in today's world, and standing strong in the difficult days ahead. They are our models for professing a biblical message of Christ to the world.

Perhaps it is worthy to note that if two of the seven churches, Smyrna and Philadelphia are the only ones to survive the Tribulation period, then the percent, or remnant, of believers would be 28%, roughly equivalent to one-third, perhaps a parallel to Zechariah 13:9, in which God says: "And I will bring the third part through the fire."

The Persecuted Church in the last days will be those Christians who will lose their lives for the Word of God and the Testimony of Jesus. We all have to die. These believers will prove to be the boldest among us.

SMYRNA

The Persecuted Church

Not Guilty

PHILADELPHIA

The Persevering Church

Not Guilty

The Persevering Church will constitute all the believers who have lived godly lives and were faithful up until their natural death or the time of the Rapture. They will be tested but not required to give their lives.

THYATIRA

The Prostituted Church

Guilty of Idolatry

PERGAMUM

The Compromising Church

Guilty of Heresy

LAODICEA

The Moderate Church

Guilty of Materialism

EPHESUS

The Loveless Church

Guilty of Traditionalism

SARDIS

The Dead Church

Guilty of Nominalism

Liberalism ←——————————————————————————→ Conservatism

The Prostituted Church on this continuum represents those believers whose consciences were seared so badly that they moved from accepted immorality to open idolatry and finally conceded to the lust of the flesh.

The Compromising Church, considered ideology to be more important than truth. They did not handle accurately the Word and therefore were unaware when false teachers entered in and seduced them into myths.

The Moderate Church may well be where many Christians are today. Materialism and prosperity have such a strong grip on our lives that we are guilty of the sins of the rich young ruler. The Christian faith is about sacrifice, and the materialistic believer is one who is dangerously close to favoring his toys and pleasures over a life of discipline, choosing to consume rather than to give.

The Loveless Church favored the traditions of men over the commandments of God. They lost their passion for caring for their fellow believers and reaching out to unbelievers. Jesus called us to selfless love.

The Dead Church was a church in name only. This church considered fellowship to be more important than truth, They worshipped the creature rather than the Creator and were no longer aware of their lifelessness.

THE TWO CROWNS AND THE TWO CHURCHES

The only crowns that are mentioned among the seven churches are the ones given to the churches of Smyrna and Philadelphia. These are the two churches that Christ acknowledged without assigning any guilt to them. Philadelphia is the Persevering Church and Smyrna is the Persecuted Church. Why do these two churches receive crowns? Because they are the overcomers. What are they overcoming? They have endured the warnings from Christ in Revelation 2 and 3, and have not compromised their convictions to the world or the attack of Satan. The sovereignty of God will protect the Philadelphian Church through the terrible time known as The Tribulation. The saints in the Church at Smyrna will personify Revelation 12:11, which says, *"they loved not their lives, even in the face of death."* They will have the glorious honor of giving up their lives as a testimony of their love and allegiance for Christ.

THE PHILADELPHIA CHURCH

*Rev 3:10 'Because you have kept the word of My perseverance, I also will keep you from the hour of testing, that hour which is about to come upon the whole world, to test those who dwell on the earth. 'I am coming quickly; hold fast what you have, so that **no one will take your crown.***

I remember the scene from Indiana Jones "Raiders of the Lost Ark" in which Indy was confronted by an Arab that was showing off his ability to spin his sword around and scare everyone. Indy understood he had no chance in a sword fight with this guy, so he pulled out his gun and shot him. Rather than allowing the "swordsmanship" to distract us, let's just cut to the chase: God will protect the Philadelphian Church during this hour of testing that we call The Tribulation Period. The Pre-Trib movement makes much of the idea that perseverance (hupomenes) doesn't mean persevere. They say it actually means "patient expectation." Really? Much attention is also given to whether 'keep you from" means 'out of' or 'through.' It seems to me that God is quite capable of preserving the Church of Philadelphia from any harm whatsoever, while still allowing them to witness and endure this traumatic time of global catastrophe. Like the lion's den and the fiery furnace, God will protect His saints.

*Rev 2:10 'Do not fear what you are about **to suffer**. Behold, **the devil** is about to cast some of you **into prison**, so that you will be tested, and you will have **tribulation for ten days**. **Be faithful** until death, **and I will give you the crown of life.***

about to suffer.   If the seven churches represent the churches at the end of the age, then the question must be asked: What is the church of Smyrna going to suffer if it is going to be raptured before the seven year period even begins?

The devil.   The Tribulation period is referred to in Revelation 12:12 as the "wrath of Satan." ("because the devil has come down to you, having great wrath, knowing that he has only a short time.") Either this prophetic statement is a general forecast of things to come throughout the centuries, or this would seem to prophesy that the devil is about to go after an entire segment of the Body of Christ (randomly of course) and persecute them to the point of death.

into prison.   Like the Romans who kept many captives alive for the purpose of sport leading to torture, these bold Christians will stand up to the test. Anyone who has suffered as a prisoner of war knows that the enemy works methodically to break the victim. But these victims have an eternal view which reaches far beyond life's brevity.

tribulation for ten days.   It is a curious thing to ignore the word "tribulation" in Chapter 3 of Revelation. The Pre-Trib movement cannot accept this word as a literal event, for fear that the argument for a pre-trib rapture begins to dissolve. The "ten days" remains a mystery, perhaps signifying a final ten day period with one more chance to repent of their sins.

Be faithful until death.   Perhaps this is just another admonition to persevere. Or, perhaps, the very words of Jesus are intended to prepare the "members" of this church to brace themselves for a torturous conclusion to their lives. We all have to die. Is it so hard to accept the reality that dying for Christ at the end of the age would be nothing less than a privilege?

the crown of life.   How can it be that those beheaded (who according to Pre-trib theology have been "left behind") - this small minority of last minute Christians, will enjoy the exclusive privilege of reigning with Christ during the millennium?

*Rev 20:4 Then I saw thrones, and they sat on them, and judgment was given to them. And I saw the souls of **those who had been beheaded** because of their testimony of Jesus and because of the Word of God, and those who had not worshiped the beast or his image, and had not received the mark on their forehead and on their hand; and they came to life and reigned with Christ for a thousand years.*

JOHN IS INVITED TO HEAVEN

Revelation Chapter 4

JOHN IS INVITED TO HEAVEN

Rev 4:1 After these things I looked, and behold, **a door standing open in heaven,** and the first voice which I had heard, like the sound of a trumpet speaking with me, said, "Come up here, and I will show you what must take place after these things."

> ***A door standing open.*** *Paul received a similar invitation 30 years earlier in 2 Corinthians 12:2 when he was caught up to the third heaven. Pre-tribulation rapture theologians use the phrase "a door standing open In heaven" and "the sound of a trumpet" to describe the timing of the rapture. This is nice symbolism, but it is a weak interpretation of the scripture. See 6:14 for the more likely timing of the rapture.*

JOHN SEES THE HEAVENLY THRONE

Rev 4:2 Immediately I was in the Spirit; and behold, a throne was standing in heaven, and One sitting on the throne.

Rev 4:3 And He who was sitting was like a jasper stone and a sardius in appearance; and there was a rainbow around the throne, like an emerald in appearance.

Rev 4:4 Around the throne were twenty-four thrones; and upon the thrones I saw **twenty-four elders** sitting, clothed in white garments, and golden crowns on their heads.

Rev 4:5 Out from the throne come flashes of lightning and sounds and peals of thunder. And there were seven lamps of fire burning before the throne, which are **the seven Spirits of God;**

Rev 4:6 and before the throne there was something like a sea of glass, like crystal; and in the center and around the throne, **four living creatures** full of eyes in front and behind.

> ***The twenty four elders*** *and thrones represent men, not angels. One theory is that the 24 represent the 12 tribes of Israel and the 12 apostles. Another theory states that the 24 represent godly men throughout history.* ***The seven spirits of God****. There are several likely interpretations. 1) The number seven merely implies the perfection or completion of the Holy Spirit. 2) The number seven refers to seven angels, cherubim or seraphim, who are defined by certain functions. One interpretation of those functions is 6 spirits in Isaiah 11:2, as follows: The Spirit of the LORD will rest on Him, The spirit of wisdom and understanding, The spirit of counsel and strength, The spirit of knowledge and the fear of the LORD.*

Rev 4:7 The first creature was like <u>a lion</u>, and the second creature like <u>a calf</u>, and the third creature had a face like that of <u>a man</u>, and the fourth creature was like <u>a flying eagle</u>.

Rev 4:8 And **the four living creatures**, each one of them having six wings, are full of eyes around and within; and day and night they do not cease to say, "HOLY, HOLY, HOLY is THE LORD GOD, THE ALMIGHTY, WHO WAS AND WHO IS AND WHO IS TO COME."

Rev 4:9 And when the living creatures give glory and honor and thanks to Him who sits on the throne, to Him who lives forever and ever,

Rev 4:10 the twenty-four elders will fall down before Him who sits on the throne, and will worship Him who lives forever and ever, and will cast their crowns before the throne, saying,

Rev 4:11 "Worthy are You, our Lord and our God, to receive glory and honor and power; for You created all things, and because of Your will they existed, and were created."

> ***The four living creatures*** *are defined as having characteristics of lion, ox, eagle and man. The lion is the* <u>*NOBLEST*</u> *of the beasts, the ox (the calf) is the* <u>*STRONGEST*</u>*, the eagle is the* <u>*SWIFTEST*</u> *and man is the* <u>*WISEST*</u>*. In Isaiah 6, these creatures are called "seraphim" which means, "the burning ones". Their fiery power is a purifying agent, and they stand before God as the guardians of flaming purity. Notice that this passage of scripture is attributing "worthiness" or value to God the Father for the act of creation. In the next chapter, you will find that there is another level of worthiness, and that is the ability to open the book, the scroll with seven seals, to reveal the judgment of mankind.*

The Four Living Creatures in Isaiah 6

Isa 6:1 In the year of King Uzziah's death I saw the Lord sitting on a throne, lofty and exalted, with the train of His robe filling the temple.

Isa 6:2 Seraphim stood above Him, each having six wings: with two he covered his face, and with two he covered his feet, and with two he flew.

Isa 6:3 And one called out to another and said, "Holy, Holy, Holy, is the LORD of hosts, The whole earth is full of His glory."

Isa 6:4 And the foundations of the thresholds trembled at the voice of him who called out, while the temple was filling with smoke.

"Covered his face", symbolizing the glory of God, which the Seraph could not gaze upon.

"Covered his feet", symbolizing the humility of man before a God of consuming fire.

WHO IS WORTHY?

REVELATION CHAPTER 5

WHO IS WORTHY? NO ONE IS WORTHY

Rev 5:1 I saw in the right hand of Him who sat on the throne **a scroll written inside** and on the back, sealed up with seven seals.

Rev 5:2 And I saw a strong angel proclaiming with a loud voice, "Who is worthy to open the scroll and to break its seals?"

Rev 5:3 And no one in heaven or on the earth or under the earth was able to open the scroll to look into it.

Rev 5:4 Then I began to weep greatly because **no one was found worthy** to open the scroll or to look into it;

> *A scroll written inside and on the back. The key to understanding the first 8 chapters of Revelation is to understand the scroll with the seven seals. In ancient times, the scroll was a legal document and each seal represented a condition that had to be met before removing the next seal. Only when all the seals were peeled off could you open the scroll to reveal its contents. Before the scroll is opened, the saints will be raptured. Upon opening the scroll, the Wrath of God is unleashed upon the defiant remnant of mankind.*
>
> *No one was found worthy. Even though John the apostle had witnessed the miraculous power of Jesus, he began to weep greatly because it appeared that even Jesus was not worthy. And then the elders removed his anxiety.*

THE LION IS WORTHY

Rev 5:5 and one of the elders said to me, "Stop weeping; behold, the Lion that is from the tribe of Judah, the Root of David, has overcome so as to open the book and its seven seals."

Rev 5:6 And I saw between the throne (with the four living creatures) and the elders a Lamb standing, as if slain, having **seven horns and seven eyes,** which are **the seven Spirits of God,** sent out into all the earth.

Rev 5:7 And He came and took the scroll out of the right hand of Him who sat on the throne.

Rev 5:8 When He had taken the scroll, the four living creatures and the twenty-four elders fell down before the Lamb, each one holding a harp and golden bowls full of incense, which are **the prayers of the saints.**

Rev 5:9 And they sang a new song, saying, "Worthy are You to take the book and to break its seals; for You were slain, and purchased for God with Your blood men from every tribe and tongue and people and nation.

Rev 5:10 "You have made them to be a kingdom and priests to our God; and they will reign upon the earth."

> **Seven horns and seven eyes.** See Revelation 17:12. Notice that Jesus has seven horns and Satan counterfeits this by having ten horns which become seven.
> **The prayers of the saints.** See Genesis 8:21. The Old Testament uses the term 'soothing aroma' to describe God's ability to smell the fragrance of a burnt offering. For the New Testament saint, God can also smell the fragrance of prayer, which is an act of worship. This verse seems to imply that acceptable prayers are even collected by God in bowls and translated into a fragrant aroma.

THE MYRIAD NUMBER OF ANGELS

Rev 5:11 Then I looked, and I heard the voice of many angels around the throne and the living creatures and the elders; and the number of them was **myriads of myriads**, and thousands of thousands,

Rev 5:12 saying with a loud voice, **"Worthy is the Lamb** that was slain to receive power and riches and wisdom and might and honor and glory and blessing."

Rev 5:13 And every created thing which is in heaven and on the earth and under the earth and on the sea, and all things in them, I heard saying, "To Him who sits on the throne, and to the Lamb, be blessing and honor and glory and dominion forever and ever."

Rev 5:14 And the four living creatures kept saying, "Amen." And the elders fell down and worshiped.

> **Myriads of myriads.** The definition of a myriad is 10,000. If you multiply 10,000 times 10,000 you get the incredible number of 100 million. Since the phrase actually says myriads of myriads, it actually means many ten thousands times many ten thousands. If you dare to try to multiply 40,000 times 25,000, the number would be 1 billion. The point is that the angels in heaven equal a number that is too vast for man to imagine. Myriads of Myriads equal BILLIONS of angels.
> **Worthy is the Lamb.** The word 'worship' is derived from the middle English word 'worth-ship', and therefore means that only those things that are worthy are to be worshipped. We use the term worthy carelessly to justify that which we think we have earned. In reality, worthiness is assigned only to God the Father for creation and Christ the Son for redemption.

The Scroll and the Seven Seals

SEAL ONE
The Conqueror

SEAL TWO
War

SEAL THREE
Famine

SEAL FOUR
Death

SEAL FIVE
Martyrdom

SEAL SIX
Cosmic Signs

SEAL SEVEN
Silence in Heaven

Beginning of Sorrows

Seals 1-3

The Tribulation

Seals 4,5

Gathering of The Elect

Seal 6

The Wrath of God

Seal 7

The key to understanding the first 8 chapters of Revelation is to understand the scroll with the seven seals. In ancient times, the scroll was a legal document and each seal represented a condition that had to be met before removing the next seal. Only when all the seals were peeled off could you open the scroll to reveal its contents. This scroll was written on both sides.

The first three seals coincide with the time Jesus called "the beginning of sorrows" or "the beginning of birth pangs." The Global Leader (seal one) rises out of the nations as a charming, compassionate and magnetic personality. He's a problem solver and a leader of leaders. His diplomatic skills will quickly thrust him to the global center stage as the "uberman" everyone has been waiting for. He may be the Secretary General of the United Nations, having risen to power as the head of one of the larger nations. Israel will likely be surrounded by her enemies and prepared for annihilation. The Global leader will galvanize three nations together to form an alliance and promise Israel protection. As part of Satan's evil plan, wars and famine (seals two and three) will continue to plague planet earth. The Global Leader will use these crises to justify his governmental imposition into everyone's life and values.

The fourth and fifth seals begin the second half of the seven year period. Birth pangs are over. The analogy of child birth now moves into the stage of painful contraction. The Global Leader now reveals himself to be the man of lawlessness, the son of perdition, the Anti-Christ. He begins a global assault against the Jews and the Christians. Global death follows and many martyrs will give their lives for the cause of Christ. Satan's fury, The Great Tribulation, would destroy all of planet earth, if not for God's plan to cut short the wrath of Satan with His return.

The sixth seal is removed and scripture says that the earth turns dark and the moon appears to turn to blood. The mountains and the islands are shaken loose from their places of majestic beauty. It is at this simultaneous moment that God seals the 144,000 who have been chosen from the 12 tribes of Israel. Then, out of the blackness of this global calamity, a blinding light appears from the heavens. Jesus comes in the sky to take the dead in Christ and His living saints to glory. Revelation 7 says that the elders in heaven marvel that the multitude which no one could count, has just arrived in white robes. Scripture says that the kings of the earth hide among the rocks because the Jesus that they have ignored and mocked and persecuted has now returned. What's that in Jesus' hand? It's the scroll with six seals removed. And now He peels off the final seal.

The seventh seal is removed at the beginning of Revelation 8 and the Lamb who is worthy opens the scroll. All of heaven is awestruck. For 30 long minutes, there is deafening silence as heaven prepares for that prophetic event called the Great and Terrible Day of the Lord. The seven Trumpet judgments are about to signal God's fury upon Satan, his demons and the unrepentant nations. God's patience and mercy are winding down as months of agonizing torment are about to be unleashed. The Potter is about to crush the clay pot and start over.

THE SEALS ARE OPENED

REVELATION CHAPTER 6

6A. THE FIRST THREE SEALS - THE BEGINNING OF SORROWS

Rev 6:1 Then I saw when the Lamb broke one of **the seven seals,** and I heard one of the four living creatures saying as with a voice of thunder, "Come."

Rev 6:2 I looked, and behold, **a white horse**, and he who sat on it had a bow; and a crown was given to him, and he went out conquering and to conquer.

Rev 6:3 When He broke **the second seal,** I heard the second living creature saying, "Come."

Rev 6:4 And another, **a red horse**, went out; and to him who sat on it, it was granted to take peace from the earth, and that men would slay one another; and a great sword was given to him.

Rev 6:5 When He broke **the third seal,** I heard the third living creature saying, "Come." I looked, and behold, **a black horse**; and he who sat on it had a pair of scales in his hand.

Rev 6:6 And I heard something like a voice in the center of the four living creatures saying, "A quart of wheat for a denarius, and three quarts of barley for a denarius; and do not damage the oil and the wine."

> *Seven Seals - It is important to understand that the Lamb is giving authority (see v8) for each of the consequences of the first 5 seals. Each of the seven seals must be removed in order to fulfill the sound of the seven trumpets.*
>
> *Seal One - The White Horse of the Global Leader. The rider of this horse is the counterfeit of Christ. King Jesus will later marshal the armies of heaven to fight the great battle of Armageddon. Just as Christ rides a white horse in Revelation 19:11, Satan will counterfeit this event by riding this white horse.*
>
> *Seal Two - The Red Horse of War. In order to justify the need for the Global Leader, the crisis of war will reach its crescendo when the very lifeblood of Israel is threatened. 'Take peace from the earth' implies that war conditions have never been as bad as this.*
>
> *Seal Three - The Black Horse of Famine. The denarius in Jesus' day was a day's wages. The implication here is that a day's worth of labor will yield only enough food to last for a day.*

Purpose of Seals

For thousands of years, kings have affixed their official seal to documents, thereby identifying them as a possession of the king. This was a unique seal that could not be duplicated, and served as an extension of the king's authority. Neither the message nor the messenger were to be harmed. We who acknowledge Jesus as Lord have been sealed permanently for our salvation.

1) In this present age we are sealed as a sign of <u>POSSESSION</u>

> **2 Co 1:22** who also SEALED us and gave us the Spirit in our hearts as a pledge.

> **Eph 1:13** In Him, you also, after listening to the message of truth, the gospel of your salvation--having also believed, you were SEALED in Him with the Holy Spirit of promise,

> **Eph 4:30** Do not grieve the Holy Spirit of God, by whom you were SEALED for the day of redemption.

2) In the last days, the twelve tribes of Israel will be sealed for their <u>PROTECTION.</u>

> **Rev 5:1** I saw in the right hand of Him who sat on the throne a book written inside and on the back, SEALED up with seven seals.

> **Rev 7:3** saying, "Do not harm the earth or the sea or the trees until we have SEALED the bond-servants of our God on their foreheads."

> **Rev 7:4** And I heard the number of those who were sealed, one hundred and forty-four thousand SEALED from every tribe of the sons of Israel:

> **Rev 7:5** from the tribe of Judah, twelve thousand were SEALED, from the tribe of Reuben twelve thousand, from the tribe of Gad twelve thousand,

> **Rev 7:8** from the tribe of Zebulun twelve thousand, from the tribe of Joseph twelve thousand, from the tribe of Benjamin, twelve thousand were SEALED.

The Seals, The Trumpets and The Bowls

THE SEALS - THE PROTECTION OF GOD.
Seals 1-3 were the "beginning of birth pangs." Yes, God is in charge but He gives Satan authority in seals 1-3 to pour out his general vengeance on mankind. In seals 4 and 5 he gives Satan authority (as with Job, and with Jesus) to test "some" of His servants during the Tribulation. But ultimately, God will seal and protect his children.

THE WRATH OF SATAN

THE WRATH OF GOD

THE TRUMPETS - THE WARNING OF GOD.
The Wrath of God begins in Chapter 8 with the Trumpet judgments. The first four judgments are directed at nature, and the final three initiate God's three woes on man himself. Though it says "they did not repent", it was still not too late to receive God's salvation. In Revelation 14:6, the angel with the eternal gospel offers one last call for redemption.

THE BOWLS - THE FINAL JUDGMENT OF GOD.

These containers of God's ultimate wrath on unrepentant man were actually shallow dishes as opposed to deep vessels, for the purpose of quickly and broadly dispensing God's wrath. Though these were the "seven last plagues," Armageddon would be the finale when God would close this chapter of Satan's rebellion. Rev 16:11 says: *"and they blasphemed the God of heaven because of their pains and their sores; and they did not repent of their deeds."* Man's seething rage against God could not even be quenched by the pain of torture.

Rev 6:7 When the Lamb broke **the fourth seal**, I heard the voice of the fourth living creature saying, "Come."

Rev 6:8 I looked, and behold, **an ashen horse**; and he who sat on it had the name Death; and Hades was following with him. Authority was given to them over a fourth of the earth, to kill with sword and with famine and with pestilence and by **the wild beasts of the earth.**

Rev 6:9 When the Lamb broke **the fifth seal**, I saw underneath the altar the souls of those who had been slain because of the word of God, and because of the testimony which they had maintained; 6:10 and they cried out with a loud voice, saying, **"How long, O Lord**, holy and true, will You refrain from judging and avenging our blood on those who dwell on the earth?" 6:11 And there was given to each of them **a white robe**; and they were told that they should rest for a little while longer, until **the number of their fellow servants** and their brethren who were to be killed even as they had been, would be completed also.

The Fourth Seal - The Pale Horse of Global Death. The Global Leader has now taken off his mask and reveals himself to be the Anti-Christ. The word "ashen" or "pale" is the Greek word "chlorous", which may imply chemical warfare, capable of taking out more than a billion people, most of whom will likely be believers.

the wild beasts of the earth - likely to be demonic inspired animals.

The Fifth Seal of Martyrdom - Tertullian said, "The blood of the martyrs is the seed of the church." God is honored by those, who in the last days, will stand strong and bear their allegiance to King Jesus, especially in the face of torture and death. These saints who give up their lives are the Church of Smyrna, the persecuted church. It is worthy to note that in the jihadist ideology, martyrdom is a great honor. Hopefully, one day, the Church will understand that also.

How long, O Lord? The martyred saints are waiting for the vengeance of God to sweep down upon the earth and avenge their death. In Chapter 8, just after the silence, the trumpets will begin to execute judgment. How can the fifth seal be God's wrath (Pre-Trib) if the saints are waiting for God to avenge them?

A white robe. It is interesting to note that the only other reference to white robes is found in Revelation in 7:9, 13 and 14, where the raptured saints have just arrived in heaven.

The number of their fellow servants. This is a difficult passage for the Pre-Trib movement to reconcile. One can rationalize that the reference is merely to "the left behind" yet martyred for the faith. BUT, this appears to be the Philadelphian Church of the Persevering, and the Smyrna Church of the Persecuted, whose lives will be completed, either by rapture or violent death. The reward for the persevering saints is the rapture. The reward for the persecuted church, the martyrs, is the millennial kingdom.

TEN WORST FAMINES IN GLOBAL HISTORY

Famine will devastate the global population, as a result of the third seal in Rev. 6:5.

1. **The Great Chinese Famine (1960-1962).** As part of the Communist strategy called "The Great Leap Forward", private land ownership was outlawed in 1958, agricultural workers were made to work in steel factories and experimental seed planting policies resulting in the death of 43 million.

2. **The Chinese Famine of 1907.** A massive storm destroyed 40,000 square miles of farmland in east-central China, causing 25 million deaths.

3. **The Chalisa Famine in Northern India.** A shift in the El Nino weather patterns in 1783 caused severe rain shortage and drought, resulting in the death of 11 million.

4. **The Soviet Famine of 1932-1933.** Joseph Stalin's strategy of "collectivization" was to confiscate the land, destroy the existing crops and redistribute among communal farmers. The result was the death of 10 million, a fact unknown to the West until the 1990s.

5. **The Bengali Famine of 1770.** The English owned East India Company forced the farmers to plant indigo and opium crops instead of their traditional rice crops. This resulted in the death of 10 million people - 1/3 of the population.

6. **The Bengali Famine of 1943.** A cyclone and 3 tidal waves destroyed 3200 square miles of valuable farmland, ultimately causing a fungus on croplands, destroying 90% of all rice At the same time, Japanese imperialism during World War II cut off trade with the Burmese, resulting in the death of 7 million.

7. **The Russian Famine of 1921.** The result of World War 1, the Bolshevik Revolution in 1917 and multiple civil wars caused soldiers to plunder the farmlands and consume all the produce. The farmers began to eat seeds instead of planting them. 5 million died.

8. **The North Korean Famine in the 1990s.** Flooding of farmlands in 1995 caused the loss of 1.5 million tons of grain reserves. Kim Jung II implemented a "Military First" strategy, providing food to soldiers over the needs of the farmers. This resulted in a mortality rate of 9.3% for babies and 4.3% for expectant mothers. 2.5 to 3 million died during 4 years.

9. **The Viet Nam Famine of 1945.** After World War II, the French colonial domination of North Viet Nam shifted to Japanese industrial expansion. Japan forced farmers to begin producing rubber instead of food. Coupled with a severe drought and torrential flooding, 2 million people died.

10. **The Irish Famine of 1845.** Potato crops were a primary source of survival to the Irish. A crop disease in 1845 caused massive starvation and was compounded by British suppression of assistance from other countries. Over an eight year period, 2 million Irish migrated elsewhere and 1.5 million were dead. One fourth of the population was gone.

Ten Worst Plagues in Global History

Plagues (pestilence) will likely be part of the fourth seal in Revelation 6:7.

1. The Black Death (also known as the Black Plague or the Bubonic Plague)

This plague (1341-1347) began in China, then spread to Russia, Europe and North Africa, and totaled 75 million dead - 25 million plus of those in Europe.

2. The Third Pandemic.

This latter strain of the bubonic plague killed 12 million people in Indian and China from 1855 to 1959. New research suggests the Black Plague is lying dormant.

3. The Plague of Justinian.

This is named for the Byzantine emperor, with capitol in Constantinople (modern day Istanbul). 5,000 died daily, ultimately killing 1/4 of the eastern Mediterranean population.

4. Great Plague of London.

From 1665-1666 there were 75-100,000 casualties throughout England. This was tagged as another strain of the bubonic plague, likely transmitted by fleas.

5. American Plagues of 16th Century.

European migration to the Americas brought a serious outbreak of measles and smallpox which infected and killed many natives throughout North and Central America.

6. Great Plague of Milan

The Thirty Years War of Europe, beginning in 1618 spread the black death into northern Italy, ultimately killing 280,000 people.

7. Plague of Athens.

The Greeks fought the Peloponnesian War in 430 bc and lost, in part due to the plague (typhus, smallpox and measles) which, in part, led to the Roman Empire

8. The Antonine Plague (165-180 ad)

Named for one of the emperors who died from this plague, much of the Roman army was decimated, resulting in 2,000 deaths per day, totaling 5 million.

9. The Great Plague of Marseilles.

From 1720 to 1722, this epidemic struck the French province, killing 100,000. In order to warn travelers and contain the disease, a stone wall was erected.

10. The Moscow Plague and Riot of 1771.

Between 50-100,000 Russians died from this disease, but the greater consequence was the civil unrest that resulted from forced quarantines and property destruction.

"I would be remiss if I gave the Anti-Christ
too much credit for his opposition against God.
The real enemy is Satan,
who has been opposed to God
ever since the garden of Eden.
Satan deceived our first parents,
but he will deceive the whole world
In his eschatalogical possession
of the man of lawlessness."

ALAN KURSCHNER
"AntiChrist Before the Day of the Lord."

2

THE TRIBULATION

"The Mask Comes Off"

At the beginning of the second 3.5 year period, the global leader now exposes his true nature as the Anti-Christ, Babylon falls and civilization begins to crumble. The fourth seal, death, is on the mind of every human being. God sends Moses and Elijah to preach redemption, but the lawless one requires every person to swear allegiance by taking the "mark of the beast". The consequence of choosing Christ over the Anti-Christ causes many to <u>defend their faith and defy his leadership,</u> facing the ultimate persecution, the fifth seal - being martyred and beheaded for their faith in Christ.

HEARTS THAT ARE COLD

Jesus made a profound statement in Matthew 24:12 that can only be understood when the breadth and depth and height of the Tribulation period finally happens. He said, "Because lawlessness is increased, most people's hearts will grow cold." Two movies come to mind that portray a glimpse of what the Tribulation could look like. These movies are rated R for violence and language, so you will be forewarned and advised to watch the network channel versions that are edited. Both of these movies were considered box office duds, due to the public's superficial hunger for feel-good movies. Both movies are a sober glimpse into a future that could well be a reflection of the time of Tribulation.

The book of Eli (Denzel Washington, Gary Oldham, 2010).

> Thirty years after a nuclear war that decimated civilization, a man begins walking westward across the United States in what can only be described as a state of single minded pursuit. He scavenges through the remains of former towns with occasional reminders of what society used to look like. He finds delight in a battery that operates an old Walkman music device; He trades a cigarette lighter for water. Along the way, he is assaulted by various evil men, whose hearts, having grown cold, are intent on stealing his possessions and his life. There is a holy nature to this man, who walks from town to town in what seems to be a supernatural protection. He carries with him a book, which is coveted by the villain of the story. As he fights off one evil assault after another, he finally arrives on the West Coast, at Alcatraz Island, where an isolated band of survivors are attempting to collect books in order to rebuild society. The book that Eli had (the villain finally stole it from him) is a braille version of the Bible, and in a mysterious way that is unexplained, Eli recites the entire Bible to the anxious guardians of man's last hope for culture, just before he dies.

The Postman (Kevin Costner, Will Patton, 1997).

> The setting is 2013 in a post apocalyptic world that has experienced nuclear war 15 years prior. The result of this carnage leads to the inevitable regression of all things civil. Horses are now a valued means of transportation, and small bands of people begin to assemble in leftover towns and villages in an attempt to rebuild society. One man (Costner) is wandering across the country trying to survive, when he is forced to join the ranks of a hostile militia group, led by an ego-driven "general" named Bethlehem. After escaping, the nomad comes across an abandoned mail truck and dons a postal cap and mailbag. When he wanders into a neighboring village, he is touched by the despair of the people, and he instantly portrays himself to be a postal

carrier for the Restored United States of America. With a bag of 15 year old letters, he unwittingly inspires the allegiance of the town, and one young man in particular, who then recruits others to be postmen. The mail becomes a symbol of hope and civilization. Bethlehem is threatened by this remnant of culture, and he sets out to destroy the Postman. In a final battle between the Postman and Bethlehem, the Postman's honor wins over the former militia, and peace allows society to advance. Thirty years later, the Postman's memory is honored as the United States appears to have regained a status of civility and purpose.

Both of these movies carry the theme of societal hopelessness and despair that is countered by one person who stands strong against the assault of anarchy. In the end times, people's hearts will grow cold, and, like the time of the US civil war, even brothers will fight against each other. 'Every man for himself' may be the motto of survival.   The Anti-Christ will rise to promi-nence, accompanied by the False Prophet. They will institute the "mark of the beast" as the new standard for societal acceptance, and the Christian will suddenly be living in a hostile world that seeks to strip him of his dignity and his faith.   The one-world government will use the one-world religion as a tool for forcing allegiance and ideology, and Jews and Christians will become demonized and hunted as outlaws. Hearts will indeed grow cold, and old friendships are no longer to be trusted.

This chapter represents a short period of time inside the seventieth week of Daniel. Jesus says the Tribulation is so intense that it is "cut short". We don't really know how long this period will be. The Bible gives us clues but we can only speculate. I suppose it is accurate to say that if you added up the evil of all the movie villains in film history, they would not begin to parallel the malice that comes from the heart of the Anti-Christ. Some of the Bible's great mysteries are in this chapter: War in Heaven, the Beast, Babylon, the mark of the beast, the false proph-et, the ten nation confederacy, the Restrainer, the third temple, the two witnesses, the fourth and fifth seal.

Yes, the Tribulation is a fascinating and horrifying study. Sure, we want answers to the these hard questions. But as I mentioned in the early pages of this book, Rule 1 in reading Revelation is that you study the positive parts of the book dealing with the return and reign of King Jesus. And then, after you have exhausted much time meditating on the wonderful mystery of Jesus' return, only then should you move to Rule 2 - to try to make sense of the ten nations and ten toes. We have learned about the Spirit of Amalek, and the Sword of Antiochus. Now it is time to learn about the Scourge of Anti-Christ.   The Son of God, who is symbolic of all that is good and wonderful about God's created order, is about to be countered and counterfeited by this Son of Satan. When the mask falls from his face, the earth will tremble.

"THE MASK COMES OFF"

A. There is War in Heaven (Revelation. 12:6-17)

> Satan is Cast out of Heaven (Rev. 12:12)
>
> The Two Witnesses Begin Their Ministry (Rev 11:3-12)
>
> Michael the Restrainer is Removed (2 Thess 2:7, Dan 12:1)

B. The Beast and the False Prophet Emerge

> The Beast and the Fatal Wound (Rev 13: 1-10)
>
> The Beast and Seven Heads (2 Thess 2:9, Daniel 7:7-8)
>
> The Four Beasts of Daniel
>
> Resurrection of the Global Leader (Rev 13:1-4)
>
> > Apostasy (2 Thess 2:1-9)
> >
> > Man of lawlessness (2 Thess 2:1-9)
> >
> > False Prophet (Rev 13:11)

C. The Abomination of Desolation Emerges (Matt. 24:15)

> The Covenant with Israel is Broken (Dan 9:24)
>
> The Anti-Christ exalts himself (2 Thess 2:4)
>
> The Mark of the Beast, 666. (Rev 13:3,4,12,14,15
>
> Fourth Seal - Death (Rev 6:7)
>
> Babylon the Great Harlot (Rev 13:3,4; 8:12-15)
>
> The Eight Empires (Revelation 17)
>
> Persecution of Israel and the Church (Dan 12:1; Matt 24:20)
>
> Fifth Seal - Martrydom

There was War in Heaven
REVELATION CHAPTER 12

12A. PAST HISTORY: A WOMAN CLOTHED WITH THE SUN

Rev 12:1 A great sign appeared in heaven: a woman clothed with the sun, and the moon under her feet, and on her head a crown of **twelve stars;**

Rev 12:2 and she was with child; and she cried out, being in labor and in pain to give birth.

Rev 12:3 Then another sign appeared in heaven: and behold, a great red dragon having **seven heads and ten horns**, and on his heads were seven diadems.

Rev 12:4 And his tail swept away **a third of the stars of heaven** and threw them to the earth. And the dragon stood before the woman who was about to give birth, so that when she gave birth he might devour her child.

Rev 12:5 And she gave birth to a son, a male child, who is to rule all the nations with a rod of iron; and her child was caught up to God and to His throne.

> *The woman . . . twelve stars* - The woman (Israel) with the twelve tribes gave birth to the son (Jesus) who would eventually rule the nations, during the millennium, and throughout eternity.
> *Seven heads and ten horns* - The dragon (Satan) is pictured with seven heads and ten horns (representing the kingdoms that were destined to dominate and try to destroy the Christ.)
> *A third of the stars* - Isaiah 14:12 tells us that the star of the morning (Lucifer) would exalt himself and seek to "raise my throne above the stars of God." In so doing he took a vast army of fallen angels with him.

2B. FUTURE PROPHECY: WAR IN HEAVEN: THE GREAT TRIBULATION

Rev 12:6 Then the woman fled into the wilderness where she had a place prepared by God, so that there she would be nourished for **one thousand two hundred and sixty days.**

Rev 12:7 And there was war in heaven, Michael and his angels waging war with the dragon. The dragon and his angels waged war,

Rev 12:8 and they were not strong enough, and there was no longer a place found for them in heaven.

Rev 12:9 And the great dragon was thrown down, the serpent of old who is called the devil and Satan, who deceives the whole world; he was thrown down to the earth, and his angels were thrown down with him.

Rev 12:10 Then I heard a loud voice in heaven, saying, "Now the salvation, and the power, and the kingdom of our God and the authority of His Christ have come, for the accuser of our brethren has been thrown down, he who accuses them before our God day and night.

Rev 12:11 "And they overcame him because of the blood of the Lamb and because of the word of their testimony, and they did not love their life even when faced with death."

Rev 12:12 "For this reason, rejoice, O heavens and you who dwell in them. Woe to the earth and the sea, because the devil has come down to you, having great wrath, knowing that he has only a short time."

Rev 12:13 And when the dragon saw that he was thrown down to the earth, **he persecuted the woman** who gave birth to the male child.

Rev 12:14 But **the two wings of the great eagle** were given to the woman, so that she could fly into the wilderness to her place, where she was nourished for **a time and times and half a time,** from the presence of the serpent.

Rev 12:15 And **the serpent poured water** like a river out of his mouth after the woman, so that he might cause her to be swept away with the flood.

Rev 12:16 But the earth helped the woman, and the earth opened its mouth and drank up the river which the dragon poured out of his mouth.

Rev 12:17 So the dragon was enraged with the woman, and went off to make war **with the rest of her children,** who keep the commandments of God and hold to the testimony of Jesus.

Revelation 12:6-17 describes the end-time scenario when Israel is protected by God for the second 3.5 year period of time during the seven year period known as the seventieth week of Daniel. As the tribulation begins in the second 3.5 year period, Michael the archangel and protector of Israel, literally fights a spiritual battle against the devil and his demonic host, which numbers 1/3 of the angels in heaven. Though Satan has been the god of this world since the curse (2 Cor 4:4) he has remained a spiritual being in the heavens. At the beginning of the tribulation, he is thrown down to earth where his demons will no doubt inhabit the lives of those who oppose Israel. Many believe the two wings of the great eagle to be America, but more likely this is a reminder from Exodus 19:4 how the Jews were swiftly delivered from the hands of the Pharaoh. Time, times and half a time is a reminder of the 3.5 year period which begins the tribulation and ends just before God's final bowl judgments. "The serpent poured water" implies that one of Satan's many ploys to destroy the Jews will be a flood. "The rest of her children" indicates that after Satan's futile attempts to destroy Israel, he will go after the believers. This reference to believers during the tribulation should make one seriously consider the likelihood of a pre-wrath rapture.

THE THIRD TEMPLE

Rev 11:1 Then there was given me a measuring rod like a staff; and someone said, "Get up and measure the temple of God and the altar, and those who worship in it.

Rev 11:2 "Leave out **the court which is outside the temple** and do not measure it, for it has been given to the nations; and they will tread under foot the holy city for forty-two months.

the court which is outside the temple. *This was the court of the Gentiles in biblical days. This was as close as the Gentiles could get to the inner court of the temple. Since this passage says "do not measure it", the implication here is that this is not a Gentile issue. The real issue here is that Israel will be allowed to rebuild this temple as a concession of the Global Leader during the first 3.5 years. The forty-two months referred to in this passage is prophesying the final 3.5 years of siege by the Anti-Christ.*

The First Temple *was Solomon's Temple. It was constructed during his reign between 970-930 bc. and is described in 2 Chronicles Chapter 2. It was destroyed in 586 bc by the Babylonian King Nebuchadnezzar, who took the majority of the Jewish population captive for seventy years.*

The Second Temple *was rebuilt in 516 bc when King Cyrus of Persia granted freedom and privilege to those returning from captivity. This modest version of the temple was later pillaged by Antiochus Epiphanes in 168 bc, and finally reconstructed by Herod the Great in 20 bc.   This temple survived until 70 ad when the Roman General Titus destroyed the temple completely, resulting in the Diaspora, the dispersion of Jews throughout the world.*

The Third Temple *is sometimes referred to as the "Tribulation Temple." It will be a simpler, smaller version of the temple constructed during the seventieth week of Daniel as a conciliatory agreement between Jews and Muslims. It will be constructed during the first 3.5 years by the Global Leader, and then desecrated during the second 3.5 year period by the Anti-Christ.*

The Fourth Temple *is referred to as "Ezekiel's Temple" and is described in Ezekiel 40-48. This will be the "Millennial Temple" constructed during the thousand year reign of Christ. It will occupy a thousand acres of land in Jerusalem, and will be the center of worship for the nations, who will serve the Jews and follow the law of King Jesus.*

Rev 11:3 "And I will grant authority to **my two witnesses,** and they will prophesy for twelve hundred and sixty days, clothed in sackcloth."

Rev 11:4 These are the **two olive trees and the two lampstands** that stand before the Lord of the earth.

Rev 11:5 And if anyone wants to harm them, **fire flows out of their mouth** and devours their enemies; so if anyone wants to harm them, he must be killed in this way.

Rev 11:6 These have the power **to shut up the sky**, so that rain will not fall during the days of their prophesying; and they have power over the waters **to turn them into blood**, and to strike the earth with every plague, as often as they desire.

Rev 11:7 When they have finished their testimony, the beast that comes up out of the abyss will make war with them, and overcome them and kill them.

Rev 11:8 And **their dead bodies** will lie in the street of the great city which mystically is called **Sodom and Egypt**, where also their Lord was crucified.

Rev 11:9 Those from the peoples and tribes and tongues and nations will look at their dead bodies for three and a half days, and will not permit their dead bodies to be laid in a tomb.

Rev 11:10 And those who dwell on the earth will rejoice over them and celebrate; and they will send gifts to one another, because these two prophets tormented those who dwell on the earth.

> **my two witnesses.** *The two witnesses are generally considered to be Elijah and Moses, since it was they who participated in the transfiguration in Matthew 17. Moses represents the law, and Elijah represents the prophets.*
>
> **Two olive trees and two lampstands.** *Zechariah 4:14 defines these two as: "the two anointed ones who are standing by the Lord of the whole earth."*
>
> **fire flows out of their mouth.** *See 1 Kings 18:23. Elijah and the prophets of Baal agreed that fire from heaven would prove whose god was real. Elijah poured water on his altar to make kindling even harder. A fire from heaven came down and lit the altar as well as licking up all the excess water. The God of Elijah won.*
>
> **To shut up the sky . . . turn them into blood.** *See Luke 4:25 and Exodus 7:19. This is another confirmation that Elijah and Moses are the two witnesses.*
>
> **their dead bodies.** *Since the two witnesses were known to be alive for 1260 days, their death would have signaled the end of the seventieth week of Daniel.*
>
> **Sodom and Egypt.** *A simple allusion to the depravity that had overtaken Jerusalem in the last days.*

Michael, the Restrainer

Dan 12:1 "Now at that time **Michael, the great prince** who stands guard over the sons of your people, will arise. And there will be **a time of distress** such as never occurred since there was a nation until that time; and at that time your people, everyone who is found written in the book, will be rescued.

Dan 12:2 "Many of **those who sleep in the dust of the ground** will awake, these to everlasting life, but the others to disgrace and everlasting contempt.

Dan 12:3 "Those who have insight will shine brightly like the brightness of the expanse of heaven, and **those who lead the many to righteousness**, like the stars forever and ever. 4 "But as for you, Daniel, conceal these words and seal up the book until the end of time; many will go back and forth, and **knowledge will increase."**

> ### WORD STUDY ON MICHAEL THE ARCHANGEL. (See Page 116.)
>
> *Dan 10:13 "But the prince of the kingdom of Persia was withstanding me for twenty-one days; then behold, Michael, one of the chief princes, came to help me, for I had been left there with the kings of Persia.*
>
> *Dan 10:21 "However, I will tell you what is inscribed in the writing of truth. Yet there is no one who stands firmly with me against these forces except Michael your prince.*
>
> *1Th 4:16 For the Lord Himself will descend from heaven with a shout, with the voice of the archangel and with the trumpet of God, and the dead in Christ will rise first.*
>
> *Jud 1:9 But Michael the archangel, when he disputed with the devil and argued about the body of Moses, did not dare pronounce against him a railing judgment, but said, "The Lord rebuke you!"*
>
> *Rev 12:7 And there was war in heaven, Michael and his angels waging war with the dragon. The dragon and his angels waged war,*
>
> *Rev 12:8 and they were not strong enough, and there was no longer a place found for them in heaven.*
>
> *Rev 12:9 And the great dragon was thrown down, the serpent of old who is called the devil and Satan, who deceives the whole world; he was thrown down to the earth, and his angels were thrown down with him.*
>
> *NOTE: Michael, the archangel, and his angelic host, appear to be stronger than the demonic host, who was thrown down. The implication is that Michael would have to "stand down", enabling Satan and the Anti-Christ to move forward.*

194

2Th 2:3 Let no one in any way deceive you, for it will not come unless the

apostasy comes first, and the man of lawlessness is revealed, the son of destruction,

2Th 2:4 who opposes and exalts himself above every so-called god or object of worship, so that he takes his seat in the temple of God, displaying himself as being God.

2Th 2:5 Do you not remember that while I was still with you, I was telling you these things?

2Th 2:6 **And you know what restrains him now**, so that in his time he will be revealed.

2Th 2:7 For the mystery of lawlessness is already at work;

only he who now restrains will do so until he is taken out of the way.

2Th 2:8 Then that lawless one will be revealed whom the Lord will slay with the breath of His mouth and bring to an end by the appearance of His coming;

2Th 2:9 that is, the one whose coming is in accord with the activity of Satan, with all power and signs and false wonders, 2Th 2:10 and with all the deception of wickedness for those who perish, because they did not receive the love of the truth so as to be saved.

2Th 2:11 For this reason God will send upon them a deluding influence so that they will believe what is false,

2Th 2:12 in order that they all may be judged who did not believe the truth, but took pleasure in wickedness.

And you know what restrains him now. *Traditional Pre-Trib theology says that the Holy Spirit is the Restrainer. The alternative theory proposes that Michael the Archangel, the guardian of Israel, is the Restrainer. John 16:8 says the job description of the Holy Spirit is to convict of sin, righteousness and judgment. Spiritual warfare doesn't seem to be the task of the Holy Spirit. It also seems a stretch to believe that the Holy Spirit, who is part of the Trinitarian Godhead, and an emissary for the Father and the Son (in this age), would evacuate planet earth. If Pre-Trib contends that there will be believers during the Tribulation Period of the Anti-Christ, then how can the Holy Spirit leave those believers without a presence? In Daniel 10:21, Michael is described as standing firmly against the forces of darkness. It is Michael that wages war against the demons, and Daniel 10:13 seems to imply that Michael is fighting battles against the leading principalities of empires, which are comprised of multiple nations. Nowhere do we see the Holy Spirit waging this kind of warfare.*

Only he who now restrains will do so until he is taken out of the way. *It is likely that Michael "stands down" at the beginning of the tribulation period, which probably coincides with Jacob's Distress. When Michael is restrained, the Anti-Christ is allowed to initiate his campaign of terror. After the Tribulation, Michael probably leads the angelic execution of the trumpet and bowl judgments, concluding with Armageddon.*

No One Believes in Me Anymore

The Rationale of Satan
Words by Keith Green
(See Youtube)

Oh, my job keeps getting easier, As time keeps slipping away
I can imitate the brightest light and make your night look just like day
I put some truth in every lie to tickle itching ears
You know I'm drawing people just like flies 'cause they like what they hear
I'm gaining power by the hour they're falling by the score
You know, it's getting very simple now, 'cause no one believes in me anymore

Oh, heaven's just a state of mind my books read on your shelf
And have you heard that God is dead? I made that one up myself
They dabble in magic spells they get their fortunes read
You know they heard the truth but turned away and followed me instead
I used to have to sneak around but now they just open their doors
You know, no ones watching for my tricks because no one believes in me anymore

Everyone likes a winner with my help, you're guaranteed to win
And hey, man, you ain't no sinner, you've got the truth within
And as your life slips by you believe the lie that you did it on your own
But don't worry I'll be there to help you share our dark eternal home

Oh, my job keeps getting easier as day slips into day
The magazines, the newspapers print every word I say
This world is just my spinning top, It's all like childs-play
You know, I dream that it will never stop, But I know it's not that way

Still my work goes on and on, Always stronger than before
I'm gonna make it dark before the dawn, Since no one believes in me anymore
Well, now I used to have to sneak around, But now they just open their doors
You know, no one watches for my tricks
Since no one believes in me anymore
Well I'm gaining power by the hour, They're falling by the score
You know, it's getting very easy now, Since no one believes in me anymore
No one believes in me anymore, No one believes in me anymore

THE THREEFOLD AGENDA OF SATAN

Genesis 4:7
*"If you do well, will not your countenance be lifted up?
And if you do not do well, sin is crouching at the door;
and its desire is for you, but you must master it."*

1 Peter 5:8
*"Be of sober spirit, be on the alert.
Your adversary, the devil, prowls around like a roaring lion, seeking someone to devour."*

1. Abuse. It is Satan's desire for parents to abuse children, for employers to abuse employees, for husbands and wives to abuse each other, for friends to abuse friends, and in general, to create discord that leads to broken relationships. Abuse begins with lack of respect and then turns into malice, deceit, hypocrisy, envy and slander (1 Peter 2:1). Satan wants to destroy your life, but he begins in small ways by creating cracks in your relationships. Perhaps Satan's ultimate abuse is to make you abuse yourself by compromising your God-given dreams and goals and general purpose in life. Satan fights hard to keep you from relationship with God.

2. Addiction. It is Satan's desire to lure you and I from the discipline of a mature life into a lifestyle that is filled with distraction leading to bondage. He doesn't care whether it is drugs or pornography or promiscuity or television or food or entertainment or gambling. He wants you to compromise your time and your money and your potential for godly living. He wants to squeeze you into a small corner of your life and convince you that your addiction is more important than family or friends or career or God. Satan has the ability to put spiritual shackles on you and reduce your life to bondage and despair.

3. Annihilation. Satan's ultimate desire for your life is to create depression leading to despair leading to self destruction. He wants to take away your purpose for living, and create so much frustration and anxiety in your life that you are convinced that suicide is your only avenue of relief. John 10:10 says that Satan is a thief and a murderer and a destroyer. He has come to steal, kill and destroy. He wants to take away your joy and fulfillment and replace it with death.

James 4:7 says: "Submit therefore to God. Resist the devil and he will flee from you." Don't try to fight Satan yourself. Let Christ fight your battles for you. When Satan knocks on your door, all he wants you to do is open it. Then he has control. Don't open the door. Resist the first urge, the first temptation, and Satan will eventually give up on you and go somewhere else.

Gog and the Battle of Jerusalem

Eze 38:1 And the word of the LORD came to me saying,

Eze 38:2 "Son of man, set your face toward **Gog of the land of Magog, the prince of Rosh, Meshech and Tubal**, and prophesy against him

Eze 38:3 and say, 'Thus says the Lord GOD, "Behold, I am against you, O Gog, prince of Rosh, Meshech and Tubal.

> ***Gog of the land of Magog.*** *Apart from an (apparently) unrelated reference to Reuben's genealogy in Genesis 10, the name Gog is only mentioned in Ezekiel 38 and 39 (8 times), then in Revelation 20:8. Gog is a leader in the region of Magog, which is eastern Turkey. The seven sons of Japheth were the following: **Gomer** - generally considered to be the area of Germany, related to the migratory Gimarru or the Cimmerians. **Magog** - generally considered to be western Turkey. See Rev 2:12 and 13 for an interesting connection between Pergamum and Magog. **Midai** - generally considered to be Media of Western Iran, associated with the Medes of the Medo-Persian Empire of Iran. **Javan** - generally considered to be the Ionians, who later became Grecians. **Tubal** - generally considered to be east central Turkey. **Meshech** - generally considered to be the Mushki tribes of north central Turkey. **Tiras** - generally considered to be northwest Turkey, or Thrace, today known as southern Bulgaria.*

> *The prince of Rosh, Meshech and Tubal.* *Popular theology has translated Rosh to be Russia, Meschech to be Moscow, and Tubal to be Tobolsk, also in Russia. But the Hebrew word for rosh is "head", as in Rosh Hashanah. Therefore, the verse could read Chief Prince instead of Prince of Russia. Notice that verse 6 identifies Beth-togarmah (in Turkey) as the remote parts of the north.*

Eze 38:4 "I will turn you about and put hooks into your jaws, and I will bring you out, and all your army, horses and horsemen, all of them splendidly attired, a great company with buckler and shield, all of them wielding swords;

Eze 38:5 **Persia, Ethiopia and Put** (Libya) with them, all of them with shield and helmet;

Eze 38:6 **Gomer** with all its troops; **Beth-togarmah** from the remote parts of the north with all its troops - many peoples with you.

Eze 38:7 "Be prepared, and prepare yourself, you and all your companies that are assembled about you, and be a guard for them.

THE BEGINNING OF TRIBULATION.

Eze 38:8 "After many days you will be summoned; in the latter years you will come into the land that is restored from the sword, whose inhabitants have been gathered from many nations to the mountains of Israel which had been a continual waste; but its people were brought out from the nations, and they are living securely, all of them.

Eze 38:9 "You will go up, you will come like a storm; you will be like a cloud covering the land, you and all your troops, and many peoples with you."

Eze 38:10 'Thus says the Lord GOD, "It will come about on that day, that thoughts will come into your mind and you will devise an evil plan,

Eze 38:11 and you will say, 'I will go up against **the land of unwalled villages.** I will go against those who are at rest, that live securely, all of them living without walls and having no bars or gates,

Eze 38:12 to capture spoil and to seize plunder, to turn your hand against the waste places which are now inhabited, and against the people who are gathered from the nations, who have acquired cattle and goods, who live at **the center of the world.'**

> **the land of unwalled villages.** *Prior to the mid-point of tribulation, the nation of Israel will be lulled into false security because the Global Leader will provide them protection from the neighboring hordes that wish to exterminate them. Then, at midpoint, the mask comes off, and the Global Leader turns on the nation of Israel.*

> **the center of the world.** *The Hebrew word "tabor" is not a geographical term, or a geometric term. Use of the word 'center' here means 'origin'. Jerusalem is the navel, or the bellybutton of planet earth.*

THE DRAGON, THE BEAST & FALSE PROPHET

REVELATION CHAPTER 13

THE BEAST OF SEVEN HEADS AND TEN HORNS

Rev 13:1 And the dragon stood on the sand of the seashore. Then I saw a beast coming up out of the sea, having **ten horns and seven heads**, and on his horns were ten diadems, and on his heads were blasphemous names.

Rev 13:2 And the beast which I saw was like a leopard, and his feet were like those of a bear, and his mouth like the mouth of a lion. And the dragon gave him his power and his throne and great authority.

Rev 13:3 I saw one of his heads as if it had been slain, and **his fatal wound was healed**. And the whole earth was amazed and followed after the beast;

Rev 13:4 they worshiped the dragon because he gave his authority to the beast; and they worshiped the beast, saying, "Who is like the beast, and who is able to wage war with him?"

Rev 13:5 There was given to him a mouth speaking arrogant words and blasphemies, and authority to act for forty-two months was given to him.

Rev 13:6 And he opened his mouth in blasphemies against God, to blaspheme His name and His tabernacle, that is, those who dwell in heaven.

Rev 13:7 It was also given to him **to make war with the saints** and to overcome them, and authority over every tribe and people and tongue and nation was given to him.

Rev 13:8 All who dwell on the earth will worship him, everyone whose name has not been written from the foundation of the world in the book of life of the Lamb who has been slain. Rev 13:9 If anyone has an ear, let him hear.

Rev 13:10 If anyone is destined for captivity, to captivity he goes; if anyone kills with the sword, with the sword he must be killed. Here is **the perseverance and the faith of the saints.**

> **ten horns and seven heads.** Ten nations will rise up to serve the beast. And of those ten, three nations will serve one leader, who will dominate the other seven.
>
> **his fatal wound was healed.** Coupled with Rev. 13:12, the Anti-Christ will die and then come back to life. Because of his satanic supernatural powers, he will create miraculous events which will deceive the unbelievers. Just as Christ died and was resurrected, Satan attempts to counterfeit even this unparalleled event.
>
> **to make war with the saints.** For those who say the church is not represented after Chapter Four, verses 7 proves they are alive at the reign of Anti-Christ.
>
> **The perseverance and faith of the saints.** This verse accurately reflects the Churches of Philadelphia and Smyrna. Some will be captured. Some will face persecution. Our most important and enduring asset is our faith.

Rev 13:11 Then I saw another beast coming up out of the earth; and he had two horns like a lamb and he spoke as a dragon.

Rev 13:12 He exercises all the authority of the first beast in his presence. And he makes the earth and those who dwell in it to worship the first beast, **whose fatal wound was healed.**

Rev 13:13 He performs great signs, so that he even makes fire come down out of heaven to the earth in the presence of men.

Rev 13:14 And he deceives those who dwell on the earth because of the signs which it was given him to perform in the presence of the beast, telling those who dwell on the earth to make an image to the beast who had the wound of the sword and has come to life.

Rev 13:15 And it was given to him **to give breath to the image** of the beast, so that the image of the beast would even speak and cause as many as do not worship the image of the beast to be killed.

Rev 13:16 And he causes all, the small and the great, and the rich and the poor, and the free men and the slaves, to be given a mark on **their right hand or on their forehead,**

Rev 13:17 and he provides that no one will be able to buy or to sell, except the one who has the mark, either the name of the beast or the number of his name.

Rev 13:18 Here is wisdom. Let him who has understanding calculate the number of the beast, for the number is that of a man; and **his number is six hundred and sixty-six.**

> *to give breath to the image.* Just as the Holy Spirit breathes life into unregenerate man, so the False Prophet gives life to this mysterious image, which is yet unrevealed to mankind; Technology will likely manufacture an end-time ID chip under the skin, with an embedded video feed directly from the person of the Anti-Christ, giving real time instruction to his "disciples" as to how to deal with those who do not worship the beast. If not the ID chip, cell phone technology places the voice of the Anti-Christ in range of most every person on the planet. He could even charge the battery remotely. *Their right hand or forehead.* Like the phylacteries of Deuteronomy 6:8 (on the left hand or forehead) this mark is another counterfeit which clearly identifies the false "believers." This ID could well be the end-time vehicle for currency, tempting believers to take the mark or starve. See Revelation 22:4.
>
> *His number is 666.* The number 7 represents perfect God. The number 6 represents imperfect man. No one knows what the mysterious 666 is. For years, we have speculated that "bar code" technology is the mark, or the social security number, or the gematria, the numerical equivalent (either English or Hebrew) of a leader's name. It is possible that the mark will be the RESULT of an ideological identity. It is possible that the "shahadah", the Islamic confession of faith could be the test of faith that is rewarded by a mark (see symbol above) which allows one to buy or sell. The symbol above is actually Arabic for the Islamic confession of faith: "There is no god but Allah and Mohammed is his prophet".

Middle East

ROM. · Bucharest
UKR.
KAZAKHSTAN
Constanța
Sevastopol'
· Krasnodar
Sofia
BULGARIA
Varna
Black Sea
Sokhumi
RUSSIA
Grozny
KAZAKHSTAN
· Aqtaū
UZBEKISTAN
· Nukus
Aral Sea
Thessaloniki
İstanbul
Bosporus
Samsun
GEORGIA
Bat'umi
T'bilisi
Caspian Sea
Turkmenbashy
Nebitdag
Bukhoro
GREECE
· Bursa
Ankara
Trabzon
ARMENIA
Erzurum
Yerevan
AZERBAIJAN
Baku
Sumqayıt
TURKMENISTAN
Ashgabat
Mary
Aegean Sea
Athens
İzmir
Denizli
Konya
TURKEY
Kayseri
Van
Tabriz
Rasht
Qazvīn
Mashhad
Herāt
Antalya
İçel (Mersin)
Adana
Gaziantep
Diyarbakır
Zanjān
Tehrān
AFGH.
Crete
Nicosia
Aleppo
Mosul
Irbīl
Karkūk
Qom
Arāk
Eşfahān
IRAN
CYPRUS
SYRIA
Hims
Baghdad
Kermānshāh
Mediterranean Sea
Beirut
Damascus
De Facto Boundary
Kermān
LEBANON
Haifa
Golan Heights
West Bank
Jerusalem
Amman
IRAQ
Ahvāz
Ābādān
Zāhedān
Alexandria
Port Said
ISRAEL
JORDAN
An Nāşirīyah
Al Başrah
Būshehr
Shīrāz
PAK.
Cairo
Al Jīzah
Suez
Gaza Strip
Al 'Aqabah
Kuwait
KUWAIT
Bandar 'Abbās
Strait of Hormuz
Gulf of Aqaba
Tabūk
Ḩafar al Bāţin
Persian Gulf
EGYPT
Ḩā'il
Al Jubayl
Ad Dammām
Dhahran
BAHRAIN
Manama
QATAR
Doha
Dubai
Abu Dhabi
OMAN
Gulf of Oman
Muscat
Yanbu' al Baḩr
Medina
Buraydah
Riyadh
SAUDI
UNITED ARAB EMIRATES
De Defined Boundary
De Facto Boundary
Aswān
Luxor
Ḩalā'ib
ARABIA
OMAN
Jiddah
Mecca
Port Sudan
Red Sea
Administrative boundary
No defined boundary
SUDAN
Abhā
Arabian Sea
Omdurman
Khartoum
Wad Madani
ERITREA
Asmera
Jizan
Al Ḩudaydah
Sanaa
Al Ghaydah
Şalālah
Al Mukallā
YEMEN
Aden
Bab el Mandeb
Gulf of Aden
Socotra (YEMEN)
DJIBOUTI
Djibouti
Berbera
Desē
Provisional Administrative Line
Addis Ababa
Hargeysa
SOMALIA
ETHIOPIA

Scale 1:21,000,000
Lambert Conformal Conic Projection, standard parallels 12°N and 38°N

0   300 Kilometers
0   300 Miles

Boundary representation is not necessarily authoritative.

* Israeli-occupied with current status subject to the Israeli-Palestinian Interim Agreement — permanent status to be determined through further negotiations.

Israel proclaimed Jerusalem as its capital in 1950, but the US, like nearly all other countries, maintains its Embassy in Tel Aviv.

802588 (R02107) 6-98

The Ten Nation Confederacy

Dan 7:6 "After this I kept looking, and behold, another one, like a leopard, which had on its back four wings of a bird; the beast also had four heads, and dominion was given to it.

Dan 7:7 "After this I kept looking in the night visions, and behold, a fourth beast, dreadful and terrifying and extremely strong; and it had large iron teeth. It devoured and crushed and trampled down the remainder with its feet; and it was different from all the beasts that were before it, **and it had ten horns.**

Dan 7:8 "While I was contemplating the horns, behold, **another horn, a little one**, came up among them, **and three of the first horns** were pulled out by the roots before it; and behold, this horn possessed eyes like the eyes of a man and a mouth uttering great boasts.

Turkey
Syria
Iraq
Iran
Saudi Arabia
Egypt
Sudan
Yemen
Oman
Ethiopia
Libya

Hopefully, the predominant Pre-Tribulation theory of the European Union as the revived Holy Roman Empire is beginning to fade into history. It should be obvious, even to the casual observer, that the assault of the Jihadist regimes of the Muslim world surrounding Israel are more likely to be the confederacy of the Anti-Christ than the ten nations listed below which constitute the EU: The United Kingdom, France, Germany, Greece, Italy, Spain, Belgium, Luxembourg, Netherlands and Portugal.

It is important to read Daniel 7:7 and understand that the first three beasts were historical while the fourth beast is future. The ancient Roman empire was not that different from the Greek empire, and must therefore be discounted as being revived. The fourth beast is different. The armies of the first 3 beasts fought differently than the fourth beast. A current understanding of the Jihadists who hide behind the guise of the Islam faith to advance their nefarious cause should make it clear that the ominous rampage of Muslim extremism is spreading like the proverbial wildfire across the planet. Though the list to the left is purely speculative, these names provide a possible end-time scenario which could easily envelope little Israel and force world diplomacy to the very brink of global destruction. Into this arena, the boastful little horn emerges, consolidating three nations, and setting in motion the beginning of worldwide tribulation.

THE MAN OF LAWLESSNESS

2 THESSALONIANS 2

THE SON OF DESTRUCTION.

2Th 2:1 Now we request you, brethren, with regard to **the coming of our Lord** Jesus Christ and our gathering together to Him,

2Th 2:2 that you not be quickly shaken from your composure or be disturbed either by a spirit or a message or a letter as if from us, to the effect that the day of the Lord has come. 3 Let no one in any way deceive you, for it will not come unless **the apostasy comes first,** and **the man of lawlessness** is revealed, the son of destruction,

2Th 2:4 who opposes and exalts himself above every so-called god or object of worship, so that he takes his seat in the temple of God, displaying himself as being God.

2Th 2:5 Do you not remember that while I was still with you, I was telling you these things? 6 And you know what restrains him now, so that in his time he will be revealed. 7 For the mystery of lawlessness is already at work; only **he who now restrains** will do so until he is taken out of the way. 8 Then that lawless one will be revealed whom the Lord will slay with the breath of His mouth and bring to an end by the appearance of His coming; 9 that is, the one whose coming is in accord with the activity of Satan, with all power and signs and false wonders,

2Th 2:10 and with all the deception of wickedness for those who perish, because they did not receive **the love of the truth** so as to be saved.

> ***The coming of our Lord.*** *It is very important to see the corollary between the "coming of our Lord" and "our gathering together to Him." On the one hand you could say this sounds like two events. On the other hand, notice that in verse 2 it further questions if "the day of the Lord has come." These three terms should be seen as sequential events at the return of Jesus: His coming, His gathering and His wrath.*
>
> ***The apostasy comes first.*** *The Greek construction of this word is apo (away from) and stasis (to stand). In other words, the apostasy is a standing away from those principles which you formerly stood upon. Many view this as the Jews of Jerusalem who capitulate to the charisma of the new global leader, since this falling away also happened in the day of Antiochus. In a general sense, this will also be a falling away of church members (not genuine Christians), whose identification is limited by a nominal profession of the mouth which does not equate to a true profession of the heart. Jesus Himself said, "Not everyone who says to me, Lord, Lord, shall enter the kingdom of heaven, but he who does the will of my Father in heaven."*
>
> ***the love of the truth.*** *the pagan community has lost the ability to seek after the pure, absolute truth found in the pages of scripture.*

the man of lawlessness. It is difficult to understand how the Pre-Trib leaders can explain "it will not come unless." Clearly, the imminent return of Christ is challenged here by the antecedent events of apostasy and man of lawlessness.

he who now restrains. The Holy Spirit is often identified as the restrainer, but the warfare is among angels. Therefore Michael, the great prince who stands guard over Israel, (Dan 12:1) Is more likely the restrainer. God is sovereign and at the end of the day, Satan is no match for the Holy Spirit of God, nor will the Holy Spirit leave His remnant. This issue is open to speculation however, and should not become a test of fellowship. See page 194.

A DELUDING INFLUENCE.

2Th 2:11 For this reason God will send upon them **a deluding influence** so that they will believe what is false,

2Th 2:12 in order that they all may be judged who did not believe the truth, but took pleasure in wickedness.

2Th 2:13 But we should always give thanks to God for you, brethren beloved by the Lord, because God has chosen you from the beginning for salvation through sanctification by the Spirit and faith in the truth.

2Th 2:14 It was for this He called you through our gospel, that you may gain the glory of our Lord Jesus Christ.

2Th 2:15 So then, brethren, stand firm and **hold to the traditions** which you were taught, whether by word of mouth or by letter from us.

2Th 2:16 Now may our Lord Jesus Christ Himself and God our Father, who has loved us and given us eternal comfort and good hope by grace,

2Th 2:17 comfort and strengthen your hearts in every good work and word.

a deluding influence. In Matthew 24:24, Satan counterfeits God by sending a deluding influence so powerful, that once and for all, the wheat would be distinguished from the chaff (Malachi 4:1 and Matthew 3:12)

hold to the traditions. We are told to hold to the faith, "once and for all, delivered to the saints." In the end-times, it will be easy to become discouraged and compromised. Christ calls us to stand firm. It is worth noting that standing firm should be based on doctrinal issues. The second coming of Christ is a doctrine of the Church. The discussion of Pre-Trib and Pre-Wrath, which relate to the timing of the rapture, are not doctrines and should never be a test of fellowship.

THE MARK OF THE BEAST

Revelation 13:18
*Here is wisdom. Let him who has understanding
calculate the number of the beast, for the number is that of a man;
and his number is six hundred and sixty-six.*

Five characteristics of the Mark of the Beast:

1. Those who submit to the will of Anti-Christ will receive a mark on their left hand or their forehead.   Rev 13:16
2. No one will be able to buy or sell unless they have the mark. Rev 13:17
3. Those with the mark will be tormented with loathsome sores at the first bowl of God's wrath. Rev. 16:12
4. Those with the mark will receive the judgment of fire and brimstone and eternal damnation. Rev 14:9-11
5. If believers will suffer through the tribulation, then believers will also be made to accept or deny the mark of the beast.

It is likely that an embedded chip could be a necessary means of identification during the end times. But the mark of the beast will NOT merely be a tattoo or a bar code or an embedded chip that is received in order to register personal identification. The mark will be a symbol of allegiance to a subversive ideology.   We are reminded that everything the Anti-Christ does is a counterfeit of God. Revelation 22:4 says of believers: "His name will be on their foreheads." Believers will have the name of their God on their forehead; therefore those who take the mark of the beast will have the mark of their god also. The confession of faith of the Christian is: "Jesus is Lord." The confession of faith of Islam, which is called the shahadatan, declares the following: "there is no god but Allah and Mohammed is his prophet." It is likely in the endtimes, that the one-world government will also be the one-world religion, dominated by the followers of Mohammed. It this is true, then it is possible that those alive during the tribulation could face the ultimate test of one confession or the other. This gives new meaning to Jesus's words in Matthew 10:33 which states: "But whoever denies Me before men, I will also deny him before My Father who is in heaven."   Be prepared to stand strong in that day, remembering Jesus's words in Matthew 12:34 - "for the mouth speaks that which fills the heart."

WILL THE REAL COUNTERFEIT PLEASE STAND UP?

The year was 1985. I had just celebrated my 35th birthday after spending a Friday evening with friends. Around 10pm, I began to feel a tightening of my chest on the left side. Odd, never felt that way before. The pain subsided and I thought nothing more about it until 8pm on Saturday evening. The pain returned, and this time it lingered - 10 or 15 minutes maybe, off and on, strong pain, then nothing. Hmmm. Is this a heart attack? But I'm only 35 years old - played a round of golf last week. I'm in good shape. Nothing to worry about. On Sunday night the pain returned again. This time, I took it seriously. My wife and I, and little boy Tyler, took off for the local emergency room in Arlington, Texas. After an hour of testing, all the while enduring more pain in my left chest, the doctor came into my triage room and gave me the news. I had a temporary inflammation of the costal cartilage which connects the ribs to the sternum. This condition is called costochondritis, a pain that is known in the medical industry as a true simulation of a heart attack. So I had a pseudo-heart attack. My body was communicating a pain to me that FELT exactly like a heart attack. What I had experienced was a counterfeit. . . . Counterfeit. It's a term we use to describe false dollar bills that look like the real thing, but are actually fake. Thieves create counterfeit IDs, knowing that they can fool the general public, creating deception that causes mistrust when confronted with identifying the real thing. The Anti-Christ is the ultimate counterfeit. A close examination of scripture will reveal many ways in which the man of lawlessness tries to counterfeit the God who is All Truth.

1) The Trinity of God the Father, Son and Spirit.	1) The Trinity of the Dragon, the Anti-Christ and the False Prophet.
2) Christ's ministry on earth was estimated at 3.5 years	2) The time of the Man of Lawlessness is 3.5 years
3) Israel (origin of the true religion) is the mother spoken of in Revelation.	3) Islam (copied from Judaism and Christianity) is likely the great Harlot.
4) Jesus has seven horns, which are seven spirits of God. Rev 5:6	4) The Anti-Christ came out of the sea, having seven heads and seven horns.
5) Jesus' name will be on the foreheads of believers. Rev. 22:4.	5) The Anti-Christ will cause all men to have the mark on their foreheads. Rev 13:16
6) Jesus was crucified and then He rose from the grave.	6) The head of the beast will be slain, and his fatal wound was healed. Rev 13:3
7) The followers of Jesus give up their lives for the sake of their testimony and their allegiance to Christ.	7) The followers of Islam today are willing to give up their lives for their faith (and 70 virgins)

BABYLON, THE GREAT HARLOT

REVELATION CHAPTER 17

THE WOMAN ON THE SCARLET BEAST

Rev 17:1 Then one of the seven angels who had the seven bowls came and spoke with me, saying, "Come here, I will show you the judgment of the great harlot who sits on many waters,

Rev 17:2 with whom the kings of the earth committed acts of immorality, and those who dwell on the earth were made drunk with the wine of her immorality."

Rev 17:3 And he carried me away in the Spirit into a wilderness; and I saw a woman sitting on a scarlet beast, full of blasphemous names, having seven heads and ten horns.

Rev 17:4 The woman was clothed in purple and scarlet, and adorned with gold and precious stones and pearls, having in her hand a gold cup full of abominations and of the unclean things of her immorality,

Rev 17:5 and on her forehead a name was written, a mystery, "BABYLON THE GREAT, THE MOTHER OF HARLOTS AND OF THE ABOMINATIONS OF THE EARTH."

Rev 17:6 And I saw the woman **drunk with the blood of the saints**, and with the blood of the witnesses of Jesus. When I saw her, **I wondered greatly.**

Rev 17:7 And the angel said to me, "Why do you wonder? I will tell you the mystery of the woman and of the beast that carries her, which has the seven heads and the ten horns.

Rev 17:8 "The beast that you saw was, and is not, and is about to come up out of the abyss and go to destruction. And those who dwell on the earth, whose name has not been written in the book of life from the foundation of the world, will wonder when they see the beast, that he was and is not and will come.

> *If the woman of Rev 12 is Israel, then the harlot must be a religious counterpart, best understood to be jihadist Islam. The religion will appear to ride the beast, the Anti-Christ, and at some point, the tide will turn and the Anti-Christ will cast off the religious system, having used it to achieve his ends. It would appear, in today's culture war in which Islam seeks to conquer the earth, that the jihadist movement has the potential to be **drunk with the blood of the saints.** What does it mean when John says, **"I wondered greatly'**? John could not imagine that the sons of Ishmael and Esau could create a religion that would ultimately seek to exterminate the sons of Israel from the face of the earth. He could not imagine that religion, which is intended to bring one closer to God, would ultimately be the tool that the Anti-Christ would use to bring the world closer to him.*

Rev 17:9 "Here is the mind which has wisdom. The seven heads are **seven mountains** on which the woman sits,

Rev 17:10 and they are **seven kings; five have fallen, one is, the other has not yet come**; and when he comes, he must remain a little while.

Rev 17:11 "The beast which was and is not, is himself also **an eighth and is one of the seven**, and he goes to destruction.

Rev 17:12 "The ten horns which you saw are ten kings who have not yet received a kingdom, but they receive authority as kings with the beast for one hour.

Rev 17:13 "These have one purpose, and they give their power and authority to the beast.

Rev 17:14 "These will wage war against the Lamb, and the Lamb will overcome them, because He is Lord of lords and King of kings, and those who are with Him *are the* called and chosen and faithful."

Rev 17:15 And he said to me, "The waters which you saw where the harlot sits, are peoples and multitudes and nations and tongues.

Rev 17:16 "And the ten horns which you saw, and the beast, **these will hate the harlot and will make her desolate and naked,** and will eat her flesh and will burn her up with fire.

Rev 17:17 "For God has put it in their hearts to execute His purpose by having a common purpose, and by giving their kingdom to the beast, until the words of God will be fulfilled.

Rev 17:18 "The woman whom you saw is the great city, which reigns over the kings of the earth.

> *The seven mountains represents kings and kingdoms (or nations) that will align themselves against Israel in the last days. To say that this symbolizes Rome, the city of seven hills, is an unfortunate interpretation that has become pervasive in Pre-Trib theology. See page 404-5.*
>
> *An eighth and is one of the seven. See the next page for a fuller explanation.*
> *These will hate the harlot. The Anti-Christ will use a false religion during the tribulation to accomplish his diabolical purpose. If this religion is the jihad of Islam, he will use them as the executioner to wage war against Israel and the Church to accomplish his purpose of beheading (Rev 20:4) the saints. Then once he has spilled the blood of many believers, he will destroy the mosques and kill the Imams, rendering Islam helpless. He will expose the false religion and claim himself to be the only true god. Religion can be a stepping stone or an obstacle to experiencing God. The Anti-Christ will eliminate religion and demand that all worship be directed to him.*

THE EIGHT BEAST KINGDOMS

REVELATION CHAPTER 17

V3. I saw a woman (the Great Harlot) sitting on a scarlet Beast (the Anti-Christ).

V9. The woman also sits on seven mountains, which are seven kingdoms of history.

(The woman, the Harlot, counterfeits the woman, Israel.

The counterfeit of Israel, the religion - is Islam, the religion.)

V18. The woman is also a city, which reigns over the kings of the earth.

V10. Five have Fallen	**Kingdom Rulers**
1. Egyptian Empire	Pharaoh
2. Assyrian Empire	Niglath Pilezer
3. Babylonian Empire	Nebuchadnezzar
4. Medo Persian Empire	Cyrus
5. Grecian Empire	Alexander

V10. One is

6. Roman Empire	Caesar

V10. The Other has not yet come.

7. Islamic Empire	Muhammed

V10. When he comes,

he must remain a little while   Muhammed's public ministry was from 613ad to 632ad, a span of 19 years.

V11. The Beast which was and is not

8. Revived Islamic Empire   The Islamic Revival can be traced to two modern events: the Arab Oil Embargo in 1973 and The Iranian Revolution in 1979. These two events empowered the oil countries (OPEC) to use oil as a weapon, and also allowed the Iranian Ayatollah to challenge the supremacy of Western cultural expansion in the Middle East.

V11. is himself also an eighth and is one of the seven, and he goes to destruction.

This is the Anti-Christ, the man of lawlessness, the son of destruction, spoken of in 2 Thessalonians 2:3.

EMPIRES	DANIEL 2	DANIEL 7	REV 17	REV 17
1. Egyptian	not included	not included	1st King	
2. Assyrian	not included	not included	2nd King	
3. Babylonian	Head of Gold	Lion	3rd King	
4. Medo-Persian	Chest of Silver	Bear	4th King	
5. Grecian	Thigh of Bronze	Leopard	5th King	
6. Roman	not included	not included	6th King	
7. Islamic	Legs of Iron	Fourth Beast	7th King	
8. Anti-Christ	Feet of Iron/Clay	Ten Horns	8th King	

*The chart above is taken from page 158 of Joel Richardson's book, **"The Mideast Beast".** Richardson has challenged the historic position that declares the seventh and eighth kingdom to be the revived Roman Empire. Typically the legs of iron and the feet of iron and clay have been attributed to the strong-arm tactics of the 1st century Roman Empire. But unlike the preceding kingdoms, Rome did not succeed in expanding Its kingdom to include all the other kingdoms. It was typical of the Roman cultural expansion to assimilate the gods of other cultures because they underestimated the power of religion. Unlike the Greek Empire, which openly sought to Hellenize the world and change its culture, religion and language, the Roman expansion was satisfied to secularize the empire and leave religion to "the primitives, who continued to practice varying forms of superstition."*

Perhaps the United States can learn a lesson from the failed policy of the Roman Empire. Since we like to compare the supremacy of the US to its ancient Roman counterparts, we should note that the American and Western post World War II culture have been systematically secularizing and removing religion as a form of influence. By diminishing the influence of Christian principles and freedoms, and emasculating the strength which accompanies the Christian faith, we have created a vacuum which now allows other religions, namely Islam, to provide a multi-cultural alternative - even a novelty - to the whimsical mass of superficial seekers who like to dabble in other religions. Islam may be a novelty to westerners today, but once it becomes an accepted optional worldview, it will gradually introduce sharia law and Islamic legalism into the intellectual cavity that has become known as American liberalism.

The Islamic Connection

Dan 7:7 "After this I kept looking in the night visions, and behold, a fourth beast, dreadful and terrifying and extremely strong; and it had large iron teeth. It devoured and crushed and trampled down the remainder with its feet; and it was different from all the beasts that were before it, and it had ten horns.

> 1. A 10 nation confederacy will rise that will have a common goal of destroying Israel.

Dan 7:8 "While I was contemplating the horns, behold, another horn, a little one, came up among them, and three of the first horns were pulled out by the roots before it; and behold, this horn possessed eyes like the eyes of a man and a mouth uttering great *boasts*.

> 2. The Global Leader will consolidate the power of three of those ten nations in a focused attempt to become the world power.

Dan 9:27 "And he will make a firm covenant with the many for one week, but in the middle of the week he will put a stop to sacrifice and grain offering; and on the wing of abominations will come one who makes desolate, even until a complete destruction, one that is decreed, is poured out on the one who makes desolate."

> 3. There will be an end-time assault against Israel by the ten nations, but the Global Leader, who is likely to be Muslim, will neutralize the attack and create a covenant of peace between Israel and her enemies.

Rev 13:8 All who dwell on the earth will worship him, everyone whose name has not been written from the foundation of the world in the book of life of the Lamb who has been slain.

> 4. At the mid-point of the seven year period, the Global Leader will reveal himself to be the Al Mahdi, the prophet of God, risen from the dead. At that time, the Islamic population around the world, moderates and jihadists alike, will be ecstatic with holy zeal to carry out the mission of the prophet. There is no one on the planet that would electrify the Muslim masses like this Twelfth Imam.

Rev 12:17 So the dragon was enraged with the woman, and went off to make war with the rest of her children, who keep the commandments of God and hold to the testimony of Jesus.

> 5. The Mahdi will institute Sharia Law, forcing all infidels (Jews and Christians) to either convert, pay the tax or die.

Rev 17:13 "These have one purpose, and they give their power and authority to the beast**.

> 6. The Al-Mahdi will use Islam for his purpose, to "Arabize" the world with one culture, one language, one government and one religion.

Dan 11:37 "He will show no regard for the gods of his fathers or for the desire of women, nor will he show regard for any other god; for he will magnify himself above them all.
Rev 17:16 "And the ten horns which you saw, and the beast, these will hate the harlot and will make her desolate and naked, and will eat her flesh and will burn her up with fire.**

> 7. Near the end of the tribulation period, the Al Mahdi will reveal to the secular leaders of the ten nations that Islam is a false religious system, and he will immediately begin a campaign to kill the Imams and destroy the mosques. He will then announce to the Muslim world that there is no longer a religion called Islam and he alone is god. According to Islam's own hadith (traditions and teaching) the follow ing will happen:

> *The sacred city of Medina will be deserted and many will be led astray by ad-Dajjal.*
> *(Masih ad Dajjal is the False Messiah, the Islamic Anti-Christ)*
> *The sacred city of Mecca will be attacked and the Kaaba will be destroyed.*
> *The Quran will be forgotten and no one will recall its verses.*
> *All Islamic knowledge will be lost and believers will babble "Allah" without knowing what they are saying.*

> *The implication of this interpretation is that the Al Mahdi will be in disguise for 3.5 years as the Global Leader. At the midpoint, he will reveal himself to be the beloved prophet, and he will electrify Muslims worldwide to follow his mission for world domination. He will then persecute Jews and Christians until God cuts short the Tribulation period. Christ then returns to rescue the Church.*

THE TRIBULATION PERIOD, UNKNOWN DURATION, BEGINNING OF LAST 3.5 YEARS

The Global Leader is Revealed to Be The Twelfth Imam, risen from the dead.	The Twelfth Imam institutes a new global standard, the mark of 666. Those who refuse the mark will suffer death. Islam will be the global religion.	The Mahdi, with his secular leaders of the ten nations, will declare that Islam is a harlot, a false religion, and then will destroy every remnant of Islam. He will declare himself to be god.	Christ returns to end the time of tribulation and to rescue the Church from the ruthless persecution of the Prophet.

THE TWELFTH IMAM

Within the religion of Islam, the Sunni tribes represent 88% of the population and the Shia represent 12%. Of the two sects, the dominant eschatology of the Shi-ites is called Twelver, so called because they believe that the Twelfth Imam will return as the Messiah during the last days of troubled life on planet earth. His name is Muhammad ibn Hasan al-Mahdī. He was born in 869 ad, and at age 5 he became an Imam whose life was lived out in hiding, and represented only by his faithful deputies. After

72 years of this hiding, which is called the "minor occultation", he was spared death and was hidden away by Allah in what is currently called his "major occultation." When this period of occultation has ended, he will return to earth, with Isa (Jesus) to rescue the world community of Islam from the dreaded hands of the Masih ad-Dajjal, known within the Christian community as the Anti-Christ. The Sunnis have a variant belief that claims the Mahdi has not yet been born. The following are some of the major signs of the last days as interpreted by the Islamic hadith (traditions and teachings).

- The Masih (Messiah) ad-Dajjal will be a one-eyed man who will claim to be God.
- The sacred city of Medina will be deserted and many will be led astray by ad-Dajjal.
- A pleasant breeze will blow from the south and all believers will die peacefully.
- The sacred city of Mecca will be attacked and the Kaaba will be destroyed.
- The Quran will be forgotten and no one will recall its verses.
- All Islamic knowledge will be lost and believers will babble "Allah" without knowing what they are saying.
- Isa (Jesus) will return to the earth to rescue the followers of Mohammed. He will forsake Christianity and then die.

> Notice that the Hadith (the traditions and teachings) of Islam prophesy that Mecca will be attacked, the Kaaba destroyed, the Quran will be forgotten and all Islamic knowledge lost. Based on Rev 17:6 (these will hate the Harlot), I personally believe that the Anti-Christ will use jihadist Islam for the purpose of persecution and execution during the tribulation. Then at some appointed time, the Anti-Christ will turn on Islam, destroy the Quran and mosques, kill the Imams and declare that Islam and Allah were a counterfeit religion. He will then set himself up as God and demand singular worship to himself alone.

AN APPEAL TO THE IMAMS OF THE WORLD

There is a strange silence today among the imams (pastors) in the Muslim world. Radical jihad, with its trademark of oppressive law leading to torturous death, has become the prominent symbol of Islam in the world. Among law abiding Muslim citizens in every country, there seems to be little, if any, outrage that demands an immediate overthrow to jihadist governments. You would hope that Muslim-led governments would arm themselves in defiance against those who stain their name and compromise their religion. But what we hear is silence from the Muslim world. Why? Because for 1400 years, Islam has spread across the planet by the force of holy war. Muslim apologists will claim that jihad is an aberrant force that is not representative of their faith. They will speak on TV in defense of their peaceful faith, but as a collective body of 1 billion believers, they seem to have no system for snuffing out this evil force that tarnishes their name. To parallel this with Christianity, if the radical KKK or neo-Nazi skinheads rose up and began to behead unbelievers in the name of Christianity, there would be an immediate and widespread backlash from the churches and pastors that would seek out justice. Law enforcement and even militia groups would immediately arm themselves to silence those who defame the name of Jesus with violence. So why are Muslims silent while jihadism continues to grow? Here is the answer.

Radical jihadism IS the tool of EVANGELISM for the Muslim religion.

Unlike the Christian Church, which grows around the world by sharing the message of the gospel, the religion of Islam uses force, or taxation, or even death, to intimidate whole communities into cultural transformation. The process begins with religious education and quickly moves toward changes in the law that suppress freedom and truth. The Christian Church grows by allowing a community to hear the gospel message that Jesus the Messiah is the answer for all the personal and global problems in the world today. Christians invite hearers to receive the gospel message and accept Christ as Lord of their lives. Coercion is not the tool of Christianity. Holy war is not the tool of Christianity. Intimidation and suppression of freedom is not the way God intended to grow a world of believers.

Islam, and the imams who are the leaders of the Muslim faith, must face the reality that their religion has always been guilty of growing through violence and intimidation. They must personally repent of their silence, and begin immediately to organize against the radicalism that has hijacked their faith. Imams of the world must stand up in defiance, or they must accept the consequence that western culture will begin to turns its back on a religion that is driven by terror and intimidation. The west will continue to welcome the Muslim, but we will not continue to tolerate a religion that seeks to spread its message through torture and death.

6B. SEALS FOUR AND FIVE - THE GREAT TRIBULATION   (See page 181 for duplication)

Rev 6:7 When the Lamb broke **the fourth seal**, I heard the voice of the fourth living creature saying, "Come."

Rev 6:8 I looked, and behold, **an ashen horse**; and he who sat on it had the name Death; and Hades was following with him. Authority was given to them over a fourth of the earth, to kill with sword and with famine and with pestilence and by the wild beasts of the earth.

Rev 6:9 When the Lamb broke **the fifth seal**, I saw underneath the altar the souls of those who had been slain because of the word of God, and because of the testimony which they had maintained;

Rev 6:10 and they cried out with a loud voice, saying, **"How long, O Lord**, holy and true, will You refrain from judging and avenging our blood on those who dwell on the earth?"

Rev 6:11 And there was given to each of them **a white robe**; and they were told that they should rest for a little while longer, until **the number of their fellow servants** and their brethren who were to be killed even as they had been, would be completed also.

> *The Fourth Seal - The Pale Horse of Global Death. The Global Leader has now taken off his mask and reveals himself to be the Anti-Christ. The word "ashen" or "pale" is the Greek word "chlorous", which may imply chemical warfare, capable of taking out more than a billion people, most of whom will likely be believers.*
>
> *The Fifth Seal of Martyrdom - Tertullian said, "The blood of the martyrs is the seed of the church." God is honored by those, who in the last days, will stand strong and bear their allegiance to King Jesus, especially in the face of torture and death. These saints who give up their lives are the Church of Smyrna, the persecuted church. It is worthy to note that in the jihadist ideology, the origin of martyrdom was modeled after the Christians throughout the ages who have given their lives in testimony of their ultimate devotion to Jesus. Hopefully, future believers will embrace that same devotion.*
>
> *How long, O Lord? The martyred saints are waiting for the vengeance of God to sweep down upon the earth and avenge their death. In Chapter 8, just after the silence, the trumpets will begin to execute judgment. How can the fifth seal be God's wrath (Pre-Trib) if the saints are waiting for God to avenge them?*
>
> *A white robe. It is interesting to note that the only other reference to white robes is found in Revelation is 7:9, 13 and 14, where the raptured saints have just arrived in heaven.*

The number of their fellow servants. This is a difficult passage for the Pre-Tribulation movement to reconcile. One can rationalize that the reference is merely to "the left behind" yet martyred for the faith. BUT, this appears, once again, to be the Philadelphian Church of the Persevering, and the Smyrna Church of the Persecuted, whose lives will be completed, either by rapture or violent death. The reward for the persevering saints is the rapture. The reward for the persecuted church, the martyrs, is the millennial kingdom.

THE SIXTH SEAL - COSMIC DISTURBANCE.

Rev 6:12 I looked when He broke the sixth seal, and there was a great earthquake; and the sun became black as sackcloth made of hair, and the whole moon became like blood;

Rev 6:13 and the stars of the sky fell to the earth, as a fig tree casts its unripe figs when shaken by a great wind.

Rev 6:14 **The sky split apart like a scroll** when it is rolled up, and every mountain and island were moved out of their places.

Rev 6:15 Then the kings of the earth and the great men and the commanders and the rich and the strong and every slave and free man hid themselves in the caves and among the rocks of the mountains;

Rev 6:16 and they said to the mountains and to the rocks, "Fall on us and **hide us** from the presence of Him who sits on the throne, and from **the wrath of the Lamb;**

Rev 6:17 for the great day of their wrath has come, and who is able to stand?"

Verse 6:14. The sky split apart like a scroll. Seven amazing words. Isaiah 34:4 echoes this prophetic statement in a passage that forecasts a future time of destruction. Perhaps this phrase is the key to the timing of the rapture! Amongst all the passages that speak of the sun turning black and the moon turning to blood, this is the ONLY New Testament verse that predicts that the sky would split apart. And why does the sky split apart? Because there is something on the other side of the sky that is coming through! In a moment of unparalleled magnificence, the sky rips open with a blinding burst of light, and a voice, and a great trumpet sound can be heard around the world.

Hide us. The kings and great men, the commanders, the rich and strong are all caught off guard and are so fearful that they hide behind the rocks, hoping that an all-seeing God is not going to see them. There is no mention of the Church because we are being snatched up to glory at that very instant. The kings of the earth know what has happened. At that very moment, the spirit of God is revealing to each of them the consequence of their arrogant rejection of Christ. The spirit of darkness is preparing their hearts to wage war against a God who would dare to challenge their independence.

The wrath of the Lamb. Though many have rejected and ignored the gospel message, they will know in an instant that the creator God of the universe and His only begotten Son are preparing for the mother of all battles. The Day of the Lord has begun.

TRIBULATION AND GREAT TRIBULATION THE SAME

Matthew 24:9,21,29

There is much confusion about the terms 'tribulation' and 'great tribulation' - and I believe much of the entire Pre-Tribulation position teeters on the narrow understanding of this single issue. In Matthew 24, Jesus uses the term tribulation (v9), then great tribulation (v21), then tribulation again (v29). Based on that simple transition, I believe that the two terms are synonymous. Yes, Jesus does make the distinction to say 'then there be will a great tribulation, such as had not occurred since the beginning of the world even till now, nor ever will.' Notice this comes just before the 'cut short' event. I believe this is merely the climactic conclusion to an already devastating sequence of global catastrophes leading to the necessity for God to cut it short. **IF** Jesus had said in v29, "after the **great** tribulation of those days', I would have concluded that there was, in fact, a tribulation event, followed by an even more intense great tribulation event. I believe that Jesus' generic use of 'tribulation' in v29 indicates that the two terms are synonymous.

When comparing Matthew 24 and Revelation 6, it appears that what Jesus calls 'birth pangs' falls into the category in Revelation 6 of the first three seals: global leader, wars, famine and earthquakes. Based on this premise, it follows that the tribulation can be summarized by the fourth and fifth seals: global death and martyrdom. It then follows that the tribulation of the fourth and fifth seals are then cut short by the cosmic disturbance and the "gathering of the elect."

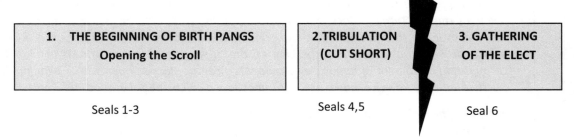

1. THE BEGINNING OF BIRTH PANGS Opening the Scroll	2.TRIBULATION (CUT SHORT)	3. GATHERING OF THE ELECT
Seals 1-3	Seals 4,5	Seal 6

It seems to me very important to weigh carefully the words of Jesus as they relate to the tribulation, the rapture and the wrath of God. This is perhaps the most misunderstood part of Christ's Second Coming. <u>You must first of all distinguish tribulation from wrath, then acknowledge that tribulation is not seven years, then acknowledge that tribulation is cut short.</u> When you have concluded these three things, you may suddenly understand that God cut short the tribulation so that Jesus could rapture the Church before the wrath of God.

TRIBULATION PRECEDES THE WRATH OF GOD

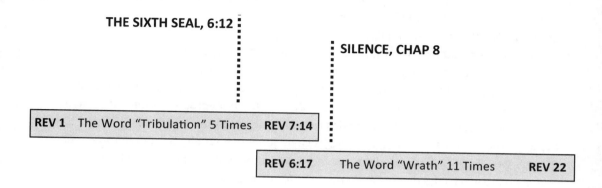

The word "tribulation" is used only 5 times in the book of Revelation; and only from Revelation 1 - 7:14. The word "wrath" is used 11 times (NASB), beginning with verse 6:17 through the end of the book. Although <u>word frequency and proximity to other words</u> are not the singular criteria for settling a scriptural issue, the reader should judge for themselves the weight of this argument.

It does appear obvious that the word "tribulation" ends and "wrath" appears to begin. The use of "tribulation" in 7:14 actually refers back to the tribulation period, which, from a pre-wrath view, occurs at Seals 4 and 5. The first reference to "wrath" occurs just after the sixth seal, the cosmic disturbance, when the sky splits open and the great men hide from what appears to be the inauguration of the "wrath" of the Lamb. The conclusion of this diagram is as follows:

1. Tribulation and Wrath appear to be two very distinct events in scripture.
2. The Tribulation event does appear to precede the Wrath event.
3. The timing of Tribulation's conclusion and wrath's commencement both appear to converge at the sixth seal, just prior to silence in heaven and the trumpet judgments.
4. Without regard to the timing of the rapture, it does appear that you cannot assign the wrath of God to the first six seals; nor can you conclude that tribulation extends past the time of the seventh seal.
5. With regard to the timing of the rapture, if wrath can be proven to begin after the seals, then the rapture can precede God's wrath, therefore legitimizing the term "pre-wrath."
6. Tribulation is not the wrath of God. Neither is the Great Tribulation the wrath of God.

The Parable of Ten Virgins

Mat 25:1 "Then **the kingdom of heaven** will be comparable to ten virgins, who took their lamps and went out to meet the bridegroom.

Mat 25:2 "Five of them were foolish, and five were prudent.

Mat 25:3 "For when the foolish took their lamps, **they took no oil with them,**

Mat 25:4 but the prudent took oil in flasks along with their lamps.

Mat 25:5 "Now while the bridegroom was delaying, they all got drowsy and began to sleep.

Mat 25:6 "But at midnight there was a shout, 'Behold, the bridegroom! Come out to meet him.' Mat 25:7 "Then all those virgins rose and trimmed their lamps.

Mat 25:8 "The foolish said to the prudent, **'Give us some of your oil,** for our lamps are going out.' Mat 25:9 "But the prudent answered, 'No, there will not be enough for us and you too; go instead to the dealers and buy some for yourselves.'

Mat 25:10 "And while they were going away to make the purchase, the bridegroom came, and those who were ready went in with him to the wedding feast; and the door was shut.

Mat 25:11 "Later the other virgins also came, saying, 'Lord, lord, open up for us.'

Mat 25:12 "But he answered, 'Truly I say to you, **I do not know you.'**

Mat 25:13 "Be on the alert then, for you do not know the day nor the hour.

the kingdom of heaven. *This is one of eleven parables Jesus told to illustrate His kingdom. (Matthew 13; 18:23; 20:1; 22:2; 25:1;). This parable is not primarily about the Rapture, or the Second Coming, or the Marriage Supper of the Lamb. This parable is about expectation and readiness of a true believer. The reference to virgins is confusing because many will say this has to imply they were all believers, but the ten virgins more likely refers to a bridal party, five of whom were church members but not born of the Spirit.*

they took no oil with them. *Oil is a common reference to the Holy Spirit. The lack of oil by 5 virgins simply implies their lack of readiness, or lack of true saving salvation. Their request to "Give us some of your oil" further implies that these members of the bridal party, whose sacred privilege was to be ready for the wedding to come, were unprepared for the very predictable coming of the groom. Going to sleep was not an indictment on the ten, but merely a reference to the normal passing of time.*

I do not know you. *Perhaps the most frightening verse in all the Bible is Matthew 7:21, which says: "Not everyone who says to me, Lord, Lord, shall enter the kingdom of heaven; but he who does the will of my Father in heaven." The door was shut, the groom refused entrance of half the bridal party. The time for compassion was past. The standard for entrance into the kingdom of heaven is not arbitrary. Awaiting Jesus' return with holy, Spirit-filled living is the non-negotiable criteria for heaven.*

GOD SPARED MY LIFE
A TESTIMONY OF GOD'S MERCY

The year was 1969. I was a student at the University of North Carolina at Charlotte. My first year in school I lived off-campus with my aunt and uncle and was dependent upon my cousin Susan to transport me to classes. Midway through the semester, I began hitchhiking to a coaching job on the other side of Charlotte. Eventually I saved enough money to buy an old pea green Fiat, which was like putting a washing machine between two bicycles. On one of my occasional 2 hour trips home to Asheville, my Fiat died, and I parked it on the side of the road, hoping someone would use it for parts. I then determined that I wanted to buy a used 1960 Austin Healey "bug-eyed" Sprite. It was a great little car - hard to believe I paid $900 for it. Today it is considered a classic. While driving to my job one day on a service road off Interstate 85, a man ran through a stop sign and ran me off the road. I fish-tailed for about 100 feet, and finally, my right rear tire hit a ditch and the car flipped over. SOMEHOW, I was now <u>under</u> the car just after the windshield was torn off at ground level. Kids today don't understand 'reaction time' when you have an accident. There is no time to react. In a matter of split seconds, I found myself sitting right side up in a ditch while my car was upside-down, on top of me. The engine was still running and I could smell gas, so I imagined that I would soon blow up in a fiery plume of smoke. I found the key and turned the engine off, and now I could hear people discussing how gruesome it would be when they flipped the car over and found my mangled body.

To their surprise, I was sitting quietly, waiting to be rescued. Sometimes when I tell that story, I still shiver at the thought of my close encounter with death.

The point of this story is that the mercy of God spared me on that very fateful day. My neck could have easily been snapped, and my life could have ended. I knew that God had a plan for my life, and I knew that my destiny was in His hands. As I reflect on the mercy of God, I understand that God is quite capable of protecting me and a billion other people from far worse than a car accident. When the Anti-Christ begins his reign of terror on planet earth, God may choose for me to die a natural death. Or, He may choose for me to experience His miraculous protection in a moment of ultimate terror. Or, my sovereign God may choose for me to stand before a firing squad and utter the final words, "Jesus is Lord", before taking me home to glory. Whatever my destiny, I trust my God to prepare me for the challenge.

BEFORE THE WRATH OF THE LAMB

The following sequence is very important to understand the Second Coming. Scripture says there are at least two signs which precede His Coming; and when He returns, the great men of the earth will fall before Him in fear, because the Church has just been raptured, and wrath is on its way.

Malachi 4:5 "Behold, I am going to send you Elijah the prophet before the coming of the great and terrible day of the LORD.
2Th 2:1 Now we request you, brethren, with regard to the coming of our Lord Jesus Christ and our gathering together to Him,
2Th 2:2 that you not be quickly shaken from your composure or be disturbed either by a spirit or a message or a letter as if from us, to the effect that the day of the Lord has come.
2Th 2:3 Let no one in any way deceive you, for it will not come unless the apostasy comes first, and the man of lawlessness is revealed, the son of destruction . . .

Mat 24:30
"And then the sign of the Son of Man will appear in the sky, and then all the tribes of the earth will mourn, and they will see the Son of Man coming on the clouds of the sky with power and great glory. Mat 24:31 "And He will send forth His angels with a great trumpet and they will gather together His elect from the four winds, from one end of the sky to the other.

Rev 6:12 I looked when He broke the sixth seal, and there was a great earthquake; and the sun became black as sackcloth made of hair, and the whole moon became like blood; Rev 6:13 and the stars of the sky fell to the earth, as a fig tree casts its unripe figs when shaken by a great wind. Rev 6:14 The sky was split apart like a scroll when it is rolled up, and every mountain and island were moved out of their places. Rev 6:15 Then the kings of the earth and the great men and the commanders and the rich and the strong and every slave and free man hid themselves in the caves and among the rocks of the mountains; Rev 6:16 and they said to the mountains and to the rocks, "Fall on us and hide us from the presence of Him who sits on the throne, and from the wrath of the Lamb;
Rev 6:17 for the great day of their wrath has come, and who is able to stand?"

> **The Coming of our Lord and Our Gathering Together in Him**

> **Elijah the Prophet Before the Day of the Lord**

> **The Apostasy Comes First and The Man of Lawlessness is Revealed**

> **Great and Terrible Day of the Lord The Wrath of the Lamb**

THE VALLEY OF THE SHADOW OF DEATH

On one of my trips to Israel I was an assistant tour host on a bus that was traveling from Jerusalem to the historic town of Jericho. Jerusalem sits on a mountain, with an elevation variance from 2,133 to 2,756 feet above sea level. Jericho has the distinction of being the lowest city on earth, at an elevation of 853 feet BELOW sea level. This accounts for a grade change ranging from 3,000 to 3,600 feet over a 23  mile descent. It was on this road that the Good Samaritan encountered the victim who had been plundered by robbers and ignored by local citizens. I was standing on the front of the bus and the wheels of the bus were located 10 feet BEHIND me. What this means is that when the bus made a turn, I would be BEYOND the turning radius of the bus. While traveling down one of the more treacherous narrow passages, the bus driver made a sharp turn over a ravine and announced the following: *"Ladies and Gentlemen, you are now passing over the Valley of the Shadow of Death. It is so deep and so dark that the bottom of the ravine can only be seen at high noon."* For me this had added significance. Since I was at the front of the bus, beyond the wheels, I was now standing on the part of the bus that was FLOATING over the ravine. My life flashed before my eyes! From my vantage point, we were about to go over the cliff. I was literally looking down into the Valley that King David made famous in Psalm 23:4 when he said: *"Even though I walk through the valley of the shadow of death, I fear no evil, for You are with me; Your rod and Your staff, they comfort me."* For David the shepherd boy, this was not just an expression. He had walked this pass with his sheep many times and probably seen wayward sheep plunge into the ravine hundreds of feet below. David epitomized in a phrase what many of us experience at some time in our lives. When tragedy or despair bring us to our knees, we feel as if we are In a deep, dark valley with no way out. Isn't it amazing how God holds our hand during those dark days and leads us with His presence and His comfort. There will come a time in human history, when the Church will experience the collective persecution of the ages. Satan's wrath will be defined as the Great Tribulation, and believers around the world will be reminded to brace themselves as they pass through the "valley of the shadow." We talk of Tribulation as if we don't deserve to pass through it. We may never experience the persecution leading to death. But some believer, sometime in the future, will stand before the enemy and proudly declare in a final act of valor, "Jesus is Lord." *Revelation 12:11 encourages us to stand strong when it says: "they loved not their lives, even when faced with death"*

"The parousia of Christ
will initiate the end of the age.
The parousia will end the time of persecution
for the surviving faithful followers of Christ
and begin a time of persecution for the wicked.
Since the end of the age, which is the harvest,
is a subset of the parousia of Christ,
God will deliver the righteous first,
followed by the punishment of the wicked.
The parousia delivers, then destroys."

CHARLES COOPER
"God's Elect and the Great Tribulation"

3

GATHERING HIS CHURCH

"The Feast of Trumpets"

The Anti-Christ and his rebel followers are about to experience the Wrath of God, but three things must precede God's vengeance.

      1) God will first seal and protect 144,000 noble Jewish warriors as the firstfruits of the millennium.

      2) Then the sixth seal, cosmic disturbance, will signal the glorious return of Christ in the sky.

      3) Then the dead in Christ, and those believers who endure the Tribulation, from every nation and tongue, will be snatched up (raptured) to heaven and clothed in white robes, about to witness God's wrath poured out on planet earth.

Pre-tribulation rapturism is
exegetically indefensible.
Some of the best theological minds
of the twentieth century have not
been able to successfully defend it.
If that statement seems exaggerated,
then listen to the admission
of John Walvoord:
"The fact is that neither post-tribulationism
nor pre-tribulationism is an explicit teaching
of scripture. The Bible does not,
in so many words, state either."

Marv Rosenthal
"The Prewrath Rapture of the Church"

THE SEQUENCE OF EVENTS

LEADING TO THE WRATH OF GOD

1) BIRTH PANGS

2) TRIBULATION

3) THE SIXTH SEAL (Revelation 6:12 and Matthew 24:29)

> A) Cosmic Disturbances
>
>> Earthquake, Sun darkened, Moon like blood, Stars fell to the earth
>
> B) Sealing the 144,000
>
>> The rapture is considered to be part of the sixth seal event, but it probably happens in Chapter 7 of Revelation, AFTER the 144,000 are sealed, since it seems reasonable to believe that God will not leave the earth without a remnant.
>
> B) The Sign of the Son of Man will appear in the sky.
>
>> Sky splits apart like a scroll
>> Jesus comes in power and great glory.
>> The Great Trumpet
>> The tribes of the earth mourn (the kings of the earth hide)
>> The great day of wrath has come.
>> Note: Great glory is the adjective 'polus', meaning better.
>>   Great wrath is the adjective 'mega', meaning bigger.

4) THE GATHERING OF THE ELECT (THE RAPTURE)

> A) The angels will gather the elect from the four winds of the earth.
> B) The great multitude no one could count,
>> Coming out of tribulation, wearing white robes.

5) SILENCE IN HEAVEN
> The 7 trumpet judgments, The Wrath of God.

THE PAROUSIA

The First Coming of Jesus Christ was recorded in Galatians 4:4, which says, "But when the fullness of time came, God sent forth His Son, born of a woman and born under the law." In Ephesian 1:10, we find similar words to describe His Second Coming. It says, "with a view to an administration suitable to the fullness of the times, that is, the summing up of all things in Christ." The fullness of time is the time that began with His first coming and will come to a climactic conclusion at His Second Coming. The disciples said to Jesus, "What will be the sign of your coming?" The specific Greek word that is used to describe the return of Jesus is the word "parousia". (pronounced 'pair-oo'-see-a'.) The meaning of this word is 'para' (alongside) and 'ousia' (being or presence). The common use for the word 'coming' was the Greek word 'erchomai' which simply means 'an arrival'. That word is used 599 times in the NT, in contrast to the word 'parousia', which was used only 8 times here to describe, more specifically, the majestic presence of a royal dignitary. These phrases indicate the variety of use in the NT.

The sign of Your coming
the promise of His coming,
The coming of the Son of Man,   **PAROUSIA**
the power and coming of our Lord Jesus,
the coming of the Lord Jesus with all His saints.
looking for and hastening the coming of the day of God.
By the appearance of His coming, the coming of the Lord is near,
that we may have confidence and not shrink away from Him in shame at His coming.

The Greek word 'epiphany' is another word to signify the Second Coming and it literally means 'a shining upon', which is interpreted to mean a sudden, brilliant presence. The following phrases are taken from the five occurrences used to describe the magnificent light that splits the skies from east to west.

By His appearing (epiphany) and His kingdom.
To all who have loved His appearing.
The appearing of our Savious Jesus Christ   **EPIPHANY**
Until the appearance of the Lord Jesus Christ
The appearing of the glory of our great God and Savior Jesus Christ.

The Greek word 'apokalupsis' comes from the root words 'apo' (away from) and 'kalupto' (a concealing), which means literally the opposite of hiding something, implying a spectacular and conspicuous revelation. The following four phrases are exclusively used in the NT to emphasize The Second Coming.

Awaiting eagerly the revelation of *our Lord Jesus Christ.*
At the revelation of His glory you may rejoice with exultation
The grace to be brought to you at the revelation of Jesus Christ.   **APOKALUPSIS**
So that your faith may be found to result in praise and glory and honor
at the revelation of Jesus Christ.

The story is told that astro-physicist Lambert Dolphin was sitting on the front row during a sermon being preached on the second coming of Christ.   When the preacher mentioned the classic passage from 1 Corinthians 15:52, "in a moment, in a twinkling of an eye", Dolphin immediately whipped out his calculator and began processing numbers. The pastor, who was a good friend of Dolphin's, stopped his preaching, looked at Dolphin and said, "what are you thinking about while I'm preaching." Mr. Dolphin, a devout Christian scholar said, "It occurred to me in the midst of the sermon what it meant to say 'the twinkling of an eye.'   The twinkling must mean the distance between the iris of the eye and the cornea of the eye. Since light travels at 186,000 miles per second, I believe that the twinkling of an eye is going to happen in 1/6 of a nano-second!"

The Parousia should be the most talked-about event in all of human history. The following passage of scripture merges Revelation 6 and Matthew 24 to give us a clue as to the dramatic timing of the Second Coming of Jesus. Seven words describe the timing of Jesus' coming: "the sky split apart like a scroll."

Rev 6:12 I looked when He broke the sixth seal, and there was a great earthquake; and the sun became black as sackcloth made of hair, and the whole moon became like blood;

Rev 6:13 and the stars of the sky fell to the earth, as a fig tree casts its unripe figs when shaken by a great wind.

*Rev 6:14 **The sky split apart like a scroll** when it is rolled up, and every mountain and island were moved out of their places.*

Mat 24:30 And then the sign of the Son of Man will appear in the sky, and then all the tribes of the earth will mourn, and they will see the Son of Man coming on the clouds of the sky with power and great glory.

Mat 24:31 And He will send forth His angels with a great trumpet and they will gather together His elect from the four winds, from one end of the sky to the other.

The Sky Split Apart Like a Scroll

THE SIXTH SEAL - COSMIC DISTURBANCE.   (See page 217 for repeat)

Rev 6:12 I looked when He broke the sixth seal, and there was a great earthquake; and the sun became black as sackcloth made of hair, and the whole moon became like blood;

Rev 6:13 and the stars of the sky fell to the earth, as a fig tree casts its unripe figs when shaken by a great wind.

Rev 6:14 **The sky split apart like a scroll** when it is rolled up, and every mountain and island were moved out of their places.

Rev 6:15 Then the kings of the earth and the great men and the commanders and the rich and the strong and every slave and free man hid themselves in the caves and among the rocks of the mountains;

Rev 6:16 and they said to the mountains and to the rocks, "Fall on us and **hide us** from the presence of Him who sits on the throne, and from **the wrath of the Lamb;**

Rev 6:17 for the great day of their wrath has come, and who is able to stand?"

> *Verse 6:14. The sky split apart like a scroll*. *Seven amazing words. Isaiah 34:4 echoes this prophetic statement in a passage that forecasts a future time of destruction. Perhaps* this phrase *is the key to the timing of the rapture! Amongst all the passages that speak of the sun turning black and the moon turning to blood, this is the ONLY New Testament verse that predicts that the sky would split apart. And why does the sky split apart? Because there is something on the* other side *of the sky that is coming through! In a moment of unparalleled magnificence, the sky rips open with a blinding burst of light, and a voice, and a great trumpet sound can be heard around the world.*
>
> *Hide us. The kings and great men, the commanders, the rich and strong are all caught off guard and are so fearful that they hide behind the rocks, hoping that an all-seeing God is not going to see them. There is no mention of the Church because we are being snatched up to glory at that very instant. The kings of the earth know what has happened. At that very moment, the spirit of God is revealing to each of them the consequence of their arrogant rejection of Christ. And, the spirit of darkness is preparing their hearts to wage war against a God who would dare to challenge their independence.*
>
> *The wrath of the Lamb. Though many have rejected and ignored the gospel message, they will know in an instant that the creator God of the universe and His only begotten Son are preparing for the mother of all battles. The Day of the Lord has begun.*

Matthew 24:29 "But immediately **after the tribulation** of those days the sun will be darkened, and the moon will not give its light, and the stars will fall from the sky, and the powers of the heavens will be shaken.

Mat 24:30 "And then **the sign** of the Son of Man will appear in the sky, and then all the tribes of the earth will mourn, and they will see the Son of Man coming on the cloud of the sky with power and great glory.

Mat 24:31 "And He will send forth His angels with **a great trumpet** and **they will gather together His elect** from the four winds, from one end of the sky to the other.

> ***After the tribulation.*** *The interpreters of the Pre-Tribulation rapture claim that this event is the second coming of Christ - not the rapture - based on the fact that their tribulation is a seven year period. This is very difficult for Pre-Trib to reconcile if you compare Revelation 6, the sixth seal, with the timing of the trumpet and bowl judgments. One of the difficulties in understanding the Pre-Tribulation argument is reconciling their use of the term "tribulation" to describe the seven year period that is more appropriately referred to as the 70th Week of Daniel. The tribulation not only ends, but is cut short, based on verse 22. How am I to be true to scripture if I can't take literally this passage? This has to be the prophetic sixth seal of Revelation chapter six. This has to be the rapture.*
>
> ***The sign.*** *This is the ultimate audio-visual moment in history. The sign will be both sight and sound - a burst of light, coupled with a shout and the blast of the Great trumpet. Can this possibly be anything but the return of the Lord Jesus?*
>
> ***a great trumpet.*** *According to scripture, only two times does God himself blow the trumpet. 1) When He gave the 10 commandments at Mt Sinai. 2) At the return of Jesus.*
>
> ***And they will gather together His elect.*** *It is amazing that we have chosen a Latin word, "rapture," over Jesus' own words to describe the snatching up of the believers into the heavens. "The Gathering of the Elect" is a beautiful term which culminates three of the most important events the world has ever witnessed: 1) the prophetic cosmic disturbance 2) the great trumpet, and 3) the coming of Christ "on the clouds" with power and great glory. Is this not the rapture? Is this not preceded by the terrible days of tribulation which was cut short in verse 22? How long will we ignore Jesus' own words to describe the end of the age?*

THE SHEKINAH GLORY OF GOD

Exo 24:15 Then Moses went up to the mountain, and the cloud covered the mountain.

Exo 24:16 **The glory of the LORD rested** on Mount Sinai, and the cloud covered it for six days; and on the seventh day He called to Moses from the midst of the cloud.

Exo 24:17 And to the eyes of the sons of Israel the appearance of the glory of the LORD was like a consuming fire on the mountain top.

> **The glory of the Lord rested.** The word 'shekinah' is used often by theologians to describe a light which symbolizes the presence of God among men. But the word 'shekinah' is so mysterious that it does not occur in scripture at all. In Exodus 24:16, the Hebrew word 'shakawn' is used to describe the 'resting' or 'dwelling' of the glory of God. In the Hebrew Talmud, the commentary on the Hebrew Bible, and also in the Targum, the paraphrases of scripture, the word 'shekinah' is used repeatedly to describe this special manifestation of God's presence among men. So our best understanding of this mysterious word is a majestic synthesis of the very presence of El Shaddai, the Most High God, coupled with the most powerful force on earth - light.

Mat 17:1 Six days later Jesus took with Him Peter and James and John his brother, and led them up on a high mountain by themselves.

Mat 17:2 And He was transfigured before them; **and His face shone like the sun**, and His garments became as white as light.

Mat 17:3 And behold, Moses and Elijah appeared to them, talking with Him.

> **and His face shone like the sun.** The ultimate manifestation of the shekinah glory of God can be found in two places: one is the transfiguration of Jesus, and the other is the time of the rapture/second coming of Christ in Matthew 24:31. Light is the purest and the most powerful form of science that mankind has ever experienced. To say that Jesus' face shone like the sun is to describe the sun itself, a force so brilliant and so powerful that it transmits warmth and energy from 93 million miles away. The very fact that light travels at 186, 000 miles per second is a fact so incredible that the human mind cannot fathom. We can measure it, we can quantify it, but we cannot understand its power. Jesus is the source of light, and when He referred to Himself as "the light of the world", He was not merely referring to a spiritual characteristic of goodness. He was giving us a clue that "in Him all things hold together", Colossians 1:17. When Christ returns, the earth, which will be temporarily shrouded in darkness, will be ablaze with an atomic blast so strong that our eyes would be vaporized if not for the tender mercy that allows us to look upon Him, who is the Savior of the World.

Rev 1:13 I saw one like a son of man, clothed in a robe reaching to the feet, and girded across His chest with a golden sash.

Rev 1:14 His head and His hair were white like white wool, like snow; and His eyes were like a flame of fire.

Rev 1:15 His feet were like burnished bronze, when it has been made to glow in a furnace, and His voice was like the sound of many waters.

Rev 1:16 In His right hand He held seven stars, and out of His mouth came:
a sharp two-edged sword . . . . and His face was like the sun shining in its strength.

> **A sharp two-edged sword.** What is the significance of the two-edged sword? The Greek word here is the word 'rompheia', which means a broadsword used for battle. Throughout the New Testament, the primary Greek word for 'sword' is the word 'machaira', which means a dagger. The machaira was the domestic tool used for cutting a limb, slicing an apple, or even doing surgery. The rompheia, however, was the implement of war. It is the rompheia which comes out of Jesus' mouth.

Rev 19:15 From His mouth comes **a sharp sword,** so that with it He may strike down the nations, and He will rule them with a rod of iron; and He treads the wine press of the fierce wrath of God, the Almighty.

John 1:14 And the Word became flesh, and dwelt among us, and we saw His glory, glory as of the only begotten from the Father, **full of grace and truth.**

> I believe that the two edges of the broadsword of Revelation 1 and 19 can be found in the words of John 1:14. Jesus was full of grace and truth. We have divided the world today along the lines of those two words. The progressive liberals of the world have taken the word grace and turned it into tolerance. Tolerance and Truth. Half the world stands for the truth and the other half of the world wants to compromise truth in favor of tolerance. Scripture says that Jesus was FULL of grace and truth. When He needed to be loving and compassionate and merciful, there was no one on the planet who exemplified these qualities like Jesus. When He needed to be direct and forceful and full of righteous indignation at the base and sinful nature of man, there was no one on the planet who could better speak with conviction and purity of truth. Our problem is that when we need to be full of truth we often take the "love" out of "tough love". And when we need to be forgiving and merciful and compassionate we get defensive because someone has not learned their lesson. Jesus was the pure embodiment of Grace and Truth. We should wake up every morning asking God to help us emulate the wonderful balance of Grace and Truth that Jesus personified.

THE SHOUT AND THE TRUMPET OF GOD.

1Thessalonians 4:16 **For the Lord Himself** will descend from heaven with **a shout, with the voice of the archangel and with the trumpet of God**, and the dead in Christ will rise first.

1Th 4:17 Then we who are alive and remain will be caught up together with them in the clouds to meet the Lord in the air, and **so we shall always be with the Lord.**

1Th 4:18 Therefore comfort one another with these words.

> *For the Lord Himself. Matthew 24:30 says that Jesus is coming in the clouds with power and great glory. It is perhaps wise for us to use our sanctified imagination at this point, because He will not present Himself as a gentle lamb, but rather as the Lion of Judah. He is coming in POWER AND GREAT GLORY! All I can say at this point is to quote 1 Corinthians 2:9. "Eyes have not seen, nor ears heard, nor entered into the hearts of man, the things which God has prepared for them that love Him." Breaking through the clouds, with an army of angels cheering him on, is the one that the Cathedral Quartet calls: "The all-time undisputed, undefeated Champion of Love."*
>
> *The shout, the voice, the trumpet. We can only speculate - our minds can only imagine - but I believe the whole world will hear these sounds while the dead in Christ and the faithful believers are rising in the air. This theory would negate the idea that the rapture will occur while the world is in amazement at the sudden absence of the entire Christian community.*
>
> *To meet the Lord in the air. Our translation could be like Christ's ascension, slowly into heavens, or it could occur rapidly, in "the twinkling of an eye", we're gone.*
>
> *so shall we always be with the Lord. There seems to be ambiguity among scholars as to where we are while Christ is rescuing the nation of Israel, then fighting the battle of Armageddon, then also reigning over the earth during the Millennium. This verse is intended as a general verse of comfort for the Church. It is not intended to confine the omnipresent Christ from superintending the universe prior to our eventual eternal home on the newly restored planet earth.*

Act 1:9 And after He had said these things, He was lifted up while they were looking on, and a cloud received Him out of their sight.

Act 1:10 And as they were gazing intently into the sky while He was going, behold, two men in white clothing stood beside them.

Act 1:11 They also said, "Men of Galilee, why do you stand looking into the sky? This Jesus, who has been taken up from you into heaven, will come in just the same way as you have watched Him go into heaven."

THE RAPTURE OR THE GATHERING?

The word "rapture" is not found in the Greek New Testament. It is found only in the Latin Vulgate version of the Bible. The words "gather" and "caught up" are better terms.

Matthew 24:30-31

And He will send forth His angels with a great trumpet
and they will <u>gather together</u> His elect from the four winds,
from one end of the sky to the other.
The word "gather together" is "epi-soon-ahgo."

$$E\pi\iota - \sigma\upsilon\nu - \alpha\gamma o$$

Meaning: "leading them together toward"

1 Thessalonians 4:17

Then we who are alive and remain
will be <u>caught up</u> together with them in the clouds
to meet the Lord in the air.
The word "caught up" is "har-po-dzo."

$$H\alpha\rho - \pi\alpha - \delta\zeta o$$

Meaning: "to seize"

The story was told recently of a woman in Australia who had a dream about the rapture of the Church. What she saw in that mysterious moment, in the twinkling of an eye, was the redeemed - who are suddenly snatched away from the gravitational constraints of the planet. What happened next is the interesting part. In her dream, she saw some people floating casually toward the clouds, and others, shot off like a rocket into the heavens. Her explanation was thought provoking: The ascension of the believers was proportional to their expectant anticipation of the coming Messiah. For those who studied and looked forward to Jesus' coming, they shot off like a rocket. For the rest, they would arrive in due time. Just a dream. But if it was true, how fast would you be launched at the time of our gathering?

THE SAINTS ARRIVE IN HEAVEN

Revelation Chapter 7

THE CALM BEFORE THE STORM

Rev 7:1 After this I saw four angels standing at the four corners of the earth, holding back the four winds of the earth, so that no wind would blow on the earth or on the sea or on any tree.

Rev 7:2 And I saw another angel ascending from the rising of the sun, having **the seal of the living God;** and he cried out with a loud voice to the four angels to whom it was granted to harm the earth and the sea,

Rev 7:3 saying, "Do not harm the earth or the sea or the trees **until we have sealed** the bond-servants of our God on their foreheads."

> *Prior to the ominous event that we call "silence in heaven", the angels give us another ominous signal: the winds of the earth cease. How much we take for granted the cool ventilation from the winds of the earth. Before The Wrath of God can begin in chapter eight, 2 things must happen: The PROTECTION of the 144,000 godly men of Israel, and, the RAPTURE of the Church. **The seal of the living God.** Ephesians 1:13 and 4:30 refer to our salvation as the sealing in Him by the Spirit of promise.*

THE 144,000 GODLY MEN OF ISRAEL

Rev 7:4 And I heard the number of those who were sealed, one hundred and forty-four thousand sealed from every tribe of the sons of Israel:

Rev 7:5 from the tribe of **Judah**, twelve thousand were sealed, from the tribe of **Reuben** twelve thousand, from the tribe of **Gad** twelve thousand,

Rev 7:6 from the tribe of **Asher** twelve thousand, from the tribe of **Naphtali** twelve thousand, from the tribe of **Manasseh** twelve thousand,

Rev 7:7 from the tribe of **Simeon** twelve thousand, from the tribe of **Levi** twelve thousand, from the tribe of **Issachar** twelve thousand,

Rev 7:8 from the tribe of **Zebulun** twelve thousand, from the tribe of **Joseph** twelve thousand, from the tribe of **Benjamin**, twelve thousand were sealed. See page 314.

> *The characteristics of the 144,000 (from Revelation 14:1-5, see page 314) are as follows: They stand on Mt. Zion. They have a mark on their forehead. They are undefiled. They follow Jesus. They are the firstfruits of the Millennium. They are blameless. Scripture is not explicit as to their purpose. They will likely be a catalyst in the nation's salvation as they look upon King Jesus. They will also likely be leaders to the nation during the wrath-filled bowl judgments - and they will provide inspiration to the nation as they begin to re-populate the thousand year Millennium.*

Rev 7:9 After these things I looked, and behold, **a great multitude which no one could count,** from every nation and all tribes and peoples and tongues, standing before the throne and before the Lamb, clothed in white robes, and palm branches were in their hands;

Rev 7:10 and they cry out with a loud voice, saying, "Salvation to our God who sits on the throne, and to the Lamb."

Rev 7:11 And all the angels were standing around the throne and around the elders and the four living creatures; and they fell on their faces before the throne and worshiped God,

Rev 7:12 saying, "Amen, blessing and glory and wisdom and thanksgiving and honor and power and might, be to our God forever and ever. Amen."

> *Nowhere else in scripture is the phrase used: "a great multitude which no one could count." This is the moment that heaven has been waiting for; when the Bride of Christ, His Church, would be rescued finally and completely from the clutches of Satan and his minions.*

THE ELDER INTRODUCES THE GREAT MULTITUDE

Rev 7:13 Then one of the elders answered, saying to me, "These who are clothed in the white robes, who are they, and **where have they come from?"**

Rev 7:14 I said to him, "My lord, you know." And he said to me, **"These are the ones who come out of the great tribulation,** and they have washed their robes and made them white in the blood of the Lamb.

Rev 7:15 "For this reason, they are before the throne of God; and they serve Him day and night in His temple; and He who sits on the throne will spread His tabernacle over them.

Rev 7:16 "They will hunger no longer, nor thirst anymore; nor will the sun beat down on them, nor any heat;

Rev 7:17 for the Lamb in the center of the throne will be their shepherd, **and will guide them to springs of the water of life;** and God will wipe every tear from their eyes."

> ***out of the Great Tribulation.*** *One of the elders asks a rhetorical question in order to declare to John the answer. He asks the question to imply that these saints have just arrived in glory. Pretribulation theology cannot explain how the "great multitude which no one could count" occurs now instead of prior to the tribulation period. This HAS TO BE the raptured saints (dead and alive) who have been snatched away, caught up, before the great and terrible day of the Lord. Coming "out of the tribulation" literally means they were raptured after the Tribulation and just before God's wrath.*
>
> ***guide them to springs of the water of life.*** *This is an important key to the activity of the saints in heaven. "At some point", Jesus will take them to paradise. I believe that Paradise and the New Jerusalem are both waiting to descend from Heaven at the appointed time.*

Four Popular Views of the Rapture

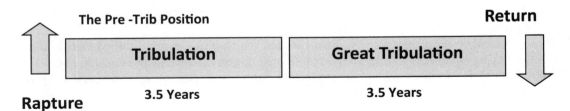

The Pre -Trib Position

Return

Tribulation   Great Tribulation

Rapture

3.5 Years   3.5 Years

The Pre-Tribulation Rapture was popularized in the early 1800's by the British evangelist J.N. Darby and the denomination known as the Plymouth Brethren. In the 1900s, it was popularized in America by theologian C.I. Scofield. This position proposes that Christ will "snatch up" all believers PRIOR to a dreadful seven year tribulation period which climaxes with the destruction of Satan and the millennial reign of Christ upon the restored earth.   This theory has become the pre-dominant theology of the 20th century, and has become a rigid ideology and a dogmatic, irrefutable test of faith for many evangelicals.

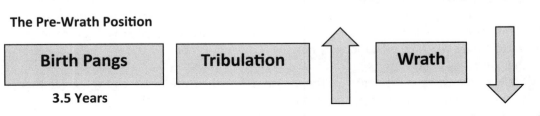

The Pre-Wrath Position

Birth Pangs   Tribulation   Wrath

3.5 Years

The Rescue of the Church   **The Rescue of Israel**

The term "Pre-Wrath rapture" was conceived by Robert Van Kampen (The Sign) and Marvin Rosenthal (The Pre-Wrath Rapture of the Church) in the 1990s. The implication is that Christ will return for His church only AFTER the church suffers through the time that Jesus called "the beginning of sorrows" and the brief tribulation of the Anti-Christ. Christ rescues the believers prior to the dreadful time known as the Wrath of God, signified by the Trumpet and Bowl judgments on the earth. This is the position held by this author, and this book will attempt to convince you of its veracity. Notice that unlike the other three positions, the Pre-Wrath Tribulation is NOT seven years in duration.

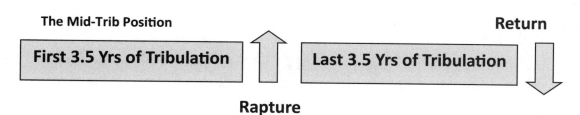

The Mid-Trib Position

First 3.5 Yrs of Tribulation | **Last 3.5 Yrs of Tribulation**

Return

Rapture

The Mid-Tribulation Rapture contends that the rapture of the church occurs immediately after the first 3.5 years of tribulation, and just before The Great Tribulation in the last half of the seven years. Mid-Trib contends that believers will suffer through the Trumpet Judgments, but not the Bowl Judgments. Like the Pre-Trib position, the rapture and the return of Christ are separated by years of tribulation.

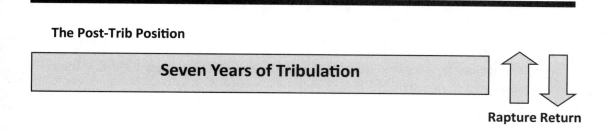

The Post-Trib Position

Seven Years of Tribulation

Rapture Return

The classic position called the Post-Tribulation rapture believes that the church will not only suffer the persecution of Tribulation, but also the horror of God's Wrath during the Trumpet and Bowl Judgments. Technically, the <u>PRE-WRATH </u>position is a Post Tribulation position, but only in the sense that the Tribulation is NOT seven years, and only in the sense that the Rapture precedes the Wrath of God during the time known as the "Day of the Lord." Pre-Wrath advocates did not use the term "post-trib" because of the ambiguity of associating with a seven year tribulation and incorrect rapture timing.

THE LOGIC (?) OF PRE-TRIBULATION RAPTURE

1. Pre-Tribulation theology believes that the tribulation is seven years in length, based on Daniel 9:27.

2. Pre-Trib theology believes that since Daniel 9:27 says that there is a first and second half of the seven year period - the first part is the tribulation and the second part is the Great Tribulation.

3. Pre-Trib theology believes that the Tribulation Period and the Wrath of God are synonymous, therefore the Wrath of God, or the Day of the Lord, must begin at the beginning of the seven years.

4. Pre-Trib theology believes that since God promised that believers are not destined for wrath, then the rapture must begin at the beginning of the seven year period.

5. Pre-Trib theology believes that since the rapture must precede the wrath of God, then the cosmic disturbance and sign of the Messiah in Matthew 24:31 must be at the end of the seven year period.

6. Pre-Trib theology believes that the thief in the night passage in 1 Thessalonians 5:2 confirms the imminency of Christ's rapture.

7. Pre-Trib theology believes that since Matthew 24:31 must be at the end of the age, then there is a two part return of Christ, with an interim period of seven years.

8. Pre-Trib theology believes that since God has promised that believers will not go through wrath, it follows that Christians will not go through tribulation.

9. Pre-Trib theology believes that Christians in every decade since Jesus have experienced persecution, but they reject the idea that Christians will go through the time of tribulation.

The Pre-Wrath Rapture position does not agree with these Pre-Tribulation theories. Jesus said to the Pharisees, "You favor the traditions of men over the commandments of God." It is imperative that the tradition of Pre-Tribulation rapture be reexamined, according to the truth of scripture.

PRE-TRIBULATION THEOLOGY & RESPONSE

Please note each Pre-Wrath Response includes a scriptural basis. It is difficult for the Pre-Tribulation Theology to provide substantive verses to affirm each position.

1. The climax of human history will be a seven year period that is called Tribulation.
    Pre-Wrath theology teaches that the Tribulation is a brief period of time within the seven years that is cut short prior to the wrath of God, based on Matthew 24:22.

2. The first 3.5 years are called tribulation and the second 3.5 years are called The Great Tribulation.
    Pre-Wrath theology teaches that the two terms are synonymous based on Matthew 24:9, 21,29 - and the tribulation begins at the mid-point of the seven years.

3. Christ will rapture the Church PRIOR to the seven year period called Tribulation.
    Pre-Wrath theology teaches that The Church will be raptured AFTER they endure the shortened period called the Tribulation, based on Matthew 24:29-31.

4. The evidence of the rapture is found in Revelation Chapter Four, where John hears a trumpet and is invited through an open door into heaven.
    Pre-Wrath theology teaches that Christ raptures the Church in Chapter 6 of Revelation after the 6th seal, based on Revelation 6:14.

5. The Seals and Trumpets and Bowls are all three considered to be the wrath of God.
    Pre-wrath theology teaches that the scroll and seals are the pre-cursor to the wrath of God, based on Revelation 8:1.

6. The return of Christ is imminent, which means it could happen at any moment.
    Pre-wrath theology teaches that there are multiple signs that believers will recognize which precede the coming of Christ, based on Malachi 4:5 and 2 Thess 2:3. But we still don't presume to know the day or the hour.

7. The Rapture will be a mysterious snatching up of believers which will leave the world unaware of the sudden disappearance of perhaps a billion people.
    Pre-wrath theology teaches that every eye will see him and the great men of the earth will hide behind the rocks in fear of the Lord. Rev 1:7 and Rev 6:16.

WHICH MAKES MORE SENSE?

One of these days when we ask Jesus all of those heavy questions about the Day of the Lord, I somehow imagine that Jesus is going to respond like this: *"The Day of the Lord means that day when I come back to rescue my Church, to deliver punishment to the unrepentant, and then to see my prodigal children, Israel, come to faith. When I say, the day, I mean that it is a continuous Day. It begins with the sky being rolled back when I gather the Church; then my wrath falls upon the unrepentant world and the pawns of Satan; and finally, I stand on Mt. Zion with my beloved Israel. That's what I mean when I say, a day."*

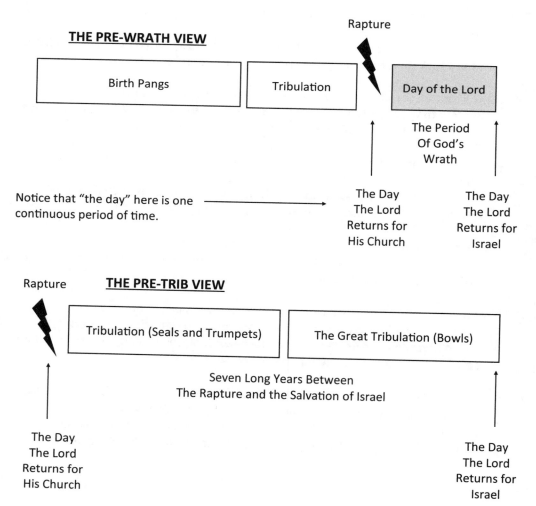

THE PRE-TRIBULATION PROPOSITION

It would seem that the entire Pre-Tribulation argument begins with one simple pre-supposition - that the tribulation period is seven years, equal to the seventieth week of Daniel. From that single idea, there are a series of events and ideas that have to take place built around that single premise. If that single premise is incorrect, the entire equation suffers. The following conditional statements are an attempt at summarizing the weakness in assuming a seven year period of tribulation.

IF . . .   The tribulation is 7 years . . .

> THEN . . . The Tribulation must also be the wrath of God, and

> IF . . .   The Tribulation is the Wrath of God

> THEN . . . The Church must experience a Pre-Tribulation Rapture

> SINCE . . . We all agree that believers will not experience the wrath of God.

BUT

IF . . . The tribulation is NOT 7 years

> AND . . . The Tribulation is cut short, as Jesus says.

> AND . . . The Wrath of God could be <u>after</u> the Tribulation.

> THEN . . . It is possible for the Rapture to occur

> > After the Tribulation and before the Wrath of God.

AND . . .

> SINCE . . . The word tribulation occurs 5 times BEFORE Revelation 7:14, and

> SINCE . . . The word wrath occurs 11 times AFTER Revelation 6:16

> THEN. . . . It would appear that the wrath of God, (The Day of the Lord)

> > does occur AFTER the sixth seal, beginning with Chapter 8.

Twenty-Two Major Problems
with the Pre-Tribulation Rapture

2 Peter 3:18 says, *"Be ready always to give an answer to every man who asks you a reason for the hope that is in you."* That verse is usually quoted in the context of apologetics regarding the basic doctrines of the Christian faith. But it must also be used in the context of end-time study because the stakes are high. Either we are exempt from tribulation or we are not. If we are not exempt, and there is a chance of enduring the tribulation, then is it not sound doctrine to hold to a theory that will expose so many believers to "a surprise ending." Titus 1:9 says, "holding fast the faithful word which is in accordance with the teaching, so that he will be able both to exhort in sound doctrine and to refute those who contradict." Listed below is a summary of twenty-two arguments that must be answered by Pre-Tribulation scholars.

1. The Olivet Discourse (Matthew 24)
Jesus' own words provide an outline of things to come:
Beginning of Sorrows, Tribulation, The Gathering and the Wrath of God.

2. The Tribulation is NOT Seven years. (Daniel 9:27)
There is a seven year period in biblical eschatology, but it is mistakenly referred to as "The Tribulation."

3. Cut Short. (Matthew 24:22)
Which is it, 3.5 years or cut short?

4. Every Eye will See Him. (Revelation 1:6)
The return of Jesus will not be a secret. The world will not suddenly be surprised to find the Christian population is absent.

5. The Overcomers of the Seven Churches (Revelation 2,3)
All seven churches were challenged to overcome. Were they just to overcome their sin, or is it more likely they were to persevere through the tribulation?

6. Door Standing Open (Revelation 4)
Compared to Matthew 24:29-31, this is a very weak argument for the rapture.

7. The Great Multitude (Revelation 7)
An innumerable host of white-robed believers just show up in heaven, coming out of the tribulation. Can this be the rapture?

8. Deliverance and Judgment (Luke 17)
The stories of Noah and Lot portray the idea that the rapture and second coming are tied together, not separated by 7 years.

9. The Rest of Her Children (Revelation 12:17)
Satan makes war with Israel and then the Church. But how can this be the Church (according to Pre-Trib theology) in the middle of the Tribulation?

10. The Thief in the Night (1 Thessalonians 5:4)
Jesus warned us that ONLY un-believers would be caught off guard.

11. The Man of Lawlessness (2 Thessalonians 2:1-3)
The timing of Jesus' second coming is clearly related to the apostasy and the advent of the Anti-Christ.

12. Not Destined for Wrath (1 Thess 5:9)
Another name for wrath is the Day of the Lord. The timing of this fearful day is the key to understanding the timing of the Rapture.

13. The Seven days of the Flood. (Genesis 7:4, 12,13)
Seven days do not automatically become seven years.

14. The Inevitability of Persecution (2 Timothy 3:12)
Jesus has called us to a life of suffering and persecution. The Tribulation is an opportunity for worldwide believers to confess their faith at the point of death.

15. How Long Will You Refrain O Lord? (Revelation 6:10)
The martyrs knew that the period of wrath was yet to come.

16. Elijah Will Come First. (Malachi 4:2-6)
If Elijah is one of the two witnesses, then the rapture cannot be Pre-Trib.

17. The Perseverance of the Saints. (Revelation 13:10)
Perseverance implies Tribulation.

18. The Hour of Testing. (Revelation 3:10)
Testing is an opportunity to display our trust in God.

19. The Jewish Wedding.
The Jewish Wedding is Not a Model for the Pre-Tribulational Rapture.

20. The Fiery Furnace. (Daniel 3:17,18; 21-25)
Perseverance Implies Tribulation.

21. The Mythology of Left Behind.
Jesus told us not to follow tradition, but rather the commandments of God.

22. Where is the Church after Chapter 4?
The Pre-Trib network contends that the Church is not mentioned after Chapter 4. You decide.

The Olivet Discourse

PROBLEM ONE
Jesus Himself identifies the Rapture <u>AFTER</u> the Tribulation.

Matthew 24

Mat 24:21 "For then there will be a great tribulation, such as has not occurred since the beginning of the world until now, nor ever will.

Mat 24:22 "Unless those days had been cut short, no life would have been saved; but for the sake of the elect those days will be cut short.

Mat 24:29 "But immediately **after the tribulation** of those days the sun will be darkened, and the moon will not give its light, and the stars will fall from the sky, and the powers of the heavens will be shaken.

Mat 24:30 "And then the sign of the Son of Man will appear in the sky, and then all the tribes of the earth will mourn, and they will see the Son of Man coming on the clouds of the sky with power and great glory.

Mat 24:31 "And He will send forth His angels with a great trumpet and they will gather together His elect from the four winds, from one end of the sky to the other.

> *"after the tribulation" - It is amazing that the clarity of this text is ignored by the scholars of Pre-Tribulation theology. The Great Tribulation begins in the second half of the seven year period, but is dramatically cut short by God, in order to spare the lives of "the elect". The Tribulation is Satan's wrath on planet earth, and because Satan would systematically exterminate all Christians, God cuts short this diabolical plan and allows the rapture as a divine means of escape. The Great Reward for suffering through the Great Tribulation is the glorious gathering by Christ and His angels at the end of the tribulation. The Pre-Trib movement would argue that the "elect" are the 1/3 of Israel that will be saved, and not the church. Clearly, the second coming of Christ will follow the tribulation, and will coincide with a cataclysmic upheaval of the sun, moon and stars. Christ will then rapture His beloved church as the Day of the Lord begins. God's wrath then burns against the world population that refuses to repent. It is incumbent upon the students of Pre-Trib rapture to look closely at the six seals in Revelation 6.*

TRIBULATION IS NOT SEVEN YEARS

PROBLEM TWO
The Tribulation Period is not seven years in length.

Mat 24:8 "But all these things are merely the beginning of birth pangs.

Mat 24:9 "Then they will deliver you to **tribulation,** and will kill you, and you will be hated by all nations because of My name.

Mat 24:21 "For then there will be a **great tribulation**, such as has not occurred since the beginning of the world until now, nor ever will.

Mat 24:22 "Unless those days had been **cut short**, no life would have been saved; but for the sake of the elect those days will be **cut short.**

Mat 24:29 "But immediately after **the tribulation** of those days THE SUN WILL BE DARKENED, AND THE MOON WILL NOT GIVE ITS LIGHT, AND THE STARS WILL FALL from the sky, and the powers of the heavens will be shaken.

Daniel 9:27 "And he will make a firm covenant with the many for one week, but in the middle of the week he will put a stop to sacrifice and grain offering; and on the wing of abominations will come one who makes desolate, even until a complete destruction, one that is decreed, is poured out on the one who makes desolate."

Rev 6:17 **for the great day of their wrath has come**, and who is able to stand?"

Pretribulation theology incorrectly teaches that the seven year period known as "the seventieth week of Daniel" is called seven years of Tribulation, and that the last 3.5 years is referred to as the Great Tribulation. Nowhere in scripture do we find reference to the seven years as "The Tribulation Period". Certainly, the beginning of birth pangs will be suffering and distress and tribulation (pressure). But the Great Tribulation begins at the midpoint of the seven year period, and is followed by the rapture - and then the Day of the Lord. It is very important to understand the distinction between the Tribulation, which is the wrath of Satan, and the Day of the Lord, which is the wrath of God. Pretribulationism does not clearly delineate these two events. Tribulation and Wrath seemed to be synonymously used to describe end-time chaos. We all agree that God has not destined us for wrath. But if the tribulation and wrath are synonymous, and many will be saved during the tribulation (or time of wrath), then how can we reconcile God allowing ANY of his children to suffer through His wrath if it is synonymous with tribulation?

CUT SHORT

PROBLEM THREE
Which is it - Seven Years or Cut Short?

Mathew 24:22
Unless those days had been cut short, no life would have been saved;
but for the sake of the elect those days will be cut short.

I began my study of Revelation 30 years ago in a seminary classroom at Southwestern Seminary. Dr. J.W. MacGorman, professor emeritus of Greek and New Testament studies, was my teacher, and I still remember the moment when he read this passage of scripture. Part of his charm was a soft, rolling Scottish brogue that always made his interpretation more interesting. When he said "cut short", he moved his arm like a machete. And then he did it again. His words, normally flowed smoothly. But this time, his words were quick and staccato like. "Cut short - amputated," he said. "Unexpectedly brief. Severely interrupted." He explained that the word 'cut short' in the Greek is the word 'kolobo-o.' It is used only twice in scripture, and both times in the context of Jesus' words about the tribulation. In Matthew we say 'cut short'. In Mark, we say 'shortened.' I later studied the root word, which is 'kolodzo'. The variant meaning for this word was "to chastise or to punish". What could that mean?

I confess I left the class confused that day. I was just taught that the tribulation had been cut short. But I was also taught that the tribulation was seven years in length. How could it be cut short?

Years later, I began to understand that the Anti-Christ would be allowed by God to control the earth for 3.5 years - 42 months, 1260 days, the second half of the Seventieth Week of Daniel. I began to realize that most of the events in Revelation are Satan's counterfeit for Jesus' ministry. For that reason, I believe that Jesus' ministry was 3.5 years in duration, and the 42 months in Revelation are intended to be a sadistic counterfeit. But this time period was cut short by God because Satan would have destroyed the elect had He not intervened. Kolobo-o means the days were cut short, but kolodzo means that Satan was chastised or interrupted by God, in order to abbreviate the rampage that was his diabolical intent. Yes, the Great Tribulation was cut short. For what reason? Because the next great event in human history, according to Jesus, was the cosmic disturbance of sun, moon and stars acting contrary to natural order. Then comes the Messiah, splitting the skies, in a flash of lightning. The sounds of the great voice and the great trumpet announce His Second Coming. And then scripture says, His angels gather the elect from the four winds of the earth. The glorious rapture of the Church, the beloved Body of Christ, has just occurred in the twinkling of an eye.

EVERY EYE WILL SEE HIM

PROBLEM FOUR
How can the Pre-Trib Rapture be a mystery if every eye will see him?

Mat 24:30 "And then the sign of the Son of Man will appear in the sky, and then all the tribes of the earth will mourn, and **they will see the Son of Man** coming on the clouds of the sky with power and great glory.

Mat 24:31 "And He will send forth His angels with a great trumpet and they will gather together His elect from the four winds, from one end of the sky to the other.

_____

Acts 1:9 And after He had said these things, He was lifted up **while they were looking on**, and a cloud received Him out of their sight.

_____

Rev 1:7 Behold He is coming with the clouds, and **every eye will see Him**, even those who pierced Him; and all the tribes of the earth will mourn over Him. So it is to be. Amen.

> *The Pre-Tribulation rapture contends that there will be an imminent, sudden, totally unexpected moment, in which the dead in Christ and those who are alive will be caught up in the skies. The popular 'Left Behind' film series depicts this event with millions of items of clothing left on the ground, having just been vacated by the occupant. According to Pre-Trib, the rest of the world won't have a clue what just happened. Those who are left behind will be confused as to what happened. How can this be? Scripture clearly says that every eye will see him.*

> *One of the difficult areas to explain in the study of Jesus' rapture and second coming is this: When does the divine text talk about Israel, and when does it refer simply to the church? When it refers to tribes, does it mean the exhaustive languages and cultures around the globe? Or is it referring to the 12 tribes of Israel? Pre-trib scholars would argue that the elect in verse 31 is referring ONLY to the 12 tribes of Israel. But further investigation will make clear that the time for Israel does not occur until the Mighty Angel holds the smaller scroll in Revelation 10.*

THE OVERCOMERS

PROBLEM FIVE
Are the Seven Churches overcoming sinful acts or the Tribulation?

Ephesus: **To him who overcomes,** I will grant to eat of the tree of life which is in the Paradise of God.'

Smyrna: **He who overcomes** will not be hurt by the second death.

Pergamum: **To him who overcomes,** to him I will give some of the hidden manna, and I will give him a white stone, and a new name written on the stone which no one knows but he who receives it.'

Thyatira: **He who overcomes,** and he who keeps My deeds until the end, to Him I will give authority over the nations.

Sardis: '**He who overcomes** will thus be clothed in white garments; and I will not erase his name from the book of life, and I will confess his name before My Father and before His angels.

Philadelphia: '**He who overcomes**, I will make him a pillar in the temple of My God, and he will not go out from it anymore; and I will write on him the name of My God, and the name of the city of My God, the new Jerusalem, which comes down out of heaven from My God, and My new name.

Laodicea: '**He who overcomes,** I will grant to him to sit down with Me on My throne, as I also overcame and sat down with My Father on His throne.

> *The origin of the word 'overcome' gives us the Greek word Nike, which means victory. Christ spoke to the seven churches and promised them various rewards in the eternal kingdom, IF they overcome, or persevere. Rev 14:12 says, "Here is the perseverance of the saints, who keep the commandments of God and their faith in Jesus." The context of this verse is taking the mark of the beast during the Tribulation. This cannot be talking about the Jews because they don't believe in Jesus. Once again, the Pre-Trib argument is that this group are the remnant that is left behind during the Tribulation. Also, keep in mind that the Pre-Trib Restrainer (that has supposedly been removed) is the Holy Spirit. The huge question for the Pre-Trib scholars is: How does one get saved by the Holy Spirit, once the Holy Spirit, the Restrainer, has been removed? And, how could the Holy Spirit be removed at the beginning of the seven years, and then later, after the seals, a multitude so vast, comes out of the tribulation?*

THE DOOR STANDING OPEN

PROBLEM SIX
Compared to Matthew 24:29-31, this is a very weak argument for the rapture.

Rev 4:1 After these things I looked, and behold, **a door standing open** in heaven, and the first voice which I had heard, like **the sound of a trumpet** speaking with me, said, "**Come up here**, and I will show you what must take place after these things."

Rev 4:2 Immediately I was in the Spirit; and behold, a throne was standing in heaven, and One sitting on the throne.

> *The door standing open has become one of the classic arguments for the Pre-Tribulation rapture position. I suppose when you combine the open door with the sound of a trumpet and a voice that says "Come up here", that should be enough to convince you and I that the rapture has just taken place. Verse 2 makes very clear that this is an actual event by one person, John, at a certain time and place. To extract from this a rapture narrative is a stretch.*
>
> *A secondary argument from this passage is the Pre-Trib idea that the Church had to be raptured because it is not mentioned after chapter four. After all, the churches have just been mentioned in chapters 2 and 3, and admittedly, the word "church" is not mentioned again until chapter 22. Actually, the church is not mentioned in ANY of the rapture passages, so the "open door, after chapter four" test doesn't work. BUT, what's another word for the church? The word 'saints.' Also in Revelation 12:17, "those who hold to the testimony of Jesus" is a reference to the Church. This "proof by absence" method is a pretty weak means of hermeneutic for a body of evangelicals who say they are committed to the accuracy of scriptural interpretation. (See page 268)*

Rev 13:7 It was also given to him to make war with the saints and to overcome them, and authority over every tribe and people and tongue and nation was given to him.

> *Yes, the Pre-Trib movement will argue that this is a "remnant", the "left behind' - those who were saved after the seven years began. But the context of this passage is the beginning of the Anti-Christ's destructive path of power. It would seem that it is too soon to have a remnant of saints that are so significant in number that the Beast would be going after them.*

THE GREAT MULTITUDE

PROBLEM SEVEN
The Great Multitude comes out of the great tribulation.

Revelation 7

v9. After these things I looked, and behold, **a great multitude** which no one could count, from every nation and all tribes and peoples and tongues, standing before the throne and before the Lamb, clothed in white robes, and palm branches *were* in their hands;

v13. who are they, and **where have they come from**?"

v14 "These are the ones who come **out of the great tribulation**, and they have washed their robes and made them white in the blood of the Lamb."

"a great multitude" - *Nowhere else in the pages of scripture do we find this phrase "which no one could count." While it is true that scripture refers to people like "the sands of the seashore" or "the stars in the sky", this phrase seems to surpass those metaphors as referring to the saints of all time, dead and alive, who have now been snatched off of planet earth to begin their eternal pilgrimage with Christ.*

"where have they come from" - *What a strange phrase to be uttered by an elder in heaven. But upon further investigation, we find that this elder is merely asking John the apostle a rhetorical question in order to hear him declare that these are the raptured saints.*

"out of the great tribulation" - *It has always been assumed by Pre-Tribulation theologians that this phrase implies those believers who were saved "during the tribulation" and only after the rapture, which precedes the 7 year period. But, if you read this with the understanding that the tribulation may NOT be seven years - AND, with the possibility of the saints going through the tribulation - you will then see the churches of Philadelphia (the persevering church) and Smyrna (the persecuted church), along with the faithful dead, who represent the great multitude from every tribe and nation.*

Does it not seem a great end-time mystery that those who come "out of the great tribulation" are also those who are a multitude "which no one could count?" I would certainly hope that the multitude too vast to count would be those who are raptured. Otherwise, the multitude which no one could count will be those unbelievers who resisted the gospel before the seven years, and were scared into heaven at the last minute by terrors of the tribulation. Is that really the Chapter Seven saints that are now celebrating their salvation? I think not.

DELIVERANCE & JUDGMENT

PROBLEM EIGHT
The Pre-Trib Rapture does not fit the biblical model of Deliverance and Judgment.

Luke 17:26 "And just as it happened in the days of Noah, so it will be also in the days of the Son of Man:

Luk 17:27 they were eating, they were drinking, they were marrying, they were being given in marriage, **until the day that Noah entered the ark**, and the flood came and destroyed them all.

Luk 17:28 "It was the same as happened in the days of Lot: they were eating, they were drinking, they were buying, they were selling, they were planting, they were building;

Luk 17:29 but **on the day that Lot went out from Sodom** it rained fire and brimstone from heaven and destroyed them all.

Luk 17:30 "It will be just the same **on the day** that the Son of Man is revealed.

> *"until the day that Noah"* - *I have always been taught that this passage is a cultural symbol - that it is merely talking about the very traditional social activities of everyday life: marrying, eating, drinking, buying, selling, planting, building. But I'm afraid we have "the em-fa-sis on the wrong sy-lab-ble." The operative words to understand this passage are the words "deliverance" and "judgment". On the day that Noah was delivered, the flood came. Deliverance, then judgment. He was raptured away (delivered) and then came judgment. The same with Lot.*
>
> ***On the very day that Lot went out*** *(raptured away or delivered) the judgment of fire and brimstone fell upon Sodom and Gomorrah.*
>
> *"on the day" - The implication here is that "on the day" that Christ is revealed, He raptures the church and sets in motion the judgment against the nations: deliverance and judgment, deliverance and judgment. The very idea that the Pre-Trib movement says that the Second Coming occurs at the end of the seven years is just not good interpretation of the basic text of scripture.*
>
> *Like two sides of a coin, deliverance and judgment are back-to-back events which also fit the model of the Great Trumpet as the "call of assembly" and the "call to war."*

THE REST OF HER CHILDREN

PROBLEM NINE
The "rest of her children" refers to the Church at the beginning of the Tribulation

Revelation 12:17
So the dragon was enraged with the woman,
and went off to make war with the rest of her children,
who keep the commandments of God and hold to the testimony of Jesus.

The paraphrase of this verse sounds like this:

> *"So Satan the dragon was enraged with Israel,*
> *and went off to make war with the Church,*
> *the adopted children of God,*
> *who live by God's commandments and the testimony of Jesus."*

The context of this verse is the beginning of the Great Tribulation. Is there any doubt that the woman is Israel, or that the 'rest of her children' is speaking about the mass of believers who love God and follow Jesus? Pre-Tribulation theology teaches that the Church will be gone by the time of the tribulation. Pre-Trib theology teaches that this verse is merely referring to the believers who are saved AFTER the tribulation begins, and that 'the rest' refers to a mere remnant of believers - not the glorious throng of believers in every country of the world, awaiting anxiously the return of Christ. Pre-Tribulation IGNORES this verse of scripture because it cannot possibly reconcile how the Church got caught in the middle of Satan's wrath. We understand that our faith, our strength, our complete reliance on God in the darkest hours, will shine like the sun before the Lord, who is honored by our loyalty to Him.

Note also that this verse refutes the idea that the Church is not mentioned after Revelation Chapter 4. See page 268 for additional verses that substantiate the clear references to the Church throughout the Tribulation period.

254

THE THIEF IN THE NIGHT

PROBLEM TEN
The scripture about Christ's surprise return is directed toward UNbelievers.

1 Thessalonians 5

1Th 5:1 Now as to the times and the epochs, brethren, you have no need of anything to be written to you.

1Th 5:2 For you yourselves know full well that the **day of the Lord will come just like a thief in the night.**

1Th 5:3 While they are saying, "Peace and safety!" then destruction will come upon them suddenly like labor pains upon a woman with child, and they will not escape.

1Th 5:4 **But you, brethren**, are not in darkness, that the day would overtake you like a thief;

1Th 5:5 for you are all sons of light and sons of day. We are not of night nor of darkness;

1Th 5:6 so then let us not sleep as others do, but let us be alert and sober.

1Th 5:7 For those who sleep do their sleeping at night, and those who get drunk get drunk at night.

1Th 5:8 But since we are of *the* day, let us be sober, having put on the breastplate of faith and love, and as a helmet, the hope of salvation.

1Th 5:9 **For God has not destined us for wrath**, but for obtaining salvation through our Lord Jesus Christ,

> *"Like a thief in the night"* - Notice that this passage says *"the day of the Lord"*. This is not the Pre-Trib rapture, but it is the Pre-Wrath rapture. It is very important that we distinguish between *"tribulation"* (the wrath of Satan) and the *"day of the Lord."* (the wrath of God.) 2 Peter 3:10, Revelation 3:3 and Revelation 16:5 also refer to Jesus' Second Coming as a thief in the night. These verses refer to those who are asleep and those who are naked, implying those unbelievers who are not prepared.
>
> *"But you, brethren* - Though we are to be ever vigilant for the return of our Master, this passage clearly says that WE (believers) are not the object of this passage, and will NOT be overtaken in surprise by the Lord's return.
>
> *"God has not destined us for wrath"* - Much of the Pre-Trib position has been built on the premise that God's wrath begins with the seven year period. If wrath does indeed come after the tribulation, then this reading takes on new meaning. Rev 6:17 clearly places the wrath of God AFTER the tribulation period.

THE MAN OF LAWLESSNESS

PROBLEM ELEVEN
Christ's "imminent" return can't be reconciled with the return of Anti-Christ.

2 Thessalonians 2:1

Now we request you, brethren, with regard to **the coming of our Lord Jesus Christ and our gathering together to Him,**

2Th 2:2 that you not be quickly shaken from your composure or be disturbed either by a spirit or a message or a letter as if from us, to the effect that the day of the Lord has come.

2Th 2:3 **Let no one in any way deceive you, for it will not come unless the apostasy comes first,** and the man of lawlessness is revealed, the son of destruction,

> *"the coming of our Lord" - It is interesting to see that The Second Coming is literally associated with the rapture, though Pre-Trib theology teaches that Christ will rapture the Church, and then seven years later will return for His official Second Coming.*
>
> *"let no one deceive you." - These words are likely directed at church leaders in the last days; but not deceptive church leaders. Perhaps the implication is that trusted pastors and traditional theology will naively believe that believers will not have to endure the tribulation.*
>
> *"for it will not come" - This phrase refers to verse 1 (the coming of our Lord) and CLEARLY says that Christ WILL NOT COME until two things have happened: the apostasy, and the revealing of the anti-Christ.   To be 'apostate' means to fall away from the faith. This falling away can begin at any time after the beginning of the 3.5 year period, but most likely will occur at the beginning of the tribulation period, when the Anti-Christ takes off his mask and reveals his satanic plot to institute the mark of the beast.*
>
> *According to Tim LaHaye, in his book, Charting the End Times, "The first seven translations of the English Bible rendered it (apostesia) as departure. No one knows why the translators of the KJV render it 'falling away', or why others translate it rebellion. A case can be made that all seven of the earliest translations of the English Bible were right in rendering it "departure", which could mean a physical departure or rapture." Comment from this author. Really? I was taught not to isogete scripture.   This is the weakest argument I have ever heard for the Pre-Trib Rapture.*

Not Destined for Wrath

PROBLEM TWELVE
The Pre-Tribulation Movement Must Define the Period Known as The Wrath of God.

1Th 5:9 For God has <u>not destined us for wrath</u>, but for obtaining salvation through our Lord Jesus Christ,

1Th 5:10 who died for us, so that whether we are awake or asleep, we will live together with Him.

Perhaps the most confusing issue in discussing Pre-Tribulation theology is the issue of wrath. The 21st century Pre-Trib believer has the idea that since we are promised protection from wrath, then we are promised protection from persecution. Jesus never exempted us from persecution. We must be careful to always distinguish between the wrath of God and the tribulation of Satan. The Greek word for tribulation is "thilipsis", which means suffering, affliction, anguish, distress or persecution. The Greek word for wrath is "thumos", which means rage, indignation or fierce anger.

When Jesus spoke of tribulation three times in Matthew 24, he always used the word for anguish, not the word for rage. God's rage is reserved for that period of time, after Revelation 6:17, when He sounds the trumpets and pours the bowls. it is also worth noting that Satan (in Revelation 12:12) comes down with "great wrath", having only a short time. Remember that Satan is a counterfeiter. If God exacts wrath, Satan is going to try to do the same. Therefore, the tribulation period - interpreted as Seals four (death) and five (martyrdom) are actually the "wrath of Satan."

The term "pre-wrath" was coined by Robert Van Kampen and Marv Rosenthal to designate the timing of the rapture as just preceding the trumpet and bowl judgments, beginning in Chapter 8. In a sense, the Pre-Tribulation movement is also pre-wrath, since we are in total agreement that no believer wants, or expects to go through the terrible time known as the wrath of God - or otherwise known as the Day of the Lord.

Titus 2:13 says that we are looking for the "blessed hope", and the appearing of the glory of our great God and Savior. The Pre-Tribulation movement and Pre-Wrath believers are in agreement. We are all looking for the blessed hope! And we also agree that we are NOT destined for wrath. The blessed hope awaits the persevering Church who have stood fast to overcome the mark of the beast.

THE SEVEN DAYS OF THE FLOOD

PROBLEM THIRTEEN
Seven Days Do Not Automatically Become Seven Years.

Gen 7:4 "For after seven more days, I will send rain on the earth forty days and forty nights; and I will blot out from the face of the land every living thing that I have made."
Gen 7:10 It came about after the seven days, that the water of the flood came upon the earth.

This passage has become a classic text among the Pre-Tribulation movement to justify the rapture at the beginning of the seven years. The logic goes like this: The seven day period is interpreted to be seven years. The end of the seven years is judgment. Noah went into the ark (the symbol of God's protection) before the seven day period, therefore escaping the wrath of God that was about to punish the rebellious generation of mankind.

There are several problems with this theory.   It is a huge stretch as Bible interpreters to dogmatically claim that the seven days are seven years. There is no precedent elsewhere in scripture. Now I know that you're thinking: what about the seventieth week of Daniel? I confess that I am not smart enough to calculate the 483 years that constitute 69 weeks that we called the "Time of the Gentiles." But it is not random interpretation that defines the 70th week as a seven year period. It is also a loose interpretation to associate the end of the seven days (judgment of the flood) with the end of the seven years. The implication is that judgment is at the end, but clearly, the trumpet judgment which begins wrath is not at the end of the seven years, but some time after the middle of the seven years. It is true that Jesus used Noah as an analogy of the endtime. In the parallel passage to the Olivet Discourse in Luke 17:23, it says, "until the day that Noah entered the ark, and the flood came. Then in v29 its says of Lot, "but on the day that Lot went out from Sodom it rained fire and brimstone." The implication in these two passages is this: For Noah and Lot, on the very day they were protected by God's grace, judgment came upon the earth. Deliverance and judgment. I do not want to believe that it takes a Bible professor to figure out for me that seven days in Genesis means seven years in Revelation. I would prefer to trust the very simple understanding of the Noah and Lot passages as a back-to-back sequence of events that reflect the reality of Jesus' second coming: Tribulation will come, and then King Jesus will split the skies in a moment of glory, to rescue the believers, just before the great and terrible "Day of the Lord" judgment.

THE INEVITABLE PERSECUTION

PROBLEM FOURTEEN
The hope of Pre-Trib is escapism, denying the possibility of persecution.

2 Timothy 3:12
Indeed, all who desire to live godly in Christ Jesus **will be persecuted**.

Philippians 3:10
That I may know Him, and the power of His resurrection,
and **the fellowship of His sufferings**, being conformed even to His death.

Romans 8:35
Who will separate us from the love of Christ? **Will tribulation,** or distress, or persecution,
or famine, or nakedness, or peril, or sword?

Matthew 5:10
"Blessed are those who have been persecuted **for the sake of righteousness,** for theirs is the
kingdom of heaven.

> ***"will tribulation"*** *- Suffering and persecution are built into the doctrine of conforming
> to the image of Christ. And yet, the present day church is GUILTY of ignoring the reality
> of suffering for our faith. We are so inculcated <u>FOR</u> comfort and so inoculated
> <u>AGAINST</u> suffering that we do not even preach and pray about persecution in other
> countries. The Greek word for tribulation is 'thilipsis" which means pressure. The an-
> cient practice was to place a heavy stone upon the chest of the victim until the pressure
> of the stone literally suffocated him. Is it possible that Paul's use of the word
> 'tribulation' in this passage is not just a generic use of the word pressure, but possibly a
> clue that points to the Great Tribulation, a time in which families will turn against each
> other and governments will begin to openly punish believers?*

How Long Will You Refrain O Lord?

PROBLEM FIFTEEN
The Martyrs Knew that the Period of Wrath was yet to Come.

Rev 6:9 When the Lamb broke the fifth seal, I saw underneath the altar the souls of those who had been slain because of the word of God, and because of the testimony which they had maintained;

Rev 6:10 and they cried out with a loud voice, saying, "How long, O Lord, holy and true, will You refrain from judging and avenging our blood on those who dwell on the earth?"

Rev 6:11 And there was given to each of them a white robe; and they were told that they should **rest for a little while longer**, until the number of their fellow servants and their brethren who were to be killed even as they had been, would be completed also.

Pre-Wrath theology teaches that the fourth and fifth seals are the time we call Tribulation. The fourth seal pours out unprecedented death upon the earth. Scripture says the Lamb broke the seal and authority was given to kill one-fourth of the earth. The Pre-Tribulation Rapture movement must face the reality that God is giving authority to Satan for 42 months to exact his own version of wrath upon planet earth and the select inhabitants called Jews and Christians. The fifth seal is the result of the fourth seal. If the population by this time is 8 billion people then Satan will successfully destroy 2 billion people. Incredible! That is the total population of South Asia today. It is also the total population of Christianity around the world. But Satan will not take out all of Christianity. There are two churches that will receive crowns for their faithfulness. God will protect the Philadelphia Church, and the Smyrna Church will join those saints of all the ages who have given their lives for the gospel of Christ. It is the Smyrna Church that asks God the question, "How long will you refrain from avenging our blood"? The only explanation for this question is that the Wrath of God has not yet come. And since we know that the children of God will not face God's wrath, we must conclude that Tribulation and Wrath are NOT the same. Notice also that verse 11 says these martyred saints must wait until the completion of their fellow saints and additional martyrs are translated as well. "The number" of fellow saints in this passage, must, by good hermeneutical practice, be the raptured saints, waiting for the sun to be darkened and the light of Christ to flood the skies.

ELIJAH WILL COME FIRST

PROBLEM SIXTEEN
If Elijah is One of the Two Witnesses, then the Rapture Cannot be Pre-Trib.

Mal 4:2 "But for you who fear My name, the sun of righteousness will rise with healing in its wings; and you will go forth and skip about like calves from the stall.

Mal 4:3 "You will tread down the wicked, for they will be ashes under the soles of your feet on the day which I am preparing," says the LORD of hosts.

Mal 4:4 "Remember the law of Moses My servant, *even the* statutes and ordinances which I commanded him in Horeb for all Israel.

Mal 4:5 "Behold, **I am going to send you Elijah** the prophet before the coming of the great and terrible day of the LORD.

Mal 4:6 "He will restore the hearts of the fathers to their children and the hearts of the children to their fathers, so that I will not come and smite the land with a curse."

For 3500 years, the Jewish people have been faithful to God in at least one regard: They have celebrated the Passover Seder as God directed them to do. After 70 ad, the ceremony changed slightly. From that point forward, the rabbis successfully modified the family seder to include three important elements. 1) The family would leave one chair vacant in the hopes that Elijah would honor them with a visit. 2) The family would set the table with one cup of wine reserved for Elijah. 3) At the appointed time, all the children would go to the door and call out for Elijah - always hoping that Elijah the prophet would miraculously step into the room, thus fulfilling this verse of prophetic scripture.

If Elijah is indeed one of the two witnesses, he will appear promptly on the first day of the second half of the seventieth week - and then minister to the Jewish people for exactly 3.5 years. If Pre-Trib believes that "the great and terrible day of the Lord" is seven years in length, then Elijah must precede the rapture event, therefore nullifying the imminent return of Christ. According to Pre-Wrath, Elijah will come at the beginning of Tribulation, to warn the Jewish people of the impending doom of the wrath of God which is yet to come.

THE PERSEVERANCE OF THE SAINTS

PROBLEM SEVENTEEN
Perseverance Implies Tribulation.

Rev 13:10 If anyone is destined for captivity, to captivity he goes; if anyone kills with the sword, with the sword he must be killed. **Here is the perseverance and the faith of the saints.**

Rev 14:12 **Here is the perseverance of the saints** who keep the commandments of God and their faith in Jesus.

> *Verse 13:10 reads like some kind of riddle. In reality, the verse is very simple. The believers who live during the tribulation period must be prepared **for captivity.** This means imprisonment of some kind. Perhaps it means becoming a slave for some form of forced labor: farm work or road work or clean up crews. Perhaps it means singling out a pastor or well known community leader and subjecting them to tremendous torture, in order to scare the rest of the community into submission. Or maybe solitary confinement is used for the fathers of each family in order to break the will of the children. Whatever the penalty for being a Christian in those days, this verse affirms that captivity is not the result of God withdrawing his love and protection. On the contrary, like those persecuted through the ages, it is God's promise of drawing close to you in the midst of fiery trials.*

1Pe 4:12 *Beloved, do not be surprised at the fiery ordeal among you, which comes upon you for your testing, as though some strange thing were happening to you;*
1Pe 4:13 *but to the degree that you share the sufferings of Christ, keep on rejoicing, so that also at the revelation of His glory you may rejoice with exultation.*
1Pe 4:14 *If you are reviled for the name of Christ, you are blessed, because the Spirit of glory and of God rests on you.*

> **with the sword he must be killed.**   *This is a reminder to believers that a Christian militia is not the way to counter the assault of the Anti-Christ. If we believe in capital punishment now, we must believe in it then. We are not to engage in all-out warfare against the forces of evil. Trust in Jesus and let him fight your battles for you.*

> **the perseverance.**   *Though the Pre-Trib movement will argue this is the left-behind believers who belatedly accepted Christ, an honest evaluation of this and other passages consistently points to the present day community of faith who must either face capture or experience death for the cause of Christ. The Greek root for perseverance, 'hupomeno' means to 'remain under', implying that we have been called, in the last days, to remain under threat of persecution, until Christ rescues us. See Daniel 3:17,18.*

The Hour of Testing

PROBLEM EIGHTEEN
Testing is an opportunity to display our trust in God.

Rev 3:10 'Because you have kept the word of My perseverance, I also will keep you from **the hour of testing**, that hour which is about to come upon the whole world, to test those who dwell on the earth.

> *the hour of testing.* *This is the highly contested phrase used by Pre-Trib rapture to prove that believers will not go through the Tribulation. The phrase "keep you from" can also be translated "keep you through" the hour of testing. It is very possible that this verse does promise the Church of Philadelphia to be strong and faithful, and "hunker down" until the storm passes over. It is very possible that miraculous events will precede those who stand strong for Jesus: It is possible that at the moment you exhibit unflinching courage in the face of the enemy, God may well miraculously cause the enemy to flee. Or, you stand strong and faithful as you stare down a firing squad, and suddenly, miraculously, the bullets bounce off your chest and the enemy flees. During this hour of testing, the focus should be on God, not on us.*

> *Perhaps the song from Andrae Crouch gives us encouragement for dark days ahead.*

> *"I've had many tears and sorrows, I've had questions for tomorrow,*
> *there's been times I didn't know right from wrong.*
> *But in every situation, God gave me blessed consolation,*
> *that my trials come to only make me strong.*

> *Through it all, through it all, I've learned to trust in Jesus, I've learned to trust in God.*
> *Through it all, through it all, I've learned to depend upon His Word.*

> *I've been to lots of places, I've seen a lot of faces,*
> *there's been times I felt so all alone.*
> *But in my lonely hours, yes, those precious lonely hours,*
> *Jesus lets me know that I was His own.*

> *I thank God for the mountains, and I thank Him for the valleys,*
> *I thank Him for the storms He brought me through.*
> *For if I'd never had a problem, I wouldn't know God could solve them,*
> *I'd never know what faith in God could do."*

> *Through it all, through it all, I've learned to trust in Jesus, I've learned to trust in God.*
> *Through it all, through it all, I've learned to depend upon His Word.*

THE JEWISH WEDDING

PROBLEM NINETEEN
The Jewish Wedding is a Model for the Pre-Wrath Rapture.

I believe that every young Christian should watch two movies as part of his or her training as a follower of Jesus. The first is *"The Ten Commandments",* which tells the story of Israel's exodus from the bondage of Egypt. The second is *"Fiddler on the Roof",* which tells the story of a Russian Jewish peasant who has three daughters that challenge the traditional values of Jewish marriage. Jesus used Jewish wedding imagery as He refers to Himself as the Bridegroom and to the Church as the Bride of Christ. There are traditionally three parts to the Jewish wedding that are used by believers to interpret Jesus' Second Coming;

> **1) The bride and the groom are betrothed.** In the ancient Jewish culture, the parents of the bride would select the perfect mate for their daughter. We would consider arranged marriages to be primitive and oppressive, but the reality is that kids in the last several generations are not doing a very good job of choosing their mates by themselves. By God's grace and His foreknowledge, we the Church, have been chosen, before the foundations of the world, to be wed to Christ, as His eternal bride. Our salvation becomes our betrothal. 2 Corinthians 11:2 says, " For I am jealous for you with a godly jealousy; for I betrothed you to one husband, so that to Christ I might present you as a pure virgin." The young man contracts with the bride's father and pays a "bride price" to show how much he values his bride. Christ paid the ultimate price for us when He died on Calvary for our sins.

> **2) The groom goes to prepare a house.** In the ancient Jewish culture, after the betrothal, the groom would begin the process of establishing a new home for his future bride. He would either build a new house or he would build an addition to his father's house. This process would sometimes take one to two years, and during this time the betrothed couple were not allowed to see each other. Traditionally, he is busy preparing for their future together. Jesus promised us that He would "go to prepare a place for us." That preparation is taking place now, as Christ prepares our heavenly home. We do not understand the meaning of 'dwelling places' in this life, but at the appointed time, we will not only have a newly resurrected body, but we will also have a new dwelling in our heavenly home. John 14:1-3 says, *"Let not your heart be troubled; you believe in God, believe also in Me. In My Father's house are many dwelling places; if it were not so, I would have told you; for I go to prepare a place for you. If I go and prepare a place for you, I will come again and receive you to Myself, that where I am, there you may be also. "*

3) The bridegroom comes for his bride, takes her to his new home - and they enjoy the marriage supper together.

In the Jewish culture, the Bridegroom and his wedding party would come unannounced to the bride's home - to take her and her wedding party to his new home. Traditionally, this was an evening event, and the bridegroom might show up at midnight, the darkest hour of the night, to take his bride. The bride's wedding party was charged with being ready also, as evidenced by the parable of the ten virgins in Matthew 25. Having your lamps trimmed would be the equivalent of having gas in the car for a long non-stop journey. Matthew 25:5 says, "Now while the bridegroom was delaying, they all got drowsy and began to sleep. 6 **"But at midnight there was a shout, 'Behold, the bridegroom! Come out to meet him.'** At this point, according to the sixth seal in Revelation 6, the sun is darkened, and in a moment of glory, Christ gathers His church to join Him in the heavens. The midnight hour is also interpreted to mean a time when least expected.

The Pre-Trib movement uses the thief in the night illustration to describe the groom's unexpected arrival. They will also make much of the supposed seven days that the couple would enjoy before the invited guests arrive. However, the seven days was a casual and very arbitrary observance that could just as likely have been two weeks in length. The Pre-Trib interpretation says that the "thief in the night" arrival proves the imminent Pre-Trib rapture, and the seven day period symbolically proves the length of seven years, representing the time from the rapture to the Marriage Supper of the Lamb. The proponents of Pre-Tribulation would also disavow any possibility of the bride going through tribulation, based on there being no analogy for a time of distress prior to the wedding.

The Jewish Wedding is a beautiful picture of the spiritual betrothal, preparation and arrival of the groom, and his return to receive His bride, the Church. BUT . . . It is probably a risky interpretation to connect a seven day honeymoon to a seven year Tribulation. The wedding parable should remain just that - a parable. We must not let the weight of scripture be shadowed by a cultural custom.

Jeremiah 33:11
"The voice of joy and the voice of gladness,
the voice of the bridegroom and the voice of the bride,
the voice of those who say, "Give thanks to the LORD of hosts,
For the LORD is good, For His lovingkindness is everlasting".

THE FIERY FURNACE

PROBLEM TWENTY
Perseverance Implies Tribulation.

Dan 3:17 "If it be so, our God whom we serve is able to deliver us from the furnace of blazing fire; and **He will deliver us** out of your hand, O king.

Dan 3:18 **"But even if He does not**, let it be known to you, O king, that we are not going to serve your gods or worship the golden image that you have set up."

———————————

Dan 3:21 Then these men were tied up in their trousers, their coats, their caps and their other clothes, and were cast into the midst of the furnace of blazing fire.

Dan 3:22 For this reason, because the king's command was urgent and the furnace had been made extremely hot, the flame of the fire slew those men who carried up Shadrach, Meshach and Abed-nego.

Dan 3:23 But these three men, Shadrach, Meshach and Abed-nego, fell into the midst of the furnace of blazing fire still tied up.

Dan 3:24 Then Nebuchadnezzar the king was astounded and stood up in haste; he said to his high officials, "Was it not three men we cast bound into the midst of the fire?" They replied to the king, "Certainly, O king."

Dan 3:25 He said, "Look! I see four men loosed and walking about in the midst of the fire without harm, and the appearance of the fourth is like a son of the gods!"

Our heroes in the Christian faith have always been those men and women in the pages of scripture who have stood firm against all odds. Their stories begin as humble, faithful, servants of God, and then they are tested with some incredible, unthinkable threat beyond comprehension. God is good. He rescues them, and elevates their faith to new heights of responsibility and reward.

Whether it be Daniel's friends in the Fiery Furnace or Daniel himself in the Lion's Den, the story is always the same. God either rescues us from persecution, or gives us the supernatural grace to endure persecution for His sake. Either way, God is honored.

*Why is it so hard for us to imagine that God would ask his end-time servants to prove their love for Him by standing strong in their faith, like our biblical heroes? Have you ever considered that perhaps in the days of end-time persecution, another Babylon may throw some of us into a furnace of fire? What kind of supernatural joy would we experience if we watched God protect us from the enemies of darkness! God may have prepared some of us for a "Shadrach" moment, to experience the exhilaration of walking out of a blast furnace, without even a hint of smoke. But, **even if** God chooses for us to serve as martyrs, we are reminded of Daniel 3:18.*

THE MYTHOLOGY OF "LEFT BEHIND"

PROBLEM TWENTY-ONE

Jesus told us to not to follow traditions, but rather, to follow the commandments of God.

Once upon a time . . .

A little row boat left the shores of England in the 1830s with a message nailed to the deck of the boat. The message was about the return of Jesus to the planet earth for the glorious purpose of restoring His kingdom and judging the nations. Now the message of Jesus' return was clear and simple. But there was also a coded commentary that accompanied the message. The coded commentary had to do with the "timing" of Jesus' return. The coded commentary taught that Jesus would return at the end of time and He would snatch up His faithful followers JUST BEFORE A TIME OF GREAT TRIBULATION. Up until that time, people had read about Jesus' return and believed that His followers would experience a severe time of persecution JUST BEFORE THE WRATH OF GOD. The coded commentary on the little boat was different. But it was much more pleasant than the message of persecution.

When the little boat reached the shores of America, the message and its commentary were passed on to a small band of believers. These believers were relieved to find that they would not have to endure the calamitous times of TRIBULATION that the Bible spoke of. They passed the message on to their friends, who passed the message on to their friends. The commentary was still coded and cryptic, and difficult to understand when compared to scripture. But by this time, the coded commentary had become so popular that cruise ships were chartered to teach the coded message. And the cruise ships kept getting larger and larger, and the captains of the largest cruise ships in America were now teaching the coded message. And the cruise ships kept going farther and farther out to sea.

Then one day, a simple man picked up the Bible, and interpreted the return of Jesus the way people had understood it hundreds of years before. He went to the captains of the cruise ships, requesting that they re-evaluate the coded message, but they scoffed at the idea that this simple man, who was not even a ship captain, would dare to challenge the coded message. By this time, the coded message was indelibly written into the official charter of every cruise ship. And the cruise ships were traveling farther and farther out to sea. Then came the time when a Pirate called "the lawless one" began to attack the ships. The people were unprepared for persecution, because the captains told them not to worry.

And it was too late to turn the big ship around.

WHERE IS THE CHURCH AFTER CHAPTER 4?

The Pre-Tribulation network contends that the Church
is not mentioned after Chapter 4. Decide for yourself.

AFTER THE FIFTH SEAL.
Rev 6:10 and they cried out with a loud voice, saying, "How long, O Lord, holy and true, will
You refrain from judging and avenging **our blood** on those who dwell on the earth?"
Rev 6:11 And there was given to each of them a white robe; and they were told that they
should rest for a little while longer, until **the number of their fellow servants and their brethren**
who were to be killed even as they had been, would be completed also.

> *These martyred saints are asking God when the Wrath will begin. "The number of
> their fellow servants and the brethren who were to be killed" seems to imply the
> believers who will face tribulation. Pre-Trib will convince you that the martyred saints
> are the newly left behind in the tribulation - already willing to give their lives for a
> gospel they didn't believe until recently. This is the Church in Chapter Six.*

THE DRAGON ATTACKS ISRAEL AND THE CHURCH.
Rev 12:17 So the dragon was enraged with the woman, and went off to make war with the
rest of her children, who keep the commandments of God and **hold to the testimony of
Jesus.**

> *The context of this verse is clearly the tribulation, and the Church is being persecuted
> after the Anti-Christ has first gone after the Jews. This is the Church in Chapter 12.*

THE ANTI-CHRST BEGINS HIS RULE.
Rev 13:7 It was also given to him to make war with **the saints** and to overcome them, and
authority over every tribe and people and tongue and nation was given to him.
Rev 13:10 If anyone is destined for captivity, to captivity he goes; if anyone kills with the
sword, with the sword he must be killed. Here is the perseverance and the faith **of the saints.**

> *This is clearly the time of the tribulation, likely the midpoint of the seven years. This is
> the Church in Chapter 13.*

REGARDING THE MARK OF THE BEAST.
Rev 14:12 Here is the perseverance **of the saints** who keep the commandments of God and
their faith in Jesus.

> *The saints here clearly identify those who have faith in Jesus. This is the Church in
> Chapter 14.*

Is This a Hill Worth Taking?

On June 6, 1944, the Allied forces of World War II participated in the largest amphibious military invasion in human history. They landed in Normandy, France, under the command of U.S. General Dwight D. Eisenhower. The first day, called D-Day, was so strategic that it was planned for months in advance, and the very mention of the timing of this event at an officers' party cost one major general a demotion and immediate retirement. The invasion began with overnight parachute and glider landings, massive air attacks  and naval bombardments. Five beaches, code-named Utah, Omaha, Gold, Juno and Sword, were the strategic points of amphibious landing. Over 300,000 Allied Forces countered the evil encroachment of Hitler's Nazi warriors, and the Normandy Invasion became the turning point for the U.S. and Allied victory. During that campaign alone, 200,000 Allied forces lost their lives in the process of taking the lives of 300,000 German soldiers. It was the planning and execution of this seminal event that favored the course of western democracy and crushed Hitler's attempt at worldwide totalitarian domination.

What's the point of this story in a book on Revelation? While teaching about the timing of the rapture at my church, my friend Dutch asked a very important question. *"Is this a hill worth taking? Is this a beach worth capturing? Is this just a debate for theologians, or does this really matter to the average Christian who is just trying to live a godly life and understand the Bible?"* My answer to Dutch was a resounding "YES, THIS IS A HILL WORTH TAKING." If the Pre-Trib-

Is the Pre-Wrath Rapture debate a hill worth taking? The answer involves my children and my grandchildren. You bet it is.

ulation rapture is true, then we will all enjoy a pre-emptive trip to glory before the assault of Satan and the Wrath of God. My thesis will be incorrect, and I'll gladly apologize for crying "Wolf!" BUT, if there's even a chance that we will endure the dark days of tribulation, then I want my children and grandchildren to be prepared to face the harsh reality of end-time persecution. And I don't want my pastor friends to wake up on the first day of Birth Pangs or Tribulation and have to explain to their church members why nobody got raptured before the events of Matthew 24. Is this a hill worth taking and a beach worth capturing? You bet it is. This may well become the major theological debate of the 21st Century.

In Summary

Six Major "Holes" in the Pre-Tribulation Argument, with Pre-Wrath Answers.

The Tribulation Period
is not 7 years (Pre-Trib)
but is a period of time
cut short by the Second
Coming of Christ.

The Tribulation Period
Is not the Wrath of God
(Pre-Trib), but should more
appropriately be called
"the wrath of Satan."

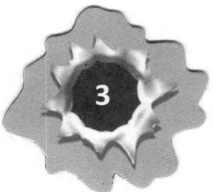

The Rapture occurs,
not before the Tribulation
(Pre-Trib), but before the
trumpet and bowl judgments,
the Wrath of the Lamb.

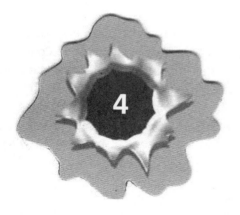

The "glorious appearing"
in Matthew 24:29-31
is not the end of the 7 years,
(Pre-Trib) but rather, it is
the return of Jesus at the 6th seal.

The return of Jesus cannot be
imminent (Pre-Trib), if Elijah,
the apostasy and the man of
lawlessness (2 Thess 2:3)
must come first.

The Rapture cannot be Pre-Trib
since Jesus compared His
Second Coming to the
Deliverance and Judgment passages
(Luke 17:26-30) of Noah and Lot.

FOUR CHALLENGES

to The Leaders of Pre-Tribulation Theology

1. **PASTOR LEADERS MUST BE DOCTRINAL,** and accept the fact that both Pre-Tribulation Rapture and Pre-Wrath Rapture are **NOT** doctrines of the Church. The Second Coming of Christ is the doctrine of the Church. You see, Pre-Tribulational Rapture has become a test of fellowship. It has become a litmus test for determining orthodoxy. Really? You mean something that is so mysterious (the timing of the rapture) and so vaguely defined is going to be a test of fellowship? Pastors, we must enthusiastically preach the second coming of Christ, and we must not allow our speculations and hypotheses to color our feelings about another interpretation of end-time theology.

2. **PASTORAL LEADERS MUST BE OBJECTIVE** in their evaluation of Pre-Tribulation and Pre-Wrath Theology. Objectivity means two things: <u>ALWAYS</u> being biblical and <u>NEVER</u> allowing tradition to legislate your theology. Objectivity is the most unused word in American politics. The American media should covet the privilege of being objective on national television. Pre-tribulationism has become "traditional theology." Jesus warned us to favor the commandments of God over the traditions of men.

3. **PASTORAL LEADERS MUCH BE COURAGEOUS** and willing to take a stand, for the sake of their grandchildren. It is easy for us to defer any controversy over end-time theology until the end-times. But we need to be training our church members and our family members to be prepared for the time when they may be forced to confess their faith in Christ or their faith in another God. The culture I currently live in does not require my confession of faith at the end of a sword. But my grandchildren may face the reality of persecution or death, depending on their ability to stand firm for their faith.

4. **PASTORAL LEADERS MUST RE-TEACH REVELATION.** It's not enough to be a closet Pre-Wrather. Ironically, pastors will find that the re-teaching of Revelation will spark a renewed interest in the Second Coming of Christ because the church members will UNDERSTAND IT like never before. Pastor, they will forgive you now for changing your theology on Pre-Trib. If you wait till later, and you're suddenly faced with the reality of tribulation, they may not forgive you then.

THE IMPLICATIONS

If the Pre-Tribulation Rapture is True.

If the Pre-Tribulation Rapture position is true, Jesus will rescue (rapture) the believers prior to the rise of the Anti-Christ and his dreadful reign of terror on the earth. The earth will be in chaos because millions of people will suddenly vanish from the earth. Pre-Wrath believers will gladly rejoice that they were wrong.

If the Pre-Wrath Rapture is True.

But, IF the Pre-Wrath position is true, believers will be caught off guard by the rise of the Anti-Christ. As wars continue to plague the nation of Israel, there will come a time when the earth will stand at the brink of nuclear holocaust. One man will emerge on the world scene who will forge an alliance between Israel and its enemies. He will then create a three-nation confederacy according to scripture that will galvanize his power throughout the world. At this stage of history, it should be apparent to biblical Christians that they are now inside the dreadful prophetic seventieth week of Daniel.

Christians will begin to ask their pastors what is happening. Suddenly, there is a mysterious world leader that has brokered peace with Israel. A wise pastor will understand what has happened. He must now prepare his people for the inevitable time of tribulation and the mark of the beast. Pastors will be held in contempt by church members who expected they would be gone before the mark of the beast became a reality. The chaos of suppressed freedom and growing discrimination against Christians, coupled with economic instability and job losses will cause the churches to suffer financially and numerically. Crime will increase, personal identities and bank accounts will be so jeopardized that the government will step in to introduce new forms of electronic identity. This new identity will be tied to banking, buying, selling, health care, etc. Then suddenly the new global leader will require allegiance to him or you will be cut off from your debit card. Organized persecution against Jews and Christians will begin, and our children and grandchildren will be completely unprepared, because the interpreters of scripture assured them this day would never come.

Quotes from Great Leaders of the Faith

The following quotes were originally introduced in Dave McPherson's book, "The Rapture Exposed." The overwhelming impact of these collective statements has to give pause to the person who has believed Pre-Trib Rapture all their lives simply because they were not introduced to any other biblical alternative.

"I am absolutely convinced that there will be no rapture before the Tribulation, but that the Church will undoubtedly be called upon to face the Antichrist. "
Oswald J. Smith (Tribulation or Rapture - Which?, p. 2).

"Christians will suffer in the Great Tribulation"
S. I. McMillen (Discern These Times, p. 55).

"There is a cowardly Christianity which still comforts its fainting heart with the hope that there will be a rapture - perhaps today - to catch us away from coming tribulation. "
Leonard Ravenhill (Sodom Had No Bible, p. 94).

"Believers of the last days will be on earth during the so-called 'Great Tribulation' "
J. Sidlow Baxter (Explore the Book, Vol. 6, p. 345).

"There is no convincing reason why John's being 'in the Spirit' and being called into heaven [Revelation 4:1-2] typifies the rapture of the church..."
Merrill C. Tenney: (Interpreting Revelation, p. 141).

"No exegetical justification exists for the arbitrary separation of the 'coming of Christ' and the 'day of the Lord.' It is one 'day of the Lord Jesus Christ' "
Harold J. Ockenga: (Christian Life, February, 1955).

"Paul makes it very clear that the Church will pass through the Great Tribulation"
Duane Edward Spencer: ("Rapture and the Tribulation)

"Soon we, in the Body of Christ, will be confronted by millions of people disillusioned by such false teaching as Pre-Tribulationism."
Pat Brooks: (Hear, O Israel, p. 186).

"Because they (The Philadelphia Church) have been faithful, He promises His sustaining grace in the tribulation."
Ray Summers (Worthy Is the Lamb, p. 123).

"Pretribulationism may be guilty of the positive danger
of leaving the Church unprepared for tribulation when Antichrist appears."
George E. Ladd: (The Blessed Hope, p. 164).

"The Christian Church on earth will face the final,
almost superhuman test of being confronted
with the apocalyptical temptation by Antichrist"
Peter Beyerhaus: (Christianity Today, April 13, 1973).

"He would not spare them from the suffering [Revelation 3:10]
but He would uphold them in it"
John R. W. Stott: (What Christ Thinks of the Church, p. 104).

"As the Church moves to meet her Lord at the parousia
world history is also moving to meet its Judge at the same parousia"
Bernard L. Ramm: (Leo Eddleman's Last Things, p. 41).

"The twentieth century has indeed witnessed a progressively
rising revolt against pre-tribulationism"
J. Barton Payne: (The Imminent Appearing of Christ, p. 38).

"Divine wrath does not blanket the entire seventieth week...
but concentrates at the close"
Robert H. Gundry (The Church and the Tribulation, p. 63).

"Frankly I favor a post-trib rapture.
I no longer teach Christians that they will NOT have to go through the tribulation"
C. S. Lovett (PC, January, 1974).

"Perhaps the Holy Spirit is getting His Church ready
for a trial and tribulation such as the world has never known"
Billy Graham: (Sam Shoemaker's Under New Management, p. 72).

"The Bible prophesies that the time will come when we cannot buy or sell,
unless we bear the sign of the Antichrist..."
Corrie ten Boom: (Tramp for the Lord, p. 187).

Hence we conclude that nowhere in Scripture
does it teach a secret or pre-tribulation Rapture"
Loraine Boettner (The Millennium, p. 168).

"There is not a line of the N.T. that declares a pre-tribulation rapture,
so its advocates are compelled to read it into certain indeterminate texts..."
James R. Graham (Watchman, What of the Night?, p. 79).

"...the time of Antichrist, when days so terrible are still to arrive for the church..."
Herman Hoeksema: (Behold, He Cometh!, p. 31).

"Nowhere do the Scriptures say that the Rapture will precede the Tribulation"
Jim McKeever (Christians Will Go Through the Tribulation, p. 55).

"I think it fair to tell you that I do not subscribe
to the happy and convenient theology
which says that God's people are going to be raptured and lifted up
when a time of tribulation and trial comes"
Arthur Katz: (Reality, p. 8).

Dr. James Merritt, pastor of Cross Pointe Church in Atlanta, and former president of the Southern Baptist Convention, tells the story of his time at Southern Seminary in Louisville, Kentucky. Dale Moody, professor of systematic theology for almost forty years, was a colorful personality on campus. His teaching was passionate and sometimes provocative. His book, *The Word of Truth,* has become a classic in systematic theology. While teaching on the book of Revelation, Dale Moody would confidently stand before the class and challenge them: "I will give $10,000 to anyone who can prove to me the solid biblical basis for the Pre-Tribulation Rapture." Dr. Merritt says no one ever stepped forward to claim the money.

"Belief in a pre-tribulational rapture contradicts all three chapters
in the New Testament that mention the tribulation and the rapture together
(Mark 13:24–27; Matt. 24:26–31; 2 Thess. 2:1–12).
The theory is so biblically bankrupt that the usual defense is made
using three passages that do not even mention a tribulation
(John 14:3; 1 Thess. 4:17; 1 Cor. 15:52).
These are important passages, but they have not had
one word to say about a pre-tribulational rapture.
Pre-tribulationism is biblically bankrupt and does not know it"
Dale Moody
The Word of Truth, 556–7.

"There is not a passage in the New Testament
to support Scofield's (argument for the Pre-Trib Rapture).
The call to John to 'come up here' has reference to mystical ecstasy,
not to a pretribulation rapture"
Dale Moody
(Spirit of the Living God, p. 203).

On October 4, 2015,
South Carolina Governor Nikki Haley
advised residents of her state
that a colossal storm, Hurricane Joaquin,
would soon produce rainfall
resulting in 24" of floodwaters
throughout the state.
Meteorologists predict
this rain was unprecedented
in the history of South Carolina.
Imagine that the Governor
had said, "Don't worry about it.
It's not likely to happen."
You may say the same thing about the Tribulation.

Why Not Be Prepared?

The Rapture Test

1. Read Matthew 24:1-31;

    Would you agree with the following order of verses 1-31:

    A. Beginning of sorrows, birth pangs

    B. Tribulation

    C. Sun will be darkened

    D. Gathering together his elect

2. Would you agree the "gathering together of His elect" sounds like the "rapture"?

3. Read 1 Thessalonians 5:1-9

    Would you agree that those who will be surprised by Christ's return will be unbelievers?

4. Would you agree that we will be raptured before the wrath of God? Read Revelation 6:17. Would you agree that the wrath of God probably follows verse 17?

5. Read 2 Thessalonians 2:1-3. Would you agree the Second Coming and the rapture are spoken of synonymously?

6. Read 2 Thessalonians 2:1-3. Would you agree that the rapture "will not come" until the man of lawlessness is revealed?

7. Read Revelation 7:9-14. Would you agree that it "appears" that the "great multitude which no one could count" just showed up in Heaven?

8. If the "great multitude which no one could count" is used only here in scripture, would you agree that this might be referring to the raptured saints of all history?

9. Read 2 Timothy 3:12 and Philippians 3:10. Would you agree that Christ has called us to a life of persecution, even a destiny of death?

10. Read Matthew 24:30 and 31. Would you agree that it "appears" tribulation and cosmic disturbance precede the Second Coming of Christ?

Conclusion:

If you answered "yes" to most of these questions,

then you have confirmed that the rapture does NOT precede the tribulation,

therefore calling into question the validity of the position called

"The Pre-Tribulation Rapture."

Continue to search the scriptures and pray that God
will give you insight to understand.

————————————

"To preach rapture before
the consummate battle of the ages is to suggest,
in military terms, being absent without leave (AWOL).
And somehow, however well intended,
men have justified that absence.
The faithful soldier volunteers for the front lines,
even when he could be permitted to stay behind.
To tell the Church that it will not be present
during a significant part of the seventieth
week of Daniel is to court disaster."

MARV ROSENTHAL
"The Pre-Wrath Rapture of the Church"

EVANGELICALS HIDE THEIR HEADS IN THE SAND

This is an actual picture of an ostrich with its head in the sand. Why do they do that? Because they bury their eggs for protection, and several times a day, they turn the eggs over to nurture the process of hatching. The good thing is that they are taking care of the family. The bad thing is they are momentarily ignoring the world around them, and totally vulnerable to attack from the enemy.

We Christians, on the other hand, have no reason or excuse for putting our heads in the sand. We use this picture as a symbol for ignoring a problem. Is the evangelical Christian community guilty of ignoring a very important principle of prophetic interpretation? Yes. We as evangelicals stand strong with conviction on the principle of scriptural accuracy. We claim to hold to a 'high view' of scripture, which requires diligent study and debate to determine the "orthodox" interpretation which most accurately reflects the very heart of God in the reading of The Word. So why is it, in the matter of interpreting the Second Coming, that we shut down the channels of open discourse related to the Rapture? I think the reason can be found in the following words . . .

SENTIMENTALITY VERSUS OBJECTIVITY

Sentimentality is a great thing in a romance. It is a wonderful way to relate to our children and our friends and our families. To be sentimental at Valentine's Day is a good thing. Even being sentimental at Christmas, for fond memories of special times is a good thing. However, being sentimental about the return of Jesus just because we don't want to go through Tribulation is not scriptural. It is not objective, and it leaves us open and vulnerable, like the ostrich, for an attack from the enemy. I encounter many people whose theology of the Second Coming is wrapped up in the simple idea that they just WANT Jesus to snatch us out of here before the dark days of Tribulation descend on us - even if it is not scriptural. Jesus was not a sentimentalist. He wants us to love Him at the risk of consequence. He told us to prepare for persecution. He blessed those who would dare to give their lives, their safety, their security for the sake of the gospel. It is time the evangelical community opens the door of dialogue to discuss the 'possibility' that the Pre-Wrath interpretation of the Second Coming is an accurate means of understanding the return of Jesus. Jesus doesn't want sentimentality. He wants us to be faithful soldiers, who are prepared to stand strong for Him in the last days, before He calls us home.

BUT WHAT ABOUT DAVID JEREMIAH?

Dr. David Jeremiah is one of my heroes in the Christian ministry. As the senior pastor of the Shadow Mountain Community Church, and a popular televangelist/author, Jeremiah provides a solid, balanced diet of sound scriptural doctrine every week to his local mega-church, as well as his worldwide audience.

So, Gordon Lawrence, how do you explain, or justify your difference of opinion with Jeremiah, and even more, how do you justify influencing the Christian community to ignore Jeremiah's teaching on the Pre-Trib Rapture in favor of your minority interpretation of the Pre-Wrath Rapture?

Good question. I often ask myself the same thing. As stated on page 19, I grew up in a conservative, evangelical church that taught the authoritative, inerrant interpretation of the holy scriptures. First of all, a Pre-Wrath Rapture view is not a liberal interpretation of eschatology. Secondly, I have always been taught to read the scriptures and allow the Holy Spirit of God to breath the inspiration of truth into my reading. That's one of the exciting things about scripture. God gives different insight to different people at different periods of time - not disconsonant, contradictory views - but always in perfect concert with God's revelation. Just like spiritual gifts, 1 Corinthians 12:11 says: *"But one and the same Spirit works all these things, distributing to each one individually just as He wills."*

The progressive revelation of God continues to unfold before our very eyes. Before 1948, most pastors thought that the Church was the total and absolute replacement for Israel. During the 1970's most pastors thought the New Age movement would be the one-world religion. In the past 30 years, the emergence of the European Union was the sure-fire, undisputed embodiment of the Ten Nation Confederacy. God continues to reveal His mysterious plan to us in small doses, and we interpret based on our limited worldview.

Pastors are men of conviction. They study, they listen, they absorb - until one day they lock into a position with unwavering conviction. Dr. Jeremiah "locked" into his position many years ago. It is very hard for international personalities to modify their position when confronted with new insight. I once heard John MacArthur say, *"Everyone's theology is flawed, including mine. If I knew where it was flawed I would change it."* Like the noble Bereans in Acts 17:11, we are to search the scriptures EAGERLY to determine the truth. It is my prayer for those who embrace Pre-Tribulation theology, that they remain O P E N to the possibility that Jesus has called us to a future that may include persecution under the worldwide scourge of the man of lawlessness. With all due respect to the Pre-Tribulation movement, I will continue to challenge them to loosen the bonds of tradition long enough to engage in meaningful dialogue about the Second Coming of the Lord Jesus.

"Although the seals will be
a time of turmoil and great pain,
these trials will be within the realm of
natural phenomena, such as war,
persecution and famine.
It is only during the cosmic
disturbances of the sixth seal
that people will realize
that something out of the ordinary
is happening."

H.L. NIGRO (Heidi Walker)
"Before God's Wrath"

4

THE WRATH OF GOD BEGINS

"The Day of the Lord"

Rom 1:18 For the wrath of God is revealed from heaven against all ungodliness and unrighteousness of men who suppress the truth in unrighteousness,

Rom 1:19 because that which is known about God is evident within them; for God made it evident to them.

Rom 1:20 For since the creation of the world His invisible attributes, His eternal power and divine nature, have been clearly seen, being understood through what has been made, so that they are without excuse.

Rom 1:21 For even though they knew God, they did not honor Him as God or give thanks, but they became futile in their speculations, and their foolish heart was darkened.

Rom 1:22 Professing to be wise, they became fools.

It's not like God didn't warn us.

"As seen repeatedly,
In the Old and New Testaments,
The Day of the Lord will see
the unleashing of God's wrath
on the wicked world,
in a final, total and climactic way.
Although this is the unequivocal
teaching of Scripture,
many today, even in the Church,
are unwilling to accept the reality
of God's wrath."

THE SIGN
Robert Van Kampen

THE WRATH OF GOD

THE BASIC ELEMENTS

1. The Wrath of God begins in Chapter 8, immediately after the silence in heaven, and with the commencement of the seven trumpet judgments.

2. The sequence of The Wrath of God begins with trumpet judgments, then bowl judgments and concludes with the Battle of Armageddon.

3. The Wrath of God is totally distinct from the preceding Tribulation Period, which is actually the Wrath of Satan.

4. We know from 1 Thessalonians 5:9 that Christians are not destined for wrath. The major arguments are: <u>When does </u>the wrath of God begin and <u>how long </u>will it be?

5. The Day of the Lord begins with the sixth seal, which inaugurates the return of Christ at the Gathering of the Elect (the rapture). Then comes the Wrath of God.

THE OUTLINE OF GOD'S WRATH

I. The Trumpet Judgments

    A. Silence in Heaven and the First Four Trumpet Judgments (Revelation 8)
    B. Trumpet Judgments Five and Six (Revelation 9)
    C. Seventh Trumpet (Revelation 11:15)

II. The Bowl Judgments   **(Part of the Day of Atonement)**

    A. The Angels with the seven bowls of plagues. (Revelation 15:6)
    B. Bowl Judgment 1 through 7. (Revelation 16)

III. The Battle of Armageddon   **(Part of the Day of Atonement)**

    A. Revelation 19:11

ANTHOLOGY OF WRATH

The word 'wrath' is referenced 183 times in scripture, (compared to the word tribulation, used 16 times). In the Old Testament, the primary Hebrew word is "chemah", and it is pronounced 'hema', which sounds like (but is unrelated to) the Greek root for blood.) So when you think of God's wrath, think of blood. Think of the blood that has been spilt throughout the generations because of sin. Think of the blood that will someday be spilt when God pours out His final wrath on mankind. And think of the blood that was shed by Jesus for your sins and mine. The definition of the word 'wrath' is chilling. It means 'rage, burning anger, fury - a venomous or poisonous indignation." There is no word in scripture that communicates God's anger like the word wrath. In the New Testament, the Greek word for wrath is 'or-gay', and is mentioned 37 times. John the Baptist used the term to describe the penalty facing the Pharisees, whom he called 'a brood of vipers.' Jesus used the term only once to describe the penalty that Jerusalem faced in the last days.

1. GOD'S ANGER BURNED AGAINST ISRAEL, CAUSING THE BABYLONIAN CAPTIVITY.

Ezr 5:12 'But because our fathers had **provoked the God of heaven to wrath**, He gave them into the hand of Nebuchadnezzar king of Babylon, the Chaldean, who destroyed this temple and deported the people to Babylon.

Lam 4:11 The LORD has accomplished His wrath, He has poured out His fierce anger; And He has kindled a fire in Zion Which has consumed its foundations.

Jer 7:20 Therefore thus says the Lord GOD, "**Behold, My anger and My wrath** will be poured out on this place, on man and on beast and on the trees of the field and on the fruit of the ground; and it will burn and not be quenched."

Jer 10:25 Pour out Your wrath on the nations that do not know You And on the families that do not call Your name; For they have devoured Jacob; They have devoured him and consumed him And have laid waste his habitation.

2. GOD'S ANGER WILL BURN AGAINST PAGAN NATIONS.

Psa 79:6 **Pour out Your wrath upon the nations** which do not know You, And upon the kingdoms which do not call upon Your name.

Eze 20:33 "As I live," declares the Lord GOD, "surely with a mighty hand and with an outstretched arm and with wrath poured out, I shall be king over you.

Zep 1:15 **A day of wrath is that day,** A day of trouble and distress, A day of destruction and desolation, A day of darkness and gloom, A day of clouds and thick darkness,

Joh 3:36 "He who believes in the Son has eternal life; but he who does not obey the Son will not see life, **but the wrath of God abides on him."**

286

3. GOD'S ANGER BURNS AGAINST THE PRESENT AGE OF UNBELIEVERS.

Rom 1:18 For the wrath of God is revealed from heaven against all ungodliness and unright-eousness of men who suppress the truth in unrighteousness.

Eph 5:6 Let no one deceive you with empty words, for because of these things **the wrath of God comes upon the sons of disobedience.**

4. GOD'S CHILDREN WILL NOT EXPERIENCE THE WRATH OF GOD.

1Th 1:10 and to wait for His Son from heaven, whom He raised from the dead, *that is* Jesus, **who rescues us from the wrath to come.**

1Th 5:9 **For God has not destined us for wrath**, but for obtaining salvation through our Lord Jesus Christ,

Rev 6:16 and they said to the mountains and to the rocks, "Fall on us and hide us from the presence of Him who sits on the throne, and from **the wrath of the Lamb;**

Rev 6:17 for the great day of their wrath has come, and who is able to stand?"

Rev 19:15 From His mouth comes a sharp sword, so that with it He may strike down the nations, and He will rule them with a rod of iron; and He treads **the wine press of the fierce wrath of God, the Almighty.**

In the movie, "Tombstone" (Kurt Russell, Val Kllmer, Sam Sheppard) Wyatt Earp's brother has just been killed by a ruthless band of outlaws. In the midst of a furious shootout, one of Wyatt's men turns to Doc Holliday and says, "Wyatt will not be satisfied till he has revenge." Doc Holliday turns to him and says, "He doesn't want revenge. He wants a 'reckoning.' "

Perhaps the word 'reckoning' best describes the wrath of God. Human history is closing up shop. God has faithfully allowed mankind for thousands of years to spit in His face - over and over again. He gave to man the gift of the creation of nature, and the inspiration of scripture, and the illumination of the Spirit and the salvation through Jesus. He gave to man the reconciliation of the Church. And still the unregenerate man did not repent.

It is vitally important to understand the difference between the wrath of Satan (which is called Tribulation) - and the wrath of God (which is called The Day of the Lord.) Jesus' analogy of birth helps us understand this process.

Birth pangs	Contractions	Hard Labor	Birth
Seals 1-3	Seals 4-5	Trumpet and Bowl Judgments	The Millennium
	Wrath of Satan	Wrath of God	

287

THE DAY OF THE LORD

Isaiah says, "Wail, for the day of the LORD is near." Ezekiel says, "It is a time of doom for the nations." Zephaniah says, "All the earth will be devoured in the fire of His jealousy." Amos says, "Will not the day of the LORD be darkness instead of light?"

Zep 1:2 "I will completely remove all things From the face of the earth," declares the LORD.

Zep 1:3 "I will remove man and beast; I will remove the birds of the sky And the fish of the sea, And the ruins along with the wicked; And I will cut off man from the face of the earth," declares the LORD.

Zep 1:7 Be silent before the Lord GOD! For the day of the LORD is near, For the LORD has prepared a sacrifice, He has consecrated His guests.

Zep 1:14 Near is **the great day of the LORD**, Near and coming very quickly; Listen, the day of the LORD! In it the warrior cries out bitterly.

Zep 1:15 **A day of wrath is that day,** A day of trouble and distress, A day of destruction and desolation, A day of darkness and gloom, A day of clouds and thick darkness,

Zep 1:16 A day of trumpet and battle cry against the fortified cities And the high corner towers.

Zep 1:17 I will bring distress on men So that they will walk like the blind, Because they have sinned against the LORD; And their blood will be poured out like dust And their flesh like dung.

Zep 1:18 Neither their silver nor their gold will be able to deliver them on **the day of the LORD'S wrath;** and all the earth will be devoured In the fire of His jealousy, For He will make a complete end, Indeed a terrifying one, of all the inhabitants of the earth.

> *Set aside for a moment the multiple prophecies by Isaiah, Jeremiah, Ezekiel, Amos, Obadiah, Joel and Malachi. If we only had ONE prophecy from ONE prophet, these words from Zephaniah would clearly define for us the gravity of this cataclysmic time in human history. It is correctly called "The Day of the Lord." Notice Zephaniah's admonition to be silent before the Lord - reminds us of Revelation 8 when the heavenly choir of angels suddenly goes mute in fearful anticipation of the impending wrath of Jehovah God. Based on the reference to "a complete end of all the inhabitants of the earth", it would seem that the only flesh that will be protected is that of the newly saved remnant of Israel and those Gentiles who have been preserved from the wrath.*

Joel 1:14, 15. Consecrate a fast, Proclaim a solemn assembly; Gather the elders *And* all the inhabitants of the land To the house of the LORD your God, And cry out to the LORD. Alas for the day! For the day of the LORD is near, And it will come as **destruction from the Almighty.**

Joel 2:30,31 "I will display wonders in the sky and on the earth, blood, fire and columns of smoke. "The sun will be turned into darkness and the moon into blood before **the great and awesome day of the LORD** comes.

> *In Revelation 6:12-17, the sixth seal sets in motion the darkened sun and the blood moon lunar eclipse. Notice that the word 'wrath' is used twice (v16 and 17), connecting the day of the Lord with the wrath of God, the first mention of wrath in the book of Revelation.*

Mal 4:5 "Behold, I am going to send you Elijah the prophet before the coming of **the great and terrible day of the LORD.**

> *The timing of Elijah's coming is a significant problem for Pre-Tribulation scholarship. If Elijah is one of the Two Witnesses, whose presence is manifested at the beginning of the second half of the seven year period . . . and, the day of the Lord coincides with the sixth seal and the rapture, then it follows that Elijah's presence must pre-empt the rapture of Christ in Matthew 24:31. The implication of this timing impacts Pre-Trib's insistence on the imminent return of Christ.*

Act 2:20 "the sun will be turned into darkness and the moon into blood, before **the great and glorious day of the Lord shall** come.

2 Peter 3:10 But the day of the Lord will come like a thief, in which **the heavens will pass away** with a roar and **the elements will be destroyed** with intense heat, and the earth and its works will be burned up.

> **The heavens will pass away.** *I believe that God will replace the stars and planets with a new palette of atmospheric colors that will make our former sunrises and sunsets look pale in comparison. It is important to understand that the heavens, plural, will be replaced with a single heaven, which apparently will serve the purpose of a colorful canopy over the new earth.*
>
> **The elements will be destroyed.** *There are 98 natural elements in the periodic table and another 20 elements that are artificially produced through the process of radioactive generation. I believe that these elements will be burned from the earth's surface - and replaced with a new form of soil (for instant growth) and a carpet of green grass. No more sandals and no more garden tools.*

AND THERE WAS SILENCE

Silence in this life can be a wonderful thing. Sometimes we call it "quiet time", or meditation, or solitude. Certainly prayer may be the most majestic example of silence on planet earth. In a world gone crazy with noise, it is refreshing to observe the beauty of silence. But . . . the silence spoken of in Revelation 8 is not pleasant, or refreshing. It is a bellwether of doom. It is a harbinger of man's darkest hour. It is a warning to prepare for the Wrath of God. Notice that this silence only occurs in heaven. We don't know exactly what the noise level is on earth. The Church has just been raptured. The kings of the earth have been stunned by the visual image of blinding light emanating from King Jesus. The world may be stunned, but it is also likely to be moaning. Paul Simon records these haunting words in his classic song, "The Sounds of Silence"

"Fools", said I, "You do not know, Silence like a cancer grows
But my words, like silent raindrops fell, And echoed in the wells of silence.
And the people bowed and prayed, To the neon god they made
And the sign flashed out its warning, In the words that it was forming
And the sign said, The words of the prophets are written on the subway walls,
and tenement halls . . . and whispered, in the sounds of silence"

Ezekiel 26:3 says, "So I will silence the sound of your songs, and the sound of your harps will be heard no more." **Amos 8:3 says:** "The songs of the palace will turn to wailing in that day," declares the Lord GOD. "Many will be the corpses; in every place they will cast them forth in silence." **Psalm 115:17 says**: The dead do not praise the LORD, Nor do any who go down into silence;

The beauty of silence has finally been transformed into terror. It is a curious thing to note that heaven will be silent for 30 minutes. The Greek term 'hemi-orion' (half an hour) is used only once in scripture, as might be expected. The angels are not only silent, but they are likely rigid with anticipation, bracing themselves for an unparalleled battle of epic proportion. We can only imagine that there were two other events in the Bible that caused the hosts of heaven to be muted and standing in silent attention. The first was the Flood, when God repented of watching man spiral downward into depravity. The other was the Crucifixion, when God's teardrop fell to earth ("The Passion of the Christ") and rocked the world with earthquakes. But this third cataclysmic event signals the end - the end of beauty, the end of joy, the end once more, of God's relentless mercy. We don't know how long the wrath of God will persist, but we do know that there will be "no holds barred" when God's wrath descends on a demonically inspired army of unbelievers. All the war movies of cinema history cannot begin to tell the sordid tale of man's last defiant attempt to spit in the face of God.

THE DAY OF THE LORD EVENTS

The Day of the Lord begins at the end of Tribulation (the sixth seal) when the sun, moon and stars signal the appearing of Christ in the sky to gather His Church. Then there is a foreboding time of silence in heaven for 30 minutes, which prepares the heavenly host of angels for the seven trumpet judgments of the Wrath of God. After the sixth trumpet, Christ, the Mighty Angel, descends on land and sea, leading the 144,000 as they collect the tribes of Israel. When Israel climbs the hill to Jerusalem with Messiah, their eyes are opened and they are saved. At the sound of the seventh trumpet, Jesus stands victoriously on Mt. Zion during the Jewish Day of Atonement. He then leads the nation to safety, before God's bowl judgment destroys earth. Jesus then rallies the armies of heaven to crush the demon warriors in the Battle of Armageddon.

1. Cosmic Disturbance (Matthew 24:29)

Revelation 6 identifies this as the sixth seal.

2. The Gathering (Matthew 24:30,31)

The raptured saints have just arrived in heaven in Chapter 7, after the sixth seal.

3. Silence in Heaven, Trumpets (Revelation 8:1,2)

The trumpets are the warning alarm. There is still time to repent.

4. The Mighty Angel (Revelation 10:1,2)

He holds in His hand the open scroll of Israel's destiny.

5. Jesus on Mt. Zion (Revelation 14:1)

Christ has finally taken back the title deed to planet earth.

6. The Bowl Judgments (Revelation 16:1)

It is too late for repentance. The potter will soon crush the clay pot and start over.

7. Armageddon (Revelation 19:11)

The armies of heaven will most likely fight the demon possessed souls of men.

THE FIRST FOUR TRUMPETS OF WRATH

REVELATION CHAPTER 8

SILENCE IN HEAVEN.

Rev 8:1 When the Lamb broke the seventh seal, there was **silence in heaven** for about half an hour.

Rev 8:2 And I saw the seven angels who stand before God, and seven trumpets were given to them.

Rev 8:3 Another angel came and stood at the altar, holding a golden censer; and much incense was given to him, so that he might add it to **the prayers of all the saints** on the golden altar which was before the throne.

Rev 8:4 And the smoke of the incense, with the prayers of the saints, went up before God out of the angel's hand.

Rev 8:5 Then the angel took the censer and filled it with the fire of the altar, and threw it to the earth; and there followed peals of thunder and sounds and flashes of lightning and an earthquake.

Rev 8:6 And the seven angels who had the seven trumpets prepared themselves to sound them.

> ***Silence in heaven*** *- The combined choir of raptured saints and a billion angels are locked in mute anticipation as final preparation begins for the Wrath of God to descend upon Planet Earth. Thirty minutes is a long time for all of creation to remain completely silent. Since the beginning of time, Heaven has always been full of thunderous and joyous celebration focused on the majesty of God the Father, the atoning work of Christ the Son and the power and passion inspired by God the Spirit. For the first time and only time in God's eternity, there is deadly silence.*

> ***Prayers of all the saints*** *- The term 'soothing aroma' is used 42 times in the Old Testament to describe an act of worship to the Lord. In this passage, a very intangible, spiritual act of prayer appears to have a literal, physical application when collected by the angels for the purpose of honoring God. It is interesting to note that the Hebrew word for soothing aroma is 'riach', which is a derivative of 'ruach', the term for wind or breath. The term ruach kodesh means 'holy spirit'. This is a beautiful picture of the reciprocal relationship between a worshipper and the Holy Spirit. When we give off the aroma (riach) of worship, the Holy Sprit breathes blessing upon us. And when we are filled with the Holy Spirit, there is a spontaneous, reciprocal sense of fragrance (2 Corinthians 2:15) that exudes from our spirits that blesses the Lord.*

THE WRAT OF GOD BEGINS.

Rev 8:7 **The first angel** sounded, and there came hail and fire, mixed with blood, and they were thrown to the earth; and a third of the earth was burned up, and a third of the trees were burned up, and all the green grass was burned up.

Rev 8:8 **The second angel** sounded, and something like a great mountain burning with fire was thrown into the sea; and a third of the sea became blood,

Rev 8:9 and a third of the creatures which were in the sea and had life, died; and a third of the ships were destroyed.

Rev 8:10 **The third angel** sounded, and a great star fell from heaven, burning like a torch, and it fell on a third of the rivers and on the springs of waters.

Rev 8:11 The name of the star is called Wormwood; and a third of the waters became wormwood, and many men died from the waters, because they were made bitter.

Rev 8:12 **The fourth angel** sounded, and a third of the sun and a third of the moon and a third of the stars were struck, so that a third of them would be darkened and the day would not shine for a third of it, and the night in the same way.

Rev 8:13 Then I looked, and I heard an eagle flying in midheaven, saying with a loud voice, "Woe, woe, woe to those who dwell on the earth, because of the remaining blasts of the trumpet of the three angels who are about to sound!"

The First Angel - The world has 57 million square miles of land area and 140 million miles of oceans. Asia represents 30% of the land mass, Africa and South America represents 32% and all the other continents represent the other 38%.   The implications of no trees or grass in any one of these areas would set in motion an unprecedented crisis of erosion creating an actual "scorched earth." If the hail follows the fire, we would witness whole continents experiencing landslides and flooding. The result would be the loss of all things born of nature.

The Second Angel - A great mountain of burning fire sounds like a fiery meteor suddenly entering the atmosphere which causes 1/3 of the sea (the equivalent of the entire land mass of the earth) to poison the sea with blood. The resultant stench of 1/3 of all oceans creatures would be a smell so repulsive that mankind could not hide from the residual odor.

The Third Angel - Man can live only about 3 days without water. Assuming that Wormwood fell in a concentrated area, and that Wormwood was bitter to the point of death, the implication is that 1/3 of mankind would quickly die of parched tongues and dehydration.

The fourth angel - The implication of this verse is that there is no electricity, no batteries, no fire to provide any kind of light source. Man will be in total and absolute darkness for 8 hours per day, in addition to another 8 hours without the moon at night. This would seem to leave 4 hours of sunlit day and 4 hours of moonlit night that man could scurry about to try to survive.

FIFTH AND SIXTH TRUMPETS OF WRATH

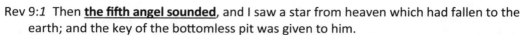

REVELATION CHAPTER 9

THE FIFTH ANGEL SOUNDS THE TORMENT OF A SCORPION

Rev 9:*1* Then **the fifth angel sounded**, and I saw a star from heaven which had fallen to the earth; and the key of the bottomless pit was given to him.

Rev 9:2 He opened the bottomless pit, and smoke went up out of the pit, like the smoke of a great furnace; and the sun and the air were darkened by the smoke of the pit.

Rev 9:3 Then out of the smoke came **locusts upon the earth**, and power was given them, as the scorpions of the earth have power.

Rev 9:4 They were told not to hurt the grass of the earth, nor any green thing, nor any tree, but only the men who do not have the seal of God on their foreheads.

Rev 9:5 And they were not permitted to kill anyone, but **to torment for five months**; and their torment was like the torment of a scorpion when it stings a man.

Rev 9:6 And in those days **men will seek death and will not find it**; they will long to die, and death flees from them.

Rev 9:7 The appearance of the locusts was like horses prepared for battle; and on their heads appeared to be crowns like gold, and their faces were like the faces of men.

Rev 9:8 They had hair like the hair of women, and their teeth were like the teeth of lions.

Rev 9:9 They had breastplates like breastplates of iron; and the sound of their wings was like the sound of chariots, of many horses rushing to battle.

Rev 9:10 They have tails like scorpions, and stings; and in their tails is their power to hurt men for five months.

Rev 9:11 They have as king over them, the angel of the abyss; his name in Hebrew is **Abaddon**, and in the Greek he has the name Apollyon.

Rev 9:12 **The first woe is past**; behold, two woes are still coming after these things.

> *locusts upon the earth.* Some end-time symbolism has tried to make helicopters out of locusts. This should be taken as a literal reference to a devastating predator.
>
> *to torment for five months.* This is the only reference to a length of time in either the tribulation or the Wrath of God.
>
> *Abaddon, the angel of the abyss, emerges from the bottomless pit of Hell with a host of demonic creatures that resemble locusts ravaging the countryside. These demon-possessed locusts sting like scorpions and this plague lasts for five full months. The intent of this pain is torture, to cause the rebellious victim to turn to God for deliverance. No doubt if these stings can be felt on earth, they can also be a sign of the eternal torment of Hell itself.*
>
> *The first woe is past.* The second woe is found in Rev 11:14.

Rev 9:13 Then **the sixth angel sounded**, and I heard a voice from the four horns of the golden altar which is before God,

Rev 9:14 one saying to the sixth angel who had the trumpet, "Release the four angels who are bound at the **great river Euphrates."**

Rev 9:15 And the four angels, who had been prepared for the hour and day and month and year, were released, so that they would kill **a third of mankind.**

Rev 9:16 The number of the armies of the horsemen was **two hundred million**; I heard the number of them.

Rev 9:17 And this is how I saw in the vision the horses and those who sat on them: the riders had breastplates the color of fire and of hyacinth and of brimstone; and the heads of the horses are like the heads of lions; and out of their mouths proceed fire and smoke and brimstone.

Rev 9:18 **A third of mankind** was killed by these three plagues, by the fire and the smoke and the brimstone which proceeded out of their mouths.

Rev 9:19 For the power of the horses is in their mouths and in their tails; for their tails are like serpents and have heads, and with them they do harm.

Rev 9:20 The rest of mankind, who were not killed by these plagues, did not repent of the works of their hands, so as not to worship demons, and the idols of gold and of silver and of brass and of stone and of wood, which can neither see nor hear nor walk;

Rev 9:21 and **they did not repent** of their murders nor of their sorceries nor of their immorality nor of their thefts.

the Great River Euphrates runs from Turkey to the Persian Gulf, a distance of 1700 miles. One of the major disputes of the Middle East today revolves around the "Southeastern Anatolia Development Project", abbreviated in the Turkish language as the "Gap" Project. There are presently 22 hydro-electric dams on the Euphrates. In Revelation 16:12, at the time of the sixth bowl, the Euphrates is dried up to make way for the kings of the east, for the battle of Armageddon.

a third of mankind. See Revelation 6:8. At the fourth seal, God gave authority to the dragon over a fourth of the earth to kill by sword, famine, pestilence and "wild beasts". The remainder of three fourths of the earth, minus the one third taken out by the sixth trumpet, would leave one half of the earth. If the world population in those days is projected at 8 billion people, then as many as 4 billion people would have been killed.

Two hundred million. This verse is often incorrectly connected to the kings of the east in Revelation 16:12. In reality, this is a demonic army released by God's angels to destroy one/third of unrepentant man.

They did not repent. Despite the cosmic disturbances, the return of Christ and the six trumpet judgments, humanity still thumbs their noses at God in open defiance.

THE WORLD POPULATION, 2013

Revelation 6:8 says that the Pale Horse will have authority (from God to Satan) over 1/4 of the earth, to kill with sword, famine, pestilence and wild beasts. Revelation 9:15 says that the sixth trumpet judgment from God will destroy another 1/3 of the earth. One fourth + one third of 75% equals one half, 50% of planet earth. Approximately 4 billion people will die, just from these two events.

ASIA TOTAL	**4.3 BILLION**
Southern	1.75 billion
Eastern	1.62 billion
Southeastern	618 mil
Central	64 mil
AFRICA TOTAL	**1.1 BILLION**
East Africa	373 mil
North	210 mil
Middle	135 mil
South	60 mil
Western	331 mil
AMERICAS TOTAL	**972 MILLION**
South America	406 mil
North America	355 mil
Central America	167 mil
Caribbean	42 mil
EUROPE TOTAL	**743 MILLION**
OCEANICA TOTAL	**38 MILLION**
WORLD TOTAL	**7.162 BILLION**

EARTHQUAKES IN THE LAST DAYS

From 2001 to 2010, there was an annual average of 27,148 earthquakes around the globe, the largest number of which was 31,777 in 2008. The average number of deaths for this 10 year period was 79,096. In 2010, the world experienced a total of 320,000 deaths. Of the following top 10 worldwide earthquakes, the average seismic impact on the Richter Scale was 8.3.

Year	Location	Index	Consequences
1960	Valdivia, Chile	9.5	6,000 deaths, equal to 1000 atomic bombs, felt 435 miles
1956	Shaanxi, China	8.0	830,000 deaths, felt in 97 countries and 520 miles away
2004	Indian Ocean	9.3	225,000 deaths, 5 tsunamis triggered
1138	Aleppo, Syria	8.5	230,000 deaths, equal to a 2.8 gigaton bomb
1976	Tangshan, China	8.2	255,000 deaths, lasted only 10 seconds
1920	Gansu, China	8.5	240,000 deaths, felt 125 miles away, aftershocks for 3 years
2010	Leogane, Haiti	7.0	316,000 deaths, 1 million people left homeless
1927	Xining, China	7.9	40,900 deaths, on the Huangshui River
856	Damghan, Iran	8.0	200,000 deaths, the town Bustam was completely leveled
2011	Tohuku, Japan	9.0	15,878 deaths, 129,000 buildings leveled, 4 nuclear plants

*** *Rev 16:18 And there were flashes of lightning and sounds and peals of thunder; and there was a great earthquake, such as there had not been since man came to be upon the earth, __so great an earthquake was it, and so mighty.__*

*Rev 16:19 The great city was split into three parts,
and the cities of the nations fell.
Babylon the great was remembered before God,
to give her the cup of the wine of His fierce wrath.
Rev 16:20 And every island fled away, and the mountains were not found.*

*** *I like to call this a Richter Scale of 16, (Chapter 16)
a logarithm that was literally 1 million times exponentially
more powerful than the strongest earthquake in all of human history.*

"The Christ who was born at Bethlehem,
walked the dusty shores of Galilee,
hung naked on a cross, was buried,
and has ascended the high hills of glory,
is coming again.
The incarnation without the coronation
would be like east without west.
It would be like an engagement
without a marriage.
We are on a collision course with destiny.
Soon the King will come,
and we cannot afford to be ignorant or indifferent."

Adrian Rogers
"Unveiling the End Times in Our Times."

5

THE DAY OF ATONEMENT

"The Prodigal Comes Home"

Christ descends to earth with one foot on land and one on sea. He appears to the 144,000 as they march from the desert to collect the remnant of Jews who have endured the Tribulation and the Trumpet Judgments. One third of the nation of Israel now looks upon the Messiah and recognizes Him as the crucified Christ, and they experience immediate salvation. Jesus ascends with the 144,000 to the top of Mt. Zion as the seventh trumpet sounds, announcing the coronation of the King. The two witnesses are resurrected, the temple in heaven is opened and the arc of the covenant is revealed. The Mount of Olives splits and the Jews are hidden in Azel while the Bowl Judgments begin, leading to the cosmic battle of the ages, Armageddon.

THE 30 DAY PERIOD - RECLAIMING AUTHORITY

Day One - The Mighty Angel The Strong Angel, the person of Christ, sets foot on land and sea, then appears at Mt Paran (Mt Sinai) on his way to Bozrah to collect the 144,000.

Day Two - The Assembly of Jacob. The nation of Israel is revived from Egypt to Assyria, and from the regions of Petra, where they have been protected for 42 months. They come out of the wilderness to follow the 144,000 - at this point unaware that the leader is Jesus Himself.

Day Three - The Journey of Ascent . The remnant nation is following their Messiah up the Jericho road to Mt Zion, while singing their annual song of ascent, Psalm 118. The Messiah (Rev 14:1) is surrounded by the 144,000. Suddenly the nation of Israel, 5 million in number, looks upon Jesus and they are saved. Like those followers on the road to Emmaus, their eyes were opened.

Day Four - The Two Witnesses are Resurrected.   Moses and Elijah, who died just days before in the streets of Jerusalem, are suddenly resurrected from the dead

Day Five - The Coronation of Jesus.   For thousands of years, the Jews have celebrated the Feast of Tabernacles (the presence of God) five days after the beginning of the Day of Atonement. The seventh trumpet sounds as Jesus and the 144,000 stand on Mt. Zion. The voices in heaven are heard to say: "the kingdom of the world has become the kingdom of our Lord." The temple in heaven is opened and the ark of the covenant is revealed.   A great earthquake destroys a tenth of the city and the Mount of Olives is split in two, providing a path to the hidden place called Azel. While the greatest of trauma is about to happen on planet earth, heaven is about to experience the greatest of joy. Christ returns to Heaven to observe the Bema seat judgment of all the raptured and resurrected believers, and immediately afterwards all of heaven will experience the Marriage Supper of the Lamb.

Day Six to Day 29 - The Seven Bowl Judgments.   The final wrath of God is unleashed on planet earth and its rebellious inhabitants.

Day 30 - The Battle of Armageddon.   Christ and the angelic armies of heaven descend to the plains of Esdraelon, in the valley of Megiddo, to wage war with the forces of Satan.   The Beast and the False Prophet were thrown into the Lake of Fire.

"THE SEVENTY FIVE DAYS OF ATONEMENT

A. The 30 Days of Reclaiming

    Day One: The Mighty Angel and Little Scroll   Rev 10
    Christ Meets the 144,000 at Mt Sinai
    Day Two: Assembling all of Jacob   Micah 2:12,13
    Marching through Petra and Bosrah   Hab 3:3-6, 13, Isa 63:1, Amos 1:1
    The Highway of Holiness   Isa 35:8,10
    Day Three: The Song of Ascent   Psalm 118:1-29; Ob 1:15,17,21
    1/3 of the Nation is Saved   Zech 12:10, Hosea 6:1,2
    Day Four: The Two Witnesses Return   Rev 11:11,12
    Day Five: The 144,000 on Mount Zion   Rev 14:1,-5
    The Seventh Trumpet   Rev 11:15
    The Coronation of King Jesus   Rev 11:15
    The Temple of the Tabernacle is Opened   Rev 15:5-8
    The Ark of the Covenant is Revealed   Rev 11:19
    The Mount of Olive Splits   Zech 14:2-4
    Day Six to 29: The Six Bowls   Rev 16:1
        One - Sores; Two - Blood in the sea;
        Three - Blood in the Rivers;
        Four - Scorching Heat; Five - torment;
        Six - Euphrates; Seventh - Earthquake;
    Day 30: Armageddon   Rev 14:14-20

B. The 45 Days of Restoration   Dan 12:11-13
    The Restoration of Jerusalem, Mt Zion   Isaiah 2:2
    The Restoration of the Nation of Israel   Is 10:20,21; 66: 18-20
    The Restoration of the Gentile Nation   Is 19:24,25; 56:6,7; Mic 7:16,17
    The Restoration of the Temple   Zechariah 6:13
    The Restoration of the Martyrs   Revelation 20:4
    The Restoration of the Sovereignty of Christ   Daniel 7:12-14
        From the Day of Atonement until the Feast of Dedication
        (or Festival of Lights, Hanukkah) there are exactly 75 days.

THE DIARY OF ASHER LEV REUBEN

Age 12.

My name is Asher Lev Reuben. I like my name. Asher Lev means "Happy Heart" in Hebrew. And my last name, Reuben, means that I am a descendent of the firstborn son of Jacob. Today I celebrated my Bar Mitzvah. I am now a "son of the covenant". I have worked very hard to study the Torah in Hebrew. My parents have taught me to love God and to live every day in anticipation that Messiah may come. My father prays every day that I might be one of the chosen warriors of the Messiah. He says that Messiah may come back any day to call the strongest and the noblest in the land of Israel. I want to be worthy of that calling. I am only 12, but I will begin praying that God will keep me pure like his servant Samuel.

Age 20.

I am a member of the Israeli army. Like every son and daughter in Israel I will fight for my country. I remember standing on top of Masada, our mountaintop training center, and crying out with thousands of young men and women: "Masada shall not fall again!" A curious thing has just taken place in the Israeli army. I have been chosen to serve in a new special forces division of the Israeli army. It is a high honor. We are called the Daniel Legion, so named because we are challenged to live the pure life that Daniel lived. I am privileged to be part of the Reuben brigade, named after my ancient descendent. I am told that there will be twelve brigades, comprised of the strongest and the noblest in the land of Israel. I will pray daily to be worthy of this calling.

Age 21.

The Reuben Brigade, like each of the twelve tribes, has just come back from special desert training. It was during this month long event that a wonderful miracle of God happened. All twelve thousand of us were participating in an intense time of prayer and singing, when suddenly, the noise of a mighty wind swirled around us, and a pillar of fire from heaven descended on each of us, and a strange mark was branded onto my forehead, and then oil miraculously poured down my head, and my body was electrified with strength and courage like I have never known before. I realized that I had been anointed by God. And then an awesome angelic warrior descended into our midst and revealed to us God's plan for the end of the age. My father had prayed that I might become one of Messiah's warriors. Each of the twelve brigades, totaling 144,000, would continue to train here at Mt Sinai, and wait for that day when Messiah would reveal Himself. And I will be a soldier in His mighty army.

Age 24.

It was 42 months ago that I was anointed by the angel and marked on my forehead as a warrior in Messiah's army. Today will likely be the most important day of my life. Each of the twelve brigades was commanded to stand in formation facing inward. Suddenly there was a blinding light and a sound like a lion's roar that caused all 144,000 to drop to our knees. When we looked up, our eyes were fixed on the most magnificent man I have ever seen. His face was like the sun, and his feet like pillars of fire. His eyes were like flaming torches and His voice was like the sound of many waters. He spoke. *"I am Y'shua whom you have crucified."* Instantaneously, we knew this was the Messiah, the Christ of the Christian faith that my family and ancestors had rejected so long ago. The Spirit of God convicted us of our sinful nature and we experienced an immediate sense of mourning for the sins of our forefathers which seemed to last for an hour. Finally, when we looked upon Him whom we had pierced, we experienced an overwhelming sense of joy that I have never known before. Today was the day of my salvation. King Jesus gave us our marching orders. We set off to collect the remnant of Israel and travel the King's Highway to the top of Mt. Zion.

Two Days Later.

What a magnificent sight. While singing "the song of ascent" millions of Jews have just looked upon the face of Y'shua and were saved, by grace, through immediate faith.

One Day Later.

My heart is stunned. Moses and Elijah, the two witnesses during the time of Jacob's distress - have just risen from the dead and are now standing next to King Y'shua. The remnant is screaming in wonderful joy at the site of these heroes of the faith.

One Day Later.

I am now standing on Mt. Zion, singing the song known only to Daniel's Legion. And now the heavens have opened and we see the long lost arc of the covenant. My heart cannot contain the joy. But now, a great earthquake has just destroyed a tenth of the city. The Mount of Olives is opening up and Messiah has directed us to follow the path to Azel. My duty now begins. We will now prepare for the final wrath of God, and then, we will watch as Jesus leads the hosts of heaven to fight the war we have all awaited . . . The Battle of Armageddon. Scripture says that I will be among the firstfruits that will become the seed of the Millennium. My father's prayer has been answered.

THE MIGHTY ANGEL

REVELATION CHAPTER 10

THE MIGHTY ANGEL AND THE LITTLE SCROLL.

Rev 10:1 I saw another angel, **a mighty angel** coming down out of heaven, clothed with a cloud; and the rainbow was upon his head, and ***his face was like the sun***, and his feet like pillars of fire;

Rev 10:2 and he had in his hand a little scroll which was open. He placed **his right foot on the sea and his left on the land;**

Rev 10:3 and he cried out with a loud voice, **as when a lion roars**; and when he had cried out, the seven peals of thunder uttered their voices.

Rev 10:4 When **the seven peals of thunder** had spoken, I was about to write; and I heard a voice from heaven saying, "Seal up the things which the seven peals of thunder have spoken and do not write them."

Rev 10:5 Then the angel whom I saw standing on the sea and on the land lifted up his right hand to heaven,

Rev 10:6 **and swore by Him who lives forever and ever**, who created heaven and the things in it, and the earth and things in it, and the sea and the things in it, that there will be delay no longer,

Rev 10:7 but in the days of the voice of the seventh angel, when he is about to sound, then ***the mystery of God is finished,*** as He preached to His servants the prophets.

> ***Mighty Angel.*** *The Greek word 'ischuros' is translated strong or mighty. In this case, the superlative word mighty MUST be used in a transcendent form which clearly communicates the unparalleled nature of Christ the Messiah. In Mark 1:7, John the Baptist describes Jesus as "one who is mightier than I".*
>
> ***His face was like the sun.*** *Throughout scripture (Ezekiel 1:27,28, Daniel 10:5,6, Rev 1:13-16) only Christ is pictured with these transcendent characteristics. Though there are differing views, this mighty angel has the characteristics of the Messiah: a face like the sun, a rainbow surrounding Him, eyes like fire and a voice like a lion. If Jesus was the only person in the universe worthy of opening the big scroll (Rev 5), then it follows that He alone would be able to open the little scroll. It is ironic that the fate of Israel is singularly dependent upon Him.*
>
> ***His right foot on the sea and his left on the land.*** *This interpretation is pure speculation by this author, based on the inspiration of Robert Van Kampen's book, "The Sign." If this verse has any explanation, it would seem plausible that Christ would be recreating the events from the exodus, where Moses crossed the Red Sea (or Sea of Aqaba) and puts his feet on dry land, on his way to Mt. Sinai.*

As when a lion roars. *Proverbs 19:12 says "the king's wrath is like the* *roaring of a lion." In "the Chronicles of Narnia" by C.S. Lewis, the messianic leader of Narnia was a majestic, all-wise and all powerful lion. Note also that Satan, the great counterfeiter, is portrayed in 1 Peter 3:8 as "a roaring lion, seeking someone to devour."*

The seven peals of thunder. *This is one of the great mysteries in the Bible. It is futile to even speculate on what these seven voices of prophecy said. It does not say, seal them till the end of time, as in Daniel. But simply, and shrouded in total mystery, it says, "Seal them up."*

And swore by Him who lives forever. *Seven words. In Daniel 12:7, the man dressed in linen was likely a christophany, an appearance of Christ. We are taught not to swear by heaven or earth. In this case, the mighty angel, Christ himself, swears as only He is allowed.*

The mystery of God is finished. *Scripture refers to the mysteries of Christ, His kingdom, His will, His church, His gospel and His gathering of the saints; the mystery of faith and godliness; the mystery of lawlessness and the woman who rides the beast. But this mystery is Romans 11:25 - the partial hardening of His chosen people, Israel, would end. The time of the Gentiles is about to be over.*

JOHN EATS THE LITTLE SCROLL

Rev 10:8 Then the voice which I heard from heaven, I heard again speaking with me, and saying, "Go, take the scroll which is open in the hand of the angel who stands on the sea and on the land."

Rev 10:9 So I went to the angel, telling him to give me **the little scroll.** And he said to me, "Take it and eat it; **it will make your stomach bitter,** but in your mouth it will be sweet as honey."

Rev 10:10 I took the little scroll out of the angel's hand and ate it, and in my mouth it was sweet as honey; and when I had eaten it, my stomach was made bitter.

Rev 10:11 And they said to me, "You must prophesy again concerning many peoples and nations and tongues and kings."

The little scroll. *The large scroll of Revelation 5 reveals the destiny of unrepentant-mankind; the little scroll reveals the destiny of Israel. Notice that the scroll is open, which indicates that the time for the Mighty Angel to rescue the nation of Israel has come.*

It will make your stomach bitter. *The scroll was sweet to the taste but bitter to the stomach. The message here is that the long awaited reunion of Christ and the nation of Israel would result in Israel's final salvation. But, the bitter stomach prophesied that 2/3 of the nation would die during the reign of terror known as the Day of the Lord, or The Wrath of God.*

THE END OF THE SEVEN YEARS.

THE TWO WITNESSES. (See page 193, cross reference.)

Rev 11:3 "And I will grant authority to **my two witnesses**, and they will prophesy for twelve hundred and sixty days, clothed in sackcloth."

Rev 11:4 These are the **two olive trees and the two lampstands** that stand before the Lord of the earth.

Rev 11:5 And if anyone wants to harm them, **fire flows out of their mouth** and devours their enemies; so if anyone wants to harm them, he must be killed in this way.

Rev 11:6 These have the power **to shut up the sky**, so that rain will not fall during the days of their prophesying; and they have power over the waters **to turn them into blood**, and to strike the earth with every plague, as often as they desire.

Rev 11:7 When they have finished their testimony, the beast that comes up out of the abyss will make war with them, and overcome them and kill them.

Rev 11:8 And **their dead bodies** will lie in the street of the great city which mystically is called **Sodom and Egypt**, where also their Lord was crucified.

Rev 11:9 Those from the peoples and tribes and tongues and nations will look at their dead bodies for three and a half days, and will not permit their dead bodies to be laid in a tomb.

Rev 11:10 And those who dwell on the earth will rejoice over them and celebrate; and they will send gifts to one another, because these two prophets tormented those who dwell on the earth.

> **my two witnesses.** *The two witnesses are generally considered to be Elijah and Moses, since it was they who participated in the transfiguration in Matthew 17. Moses represents the law, and Elijah represents the prophets.*
> **fire flows out of their mouth.** *See 1 Kings 18:23. Elijah and the prophets of Baal agreed that fire from heaven would prove whose god was real. Elijah poured water on his altar to make kindling even harder. A fire from heaven came down and lit the altar as well as licking up all the excess water. The God of Elijah won.*
> **Two olive trees and two lampstands.** *Zechariah 4:14 defines these two as: "the two anointed ones who are standing by the Lord of the whole earth."*
> **To shut up the sky . . . turn them into blood.** *See Luke 4:25 and Exodus 7:19. This is another confirmation that Elijah and Moses are the two witnesses.*
> **their dead bodies.** *Since the two witnesses were known to be alive for 1260 days, their death would have signaled the end of the seventieth week of Daniel.*
> **Sodom and Egypt.** *A simple allusion to the depravity that had overtaken Jerusalem in the last days.*

The following narrative was inspired by research from Robert Van Kampen's book, "The Sign." The intent is to tie together scriptures which logistically provide a "possible path" for the mighty angel to travel up the King's Highway into Jerusalem to the top of Mt. Zion, just before the nation is led into hiding in the mysterious Azel. The 30 days coincide with the Day of Atonement, which then climaxes five days later at the beginning of the Feast of Tabernacles.

DAY ONE. CHRIST AND THE 144,000

A. CHRIST, THE MIGHTY ANGEL, APPEARS ON EARTH

Rev 10:1 I saw another angel, a mighty angel coming down out of heaven, clothed with a cloud; and the rainbow was upon his head, and his face was like the sun, and his feet like pillars of fire;

Rev 10:2 and he had in his hand a little scroll which was open. **He placed his right foot on the sea and his left on the land;**

> *Only Christ fits this majestic description in scripture. Rev 1:14-15 says: His head and His hair were white like white wool, like snow . . . and His eyes were like a flame of fire. 15 His feet were like burnished bronze, and His face was like the sun shining in its strength. Nowhere in scripture are these the attributes of a created angelic being. Only In Revelation on 3 occasions do we see this mighty angel. On all three occasions (5:2, 10:1, 18:21) we see a veiled reference to Christ. He speaks in Heaven, He walks on the Earth and He alone passes final judgment on the unrepentant.*

> ***Right foot on sea and left foot on land.*** *There is NO indication in scripture as to where this place might be. It could be symbolic or it could be an end-time clue that we won't know until it happens. We can only speculate. But what if Christ was attempting to recreate the journey where the children of Israel found safety on the other side of the Red Sea? If He stepped out in the Gulf of Aqaba, his right foot might orient him south-ward toward Mt. Sinai. This is just sanctified imagination, but it is possible. More importantly, it paints a picture, a possible scenario that helps us better imagine the transcendent person of Christ on his way to rescue the remnant nation of Israel.*

> *We can only imagine that Mt. Sinai could be the strategic first stop that Christ would make on his way to Jerusalem. What better place could there be to assemble God's noble 144,000 than to rally at the base of the mountain where Moses delivered the ten commandments to the children of Israel. Revelation 14:4 says "they follow the Lamb wherever He goes." What a picture, to see the future Promise Keepers assembled be-fore King Jesus - the equivalent of two stadiums full of Israel's noblest young men.*

THE JOURNEY OF THE MIGHTY ANGEL

LEBANON

Mediterranean

Sea

SYRIA

IRAQ

JORDAN

Jericho
Jerusalem ★ ● ● Amman
Nebo
Madaba

ISRAEL

Kerak

Buseira (Bozrah)

EGYPT

Petra

Teman

The
Mighty
Angel

– – – The King's Highway

Gulf of Aqaba

Mt Sinai
Rephidim

SAUDI ARABIA

RED SEA

Habakkuk 3:3,4 says: "God comes from **HAB 3, IS 63** Teman, And the Holy One from Mount Paran. Selah. His splendor covers the heavens, And the earth is full of His praise. His radiance is like the sunlight; He has rays flashing from His hand, And there is the hiding of His power." 13 You went forth for the salvation of Your people, For the salvation of Your anointed.

Mt. Paran is synonymous with Mt. Sinai, and the next stop is Teman, which Is likely the modern Jordanian town of Ma'an. Today the city houses 50,000 residents, most of whom are Sunni Muslims. We get a glimpse of the majestic Christ, radiant like sunlight, with His full power and glory still veiled and disguised until His encounter with the nation. I can hear the cadence of drums and trumpets as Christ the Messiah leads the 144,000 on their mission to collect the sons of Israel who are about to experience their long awaited salvation.

B. CHRIST LEADS THE 144,000 FROM EDOM AND BOSRAH

Isa 63:1 Who is this who comes from Edom, With garments of glowing colors from Bozrah, This One who is majestic in His apparel, marching in the greatness of His strength? "It is I who speak in righteousness, mighty to save."

Bozrah was the ancient capital of Edom, and strategically located on the Kings Highway, the main trade route from Egypt to the Euphrates River. Rev. 12:6 says, "Then the woman fled into the wilderness where she had a place prepared by God, so that there she would be nourished for one thousand two hundred and sixty days. Petra may be the place in the wilderness where God protects the nation of Israel until the Messiah gathers them together for their momentous journey of salvation. This picture is the treasury building inside the red-rock fortress of Petra. This building was filmed in Indiana Jones' "Last Crusade". Unlike the illusion in the film, this building is only about 30 feet deep.

DAY TWO. THE MESSIAH GATHERS THE REMNANT OF ISRAEL. (See Hosea 6:2, next page)

A. THE REMNANT OF ISRAEL BEGINS TO GATHER

Mic 2:12 "I will surely assemble all of you, Jacob, I will surely gather the remnant of Israel. I will put them together like sheep in the fold; Like a flock in the midst of its pasture They will be noisy with men.

Mic 2:13 "The breaker goes up before them; They break out, pass through the gate and go out by it. So their king goes on before them, And the LORD at their head."

The word for sheepfold in this passage is actually the word "bosrah", most likely a double meaning to describe the location AND the congregation that are beginning to assemble as they hear that the Messiah is coming to town. Exodus 12:37 says that the original exodus had 600,000 men and likely another 1.8 million women and children. What a sight to see! Like the biblical days when Jesus was followed by His disciples and a throng of people, now the event is magnified, with 144,000 disciples and a throng of 2 million or more Jewish followers. The Jews know that the Messiah just showed up, but they still don't know WHO the Messiah is! One of the great mysteries in biblical history is about to explode with joy.

B. THE REMNANT WILL ONLY BE ONE THIRD OF THE NATION.

Zec 13:8 "It will come about in all the land," declares the LORD, "That two parts in it will be cut off and perish; But the third will be left in it.

Zec 13:9 "And I will bring **the third part through the fire**, Refine them as silver is refined, And test them as gold is tested. They will call on My name, And I will answer them; I will say, 'They are My people,' And they will say, 'The LORD is my God.'"

The implication of this passage is that God will spare one third of the nation of Israel to experience salvation by the Messiah. These four groups will enter the millennium.

!) the 144,000 (the firstfruits of the millennium, Revelation 14:4)
2) the remnant of Israel
3) the martyrs beheaded during the Great Tribulation, and
4) the Gentiles who did not take the mark of the beast (the sheep judgment)

Rev 20:4 Then I saw thrones, and they sat on them, and judgment was given to them. And I *saw* the souls of those who had been beheaded because of their testimony of Jesus and because of the word of God, and those who had not worshiped the beast or his image, and had not received the mark on their forehead and on their hand; and they came to life and reigned with Christ for a thousand years.

C. THE REMNANT NATION FOLLOWS THE MESSIAH ON THE KING'S HIGHWAY.

Isa 35:8 A highway will be there, a roadway, And it will be called the Highway of Holiness. The unclean will not travel on it, But it will be for him who walks that way, And fools will not wander on it.

Isa 35:9 No lion will be there, Nor will any vicious beast go up on it; These will not be found there. But the redeemed will walk there,

Isa 35:10 And **the ransomed of the LORD** will return And come with joyful shouting to Zion, With everlasting joy upon their heads. They will find gladness and joy, And sorrow and sighing will flee away.

Along the King's Highway, in the town of Kerak, there stands a silent memorial to the Crusades called "The Castle of the Raven." Jesus will lead the Jews past this fortress on the way to Amman, then Jericho, then Jerusalem.

The ransomed of the Lord. *Isaiah uses this verse twice. See Isaiah 51:11. Notice the word 'joy' occurs three times to describe this unparalleled experience.*

DAY THREE. THE REMNANT NATION IS SAVED.

A. THE THIRD DAY.

Hos 6:1 "Come, let us return to the LORD. For He has torn *us,* but He will heal us; He has wounded *us,* but He will bandage us.

Hos 6:2 "He will revive us after two days; He will raise us up on the third day, That we may live before Him.

It is the third day since the Mighty Angel put His feet on land and sea. Just as Christ was raised from the dead on the third day, so He will raise the nation of Israel on this day. In ancient times the Jews would travel this road in anticipation of the great feast called Tabernacles, which was celebrated five days after Atonement.   As the multitude walks up the Jericho Road toward Jerusalem, they are singing the traditional Psalm of Ascent from Psalm 118:

"Give thanks to the Lord, for He is good.
His lovingkindness is everlasting."

B. THE NATION SUDDENLY RECOGNIZES JESUS AS MESSIAH.

Zec 12:9 "And in that day I will set about to destroy all the nations that come against Jerusalem.

Zec 12:10 "I will pour out on the house of David and on the inhabitants of Jerusalem, the Spirit of grace and of supplication, so that they will look on Me whom they have pierced; and they will mourn for Him, as one mourns for an only son, and they will weep bitterly over Him like the bitter weeping over a firstborn.

Psalm *118: 21-24* say this:
I shall give thanks to You, for You have answered me,
And You have become my salvation.
The stone which the builders rejected has become the chief corner stone.
This is the LORD'S doing; It is marvelous in our eyes.
This is the day which the LORD has made; Let us rejoice and be glad in it."

It is at this moment that the veil is lifted from their eyes, their hearts are softened, and they acknowledge Jesus as their Messiah.

C. THE NATION OF ISRAEL IS SAVED.

Rom 11:25 For I do not want you, brethren, to be uninformed of this mystery--so that you will not be wise in your own estimation - that **a partial hardening** has happened to Israel until the fullness of the Gentiles has come in;

Rom 11:26 and so **all Israel will be saved;** just as it is written, "The Deliverer will come from Zion; He will remove ungodliness from Jacob."

Rom 11:27 "This is my covenant with them, when I take away their sins."

A partial hardening. Israel is one of the great mysteries of the Bible. Like the Road to Emmaus in Luke 24, each generation of Israel remains bound to their law and their traditions until at last, God removes the scales from their eyes and they see Jesus as He is - their true Messiah.

All Israel will be saved. This is a generalization which is not intended to refute the prophecy of Zechariah 13:8,9. It is more practical to believe that most of the Jews living in the that day will be caught up in the deception of the Anti-Christ. Romans 9:6 says that "they are not all Israel who are descended from Israel." God knows the heart. Perhaps "all Israel" - means those who are truly waiting for Messiah - will be the true and only Israel in the latter days.

DAY FOUR. THE TWO WITNESSES ARE RESURRECTED.

Rev 11:11 But **after the three and a half days,** the breath of life from God came into them, and they stood on their feet; and great fear fell upon those who were watching them.

Rev 11:12 And they heard a loud voice from heaven saying to them, "Come up here." Then they went up into heaven in the cloud, and their enemies watched them.

Rev 11:13 And in that hour there was **a great earthquake**, and a tenth of the city fell; seven thousand people were killed in the earthquake, and **the rest were terrified** and gave glory to the God of heaven.

Rev 11:14 **The second woe** is past; behold, the third woe is coming quickly.

after the three and a half days. The two witnesses, presumed to be Moses and Elijah, were killed on the last day of the seventieth week. On the fourth day they are resurrected. It appears that they are translated into heaven shortly after being raised. For the Anti-Christ, they were symbolic of his victory. Now, he is shaken by the news that the power of God has once again reminded him of his defeat.

a great earthquake. This was indeed a great earthquake, but it was not the great earthquake, which occurs in Revelation 16:18. See page 325.

the rest were terrified. In the sovereignty of God, even this event, this earthquake in Jerusalem, was a vehicle for what appears to be the last minute salvation of repentant Jews.

the second woe. The three woes are as follows:

Revelation 9:1-12. the fifth trumpet. The angel of the abyss rallies demonic locusts, who have the ability to torture the unrepentant with the sting of a scorpion for a period of five months.

Revelation 11:13,14. the sixth trumpet. 200 million demonic horsemen execute 1/3 of mankind (with three torturous plagues) when the angels are released at the Euphrates. Later (Rev 16:12) at the 6th bowl, the Euphrates dries up to make way for the kings of the east.

Revelation 16:16. the seventh bowl. In the seventh trumpet, God pours out all seven bowls, full of the wrath of God.

DAY FIVE. THE LAMB ON MT ZION.

A. THE LAMB WITH THE 144,000

Rev 14:1 Then I looked, and behold, the Lamb was standing on Mount Zion, and with Him one hundred and forty-four thousand, having His name and the name of His Father written on their foreheads.

Rev 14:2 And I heard a voice from heaven, like the sound of many waters and like the sound of loud thunder, and the voice which I heard was like the sound of harpists playing on their harps.

Rev 14:3 And they sang a new song before the throne and before the four living creatures and the elders; and no one could learn the song except the one hundred and forty-four thousand who had been purchased from the earth.

Rev 14:4 These are the ones who have not been defiled with women, for they have kept themselves chaste. These are the ones who follow the Lamb wherever He goes. These have been purchased from among men as first fruits to God and to the Lamb.

Rev 14:5 And no lie was found in their mouth; **they are blameless.**

The Temple Mount With The
Temple in its Midst

Wouldn't it be easy to prove the Bible wrong if all 144,000 men couldn't fit on the Temple Mount? Check it out. The Temple Mount in Jerusalem is 37 acres in size. An acre is 43,560 sf x 37 acres = 1,611,720 sf. When you divide this number by the 144,000 men, you get 11.19 sf per person or 3'-4" square per person, a perfect size for a legion of soldiers to stand side by side. It is not likely the Dome of the Rock will still be standing at this time, but if you calculate its footprint size of 8.7 acres (or 380,000 sf) and subtract this from our total, you still get 1,231,720 sf of area, or 2'-11' square per person. Imagine seeing King Jesus standing on the Temple Mount with two entire stadiums full of God's noblest warriors.

B. THE ANGEL SOUNDS THE SEVENTH TRUMPET.

Rev 11:15 Then **the seventh angel sounded**; and there were loud voices in heaven, saying, "The kingdom of the world has become the kingdom of our Lord and of His Christ; and He will reign forever and ever."

Rev 11:16 And the twenty-four elders, who sit on their thrones before God, fell on their faces and worshiped God,

Rev 11:17 saying, "We give You thanks, O Lord God, the Almighty, who are and who were, because You have taken Your great power and have begun to reign.

Rev 11:18 "And the nations were enraged, and Your wrath came, and the time came for the dead to be judged, and the time to reward Your bond-servants the prophets and the saints and those who fear Your name, the small and the great, and to destroy those who destroy the earth."

Rev 11:19 And the temple of God which is in heaven was opened; and **the ark of His covenant** appeared in His temple, and there were flashes of lightning and sounds and peals of thunder and an earthquake and a great hailstorm.

The seventh angel sounded. 1 Corinthians 1:22 says that Jews look for signs and Greeks seek wisdom. Yesterday, the Jews saw Moses and Elijah rise from the dead and then ascend to heaven. Today, Jesus is standing on Mt. Zion with The 144,000. Then the seventh angel sounds the seventh trumpet to declare that Jesus has just taken back the title deed to planet earth. As the trumpet sounds, millions of people immediately bow down before King Jesus.

The ark of His covenant. As they rise, the heavens open to display the earthly symbol of the presence of God: Their hallowed ark of the covenant. lost for thousands of years (but not in a warehouse, by the way). For a brief time, the nation of Israel breaks out in in a thunderous joy that far surpasses any sacred feast or wedding celebration. Their Messiah, Yshua ha Meshiach, has finally come to rescue them from ages of bondage.

C. THE MOUNTAIN SPLITS ON THE WAY TO AZEL.

Zec 14:1 Behold, a day is coming for the LORD when the spoil taken from you will be divided among you.

Zec 14:2 For I will gather all the nations against Jerusalem to battle, and the city will be captured, the houses plundered, the women ravished and half of the city exiled, but the rest of the people will not be cut off from the city.

Zec 14:3 Then the LORD will go forth and fight against those nations, as when He fights on a day of battle.

Zec 14:4 In that day **His feet will stand on the Mount of Olives**, which is in front of Jerusalem on the east; **and the Mount of Olives will be split** in its middle from east to west by a very large valley, so that half of the mountain will move toward the north and the other half toward the south.

Zec 14:5 You will flee by the valley of My mountains, for the valley of the mountains will **reach to Azel;** yes, you will flee just as you fled before the earthquake in the days of Uzziah king of Judah. Then the LORD, my God, will come, and all the holy ones with Him!

> ***His feet will stand on the Mount of Olives***. *This view below is the Mount of Olives as seen from the Temple Mount across the Kidron Valley. This is one of the most majestic images in the Bible. Rising 2600 feet above sea level, this mountain has been the resting place of 150,000 Jewish graves over a period of 3,000 years. From this place Christ ascended and to this place He will return in the last days to split the earth and make an avenue of protection for the Jewish remnant. The Garden of Gethsemane is at the base of this mountain and Jesus' Olivet Discourse took place on this mountainside.*

Reach to Azel. *This place is mentioned nowhere else in scripture. Traditional Pre-Trib theology teaches that Petra will be the place of Azel, but it is more likely that Petra is the place the Jews come from, NOT where they go to. Logic would suggest that this special hiding place is not likely to be*  *revealed until Christ sends the newly saved remnant of Israel to this mysterious hiding place as the judgment of bowls begins. It is worth noting that Mt Nebo, where Moses stood to look down upon the promised land, is due east of the Mt of Olives.*

In the days of Uzziah. *Perhaps the key to the location of Azel is found in this passage, which appears to have no simple explanation. The reference by Zechariah was made 250 years after the death of Uzziah. See Isaiah 6.*

ZECH 14, REV 15

DAY SIX TO DAY THIRTY

A. PREPARING FOR THE BOWL JUDGMENTS.

Rev 15:5 After these things I looked, and the temple of the tabernacle of testimony in heaven was opened,

Rev 15:6 and the seven angels who had the seven plagues came out of the temple, clothed in linen, clean and bright, and girded around their chests with golden sashes.

Rev 15:7 Then one of the four living creatures gave to the seven angels seven golden bowls full of the wrath of God, who lives forever and ever.

Rev 15:8 And the temple was filled with smoke from the glory of God and from His power; and no one was able to enter the temple until the seven plagues of the seven angels were finished.

The Day of Atonement (Yom Kippur) is celebrated on the tenth day of the fall month. In modern times, the celebration begins on the first of the month with Rosh Hashanah (the civil new year) for a period called "the ten days of Awe." Five days after Yom Kippur, the Jews celebrate the last feast of the year, the feast of Tabernacles or Sukkot. The timing of the end of the seven year period, and the beginning of the 30 day period coincides with the five day period between Yom Kippur and Sukkot. In other words, Day One is Yom Kippur when the Mighty Angel arrives to cleanse their sins and Day Five is Sukkot - the climax of the celebration when Christ stands on the temple mount and reclaims his rightful ownership of all creation.

B. CHRIST RETURNS TO HEAVEN FOR THE MARRIAGE SUPPER OF THE LAMB.

Rev 19:6 Then I heard something like the voice of a great multitude and like the sound of many waters and like the sound of mighty peals of thunder, saying, "Hallelujah! For the Lord our God, the Almighty, reigns.

Rev 19:7 **"Let us rejoice** and be glad and give the glory to Him, for **the marriage of the Lamb has come** and His bride has made herself ready."

Rev 19:8 It was given to her to clothe herself in fine linen, bright and clean; for the fine linen is **the righteous acts of the saints.**

Rev 19:9 Then he said to me, "Write, 'Blessed are those who are invited to the marriage supper of the Lamb.'" And he said to me, "These are true words of God."

Rev 19:10 Then I fell at his feet to worship him. But he said to me, "Do not do that; I am a fellow servant of yours and your brethren who hold the testimony of Jesus; worship God. For the testimony of Jesus is the spirit of prophecy."

> **Let us rejoice.** *In the annals of Heavenly history, this is one of those monumental moments. The seventh trumpet has sounded. Christ has taken back the title deed to planet earth, and now He goes to celebrate with his beloved raptured saints.*
>
> ***The marriage of the Lamb has come.*** Ephesians 5:25 is the primary passage for understanding the marriage supper. "Husbands, love your wives . . . " One question looms large as we investigate this mysterious marriage supper. Why is Israel not part of the marriage supper? It would seem that Christ would want Israel and the Church to celebrate together. We assume that the context of this passage places the timing of the marriage supper just before the battle of Armageddon. Based on that assumption, the noble husband/warrior goes off to make war with the enemy in order to usher in the next event, which is the millennium. We can only presume that Christ celebrates the marriage supper at this point for two reasons: one, to allow the church to celebrate the salvation of Israel, just before they (Israel) enter the millennial period; and two, to preempt the counterfeiter, Satan, who is about to experience his own version of the supper: "the great supper of God"; It is this author's speculation that the wedding gift from the bridegroom will be the glorious new city of Jerusalem, which seems to be intrinsically linked to the bride. (Revelation 21:9).
>
> ***the righteous acts of the saints.*** *Isaiah 61:10 says that we are clothed in garments of salvation and wrapped in a robe of righteousness. These righteous acts are not the work that got us into heaven, but rather are the result of Christ's generous act of grace. If my righteous works were the threads of my garment in heaven, I would likely be wearing rags. And all God's people said, "Amen."*

C. PREPARING FOR ARMAGEDDON.

Rev 19:11 And I saw heaven opened, and behold, a white horse, and He who sat on it is called Faithful and True, and in righteousness He judges and wages war.

Rev 19:12 His eyes are a flame of fire, and on His head are many diadems; and He has **a name written** on Him which no one knows except Himself.

Rev 19:13 He is clothed with a robe dipped in blood, and His name is called The Word of God.

Rev 19:14 And the armies which are in heaven, clothed in fine linen, white and clean, were following Him on white horses.

Rev 19:15 From His mouth comes a sharp sword, so that with it He may strike down the nations, and He will rule them with a rod of iron; and He treads the wine press of the fierce wrath of God, the Almighty.

Rev 19:16 And on His robe and on His thigh He has **a name written**, "KING OF KINGS, AND LORD OF LORDS."

Rev 19:17 Then I saw an angel standing in the sun, and he cried out with a loud voice, saying to all the birds which fly in midheaven, "Come, assemble for **the great supper of God,**

Rev 19:18 so that you may eat the flesh of kings and the flesh of commanders and the flesh of mighty men and the flesh of horses and of those who sit on them and the flesh of all men, both free men and slaves, and small and great."

Rev 19:19 And I saw the beast and the kings of the earth and their armies assembled to make war against Him who sat on the horse and against His army.

Rev 19:20 And **the beast was seized**, and with him the false prophet who performed the signs in his presence, by which he deceived those who had received the mark of the beast and those who worshiped his image; these two were **thrown alive into the lake of fire** which burns with brimstone.

Rev 19:21 And **the rest were killed** with the sword which came from the mouth of Him who sat on the horse, and all the birds were filled with their flesh.

> *a name written.* The name in verse 12 is not the same as the name in verse 16.
>
> *the great supper of God.* Satan wants to counterfeit God's marriage supper, so God gives him a supper. Only this supper is the birds of the air feasting on the remains of the unrepentant demonic hoards.
>
> *the beast was seized.* You have to wonder why Satan, who knows scripture, would risk going to war with Jesus, when he knows that his destiny will be eternal torment.
>
> *the rest were killed.* Finally, we can used the term, "a massacre of biblical proportion." The armies of heaven never lifted a sword. As always, Jesus is willing to fight our battles for us if we will only allow Him.

THE FINAL WARNING.   (Continued from p314, Revelation 14:1-5)

Rev 14:6 And I saw **another angel** flying in midheaven, having **an eternal gospel** to preach to those who live on the earth, and to every nation and tribe and tongue and people;

Rev 14:7 and he said with a loud voice, "Fear God, and give Him glory, because the hour of His judgment has come; worship Him who made the heaven and the earth and sea and springs of waters."

Rev 14:8 And **another angel**, a second one, followed, saying, "Fallen, **fallen is Babylon** the great, she who has made all the nations drink of the wine of the passion of her immorality."

Rev 14:9 Then **another angel**, a third one, followed them, saying with a loud voice, **"If anyone worships the beast** and his image, and receives a mark on his forehead or on his hand,

Rev 14:10 he also will drink of the wine of the wrath of God, which is mixed in full strength in the cup of His anger; and he will be tormented with fire and brimstone in the presence of the holy angels and in the presence of the Lamb.

Rev 14:11 "And the smoke of their torment goes up forever and ever; they have no rest day and night, those who worship the beast and his image, and whoever receives the mark of his name."

Rev 14:12 Here is **the perseverance of the saints** who keep the commandments of God and their faith in Jesus.

Rev 14:13 And I heard a voice from heaven, saying, "Write, **'Blessed are the dead who die in the Lord from now on!'"** "Yes," says the Spirit, "so that they may rest from their labors, for their deeds follow with them."

> *An eternal gospel.* Mat 24:14 says, *"This gospel of the kingdom shall be preached in the whole world as a testimony to all the nations, and then the end will come." Mankind does not hasten the end by preaching the gospel to the nations. This is the final curtain call, God's last appeal to mankind to come into the kingdom before he closes the door. The reference to the gospel, Babylon and the mark of the beast is probably not a chronological statement, but rather a summary statement, a final reminder to receive the gospel of Christ or suffer the penalty.*
>
> *Blessed are the dead who die in the Lord from now on.* The seventh trumpet has sounded. There is no more persecution and no more tribulation. The only death yet to happen is the death of the unrepentant masses who will experience the bowl judgments and the fateful battle of Armageddon. Death for the believer will happen sparingly in the Millennium, and completely under the sovereignty of God.

THE HARVEST OF WHEAT AND TARES.

Rev 14:14 Then I looked, and behold, a white cloud, and sitting on the cloud was one like a son of man, having a golden crown on His head and a sharp sickle in His hand.

Rev 14:15 And **another angel** came out of the temple, crying out with a loud voice **to Him who sat on the cloud,** "Put in your sickle and reap, **for the hour to reap has come**, because the harvest of the earth is ripe."

Rev 14:16 Then He who sat on the cloud swung His sickle over the earth, and the earth was reaped.

Rev 14:17 And **another angel** came out of the temple which is in heaven, and he also had a sharp sickle.

Rev 14:18 Then **another angel**, the one who has power over fire, came out from the altar; and he called with a loud voice to him who had the sharp sickle, saying, "Put in your sharp sickle and gather the clusters from the vine of the earth, because her grapes are ripe."

Rev 14:19 So the angel swung his sickle to the earth and gathered the clusters from the vine of the earth, and threw them into the great wine press of the wrath of God.

Rev 14:20 And the wine press was trodden outside the city, and blood came out from the wine press, up to the horses' bridles, for a distance of two hundred miles.

to him who sat on a cloud. The angel has just received instructions from the Father to be given to the Son regarding the end of the age. Matthew 24:36 says, "But of that day and hour no one knows, not even the angels of heaven, nor the Son, but the Father alone." This is one of the great mysteries in the Bible. Perhaps this is the only thing in the universe that the Son does not know.

the hour to reap has come. Two angels came out of the temple and spoke. The first angel instructed Christ to harvest the good wheat. The second angel instructed the third angel to gather the clusters of the vine for the wrathful winepress of God. The timing of this event is the seventh trumpet. Since the raptured saints are already in heaven, the harvest spoken of here must relate to Israel, who is about to be escorted to Azel, the hiding place, while the bowl judgments and Armageddon finalize the dark destiny of the tares. Mat 13:30 'Allow both to grow together until the harvest; and in the time of the harvest I will say to the reapers, "First gather up the tares and bind them in bundles to burn them up; but gather the wheat into my barn."

See page 326 for cross reference.

BEFORE THE BOWLS

REVELATION CHAPTER 15

THE VICTORIOUS SING TO THE LAMB

Rev 15:1 Then I saw another sign in heaven, great and marvelous, seven angels who had seven plagues, which are the last, because in them the wrath of God is finished.

Rev 15:2 And I saw something like a sea of glass mixed with fire, and those who had been victorious over the beast and his image and the number of his name, standing on the sea of glass, holding **harps of God.**

Rev 15:3 And they sang the song of Moses, the bond-servant of God, and the song of the Lamb, saying, "Great and marvelous are Your works, O Lord God, the Almighty; Righteous and true are Your ways, King of the nations!

Rev 15:4 "Who will not fear, O Lord, and glorify Your name? For You alone are holy; For All the nations will come and worship before You, for Your righteous acts have been revealed."

> ***harps of God.*** *In biblical times, celebrations consisted of strings and brass and percussion, much like the band of today. Perhaps the heavenly celebration will resemble an infinite string quartet - consisting of guitars, violins, violas and bass fiddles. This incredible sight gives new meaning to the term "jammin'.*

THE TEMPLE OF THE TABERNACLE IS OPENED

Rev 15:5 After these things I looked, and **the temple of the tabernacle of testimony** in heaven was opened,

Rev 15:6 and the seven angels who had the seven plagues came out of the temple, clothed in linen, clean and bright, and girded around their chests with golden sashes.

Rev 15:7 Then one of the four living creatures gave to the seven angels seven golden bowls full of the wrath of God, who lives forever and ever.

Rev 15:8 And the temple was filled with smoke from the glory of God and from His power; and no one was able to enter the temple until the seven plagues of the seven angels were finished.

> ***the temple of the tabernacle of testimony.*** *Only once in scripture do we find this phrase used. And only one other place, Isaiah's vison in Isaiah 6, do we find the temple in heaven filled with smoke. Like the silence in heaven in Chapter 8, God's wrath was so severe that the temple "was closed" until further notice. It would appear that this was the heavenly equivalent to the first and second earthly temple. Ezekiel's temple, found in Ezekiel 40, is yet to come.*

THE VOICE OF THE GREAT MULTITUDE

Rev 19:1 After these things I heard something like **a loud voice of a great multitude** in heaven, saying, "Hallelujah! Salvation and glory and power belong to our God;

Rev 19:2 because His judgments are true and righteous; for He has judged the great harlot who was corrupting the earth with her immorality, and He has avenged the blood of His bond-servants on her.

Rev 19:3 And a second time they said, "Hallelujah! Her smoke rises up forever and ever."

Rev 19:4 And the twenty-four elders and the four living creatures fell down and worshiped God who sits on the throne saying, "Amen. Hallelujah!"

Rev 19:5 And a voice came from the throne, saying, "Give praise to our God, all you His bond-servants, you who fear Him, the small and the great."

> *See Revelation 7:9. Though the Bible does use the term "great multitude" to speak of a large crowd, this great multitude must be the multitude "that no one could count. "*

THE MARRIAGE SUPPER OF THE LAMB

Rev 19:6 Then I heard something like the voice of a great multitude and like the sound of many waters and like the sound of mighty peals of thunder, saying, "Hallelujah! For the Lord our God, the Almighty, reigns.

Rev 19:7 "Let us rejoice and be glad and give the glory to Him, for the marriage of the Lamb has come and His bride has made herself ready."

Rev 19:8 It was given to her to clothe herself in fine linen, bright and clean; for the fine linen is the righteous acts of the saints.

Rev 19:9 Then he said to me, "Write, 'Blessed are those who are invited to **the marriage supper of the Lamb.**'" And he said to me, "These are true words of God."

Rev 19:10 Then I fell at his feet to worship him. But he said to me, "Do not do that; I am a fellow servant of yours and your brethren who hold the testimony of Jesus; worship God. **For** the testimony of Jesus is the spirit of prophecy."

> ***the marriage supper of the Lamb.*** *The Church has generally been considered to be the bride of Christ, but Rev 21:19 says that Jerusalem is the wife of the Lamb. Our best understanding should be this: just as the woman and Israel could not be separated, nor the harlot and the great city, so should we understand that the Church and the New Jerusalem are intrinsically linked together to be the adorned bride whom Christ the groomsman has prepared (since the beginning of time) to be bonded together for eternity. See page 327 for Revelation 19:11.*

SEVEN BOWLS OF GOD'S WRATH
REVELATION CHAPTER 16

THE CONCLUSION OF GOD'S   **WRATH.**

Rev 16:1 Then I heard a loud voice from the temple, saying to the seven angels, "Go and pour out on the earth the seven bowls of the wrath of God."

TRUMPETS	BOWLS
1) 1/3 of earth, trees, grass burned up	bodily sores
2) 1/3 of sea became blood	The seas full of blood
3) 1/3 of waters were bitter	The rivers full of blood.
4) 1/3 of day and night darkened	Men scorched with heat from the sun
5) Locusts torment for 5 months	Their pain was great
6) 1/3 of Mankind Killed	Euphrates dried up for the kings of east
7) Coronation of King Jesus	Reaping of the Earth

Rev 16:2 So **the first angel** went and poured out his bowl on the earth; and it became a loathsome and malignant sore on the people who had the mark of the beast and who worshiped his image.

Rev 16:3 **The second angel** poured out his bowl into the sea, and it became blood like that of a dead man; and every living thing in the sea died.

Rev 16:4 Then **the third angel** poured out his bowl into the rivers and the springs of waters; and they became blood.

Rev 16:5 And I heard the angel of the waters saying, "Righteous are You, who are and who were, O Holy One, because You judged these things;

Rev 16:6 for they poured out the blood of saints and prophets, and You have given them blood to drink. They deserve it."

Rev 16:7 And I heard the altar saying, "Yes, O Lord God, the Almighty, true and righteous are Your judgments."

Rev 16:8 **The fourth angel** poured out his bowl upon the sun, and it was given to it to scorch men with fire.

Rev 16:9 Men were scorched with fierce heat; and they blasphemed the name of God who has the power over these plagues, and they did not repent so as to give Him glory.

Rev 16:10 Then **the fifth angel** poured out his bowl on the throne of the beast, and his kingdom became darkened; and they gnawed their tongues because of pain,

Rev 16:11 and they blasphemed the God of heaven because of their pains and their sores; and they did not repent of their deeds.

Rev 16:12 **The sixth angel** poured out his bowl on the great river, the Euphrates; and its water was dried up, so that the way would be prepared for the kings from the east.

Rev 16:13 And I saw coming out of the mouth of the dragon and out of the mouth of the beast and out of the mouth of the false prophet, **three unclean spirits like frogs;**

Rev 16:14 for they are spirits of demons, performing signs, which go out to the kings of the whole world, to gather them together for the war of the great day of God, the Almighty.

Rev 16:15 ("Behold, I am coming like a thief. Blessed is the one who stays awake and keeps his clothes, so that he will not walk about naked and men will not see his shame.")

Rev 16:16 And they gathered them together to the place which in Hebrew is called **Har-Magedon.**

See Revelation 19:11 for details of this great war, and Rev 14:20 for the result of the war. The Mount of Megiddo, and the adjacent valley of Jezreel, will be the location of this great war between Heaven's angels and the demons of Hell.

Rev 16:17 Then **the seventh angel** poured out his bowl upon the air, and a loud voice came out of the temple from the throne, saying, "It is done."

Rev 16:18 And there were flashes of lightning and sounds and peals of thunder; and there was a **great earthquake**, such as there had not been since man came to be upon the earth, so great an earthquake was it, and so mighty.

Rev 16:19 The great city was split into three parts, and the cities of the nations fell. Babylon the great was remembered before God, to give her the cup of the wine of His fierce wrath.

Rev 16:20 And every island fled away, and the mountains were not found.

Rev 16:21 And huge hailstones, about one hundred pounds each, came down from heaven upon men; and men blasphemed God because of the plague of the hail, because its plague was extremely severe.

A great earthquake. The Richter Scale is a base 10 logarithm, which means that the energy from an earthquake is magnified by 10 for each succeeding unit. A 5.0 is thus 10 times more powerful than a 4.0. The number 10 is the highest, most devastating earthquake. I like to call this earthquake a 16 on the Richter Scale, because it is expo-nentially more devastating than anything man has ever seen.   This means that a 10 on the Richter Scale would be one million times more powerful than a 5 - and a 16 (theoretically) would be one million times more powerful than a 10. The key to under-standing the power of this earthquake is found in the phrase "every island fled away". Apparently, the islands would sink into the ocean and the mountains would be leveled.

THE BATTLE OF ARMAGEDDON

THE BEGINNING OF THE BOWL JUDGMENTS.

Rev 14:14 Then I looked, and behold, a white cloud, and sitting on the cloud was one like a son of man, having a golden crown on His head and a sharp sickle in His hand.

Rev 14:15 And another angel came out of the temple, crying out with a loud voice to Him who sat on the cloud, "Put in your sickle and reap, for the hour to reap has come, because the harvest of **the earth is ripe."**

Rev 14:16 Then He who sat on the cloud swung His sickle over the earth, and **the earth was reaped.**

> *the earth is ripe.* *The Greek word for ripe, xeros, implies a withered or rotten harvest. Ripe in this context does not mean mature or prime, but rather spoiled.*
> *the earth was reaped.* *In this passage the angel appears to be giving Christ (the son of man) instruction from God the Father. The final stage of God's judgment is about to be fulfilled. The reaping of the earth is synonymous with the bowl judgment.*

THE REAPING OF BATTLE.

Rev 14:17 And another angel came out of the temple which is in heaven, and he also had a sharp sickle.

Rev 14:18 Then another angel, the one who has power over fire, came out from the altar; and he called with a loud voice to him who had the sharp sickle, saying, "Put in your sharp sickle and **gather the clusters** from the vine of the earth, because her grapes are ripe."

Rev 14:19 So the angel swung his sickle to the earth and gathered the clusters from the vine of the earth, and threw them into the great wine press of the wrath of God.

Rev 14:20 And the wine press was trodden outside the city, and blood came out from the wine press, up to the horses' bridles, for a distance of **two hundred miles.**

> *gather the clusters.* *The reaping of v14 was judgment upon the earth. This reaping is final judgment upon mankind. As if the seven bowls were not enough, the Beast and the False Prophet now rallied their legion of demon-possessed rebels to fight the final battle. Joel 3:13 says, "Put in the sickle, for the harvest is ripe. Come, tread, for the wine press is full; The vats overflow, for their wickedness is great."*
>
> *Two hundred miles. Verse 20 has always fascinated scholars. Here is the essence of the blood up to the horses' bridles: Israel is 200 miles long. The blood began to splash as high as a horses' bridle and when it spread across the land, it covered the entire land of Israel - 10,733 sq miles, averaging 53.6 miles wide. This equates to 199,479,240 men whose blood was an inch thick over the entire surface of the land of Israel. Every square inch of the land of Israel was soaked in blood.*

GATHERING FOR BATTLE.

Rev 16:16 And they gathered them together to the place which in Hebrew is called Har-Magedon.

> **Har Magedon.** *Har in Hebrew means a mount. This is a build-up mound in northeast Israel which overlooks the valley of Jezreel, also known as the plain of Esdraelon. Napoleon said this was the greatest battlefield in the world.*

JESUS AND HIS ARMIES GO TO WAR.

Rev 19:11 And I saw heaven opened, and behold, a white horse, and He who sat on it is called Faithful and True, and in righteousness He judges and wages war.

Rev 19:12 His eyes are a flame of fire, and on His head are many diadems; and He has **a name written on Him** which no one knows except Himself.

Rev 19:13 He is clothed **with a robe dipped in blood**, and His name is called The Word of God.

Rev 19:14 And the armies which are in heaven, clothed in fine linen, white and clean, were following Him on white horses.

Rev 19:15 From His mouth comes a sharp sword, so that with it He may strike down the nations, and He will rule them with a rod of iron; and He treads the wine press of the fierce wrath of God, the Almighty.

Rev 19:16 And on His robe and on His thigh He has a name written, "KING OF KINGS, AND LORD OF LORDS."

Rev 19:17 Then I saw an angel standing in the sun, and he cried out with a loud voice, saying to all the birds which fly in midheaven, "Come, assemble for **the great supper of God,**

Rev 19:18 so that you may eat the flesh of kings and the flesh of commanders and the flesh of mighty men and the flesh of horses and of those who sit on them and the flesh of all men, both free men and slaves, and small and great."

Rev 19:19 And I saw the beast and the kings of the earth and their armies assembled to make war against Him who sat on the horse and against His army.

Rev 19:20 And the beast was seized, and with him the false prophet who performed the signs in his presence, by which he deceived those who had received the mark of the beast and those who worshiped his image; these two were **thrown alive** into the lake of fire which burns with brimstone.

Rev 19:21 And the rest were killed with the sword which came from the mouth of Him who sat on the horse, and all the birds were filled with their flesh.

> **A name written on Him.** *We look forward to this mysterious name.*
> **with a robe dipped in blood.** *Note that the robe of Christ is dipped in blood, likely from the martyred saints. The armies that follow Him are angels prepared to fight a spiritual battle with the demonic host.*
> **The great supper** *of God is an ironic parallel to the Anti-Christ's desire to replicate the life of Christ. Since the marriage supper of the Lamb has just occurred, God the Father has chosen to give the beast the supper he deserves.* **Thrown alive.** *We need to be reminded that the lake of fire is a literal place where those who stood with the beast will suffer eternal torment.*

GOG AND THE BATTLE OF ARMAGEDDON
Ezekiel 38b and 39

Eze 38:15 "You will come from your place out of **the remote parts of the north**, you and many peoples with you, all of them riding on horses, a great assembly and a mighty army;

Eze 38:16 and you will come up against My people Israel like a cloud to cover the land. It shall come about **in the last days** that I will bring you against My land, so that the nations may know Me when I am sanctified through you before their eyes, O Gog."

———————————

Eze 39:1 "And you, son of man, prophesy against Gog and say, 'Thus says the Lord GOD, "Behold, I am against you, O Gog, prince of Rosh, Meshech and Tubal;

Eze 39:2 and I will turn you around, drive you on, take you up from the remotest parts of the north and bring you against the mountains of Israel.

Eze 39:3 "I will strike your bow from your left hand and dash down your arrows from your right hand.

Eze 39:4 "You will fall on the mountains of Israel, you and all your troops and the peoples who are with you; I will give you **as food to every kind of predatory bird** and beast of the field.

Eze 39:5 "You will fall on the open field; for it is I who have spoken," declares the Lord GOD.

Eze 39:6 "And I will send fire upon Magog and those who inhabit the coastlands in safety; and they will know that I am the LORD.

Eze 39:7 "My holy name I will make known in the midst of My people Israel; **and I will not let My holy name be profaned anymore**. And the nations will know that I am the LORD, the Holy One in Israel.

Eze 39:8 "Behold, it is coming and it shall be done," declares the Lord GOD. "That is the day of which I have spoken.

Eze 39:9 "Then those who inhabit the cities of Israel will go out and make fires with the weapons and burn them, both shields and bucklers, bows and arrows, war clubs and spears, and **for seven years** they will make fires of them.

Eze 39:10 "They will not take wood from the field or gather firewood from the forests, for they will make fires with the weapons; and they will take the spoil of those who despoiled them and seize the plunder of those who plundered them," declares the Lord GOD.

Eze 39:11 "On that day I will give Gog **a burial ground there in Israel**, the valley of those who pass by east of the sea, and it will block off those who would pass by. So they will bury Gog there with all his horde, and they will call it **the valley of Hamon-gog.**

Eze 39:12 **"For seven months** the house of Israel will be burying them in order to cleanse the land.

Eze 39:13 "Even all the people of the land will bury them; and it will be to their renown on the day that I glorify Myself," declares the Lord GOD.

Eze 39:14 "They will set apart men who will constantly pass through the land, burying those who were passing through, even those left on the surface of the ground, in order to cleanse it. At the end of seven months they will make a search.

Eze 39:15 "As those who pass through the land pass through and anyone sees a man's bone, then he will set up a marker by it until the buriers have buried it in the valley of Hamon-gog.

Eze 39:16 "And even the name of the city will be Hamonah. So they will cleanse the land."'

for seven years/seven months. At the end of Armageddon, the people of Israel will begin a seven year process of burning the weapons of warfare, but for seven months they will search the land and bring all the dead bodies, and the loose bones, to the place known as Hamon-Gog.

a burial ground there in Israel. Hamon-Gog is better known as Gehenna, the valley also known as the valley of Jehoshaphat and the Hinnom Valley. This valley connects to the Kidron Valley, which separated the Mount of Olives from the Temple Mount.

the valley of Hamon-gog. It is worth noting that the name Haman, the sinister Amalekite from the book of Esther, and this valley, both come from the same root word, "ha-maw", which literally means "to make a loud noise, to incite to rage or war." Remember that Numbers 24:20 referred to Amalek as the "first of the nations" whose end shall be destruction. Exodus 17:6 says "the LORD will have war against Amalek from generation to generation."

The big question here is this: Are we saying that Gog and the Anti-Christ are the same person? And if so, how do you reconcile Revelation 19:20 and 20:10, which both say that the Beast (Anti-Christ) and the False Prophet are thrown alive into the lake of fire? If Gog is buried in Hamon-Gog, can this be the Anti-Christ who is thrown alive, not buried? At this point, we turn to Revelation 22:15 and the term "outside the gates". See the explanation on page 374. I believe it is possible that Hamon-Gog is the lake of fire described in Revelation 22:15, which is located outside the gates of the city of Jerusalem. It is "possible" that Hamon-Gog is also the valley of Hinnom, which was the Old Testament symbol of Hell. And, that this burial ground is actually the lake of fire, which, in Millennial days will become a physical valley, but then later, at the end of the Millennium, will be transformed into its final state, a lake of fire, as the permanent abode of the devil and his angels, the beast and the false prophet, and all those whose name was not written in the book of life.

THE BIRDS AND THE BEASTS WILL EAT THE FLESH OF MEN.

Eze 39:17 "As for you, son of man, thus says the Lord GOD, 'Speak **to every kind of bird and to every beast of the field,** "Assemble and come, gather from every side to My sacrifice which I am going to sacrifice for you, as a great sacrifice on the mountains of Israel, that you may eat flesh and drink blood.

Eze 39:18 "You will eat the flesh of mighty men and drink the blood of the princes of the earth, as though they were rams, lambs, goats and bulls, all of them fatlings of Bashan.

Eze 39:19 "So you will eat fat until you are glutted, and drink blood until you are drunk, from My sacrifice which I have sacrificed for you.

Eze 39:20 "You will be glutted at My table with horses and charioteers, with mighty men and all the men of war," declares the Lord GOD.

> **Cross Reference** this passage with Revelation 19, which also describes the consequences of Armageddon. While Revelation only mentions the birds of the sky who scavenge the remains of the final war, Ezekiel also says that the beasts of the field will be part of this massive cleanup of humanity's worst war in history.
>
> *Rev 19:17 Then I saw an angel standing in the sun, and he cried out with a loud voice, saying to **all the birds which fly in midheaven**, "Come, assemble for the great supper of God, Rev 19:18 so that you may eat the flesh of kings and the flesh of commanders and the flesh of mighty men and the flesh of horses and of those who sit on them and the flesh of all men, both free men and slaves, and small and great."*
>
> *Rev 19:19 And I saw the beast and the kings of the earth and their armies assembled to make war against Him who sat on the horse and against His army.*
>
> *Rev 19:20 And the beast was seized, and with him the false prophet who performed the signs in his presence, by which he deceived those who had received the mark of the beast and those who worshiped his image; these two were thrown alive into the lake of fire which burns with brimstone.*
>
> *Rev 19:21 And the rest were killed with the sword which came from the mouth of Him who sat on the horse, and all the birds were filled with their flesh.*

Eze 39:21 "And I will set My glory among the nations; and all the nations will see My judgment which I have executed and My hand which I have laid on them.

Eze 39:22 **"And the house of Israel will know** that I am the LORD their God from that day onward.

Eze 39:23 "The nations will know that the house of Israel went into exile for their iniquity because they acted treacherously against Me, and I hid My face from them; so I gave them into the hand of their adversaries, and all of them fell by the sword.

Eze 39:24 "According to their uncleanness and according to their transgressions I dealt with them, and I hid My face from them."'"

Eze 39:25 Therefore thus says the Lord GOD, "**Now I will restore the fortunes of Jacob** and have mercy on the whole house of Israel; and I will be jealous for My holy name.

Eze 39:26 "They will forget their disgrace and all their treachery which they perpetrated against Me, when they live securely on their own land with no one to make them afraid.

Eze 39:27 "When I bring them back from the peoples and gather them from the lands of their enemies, then I shall be sanctified through them in the sight of the many nations.

Eze 39:28 "Then they will know that I am the LORD their God because I made them go into exile among the nations, and then gathered them again to their own land; and I will leave none of them there any longer.

Eze 39:29 "I will not hide My face from them any longer, for **I will have poured out My Spirit on the house of Israel,"** declares the Lord GOD.

> *Notice the sequence of events that God portrays in the very necessary path of Israel's deliverance. First there is the treachery of the nation, where God clearly instructed Israel and they disobeyed. Then they are sent into exile as punishment for their sin. Then God hides His face from them, and they are delivered into the hands of enemies. Finally, he extends mercy to them, gathers them from all the lands of exile, restores their fortunes and pours out His Spirit upon the whole house of Israel.*
>
> *This is near-far prophecy that foresees the Babylonian Captivity and all its sadness for the nation, but stops short of restoring the fortunes and pouring out the Spirit upon the nation. This will only happen in the last days, when Armageddon is complete, and Israel is once again the perfect embodiment of the "apple of God's eye."*

BEAT YOUR PLOWSHARES INTO SWORDS

Joel 3:1 "For behold, in those days and at that time, when I restore the fortunes of Judah and Jerusalem,

Joel 3:2 I will gather all the nations And bring them down to **the valley of Jehoshaphat**. Then I will enter into judgment with them there on behalf of My people and My inheritance, Israel, whom they have scattered among the nations; **and they have divided up My land.**

Joel 3:3 "They have also cast lots for My people, Traded a boy for a harlot And sold a girl for wine that they may drink.

> ***the valley of Jehoshaphat.*** *This valley is generally considered to be the Hinnom Valley or the ancient place called Gehenna. See page 329.*
>
> ***and they have divided up my land.*** *Part of the resolution to make Israel a nation-state included the proposal to give the Arabs 44% of the land which today comprises The West Bank and the Gaza Strip. The Arabs refused this agreement and consequently postponed statehood, preferring not to share the land with Israel. In the 1967 Six Day War, the Jews fought to retain control of Jerusalem. The official partitioning of Israel has not yet come to pass.*

Joel 3:4 "Moreover, what are you to Me, O Tyre, Sidon and all the regions of Philistia? Are you rendering Me a recompense? But if you do recompense Me, swiftly and speedily I will return your recompense on your head.

Joel 3:5 "Since you have taken My silver and My gold, brought My precious treasures to your temples,

Joel 3:6 and sold the sons of Judah and Jerusalem to the Greeks in order to remove them far from their territory,

Joel 3:7 behold, I am going to arouse them from the place where you have sold them, and return your recompense on your head.

Joel 3:8 "Also I will sell your sons and your daughters into the hand of the sons of Judah, and they will sell them to **the Sabeans**, to a distant nation," for the LORD has spoken.

> **the Sabeans.** An ancient region that is known today as Yemen. This region was also known in biblical days as Sheba.

Joel 3:9 Proclaim this among the nations: Prepare a war; rouse the mighty men! Let all the soldiers draw near, let them come up!

Joel 3:10 **Beat your plowshares into swords** And your pruning hooks into spears; Let the weak say, "I am a mighty man."

Joel 3:11 Hasten and come, all you surrounding nations, And gather yourselves there. Bring down, O LORD, Your mighty ones.

Joel 3:12 Let the nations be aroused and come up to **the valley of Jehoshaphat**, For there I will sit to judge all the surrounding nations.

Joel 3:13 Put in the sickle, for the harvest is ripe. Come, tread, for **the wine press is full;** The vats overflow, for their wickedness is great.

Statue of Joel 3:10 created by Soviet sculptor and given to the United Nations in 1959.

The wine press is full. See Rev 14:19,20 and Rev 19:15.

Joel 3:14 Multitudes, multitudes in the valley of decision! For the day of the LORD is near in the valley of decision.

Joel 3:15 **The sun and moon grow dark** And the stars lose their brightness. (See Matt. 24:29)

Joel 3:16 The LORD roars from Zion And utters His voice from Jerusalem, And the heavens and the earth tremble. But the LORD is a refuge for His people And a stronghold to the sons of Israel.

Joel 3:17 Then you will know that I am the LORD your God, Dwelling in Zion, My holy mountain. So Jerusalem will be holy, And strangers will pass through it no more.

Joel 3:18 **And in that day** The mountains will drip with sweet wine, And the hills will flow with milk, And all the brooks of Judah will flow with water; And a spring will go out from the house of the LORD to water the valley of Shittim (pronounced Sh-teem)

Joel 3:19 Egypt will become a waste, And Edom will become a desolate wilderness, Because of the violence done to the sons of Judah, In whose land they have shed innocent blood.

Joel 3:20 **But Judah will be inhabited forever** And Jerusalem for all generations.

Joel 3:21 And I will avenge their blood which I have not avenged, For the LORD dwells in Zion.

> ***And in that day . . . But Judah will be inhabited forever.*** *This end-time snapshot prophesies a panoramic view of events from Jesus' rapture (sun and moon grow dark) to the wrath of God (the Lord roars from Zion), to Armageddon (valley of Jehoshaphat) up to the millennial kingdom, when Judah will be at peace and God will inhabit Zion.*

GREAT JUMPIN' JEHOSHAPHAT

Don Francisco, singer, songwriter

This story is told in 2 Chronicles 20:15-32. Please listen on Youtube.

Now Jehoshaphat was king in Jerusalem a long long time ago
When the children of Judah all worshiped the Lord, from the high on down to the low
And Judah was a wealthy kingdom - everybody's children were fed
'Cause Jehoshaphat studied the Word of the Lord and did everything He said.

But out the east came an army one day after Jehoshaphat's gold
And they were marching right straight to Jerusalem and Jehoshaphat soon was told
So he called all the people together and everyone fasted and prayed
The Lord God answered the people and He said there's no need for you to be afraid

Because the battle is mine tomorrow, it's not yours and it's not the king's
And all you got to do is just stand and watch to see the salvation I bring
Just believe that what I told you is exactly what I'm going to do
And go out tomorrow against them now because the Lord's gonna fight for you.

Great Jumpin' Jehoshaphat!

Well the army rose early next morning marched on out with the king
Jehoshaphat chose some singers, and he told those singers to sing
And they praised the beauty of holiness instead of shouting out a battle cry
And all the way down to the enemy's camp they sang to the Lord on high

They were singing: Praise ye the Lord, His mercy endures forever and ever
Praise ye the Lord, His mercy endures forever and ever
Praise ye the Lord, His mercy endures forever and ever
Praise ye the Lord our God - His mercy will never end.

Well the Lord God set up an ambush, He got the enemy all turned around
And they started into killing each other you know till they all laid dead on the ground
And the riches and the jewels that they left behind, it took them three whole days to haul
The children of Judah all praised the Lord 'cause He saved them one and all

If the parallel's not real obvious now, I'll spell it right out for you
When you see trouble comin' to rip you off here's all that you need to do
Just pray to your heavenly Father and believe that His Word is true
And then step out and shout the salvation of God 'cause He'll win that battle for you

The Bride of the Lamb

Conventional wisdom tells us that the Church is the bride and Jesus is the bridegroom. In the parable of the ten virgins, Matthew 25, the five virgins are symbolically the Church, awaiting the return of the bridegroom, who will then take His bride to the wedding party. But in Revelation, there is no mention of the Church as the bride of Christ - only the holy city. Perhaps the best interpretation of this is to understand the intrinsic link between ancient Israel and ancient Jerusalem - and, modern Israel and modern Jerusalem. The people must have a dwelling place and God is married to the idea that people and city are bonded together as His beloved. Notice below that scripture is consistent in presenting the harlot of Revelation with a city. In the future kingdom of God, the people will be His Children - Church and Chosen together - in the holy city, as the bride of Jesus.

2 Corinthians 11:2 For I am jealous for you with a godly jealousy; for **I betrothed you** to one husband, so that to Christ I might present you as a pure virgin.

Ephesians 5:23 For the husband is the head of the wife, as Christ also is the head of the church . . .

Revelation 19:7 "Let us rejoice and be glad and give the glory to Him, for the marriage of the Lamb has come and **His bride has made herself ready."**

Rev 19:8 It was given to her to clothe herself in fine linen, bright and clean; for the fine linen is the righteous acts of the saints.

Revelation 21:2

And I saw the holy city, new Jerusalem, coming down out of heaven from God, made ready **as a bride adorned for her husband.**

Rev 21:9 Then one of the seven angels who had the seven bowls full of the seven last plagues came and spoke with me, saying, "Come here, **I will show you the bride**, the wife of the Lamb."

Rev 21:10 And he carried me away in the Spirit to a great and high mountain, **and showed me the holy city, Jerusalem,** coming down out of heaven from God,

The woman (Israel)	and	Jerusalem
The Harlot (Islam)	and	The Great City Babylon
The Church and Israel	and	The New Jerusalem.

Babylon, the One World Government

BABYLON THE GREAT IS FALLEN.

Rev 18:1 After these things I saw another angel coming down from heaven, having great authority, and the earth was illumined with his glory.

Rev 18:2 And he cried out with a mighty voice, saying, **"Fallen, fallen is Babylon the great**! She has become a dwelling place of demons and a prison of every unclean spirit, and a prison of every unclean and hateful bird.

Rev 18:3 "For all the nations have drunk of the wine of the passion of her immorality, and the kings of the earth have committed acts of immorality with her, and the merchants of the earth have become rich by the wealth of her sensuality."

Rev 18:4 I heard another voice from heaven, saying, **"Come out of her, my people**, so that you will not participate in her sins and receive of her plagues;

Rev 18:5 for her sins have piled up as high as heaven, and God has remembered her iniquities.

Rev 18:6 "Pay her back even as she has paid, and give back to her double according to her deeds; in the cup which she has mixed, mix twice as much for her.

Rev 18:7 "To the degree that she glorified herself and lived sensuously, to the same degree give her torment and mourning; for she says in her heart, *"I sit as a queen and I am not a widow, and will never see mourning."*

Rev 18:8 "For this reason in one day her plagues will come, pestilence and mourning and famine, and she will be burned up with fire; for the Lord God who judges her is strong.

Rev 18:9 "And the kings of the earth, who committed acts of immorality and lived sensuously with her, will weep and lament over her when they see the smoke of her burning,

Rev 18:10 standing at a distance because of the fear of her torment, saying, 'Woe, woe, the great city, Babylon, the strong city! For **in one hour** your judgment has come.'

> ***fallen, fallen is Babylon the great.*** *Revelation 17:5 identifies Babylon the Great as a mystery. Some of the possibilities for Babylon, the great city, are as follows:*
> 1) *ROME, based on the belief (by some) that the Pope is the lawless one.*
> 2) *AMERICA, based on the downward spiral into immorality and idolatry.*
> 3) *BABYLON, the ancient city, although today it lies in ruins as ordained by God.*
> 4) *NEW YORK CITY, based on the belief that is considered to be the worlds great city.*
> 5) *DUBAI, based on the belief that it may be the next New York City.*
> 6) *MECCA. based on the reality that it is the most sacred Muslim city in the world.*
> 7) *IRAQ, based on the fact that this middle eastern state was ancient Babylonia.*
> 8) *JERUSALEM, the possibility that the AntiChrist completely corrupts the holy city.*

Rev 18:11 "And the merchants of the earth weep and mourn over her, because no one buys their cargoes any more-

Rev 18:12 cargoes of gold and silver and precious stones and pearls and fine linen and purple and silk and scarlet, and every kind of citron wood and every article of ivory and every article made from very costly wood and bronze and iron and marble,

Rev 18:13 and cinnamon and spice and incense and perfume and frankincense and wine and olive oil and fine flour and wheat and cattle and sheep, and cargoes of horses and chariots and slaves and human lives.

Rev 18:14 "The fruit you long for has gone from you, and all things that were luxurious and splendid have passed away from you and men will no longer find them.

Rev 18:15 "The merchants of these things, who became rich from her, will stand at a distance because of the fear of her torment, weeping and mourning,

Rev 18:16 saying, **'Woe, woe, the great city,** she who was clothed in fine linen and purple and scarlet, and adorned with gold and precious stones and pearls;

Rev 18:17 for **in one hour** such great wealth has been laid waste!' And every shipmaster and every passenger and sailor, and as many as make their living by the sea, stood at a distance,

Rev 18:18 and were crying out as they saw the smoke of her burning, saying, **'What city is like the great city?'**

Rev 18:19 "And they threw dust on their heads and were crying out, weeping and mourning, saying, 'Woe, woe, the great city, in which all who had ships at sea became rich by her wealth, for in one hour she has been laid waste!'

Rev 18:20 "Rejoice over her, O heaven, and you saints and apostles and prophets, because God has pronounced judgment for you against her."

> ***Woe, woe, the great city . . . What city is like the great city.***   *Throwing dust on their heads was an ancient middle eastern mourning tradition. Does 'ships at sea' literally mean a seaport? Is the selling of ivory a key to understanding the great city? Is it also possible that the great city is more than just a city, but perhaps symbolic of all great cities, therefore representing the arrogance of civilization to build towers to the sky in a symbolic gesture to defy the God of the heavens. Genesis 10:12 first identifies "the great city": as the kingdom of Babel and the land of Shinar, which is understood to be Iraq. Though Jerusalem is considered to be the city that split in three parts (Rev 16:19), it is worth noting that Jerusalem is generally referred to in scripture as "the holy city." It is also possible that God could withdraw the curse of Jeremiah 50:39 to allow the ancient city of Babylon (which sits on the Euphrates) to rise in power in the last days.*

THE STRONG ANGEL THROWS THE MILLSTONE.

Rev 18:21 Then a strong angel took up a stone like **a great millstone** and threw it into the sea, saying, "So will Babylon, the great city, be thrown down with violence, and will not be found any longer.

Rev 18:22 "And **the sound of harpists** and musicians and flute-players and trumpeters will not be heard in you any longer; **and no craftsman** of any craft will be found in you any longer; and the sound of a mill will not be heard in you any longer;

Rev 18:23 and **the light of a lamp** will not shine in you any longer; and the voice of the bridegroom and bride will not be heard in you any longer; for your merchants were **the great men of the earth,** because all the nations were deceived by your sorcery.

Rev 18:24 "And **in her was found the blood of prophets** and of saints and of all who have been slain on the earth."

a great millstone.   *In Matthew 18:6, Jesus condemned those who become a negative influence or a stumbling block to little children. The analogy He used was tying a millstone around their neck and casting them into the sea. There are two parts to the typical millstone: the bedstone, which serves as the base for the runner stone which then crushes and refines the grain.   A typical bedstone could weigh as much as 3300 pounds. The strong angel in this passage was sending a strong message that Babylon, with all its associated evil, would be condemned to a violent end.*

the sound of harpists . . . no craftsman.   *Music and craftsmanship are two of the wonderful symbols of a civilized society. Babylon the great city is symbolic of civilization. When civilization is finally sabotaged, the arts will be destroyed and replaced by some form of mechanized entertainment. Craftsmanship and the trade associated with the production of products in the marketplace will also be reduced to primitive forms bartering for survival. Like the tower of Babel in Genesis 11:9, the focus on civilization instead of God will eventually lead to anarchy.*

the light of a lamp. *Coupled with the analogy of a bride and groom, this signifies the lack of joy and happiness that comes with the numbing affect of losing all connection to the civilization that we have all become accustomed. Life will be reduced to nothing more than animal survival.*

in her was found the blood of prophets.   *Revelation 17:6 says: "And I saw the woman drunk with the blood of the saints, and with the blood of the witnesses of Jesus. When I saw her, I wondered greatly."   This will not be humanism or secularism that attempts to eradicate the testimony of Jesus. This will be a religion, most likely Islam, which will call the Christian community infidels, and seeks to suppress freedom of religion, until finally enforcing new laws upon the unsuspecting community.*

Regarding the timing of God's wrath, we know that the tribulation initiates the second half of the seventieth week of Daniel. The tribulation is an unknown period of time which ends with the coming of Christ in Matthew 24:30. Immediately after the silence in heaven, the time of God's wrath begins, inaugurating The Day of the Lord trumpet judgments. Since our focus is so much on the division of two 3.5 year periods of time, we tend to overlook the timeframe simply known as the seventh year, which represents the final and climactic year of history's consummation. Based on our understanding of the year of Shemitah, is it possible, based on Isaiah 34 and 63, that the final year also coincides with God's wrath?

Isaiah 34:8 says:
"For the LORD has a day of vengeance,
a year of recompense for the cause of Zion."

Isaiah 63:4 says:
"For the day of vengeance was in My heart,
And **My year of redemption** has come.

This is merely theological forecasting, not really an attempt at calculating the timing of end-time events. The only clue that we have regarding the duration of the trumpet judgments is the fifth trumpet, in which God allows locusts, with the sting of a scorpion, to torment for five months. Based on this verse alone, and the hypothesis that the trumpet judgments last for one year, then the other trumpet judgments would endure for 7 more months.

Rev 9:3 Then out of the smoke came locusts upon the earth, and power was given them, as the scorpions of the earth have power.

Rev 9:4 They were told not to hurt the grass of the earth, nor any green thing, nor any tree, but only the men who do not have the seal of God on their foreheads.

Rev 9:5 And they were not permitted to kill anyone, but to torment **for five months;** and their torment was like the torment of a scorpion when it stings a man.

It is also possible that if the duration of God's wrath is one year, then this could be inclusive of the 30 day period after the seventh trumpet. The implication is that the duration of the trumpet judgments is now eleven months instead of twelve.

Does this really matter? No, this is merely speculation, but it does allow us to paint a picture of the severity of this "time of Jacob's trouble." Perhaps the terms 'year of recompense' and 'year of redemption' point specifically to the final year of man's willful defiance to a loving God. We do not know. We can only speculate.

THE 45 DAY PERIOD OF RESTORING AUTHORITY

The simplest way to explain this complex time is to compare it to Hanukkah, or the Feast of Dedication. Jesus Himself celebrated this feast, which remembered the cleansing of the temple after the terror of Antiochus in 165 bc. This 45 day period is a cleansing and preparing as the people prepare for the Millennial reign of Christ. Three groups of people will enter the Millennium: the remnant of Israel, the Gentile nations who did not take the mark of the beast and the martyrs who were slain during the Tribulation period. This period will climax with the Sheep and Goat judgment, in which the nations will be judged. Jesus is always the standard, but grace is extended according to the mercy of God.

JERUSALEM AND MT. ZION WILL BE RESTORED.

Isaiah 2:2, Micah 4: 1-3. Now it will come about that In the last days the mountain of the house of the LORD will be established as the chief of the mountains, and will be raised above the hills; And all the nations will stream to it.

THE NATION OF ISRAEL WILL BE RESTORED.

Isa 10:20 Now in that day the remnant of Israel, and those of the house of Jacob who have escaped, will never again rely on the one who struck them, but will truly rely on the LORD, the Holy One of Israel.

Isa 10:21 A remnant will return, the remnant of Jacob, to the mighty God.

Isa 66:18 "For I know their works and their thoughts; the time is coming to gather all nations and tongues. And they shall come and see My glory.

Isa 66:19 "I will set a sign among them and will send survivors from them to the nations: Tarshish, Put, Lud, Meshech, Tubal and Javan, to the distant coastlands that have neither heard My fame nor seen My glory. And they will declare My glory among the nations.

Isa 66:20 "Then they shall bring all your brothers from all the nations as a grain offering to the LORD, on horses, in chariots, in litters, on mules and on camels, to My holy mountain Jerusalem," says the LORD, "just as the sons of Israel bring their grain offering in a clean vessel to the house of the LORD.

THE GENTILE NATIONS WILL BE RESTORED.

Isa 19:24 In that day Israel will be the third party with Egypt and Assyria, a blessing in the midst of the earth,

Isa 19:25 whom the LORD of hosts has blessed, saying, "Blessed is Egypt My people, and Assyria the work of My hands, and Israel My inheritance."

Isa 56:6 "Also the foreigners who join themselves to the LORD, to minister to Him, and to love the name of the LORD, to be His servants, every one who keeps from profaning the sabbath And holds fast My covenant;

Isa 56:7 Even those I will bring to My holy mountain And make them joyful in My house of prayer. Their burnt offerings and their sacrifices will be acceptable on My altar; For My house will be called a house of prayer for all the peoples."

Mic 7:16 Nations will see and be ashamed of all their might. They will put *their* hand on *their* mouth, Their ears will be deaf.

Mic 7:17 They will lick the dust like a serpent, Like reptiles of the earth. They will come trembling out of their fortresses; To the LORD our God they will come in dread And they will be afraid before You.

THE TEMPLE WILL BE RESTORED.

Zechariah 6:13 "Yes, it is He who will build the temple of the LORD, and He who will bear the honor and sit and rule on His throne. Thus, He will be a priest on His throne, and the counsel of peace will be between the two offices."'

THE MESSIAH'S SOVEREIGNTY OVER EARTH WILL BE RESTORED.

Dan 7:12 "As for the rest of the beasts, their dominion was taken away, but an extension of life was granted to them for an appointed period of time.

Dan 7:13 "I kept looking in the night visions, And behold, with the clouds of heaven One like a Son of Man was coming, And He came up to the Ancient of Days And was presented before Him.

Dan 7:14 "And to Him was given dominion, Glory and a kingdom, That all the peoples, nations and *men of every* language Might serve Him. His dominion is an everlasting dominion which will not pass away; And His kingdom is one which will not be destroyed.

THE MARTYRS WILL BE RESTORED.

Rev 20:4 Then I saw thrones, and they sat on them, and judgment was given to them. And I *saw* the souls of those who had been beheaded because of their testimony of Jesus and because of the word of God, and those who had not worshiped the beast or his image, and had not received the mark on their forehead and on their hand; and they came to life and reigned with Christ for a thousand years.

"The other nations of the earth
will not only serve and glorify God,
but they will also serve His chosen nation Israel,
rather than afflict them again,
as they have done for thousands of years
in the past.
ROBERT VAN KAMPEN
"THE SIGN"

6

THE MILLENNIUM

"They Will Lick the Dust of Your Feet"

Earth has just been destroyed by God's wrath. The angel now seizes Satan and casts him into a pit of darkness for a thousand years. God then miraculously restores part of planet earth, leaving some parts as memorials. There are three remnants of mankind that remain: the Jews who survived the Tribulation, the nations (Gentiles) who did not take the mark of the beast and those who were beheaded for their faith. Christ now begins His rule over the earth, with David as prince over the land of Israel. You've heard it said that the lion and the lamb will lie down together? That statement has been confused with the two persons of Jesus: the lion and the lamb. Isaiah 11:6 actually says: *"And the wolf will dwell with the lamb . . ."* Earth will experience the Garden of Eden for a thousand years. Satan is released from the pit long enough to tempt man into rebellion once more before being cast into the lake of fire.

The apostolic church thought more about
the Second Coming of Jesus Christ
than about death and heaven.
The early Christians were looking,
not for a cleft in the ground called a grave,
but for a cleavage in the sky called Glory.
Alexander MacLaren

THE MILLENNIUM
RESTORING THE FORTUNES OF JUDAH

This chapter will probably provoke more questions than answers. The Millennium can only be understood by one who is willing to acknowledge that the chosen remnant of Israel will indeed flourish for a thousand years at the expense of all the nations that sought their extermination. For those who think Zionism (restoring Israel's ownership of Jerusalem) is a political oppression of the Palestinians, you won't like this chapter. After all the drama of the Tribulation, and the Second Coming, and the Wrath of God, you would think that God's theater of man's redemption was ready to close the curtain for the final song. But God has one more message to the nations. Like Joseph, who rose from slavery to become great in the land of pharaoh - so the remnant of Israel will rise from the ashes of the Holocaust, and rise from the world's bigotry, and rise from the days of Tribulation, to show the world what it is like to worship King Jesus. The story of the Prodigal Son comes to mind. Israel, the Prodigal, has returned home; and the Father will put a ring on their collective finger. They will celebrate while singing 'Amazing Grace': *"I once was lost but now I'm found, was blind, but now I see."*

Restoring the Fortunes
REVELATION CHAPTER 20

THE DRAGON IS BOUND.

Rev 20:1 Then I saw an angel coming down from heaven, holding **the key of the abyss** and a great chain in his hand. Rev 20:2 And he laid hold of the dragon, the serpent of old, who is the devil and Satan, and **bound him** for a thousand years; Rev 20:3 and he threw him into the abyss, and shut it and sealed it over him, so that he would not deceive the nations any longer, until the thousand years were completed; after these things he must be released for a short time.

> ***the key of the abyss.*** *Notice that the abyss is not the lake of fire. Satan will not be cast into the lake of fire until v10, after the millennium. The Greek word 'bussos' means deep. The prefix 'a' means that this deep is actually boundless or bottomless. The abyss is a holding cell for the demons until the final judgment in the lake of fire.*
> ***bound him.*** *It has become popular to 'bind Satan' through the act of intense prayer in order to limit his power over a particular circumstance. We pray in faith, we pray with power, but the reality is Satan can only be bound by an angel who is commissioned by God. It is good to pray against the forces of darkness but Satan cannot be bound, only restricted.*

THE MILLENNIEL REIGN OF CHRIST.

Rev 20:4 Then I saw thrones, and they sat on them, and **judgment** was given to them. And I saw the souls of those who had been **beheaded** because of their testimony of Jesus and because of the word of God, and those who had not worshiped the beast or his image, and had not received the mark on their forehead and on their hand; and they came to life and reigned with Christ for a thousand years.
Rev 20:5 The rest of the dead did not come to life until the thousand years were completed. This is **the first resurrection.** Rev 20:6 Blessed and holy is the one who has a part in the first resurrection; over these the second death has no power, but they will be priests of God and of Christ and will reign with Him for a thousand years.

> ***judgment.*** *The Greek word is bema, which means the mercy seat in 2 Cor. 5:10. This Is the sheep and goat judgment of Matt 25.*
> ***beheaded.*** *Perhaps the most violent form of execution, this practice still continues to day by radical jihadists.*
> ***the first resurrection*** *is for the dead in Christ, the raptured and those who have died in the Tribulation, having been judged innocent by the blood of Christ. At the 7TH trumpet, the unrighteous are judged, awaiting sentencing at the Great White Throne.*

SATAN IS RELEASED.

Rev 20:7 When the thousand years are completed, Satan will be released from his prison,

Rev 20:8 and will come out to deceive the nations which are in the four corners of the earth, **Gog and Magog**, to gather them together for the war; the number of them is like the sand of the seashore.

Rev 20:9 And they came up on the broad plain of the earth and surrounded the camp of the saints and the beloved city, and **fire came down** from heaven and devoured them.

Rev 20:10 And the devil who deceived them was thrown into the lake of fire and brimstone, where the beast and the false prophet are also; and they will be tormented day and night forever and ever.

> ***Gog and Magog.*** *The name Gog is used 8 of 10 times in Ezekiel 38 and 39. See explanation on page 198 and 326.*
>
> ***Fire came down.*** *The climax of human history shows the sons of Adam, once more deceived by the devil. Isaiah 30:33 describes the Lord's breath as fire and brimstone.*

THE BOOK OF LIFE IS OPENED.

Rev 20:11 Then I saw a **great white throne** and Him who sat upon it, from whose presence earth and heaven fled away, and no place was found for them.

Rev 20:12 And I saw the dead, the great and the small, standing before the throne, and books were opened; and another book was opened, which is **the book of life**; and the dead were judged from the things which were written in the books, according to their deeds.

Rev 20:13 And the sea gave up the dead which were in it, and death and Hades gave up the dead which were in them; and they were judged, every one of them according to their deeds.

Rev 20:14 Then death and Hades were thrown into the lake of fire. This is the second death, the lake of fire.

Rev 20:15 And if anyone's name was not found written in the book of life, he was thrown into the lake of fire.

> ***great white throne.***   *This final judgment is for three groups: the dead unbelievers of all time, the defiant unbelievers in the millennium who are now dead, and the remnant of saints who were faithful in spite of Satan's deception.*
>
> ***the book of life.***   *Exodus 32:33 says that sinners (unless saved by the blood of Christ) are blotted out of the book. Rev 13:8 and 17:8 say that the book was recorded before the foundations of the world.*

ISAIAH'S MILLENNIAL VISION

THE NATIONS WILL BOW BEFORE ISRAEL.

Isa 49:22 Thus says the Lord GOD, "Behold, I will lift up My hand to the nations And set up My standard to the peoples; And they will bring your sons in their bosom, And your daughters will be carried on their shoulders.

Isa 49:23 "Kings will be your guardians, And their princesses your nurses. They will bow down to you with their faces to the earth **and lick the dust of your feet;** And *you* will know that I am the LORD; Those who hopefully wait for Me will not be put to shame.

> ***and lick the dust of your feet.*** *The ultimate forgiveness has taken place. God has forgiven His beloved Israel of their sinfulness, and now He restores them to a place of honor. Throughout the millennium, His "chosen people" will be served by kings and princesses. This would imply that the nations are not all believers, and probably serve Jesus as King of the earth with some reluctance.*

THE MILLENNIEL GENERATION

Isa 65:20 "No longer will there be in it **an infant who lives but a few days**, or an old man who does not live out his days; For the youth will die at the age of one hundred And the one who does not reach the age of one hundred will be thought accursed.

Isa 65:21 "They will build houses and inhabit them; They will also plant vineyards and eat their fruit.

Isa 65:22 "They will not build and another inhabit, They will not plant and another eat; For as the lifetime of a tree, so will be the days of My people, And **My chosen ones** will wear out the work of their hands.

Isa 65:23 "They will not labor in vain, Or bear children for calamity; For they are the offspring of those blessed by the LORD, And their descendants with them.

Isa 65:24 "It will also come to pass that before they call, I will answer; and while they are still speaking, I will hear.

Isa 65:25 **"The wolf and the lamb** will graze together, and the lion will eat straw like the ox; and dust will be the serpent's food. They will do no evil or harm in all My holy mountain," says the LORD.

> ***An infant who lives but a few days.*** *The millennium will be a re-enactment of what God intended for the Garden of Eden. Adam lived to be 930. It is likely that God will allow those who entered the millennium to return to the "age of longevity", meaning that 100 years will appear to be youthful.*
>
> ***My chosen ones.*** *It is most likely that this expression identifies the Jewish nation whom God allowed to enter the millennium. The implication here is that wooden houses and artifacts will deteriorate long before the owner of the house.*

348

> **The wolf and the lamb.** *This is the classic imagery that portrays*
> *"the mild and the wild" co-habiting in the future animal kingdom. This*
> *verse is often confused with the expression "the lion and the lamb" will lie down*
> *together. Actually, the lion and the lamb are not a reference to the millennial*
> *kingdom, but rather a composite image of Christ as both the lamb of God and the lion*
> *of Judah.*

JEREMIAH'S MILLENNIAL VISION

RESTORING THE FORTUNES OF JACOB.

Jer 29:14 'I will be found by you,' declares the LORD, 'and **I will restore your fortunes** and will gather you from all the nations and from all the places where I have driven you,' declares the LORD, 'and I will bring you back to the place from where I sent you into exile.'

Jer 30:3 'For behold, days are coming,' declares the LORD, 'when **I will restore the fortunes** of My people Israel and Judah.' The LORD says, 'I will also bring them back to the land that I gave to their forefathers and they shall possess it.'"

Jer 30:18 "Thus says the LORD, 'Behold, **I will restore the fortunes** of the tents of Jacob And have compassion on his dwelling places; And the city will be rebuilt on its ruin, And the palace will stand on its rightful place.

Jer 31:23 Thus says the LORD of hosts, the God of Israel, "Once again they will speak this word in the land of Judah and in its cities **when I restore their fortunes**, 'The LORD bless you, O abode of righteousness, O holy hill!'

Jer 33:7 '**I will restore the fortunes of Judah** and the fortunes of Israel and will rebuild them as they were at first.

> **I will restore the fortunes.** *This term is used 11 times in Jeremiah, and only 1 other time in each of the books of Ezekiel, Hosea, Joel, and Zephaniah. This is called "near/far" prophecy, and relates to both imminent events and also end-time events.*
>
> *1) It applies first of all to the restoration of Jerusalem after the Babylonian captivity.*
>
> *2) It also applies to the restoration of Israel in 1948.*
>
> *3) It also applies to the restoration of Israel during the Millennium.*
>
> *Like the Hittites and the Jebusites, Israel could have been a footnote in history. Instead It will become a global monument to remember and revere the God of Israel.*

Zechariah's Millennial Vision

B. JESUS WILL BE KING OF THE EARTH.

Zec 14:8 And in that day **living waters** will flow out of Jerusalem, half of them toward the eastern sea and the other half toward the western sea; it will be in summer as well as in winter.

Zec 14:9 And the LORD will be **king over all the earth;** in that day the LORD will be the only one, and His name the only one.

Zec 14:10 All the land will be changed into a plain from Geba to Rimmon south of Jerusalem; but Jerusalem will rise and remain on its site from Benjamin's Gate as far as the place of the First Gate to the Corner Gate, and from the Tower of Hananel to the king's wine presses. Zec 14:11 People will live in it, and there will no longer be a curse, for Jerusalem will dwell in security.

> *living waters*. Jerusalem's only water source is the Gihon Spring, which is mentioned in Genesis chapter two as one of the four rivers flowing from the Garden of Eden. The primary water source for the city comes from water pumped in from coastal aquifers. These waters flowing toward the west and toward the east indicate new sources of water not known to the biblical residents of Jerusalem. In 2011, while planning for a major subway under Jerusalem, geologists unearthed a huge underground river. God has sources we know not of.
>
> *king over all the earth*. Jesus will literally rule the earth as intended in the original Garden of Eden. See references for Revelation 12:5 and 19:15. It is prophesied that Jesus will rule with a rod of iron, but these refer only to the Millennium when mankind still has the freedom to sin and to disobey.
>
> Rev 12:5 And she gave birth to a son, a male child, **who is to rule all the nations with a rod of iron**; and her child was caught up to God and to His throne.
> Rev 19:15 From His mouth comes a sharp sword, so that with it He may strike down the nations, **and He will rule them with a rod of iron**; and He treads the wine press of the fierce wrath of God, the Almighty.

C. A VISION OF ARMAGEDDON.

Zec 14:12 Now this will be the plague with which the LORD will strike all the peoples who have gone to war against Jerusalem; **their flesh will rot** while they stand on their feet, and their eyes will rot in their sockets, and their tongue will rot in their mouth.

Zec 14:13 It will come about in that day that a great panic from the LORD will fall on them; and they will seize one another's hand, and the hand of one will be lifted against the hand of another.

Zec 14:14 Judah also will fight at Jerusalem; and the wealth of all the surrounding nations will be gathered, gold and silver and garments in great abundance.

Zec 14:15 So also like this plague will be the plague on the horse, the mule, the camel, the donkey and all the cattle that will be in those camps.

> **their flesh will rot.** *Director Steven Spielburg obviously read this passage of Scripture during the filming of the Indiana Jones' episode "Raiders of the Lost Ark." When the Germans opened the ark, expecting to capitalize on the power of God, their flesh rotted from their faces.*

D. THE NATIONS WILL WORSHIP JESUS.

Zec 14:16 Then it will come about that **any who are left** (of all the nations that went against Jerusalem) will go up from year to year to worship the King, the LORD of hosts, and to celebrate **the Feast of Booths.**

Zec 14:17 And it will be that whichever of the families of the earth does not go up to Jerusalem to worship the King, the LORD of hosts, there will be **no rain on them.**

Zec 14:18 If the family of Egypt does not go up or enter, then no rain will fall on them; it will be the plague with which the LORD smites the nations who do not go up to celebrate the Feast of Booths.

Zec 14:19 This will be the punishment of Egypt, and the punishment of all the nations who do not go up to celebrate the Feast of Booths.

Zec 14:20 In that day there will be inscribed on the bells of the horses, "HOLY TO THE LORD." And the cooking pots in the LORD'S house will be like the bowls before the altar.

Zec 14:21 Every cooking pot in Jerusalem and in Judah will be holy to the LORD of hosts; and all who sacrifice will come and take of them and boil in them. And there will no longer be a Canaanite in the house of the LORD of hosts in that day.

> **any who are left.** *This refers to those Gentiles who did not take the mark of the beast, and were allowed by God to be the seed of the Gentile nations that would inhabit the Millennium.*
>
> **the Feast of Booths.** *It is likely that the Jews (and likely believers) will be celebrating ALL the seven feasts of Israel, and the Gentile nations will be required to celebrate at least the final feast which symbolizes that God dwells in the midst of His people.*
>
> **no rain for them.** *It is interesting that the Millennium will be a time in which the nations will still have the freedom to choose to do right or wrong. The government of the Millennium will be a theocracy, in which Christ will be the King.*

EZEKIEL'S MILLENNIAL VISION

THE PROPHETIC TEMPLE

Eze 40:1 In **the twenty-fifth year of our exile**, at the beginning of the year, on the tenth of the month, in the **fourteenth year after the city was taken**, on that same day the hand of the LORD was upon me and He brought me there.

Eze 40:2 In the visions of God He brought me into the land of Israel and set me on a very high mountain, and on it to the south there was a structure like a city.

Eze 40:3 So He brought me there; and behold, there was a man whose appearance was like the appearance of bronze, with a line of flax and a measuring rod in his hand; and he was standing in the gateway.

Eze 40:4 The man said to me, "Son of man, see with your eyes, hear with your ears, and give attention to all that I am going to show you; for you have been brought here in order to show it to you. Declare to the house of Israel all that you see."

Eze 40:5 And behold, there was a wall on the outside of **the temple** all around, and in the man's hand was a measuring rod of six cubits, each of which was **a cubit and a hand-breadth.** So he measured the thickness of the wall, **one rod;** and the height, one rod.

> **twenty-fifth year of our exile . . . Fourteenth year after the city was taken.** *Jerusalem was "taken" (destroyed) in 586 bc. Fourteen years after that year would be 572-573 bc. The twenty-fifth year exile would be 598 bc. This verse, among many others, details the precision with which the Jewish people recorded their existence.*
>
> **the temple.** *This is referred to as the Third Temple or the Millennial Temple. If you include the Tribulation Temple, this is actually the fourth.*
>
> **a cubit and a handbreadth.** *The common cubit is generally considered to be 18", the length from the elbow to the fingertip. The handbreadth was usually 3 fingers, equaling 3". The royal cubit of Babylon was considered to be 21".*
>
> **one rod.** *Six royal cubits would equal 10.5 feet.*

Eze 43:10 "As for you, son of man, **describe the temple** to the house of Israel, that they may be ashamed of their iniquities; and let them measure the plan.

> **describe the temple.** *Chapters 40 through 48 describe with incredible detail this temple that will stand for a thousand years.   Note the size differential. This temple will have to accommodate millions of people from many nations.*

Eze 48:30 "These are the exits of the city: on the north side, **4,500 cubits** by measurement,

Eze 48:31 shall be the gates of the city, named for the tribes of Israel, three gates toward the north: the gate of Reuben, one; the gate of Judah, one; the gate of Levi, one.

Eze 48:32 "On the east side, 4,500 cubits, shall be three gates: the gate of Joseph, one; the gate of Benjamin, one; the gate of Dan, one.

Eze 48:33 "On the south side, 4,500 cubits by measurement, shall be three gates: the gate of Simeon, one; the gate of Issachar, one; the gate of Zebulun, one.

Eze 48:34 "On the west side, 4,500 cubits, shall be three gates: the gate of Gad, one; the gate of Asher, one; the gate of Naphtali, one.

Eze 48:35 **"The city shall be 18,000 cubits round about**; and the name of the city from that day shall be, **'The LORD is there.'"**

> **4500 cubits . . . 18,000 cubits.** *The equivalent of 6750 feet or 1.28 miles on each side; The total area of the temple itself would be 1046 acres. If by chance, these were royal cubits, each side would be 1.5 miles and 1423 acres.*
>
> **The Lord is there.** *The Hebrew translation is 'Jehovah Shom.' The implication of this statement is that Christ will inhabit this temple as the Messiah. He will walk among the people as He did 2,000 years ago. But this time, He will walk among them as the Creator God.*

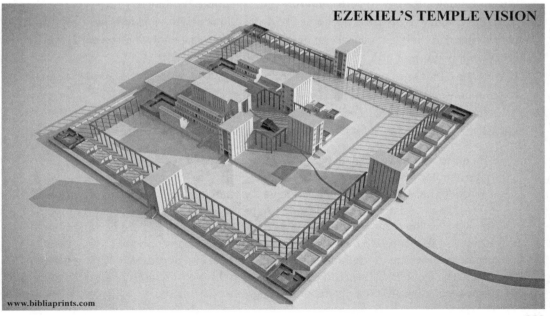

EZEKIEL'S TEMPLE VISION

www.bibliaprints.com

A Day is Like a Thousand Years

THE HEAVENS AND THE EARTH WILL BE BURNED UP.

2 Peter 3:1 This is now, beloved, the second letter I am writing to you in which I am stirring up your sincere mind by way of reminder,

2Pe 3:2 that you should remember the words spoken beforehand by the holy prophets and the commandment of the Lord and Savior spoken by your apostles.

2Pe 3:3 Know this first of all, that **in the last days mockers will come** with their mocking, following after their own lusts,

2Pe 3:4 and saying, "Where is the promise of His coming? For ever since the fathers fell asleep, all continues just as it was from the beginning of creation."

2Pe 3:5 For when they maintain this, it escapes their notice that by the word of God the heavens existed long ago and the earth was formed out of water and by water,

2Pe 3:6 through which the world at that time was destroyed, being flooded with water.

2Pe 3:7 But by His word the present heavens and earth are being reserved for fire, kept for the day of judgment and destruction of ungodly men.

2Pe 3:8 But do not let this one fact escape your notice, beloved, that with the Lord **one day is like a thousand years,** and a thousand years like one day.

2Pe 3:9 The Lord is not slow about His promise, as some count slowness, but is patient toward you, not wishing for any to perish but for all to come to repentance.

2Pe 3:10 But the day of the Lord will come like a thief, in which the heavens will pass away with a roar and the elements will be destroyed with intense heat, and **the earth and its works will be burned up.**

2Pe 3:11 Since all these things are to be destroyed in this way, what sort of people ought you to be in holy conduct and godliness,

2Pe 3:12 looking for and hastening the coming of the day of God, because of which the heavens will be destroyed by burning, and the elements will melt with intense heat!

The earth and its works will be burned up. The likely scenarios to imagine this natural holocaust could be nuclear warfare or a meteor shower from the heavens. Currently there are 8 countries that have detonated nuclear weapons: The United States, The Russian Federation, China, United Kingdom, and France are members of the Non Proliferation Treaty; Indian, Pakistan and North Korea are non-members. Israel also is reputed to have nuclear weapons, while Iran continues to say their uranium enrichment program will be used for peaceful purposes only. Five other countries, Germany, Italy, Turkey, Belgium and the Netherlands have access to nuclear arms through a NATO nuclear sharing program.

2Pe 3:13 But according to His promise we are looking for **new heavens and a new earth,** in which righteousness dwells.

2Pe 3:14 Therefore, beloved, since you look for these things, be diligent to be found by Him in peace, spotless and blameless,

2Pe 3:15 and regard the patience of our Lord as salvation; just as also our beloved brother Paul, according to the wisdom given him, wrote to you,

2Pe 3:16 as also in all his letters, speaking in them of these things, in which are some things hard to understand, which the untaught and unstable distort, as they do also the rest of the Scriptures, to their own destruction.

2Pe 3:17 You therefore, beloved, knowing this beforehand, be on your guard so that you are not carried away by the error of unprincipled men and fall from your own steadfastness,

2Pe 3:18 but grow in the grace and knowledge of our Lord and Savior Jesus Christ. To Him be the glory, both now and to the day of eternity. Amen.

Question. If believers are raptured from the earth, will they remain in heaven for months or years or decades or centuries until they are finally allowed to become part of the New Jerusalem? Is it possible that the key to this verse is simply: **a day in heaven is a thousand years on earth.** Could that be the interpretation of 2 Peter 3:8? Is it possible that we who have just been raptured into the realm of glory will only dwell there for what seems like a brief time, and then we will experience the joy of Eden in the New Jerusalem. Isn't it likely that Jesus, who has just come back to rapture us out of the tribulation, will not wait years before returning with His angels to fight the great battle? Does it not make sense that during the millennium, the raptured saints will enjoy the garden from our heavenly home? Then, what seems like a day later (1000/1 comparison) the garden paradise and the great City, will descend to planet earth, at the appointed time, to unite the Church and the Chosen in becoming the Children that God had intended "in the beginning."

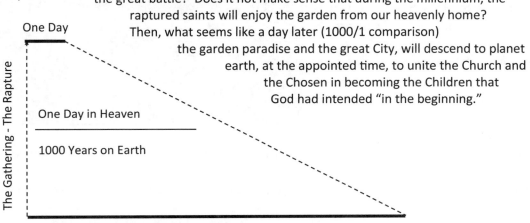

One Day

The Gathering - The Rapture

One Day in Heaven

1000 Years on Earth

A Thousand Years - The Millennium

THE SHEEP AND GOAT JUDGMENT

Mat 25:31 "But **when the Son of Man comes** in His glory, and all the angels with Him, then He will sit on His glorious throne.

Mat 25:32 "All the nations will be gathered before Him; and He will separate them from one another, **as the shepherd separates the sheep from the goats;**

Mat 25:33 and He will put the sheep on His right, and the goats on the left.

Mat 25:34 "Then the King will say to those on His right, 'Come, you who are blessed of My Father, inherit the kingdom prepared for you from the foundation of the world.

Mat 25:35 'For I was hungry, and you gave Me something to eat; I was thirsty, and you gave Me something to drink; I was a stranger, and you invited Me in;

Mat 25:36 naked, and you clothed Me; I was sick, and you visited Me; I was in prison, and you came to Me.'

Mat 25:37 "Then the righteous will answer Him, 'Lord, when did we see You hungry, and feed You, or thirsty, and give You something to drink?

Mat 25:38 'And when did we see You a stranger, and invite You in, or naked, and clothe You?

Mat 25:39 'When did we see You sick, or in prison, and come to You?'

Mat 25:40 "The King will answer and say to them, 'Truly I say to you, to the extent that you did it to **one of these brothers of Mine**, *even* the least *of them,* you did it to Me.'

Mat 25:41 "Then He will also say to those on His left, 'Depart from Me, accursed ones, into the eternal fire which has been prepared for the devil and his angels;

Mat 25:42 for I was hungry, and you gave Me nothing to eat; I was thirsty, and you gave Me nothing to drink;

Mat 25:43 I was a stranger, and you did not invite Me in; naked, and you did not clothe Me; sick, and in prison, and you did not visit Me.'

Mat 25:44 "Then they themselves also will answer, 'Lord, when did we see You hungry, or thirsty, or a stranger, or naked, or sick, or in prison, and did not take care of You?'

Mat 25:45 "Then He will answer them, 'Truly I say to you, to the extent that you did not do it to one of the least of these, you did not do it to Me.'

Mat 25:46 "These will go away into eternal punishment, but the righteous into eternal life."

As the Millennium begins, there will be Gentile survivors of the Tribulation and the Wrath. God refers to the Gentiles (non-Jews) as the 'nations' (the Greek word 'ethnos). These survivors will be in two categories: those that took the mark and those that didn't. Those who took the mark of the beast will be condemned as goats to eternal punishment. Those that didn't take the mark (that helped the Jews) will constitute the newly founded nations of the earth. Jesus statement "I was hungry and you gave me something to eat" is a reference to those Gentiles who helped the Jews during the time of Tribulation and Wrath. Jesus says: "When you did it to the least of these, you did it to me." The context of this statement was judgment.

THE TIMING OF SHEEP AND GOAT JUDGMENT

A review of both the Rapture and the Second Coming of Christ indicates that the account given in **Matthew 25:31-46** cannot refer to the Rapture. And as previously discussed, the judgment mentioned in this passage is not to be confused with the Great White Throne Judgment depicted in **Revelation 20:11-15**.

It is also important to understand that the Sheep and Goat Judgment is not the "Bema Seat Judgment" or "Judgment Seat of Christ," at which the works of all Christians will be evaluated for either loss or gain of "rewards" (**Romans 14:10; 2 Corinthians 5:10; 1 Corinthians 3:10-15; John 5:22, 27; Colossians 3:23-25**).

At that judgment it is important to understand that the judgment of sin for one's salvation is not in question; since this was an issue settled at the cross in the person of his substitute, the Lord Jesus Christ (**Romans 8:3; 2 Corinthians 5:21; Hebrews 9:28; 1 Peter 2:24**). The issue is strictly one of rewards based on a Christian's quality of service.

The Three Judgments of Revelation

THE BEMA SEAT JUDGMENT

Romans 14:10 But you, why do you judge your brother? Or you again, why do you regard your brother with contempt? For **we will all stand before the judgment seat** of God.

2 Corinthians 5:10 For we must all appear before **the judgment seat of Christ**, so that each one may be recompensed for his deeds in the body, according to what he has done, whether good or bad.

1 Corinthians 3:13 each man's work will become evident; for the day will show it because it is to be revealed with fire, and the fire itself will test the quality of each man's work. 14 If any man's work which he has built on it remains, he will receive a **reward.**

Joh 5:22 "For not even the Father judges anyone, but **He has given all judgment to the Son.**

Col 3:23 Whatever you do, do your work heartily, as for the Lord rather than for men, knowing that from the Lord **you will receive the reward** of the inheritance. It is the Lord Christ whom you serve.

James 1:12 Blessed is the man who remains steadfast under trial, for when he has stood the test he will receive **the crown of life,** which God has promised to those who love him.

1 Corinthians 3:14, 15. If any man's work which he has built on it remains, **he will receive a reward.** If any man's work is burned up, he will suffer loss; but he himself will be saved, yet so as through fire.

> *The term 'judgment seat' is the Greek word 'bema'. In ancient Greece, the bema was the judge's stand beyond the finish line. This judge was responsible for presenting awards to those (only believers) who faithfully finished the race. The criteria for receiving a crown was the good works of victory. Jesus refers to these good works as the residue left from burning of hay, wood and straw. The bema seat will occur some-time after the seventh trumpet. While crowns are being awarded in heaven to the faithful, the bowl judgments are executed upon the unrepentant nations. Just as the twenty-four elders (Rev 4:10) cast their crowns before the throne, it is likely that the believers will humbly bow before King Jesus and gladly give the glory of their newly received crowns back to Him.*

		BEMA ▼	SHEEP GOAT ▼	GREAT WHITE THRONE ▼	
Birth Pangs	Tribulation/Wrath	75	1000		Eternity

THE SHEEP AND GOAT JUDGMENT

Matthew 25:32 "All the nations will be gathered before Him; and He will separate them from one another, **as the shepherd separates the sheep from the goats;**
Mat 25:40 "The King will answer and say to them, 'Truly I say to you, to the extent that you did it to **one of these brothers of Mine**, even the least of them, you did it to Me.'

> *The time is just prior to the Millennium. The bowl judgments and Armageddon have destroyed much of the demonic hoardes who followed the beast. There are still many among the Gentiles who have not taken the mark, and also many who have shown sympathy to the Jews during the time known as 'Jacob's distress'. They will enter into the millennial kingdom with the martyrs and the Jewish remnant who were saved. The goats are those who have not taken the mark, yet have proven to be hypocrites among the faithful. They will be singled out and cast into eternal judgment.*

THE GREAT WHITE THRONE JUDGMENT. (Revelation 20:11-15))

Rev 20:11 Then I saw a great white throne and Him who sat upon it, from whose presence earth and heaven fled away, and no place was found for them.
Rev 20:12 And I saw the dead, the great and the small, standing before the throne, and books were opened; and another book was opened, which is the book of life; and **the dead were judged** from the things which were written in the books, according to their deeds.
Rev 20:13 And the sea gave up the dead which were in it, and death and Hades gave up the dead which were in them; and they were judged, every one of them according to their deeds.
Rev 20:14 Then death and Hades were thrown into the lake of fire. This is the second death, the lake of fire.
Rev 20:15 And if anyone's name was not found written in the book of life, he was thrown into the lake of fire.

> ***The dead were judged***. *A thousand years have passed since the sheep and goat judgment. The dead from ages past, along with those who were killed during the bowls, Armageddon and final millennial battle, will be judged at this time. Since Satan once again deceives the Gentile nations at the end of the millennium, there will be many who will stand before God at this judgment to receive their eternal punishment. This is not a judgment for raptured believers, nor is this a judgment for believers in the Millennium (both Jews and Gentiles.)*

> *In summary, the raptured saints, the Gentiles who survived Tribulation and Millennium, and the Jewish remnant will be spared the Great White Throne. All others, the past dead and the Millennial dead will be judged and then condemned to Satan's abode.*

THE VALLEY OF DRY BONES

A. THE PROPHECY OF DRY BONES - THE REBIRTH OF ISRAEL 1948

Eze 37:1 The hand of the LORD was upon me, and He brought me out by the Spirit of the LORD and set me down in the middle of the valley; and it was full of bones.

Eze 37:2 He caused me to pass among them round about, and behold, there were very many on the surface of the valley; and lo, they were very dry.

Eze 37:3 He said to me, "Son of man, can these bones live?" And I answered, "O Lord GOD, You know."

Eze 37:4 Again He said to me, "Prophesy over these bones and say to them, 'O dry bones, hear the word of the LORD.'

Eze 37:5 "Thus says the Lord GOD to these bones, 'Behold, I will cause breath to enter you that you may come to life.

Eze 37:6 'I will put sinews on you, make flesh grow back on you, cover you with skin and put breath in you that you may come alive; and you will know that I am the LORD.'"

Eze 37:7 So I prophesied as I was commanded; and as I prophesied, there was a noise, and behold, a rattling; and **the bones came together**, bone to its bone.

Eze 37:8 And I looked, and behold, sinews were on them, and flesh grew and skin covered them; but **there was no breath in them.**

> **the bones came together.** *Prophecy scholars seem to agree that the rebirth of Israel on May 14,1948 was the historic fulfilment of Ezekiel 37a. "Can a land be born in one day? Can a nation be brought forth all at once?" (Isaiah 66:8) Notice that the bones came together but there was no breath in them.*
>
> *The fulfillment of the bones coming together began in 1948 and climaxed in 1967 during the Arab Israeli War (also called the Six Day War) in which the surrounding nations tried to destroy Israel. In this miraculous event, Israel fought off Egypt, Syria and Jordan, regaining control of the city of Jerusalem.*
>
> **there was no breath in them.** *This prophecy will not be fulfilled until the time of the Gentiles is ended and the national remnant is redeemed by the Messiah. This will occur at the end of the seven year period during Yom Kippur, the Day of Atonement. At that time, God will remove the scales from their eyes and soften their hearts and breathe redemption into them. The Messianic movement (Jews who accept Jesus as the Messiah) is a foreshadowing of this future event. "Completed Jews" have the breath of God in them, and they represent the phenomenon of a people who have rejected Jesus for 2,000 years, and suddenly come to life, to enjoy the breath of the Spirit of God.*

B. THE DRY BONES COME TO LIFE - THE SPIRITUAL REBIRTH OF ISRAEL - FUTURE.

Eze 37:9 Then He said to me, "Prophesy to the breath, prophesy, son of man, and say to the breath, 'Thus says the Lord GOD, "Come from the four winds, O breath, and breathe on these slain, that they come to life.'"

Eze 37:10 So I prophesied as He commanded me, and the breath came into them, and they came to life and stood on their feet, **an exceedingly great army.**

Eze 37:11 Then He said to me, "Son of man, these bones are **the whole house of Israel;** behold, they say, 'Our bones are dried up and our hope has perished. We are completely cut off.'

Eze 37:12 "Therefore prophesy and say to them, 'Thus says the Lord GOD, "Behold, I will open your graves and cause you to come up out of your graves, My people; and I will bring you into the land of Israel.

Eze 37:13 "Then you will know that I am the LORD, when I have opened your graves and caused you to come up out of your graves, My people.

> *an exceedingly great army.*   *Exodus 12:37 estimates that there were 600,000 men, In addition to children (and most likely women also) who made the exodus trip out of Egypt. Most estimates say there were 2 million total. Today there are approximately 15 million Jews through the world. If 1/3 of them are the saved remnant, then there would be approximately 5 million who would experience salvation, and ultimately be the heirs of the millennium.*

> *the whole house of Israel. It is noteworthy to remember that the growing Messianic movement around the world today will not be part of this seventh trumpet event because they will already have been raptured at the time of the sixth seal, after the tribulation, and just prior to the trumpet judgment of God's wrath.*

C. THE DRY BONES FIND FULFILLMENT IN THE MILLENNIUM.

Eze 37:14 "I will put My Spirit within you and you will come to life, **and I will place you on your own land.** Then you will know that I, the LORD, have spoken and done it," declares the LORD.'"

> *and I will place you on your own land.   This is a reference to the spiritually "saved" remnant of Israel who "will" (future tense) be placed on their own land during the time of the Millennium. The purpose of the Millennium is to show the Jews what life would have been like if they had not disobeyed God the first time, and they had not denied Jesus the Messiah. During the Millennium they will truly be the "chosen people", and the nations of the earth will serve them. One of the questions to be asked about the Millennium is this: Will God restore the history of mankind during the Millennium? In other words, will the nations who will then serve the Jews have a historical understanding of how they persecuted, and tried to exterminate the Jewish people for 2,000 years?*

TWO STICKS OF ISRAEL AND JUDAH.

Eze 37:15 The word of the LORD came again to me saying,

Eze 37:16 "And you, son of man, take for yourself one stick and write on it, **'For Judah and for the sons of Israel,** his companions'; then take another stick and write on it, **'For Joseph, the stick of Ephraim** and all the house of Israel, his companions.'

Eze 37:17 "Then join them for yourself one to another into one stick, that they may become one in your hand.

Eze 37:18 "When the sons of your people speak to you saying, 'Will you not declare to us what you mean by these?'

Eze 37:19 say to them, 'Thus says the Lord GOD, "Behold, I will take the stick of Joseph, which is in the hand of Ephraim, and the tribes of Israel, his companions; and I will put them with it, with the stick of Judah, and make them one stick, and they will be one in My hand."'

Eze 37:20 "The sticks on which you write will be in your hand before their eyes.

Eze 37:21 "Say to them, 'Thus says the Lord GOD, "Behold, I will take the sons of Israel from among the nations where they have gone, and I will gather them from every side and bring them into their own land;

Eze 37:22 and I will make them one nation in the land, on the mountains of Israel; and one king will be king for all of them; and they will no longer be two nations and no longer be divided into two kingdoms.

Eze 37:23 "They will no longer defile themselves with their idols, or with their detestable things, or with any of their transgressions; but I will deliver them from all their dwelling places in which they have sinned, and will cleanse them. <u>And they will be My people, and I will be their God.</u>

Eze 37:24 "**My servant David will be king** over them, and they will all have one shepherd; and they will walk in My ordinances and keep My statutes and observe them.

Eze 37:25 "They will live on the land that I gave to Jacob My servant, in which your fathers lived; and they will live on it, they, and their sons and their sons' sons, forever; **and David My servant will be their prince forever.**

Eze 37:26 "I will make a covenant of peace with them; it will be an everlasting covenant with them. And I will place them and multiply them, and will set My sanctuary in their midst forever. Eze 37:27 "My dwelling place also will be with them; and I will be their God, and they will be My people.

Eze 37:28 "And the nations will know that I am the LORD who sanctifies Israel, when My sanctuary is in their midst forever."'"

Eze 34:23 "Then I will set over them one shepherd, My servant David, and he will feed them; he will feed them himself and be their shepherd.

Eze 34:24 "And I, the LORD, will be their God, and My servant David will be prince among them; I the LORD have spoken.

two sticks. The Mormon church distorts the meaning of this passage. They claim that Judah is the Bible and the Book of Mormon is Joseph, and that both sticks are necessary for the proper interpretation of God's revelation. The two house movement, a minority view within the Messianic community, claims that the northern 10 tribes of Israel, though mingled and dispersed among the Gentile nations, will soon begin to migrate to The Holy Land, thus completing the nation of Israel. This view is also a minority view within the evangelical community.

Only God knows the pure DNA of the twelve tribes of Israel. And at the appointed time, He will raise up an army comprised of 144,000 total from each of the twelve tribes. These anointed warriors of the Messiah will be the firstfruits of those who will enjoy the thousand year reign of Christ called the Millennium.

Notice to the right the northern kingdom, known as Israel, headquartered in Samaria, and the southern kingdom, known as Judah, (the region of Judea) is headquartered in Jerusalem.

> ## "If the Jews had accepted Jesus in the first place, they would have enjoyed the Millennium 2000 years ago."

David My servant will be their prince forever. David the shepherd boy became the king who ruled Israel for forty years during its golden era. In Acts 13:22 God refers to David as

"a man after My own heart, who will do all My will." Despite David's adulterous and murderous activities, there was something about his heart that was both innocent and passionate. In David's famous psalm of repentance (Ps 51), David asks God to "create in me a clean heart, O God, and renew a steadfast spirit within me." The throne of David was prophesied throughout each generation as being the line of the Messiah. While Christ will rule the earth, King David will be given authority to rule over Israel forever and ever.

L' ENVOI

When Earth's last picture is painted, and the tubes are twisted and dried,
When the oldest colors have faded, and the youngest critic has died,
We shall rest, and, faith, we shall need it-lie down for an aeon or two,
'Til the Master of All Good Workmen shall set us to work anew!

And those that were good will be happy: they shall sit in a golden chair;
They shall splash at a ten-league canvas with brushes of comets' hair;
They shall find real saints to draw from-Magdalene, Peter and Paul;
They shall work for an age at a sitting and never be tired at all!

And only the Master shall praise us, and only the Master shall blame;
And no one shall work for money, and no one shall work for fame,
but each for the joy of the working, and each, in his separate star,
Shall draw the thing as he sees it for the God of things as they are!

Rudyard Kipling

7

UNITING HIS CHILDREN

"Return to Eden and the New Jerusalem"

Sin and death were finally destroyed at the end of the millennium. God now restores the earth to its original pristine paradise. The holy city Jerusalem comes down from heaven, revealing walls and foundation constructed from the most precious jewels and minerals the world has ever known. Outside the gates of the city is the lake of fire, a silent invisible memorial to Satan's doom. The Jews will inhabit the golden city, while the Church, the Gentile nations, who live in the new garden paradise of the restored Eden, will enter the gates to worship God forever and ever. Gardening may become the ultimate occupation. Forever and ever. Amen.

"I Can Only Imagine"

(See Youtube, Mercy Me, I Can Only Imagine)

I can only imagine
What it will be like
When I walk by your side
I can only imagine
What my eyes will see
When your face is before me.
I can only imagine.

Surrounded by your glory, what will my heart feel,
Will I dance for You, Jesus, or in awe of You be still?
Will I stand in Your presence or to my knees will I fall?
Will I sing Hallelujah, will I be able to speak at all?
I can only imagine, I can only imagine.

I can only imagine when that day comes
And I find myself standing in the Son
I can only imagine when all I will do.
Is forever worship You.

"And God shall wipe away all tears from their eyes;
And there shall be no more death,
Neither sorrow, nor crying
Neither shall there be any more pain.
For the former things are passed away."
Revelation 21:4

"Uniting His Children"

A. The New Heaven and New Earth

    1. The New Earth — Rev. 21:1

    2. The Holy City Coming Down — Rev 21:2-7

        A. The Lake that Burns with Fire and Brimstone — Rev 21:8

        B. Description of the New Jerusalem — Rev 21:9-11

        C. The Features of the Holy City of Jerusalem — Rev 21:12-27

        D. The River of the Water of Life — Rev 22:1-7

        E. 12 fruits, healing of the nations — Rev 22:2

    3. John Responds to the Vision — Rev 22:8-11

    4. Jesus, the Alpha and the Omega — Rev 22:12-14

    5. Outside the Gates of the City — Rev 22:15-17

    6. Adding or Taking Away from Scripture — Rev 22:18-21

B. Living in Paradise

    The City of 2 Million Square Miles

    Evening and Morning, The First Day

    The Heavenly Concept of Innocence

    The Heavenly Concept of Nature

    The Heavenly Concept of Food

    The Heavenly Concept of Animals

    The Heavenly Concept of Activity

    The Heavenly Concept of Music

    The Heavenly Concept of Worship

    The Heavenly Concept of Culture

THE NEW HEAVEN AND NEW EARTH.

Rev 21:1 Then I saw a new heaven and a new earth; for the first heaven and the first earth passed away, and there is **no longer any sea.**

Rev 21:2 And I saw the holy city, new Jerusalem, **coming down out of heaven** from God, made ready **as a bride adorned** for her husband.

Rev 21:3 And I heard a loud voice from the throne, saying, "Behold, the tabernacle of God is among men, and He will dwell among them, and they shall be His people, and God Himself will be among them,

Rev 21:4 and He will wipe away every tear from their eyes; and there will no longer be any death; there will no longer be any mourning, or crying, or pain; the first things have passed away."

Rev 21:5 And He who sits on the throne said, "Behold, I am making all things new." And He said, "Write, for these words are faithful and true."

Rev 21:6 Then He said to me, "It is done. I am the Alpha and the Omega, the beginning and the end. I will give to the one who thirsts from the spring of the water of life without cost.

Rev 21:7 "He who overcomes will inherit these things, and I will be his God and he will be My son.

Rev 21:8 "But for the cowardly and unbelieving and abominable and murderers and immoral persons and sorcerers and idolaters and all liars, their part will be in the lake that burns with **fire and brimstone**, which is the second death."

> *no longer any sea. The oceans will no longer exist, having been the last remnant of the flood's catastrophic signature on the planet. The salty, undrinkable water has always been a mystery, but perhaps God will allow the sea creatures to continue on as fresh water angelfish and jellyfish and sea horses.*
>
> *coming down out of heaven. There seems to be a prevailing theory that the new Jerusalem will hover over the earth. I don't agree.*
>
> *as a bride adorned. Note that both the Church and the City are referred to as the bride of Christ. See Revelation 19:7 in reference to the marriage supper of the Lamb.*
>
> *fire and brimstone. Eight characteristics are listed here to describe the souls throughout history that have thumbed their noses at God, and allowed Satan to drive them into the depths of depravity. God instituted three strikes of fire and brimstone in scripture. In Genesis 19 rained f/b on Sodom and Gomorrah. In Revelation 9, the sixth trumpet, the 200 million demonic horses breathed f/b from their mouths and killed 1/3 of mankind. Finally, the false trinity, his demons and vast throng of defiant unbelievers, are hopelessly cast into the eternal lake of burning sulfur.*

Rev 21:9 Then one of the seven angels who had the seven bowls full of the seven last plagues came and spoke with me, saying, "Come here, I will show you the bride, the wife of the Lamb."

Rev 21:10 And he carried me away in the Spirit to a great and high mountain, and showed me the holy city, Jerusalem, coming down out of heaven from God,

Rev 21:11 having the glory of God. Her brilliance was like a very costly stone, as a stone of crystal-clear jasper.

Rev 21:12 It had a great and high wall, with **twelve gates**, and at the gates twelve angels; and names were written on them, which are the names of the twelve tribes of the sons of Israel.

Rev 21:13 There were three gates on the east and three gates on the north and three gates on the south and three gates on the west.

Rev 21:14 And the wall of the city had twelve foundation stones, and on them were the twelve names of the twelve apostles of the Lamb.

Rev 21:15 The one who spoke with me had a gold measuring rod to measure the city, and its gates and its wall.

Rev 21:16 The city is laid out as a square, and its length is as great as the width; and he measured the city with the rod, **fifteen hundred miles;** its length and width and height are equal.

Rev 21:17 And he measured its wall, **seventy-two yards**, according to human measurements, which are also angelic measurements.

Twelve gates. If the gates of the city were each 100 miles wide, there would be 300 miles between the gates, in order to allow the billions of people to flow into the city to worship.

fifteen hundred miles. the approximate area of this city is roughly from New York City to Dallas, Texas - from Minneapolis to Orlando, Florida. 1500 miles square is 60% of the area of the U.S. Of more interest is to know that this area is the equivalent of the areas of Iraq, Iran, Saudi Arabia, Turkey, Yemen, Oman, Syria, Jordan and Israel. In other words, the entire area of the middle east. The height of the city rises above the troposphere, the mesosphere, the thermosphere, and the ionosphere another 900 miles.

seventy two yards. the equivalent of 216 feet or 2/3 of a football field. The thickness of the wall was not for protection, but rather to support a wall which is 1500 miles high. Yes, God could create a wall one foot thick if He wanted to, but this incredible wall was built for majesty more than strength.

THE MATERIALS OF THE CITY.

Rev 21:18 The material of the wall was jasper; and the city was pure gold, like clear glass.

Rev 21:19 The foundation stones of the city wall were adorned with every kind of precious stone. The first foundation stone was jasper; the second, sapphire; the third, chalcedony; the fourth, emerald;

Rev 21:20 the fifth, sardonyx; the sixth, sardius; the seventh, chrysolite; the eighth, beryl; the ninth, topaz; the tenth, chrysoprase; the eleventh, jacinth; the twelfth, amethyst.

> *Hebrews 11:10 gives us a clue to the construction of this amazing city: "whose architect and builder was God." It should be worth noting that God does not use alien materials to construct his beloved eternal city. He uses the very substances of planet earth. We don't know whether these stones were horizontally layered or whether each huge stone was placed side by side, alternating around the 6,000 mile perimeter. Remember that the monthly birthstones celebrated by people around the world originated with* the biblical stones that are found, not only in the eternal city, but also in the breastplate of the high priest.

THE BREASTPLATE OF THE HIGH PRIEST

Exodus 28:17-20. You shall mount on it four rows of stones; the first row shall be a row of ruby, topaz and emerald; and the second row a turquoise, a sapphire and a diamond; and the third row a jacinth, an agate and an amethyst; and the fourth row a beryl and an onyx and a jasper; they shall be set in gold filigree.

> *The intricacies of the biblical detail regarding the temple and all its ceremony and ornamentation is almost beyond description. Each stone represents one of the twelve tribes of Israel. Even the Temple Institute in Jerusalem is not sure of the profound meaning that each of these stones had for the 12 tribes. Note also that Lucifer himself, as the worship leader in heaven, was first adorned with these jewels in Ezekiel 38. To view the most creative expression of these twelve stones that I have ever seen, (made for children) go to the the website* **rainbowcastle.org**.

Rev 21:21 And the twelve gates were twelve pearls; each one of the gates was a single pearl. And the street of the city was pure gold, like transparent glass.

Rev 21:22 I saw no temple in it, for the Lord God the Almighty and the Lamb are its temple.

Rev 21:23 And the city has no need of the sun or of the moon to shine on it, for the glory of God has illumined it, and its lamp is the Lamb. 24 The nations will walk by its light, and **the kings of the earth** will bring their glory into it.

Rev 21:25 In the daytime (for there will be no night there) its gates will never be closed;

SARDIUS (RUBY)
(RED/BLACK VEINS)

TOPAZ
(BRIGHT BLUE)

EMERALD
(DEEP GREEN)

CHRYSOPHASE
(APPLE GREEN)

SAPPHIRE
(DEEP BLUE)

DIAMOND
(CHRYSOLITE)

Rev 21:26 and they will bring the glory and **the honor of the nations** into it;

Rev 21:27 and nothing unclean, and no one who practices abomination and lying, shall ever come into it, but only those whose names are written in the Lamb's book of life.

JACINTH
(SPARKLING RED)

AGATE
(CHALCEDONY)

AMETHYST
(BRIGHT GREEN)

BERYL
(GOLDEN)

ONYX
(STRIATED RED)

JASPER
(VARIED COLORS)

the kings of the earth . . . the honor of the nations. *One of the great mysteries in the Bible is how there could be kings and nations AFTER the Millennium, and during the glorious days of eternity. The answer must be this: God loves the variety of his creation, and He wants to celebrate the diversity of the nations into the eternal age. The further implication of bringing their glory 'into' the New Jerusalem leaves the possibility that the 'nations' (ethnos, goyim) will live outside the city, in the "suburbs" of the pristine Garden of Eden - while the Children of Israel will superintend the city and perpetuate the Feasts of Israel that they have faithfully celebrated throughout the present age.*

FOREVER IN THE KINGDOM

Revelation Chapter 22

THE RIVER OF THE WATER OF LIFE.

Rev 22:1 Then he showed me a river of the water of life, clear as crystal, coming from the throne of God and of the Lamb,

Rev 22:2 in the middle of its street. On either side of the river was **the tree of life,** bearing **twelve kinds of fruit,** yielding its fruit every month; and the leaves of the tree were for **the healing of the nations.**

Rev 22:3 **There will no longer be any curse;** and the throne of God and of the Lamb will be in it, and His bond-servants will serve Him;

Rev 22:4 they will see His face, and **His name will be on their foreheads.**

Rev 22:5 And there will **no longer be any night;** and they will not have need of the light of a lamp nor the light of the sun, because the Lord God will illumine them; and they will reign forever and ever.

Rev 22:6 And he said to me, "These words are faithful and true"; and the Lord, the God of the spirits of the prophets, sent His angel to show to His bond-servants the things which must soon take place.

Rev 22:7 "And behold, I am coming quickly. Blessed is he who heeds the words of the prophecy of this book."

Rev 22:8 I, John, am the one who heard and saw these things. And when I heard and saw, I fell down to worship at the feet of the angel who showed me these things.

Rev 22:9 But he said to me, "Do not do that. I am a fellow servant of yours and of your brethren the prophets and of those who heed the words of this book. Worship God."

Rev 22:10 And he said to me, "Do not seal up the words of the prophecy of this book, for the time is near.

Rev 22:11 "Let the one who does wrong, still do wrong; and the one who is filthy, still be filthy; and let the one who is righteous, still practice righteousness; and the one who is holy, still keep himself holy."

Rev 22:12 "Behold, I am coming quickly, and My reward *is* with Me, to render to every man according to what he has done.

Rev 22:13 "I am **the Alpha and the Omega,** the first and the last, the beginning and the end."

Rev 22:14 Blessed are those who wash their robes, so that they may have the right to the tree of life, and may enter by the gates into the city.

The tree of life. In Genesis 3:22 we find that the tree of life causes those who eat of it to live forever.

Twelve kinds of fruit. Your mom always said, *"Eat your fruits and vegetables."* Well, you may as well begin on earth, because they are going to be your heavenly menu.

The healing of the nations. As in the Edenic days prior to the eating of meat, the New Eden will be landscaped with the mystical *"tree of life"* providing twelve *"flavors of the month."* It is possible that we will be sustained by food and water in the New Eden, just as God has provided for us throughout the ages. It is possible that God intended for leaves and plants to be a supernatural healing agent that fuel the human body with boundless energy and eternal immunity. Since disease no longer exists, the leaves would be a supernatural vitamin that everyone would consume to attest to the plan that God originally had for the planet. It is also possible that our resurrected bodies will be a human form perfected by Eden's standards.

There will no longer be any curse. Seven words that mankind has hungered to hear for thousands of years.

His name will be on their foreheads. We readily identify that the mark of the beast will be on the foreheads of those who concede their principles and reveal their compromised heart - but we should always remember that the mark on the forehead is foremost a mark of identification with the Lord Jesus.

no longer any night. It stretches the human mind to imagine that there will be no night. This implies that there will be no sleeping or need for regenerating the body. There will be no stars.

the alpha and the omega. Three times (Revelation 1:8, 21:6 and 22:13) these letters are used to describe the eternal, transcendent Christ. Representing the first and last letters of the Greek Alphabet, they have become a part of Christian art through the ages, often appearing to the left and right of Jesus' head. Colossians 1:15-19 reminds us of the sublime nature of Jesus the carpenter of Nazareth.

Col 1:15 He is the image of the invisible God, the firstborn of all creation.

Col 1:16 For by Him all things were created, both in the heavens and on earth, visible and invisible, whether thrones or dominions or rulers or authorities--all things have been created through Him and for Him.

Col 1:17 He is before all things, and in Him all things hold together.

Col 1:18 He is also head of the body, the church; and He is the beginning, the firstborn from the dead, so that He Himself will come to have first place in everything.

Col 1:19 For it was the Father's good pleasure for all the fullness to dwell in Him.

OUTSIDE THE GATES OF THE CITY.

Rev 22:15 **Outside** are the dogs and the sorcerers and the immoral persons and the murderers and the idolaters, and everyone who loves and practices lying.

> **Outside.** *It is amazing to me that just seven verses before the end of the Bible, we find reference to a place that is inhabited by dogs and sorcerers - the immoral and the idolaters. If you look at verse 14, it refers to the gates of the New Jerusalem. Therefore, in verse 15, the correct language could read, "outside the gates are the dogs and sorcerers, etc.* What could possibly be the meaning of this passage? Rarely does any commentary, or any study Bible address this passage. Why? Perhaps this interpretation will make sense of Rev 22:15.*
>
> *The Old Jerusalem city sits on a mountain.*
> *The New Jerusalem will also sit on a mountain.*
>
> *The Old Jerusalem had walled gates all around the city.*
> *The New Jerusalem will also have walled gates all around the city.*
>
> *The Old Jerusalem had a place called "Gehenna" outside the city gates. It was the most repulsive location in all of Jerusalem because it was not only the city landfill but also a place of human sacrifice. It was also called the Valley of Hinnom, and it may likely be the Valley of Hamon-Gog, where Gog himself will be buried. Verse 15 says "outside the city gates" of the new perfect eternal Jerusalem will be the dogs and sorcerers. What are they doing in this heavenly version of God's perfect city, anywhere close to the saints of all eternity?*
>
> *I believe that Hell will be outside the gates of the New Jerusalem.*
>
> *I believe it will be a pit, an abyss, just as Gehenna was. I believe it will be a lake of fire, just as gehenna was - a smouldering pit of flames, always burning from the discarded refuse of Jerusalem's residents. I believe this lake of fire will house those who have been condemned to spend eternity with the false trinity - Satan, the Beast, the False Prophet - and all those who refused to name Jesus as the Messiah.*
>
> *I believe they will occasionally rise from the abyss - the pit - to cry out at the edge of the lake of fire as the "saints go marching by", on their way through the gates of the golden translucent city. I believe they will be invisible to the eyes and ears of the multitude of believers who will pass through the gates. The saints will be unable to hear the silent wailing and screams of anguish that will rise from the lake of fire. Hell is not in the counter-opposite end of the universe. What greater hell could there be than looking at the golden city and knowing that you scorned the opportunity to acknowledge Jesus as the Lord of this life. "Every knee shall bow, and every tongue confess." What a tragic way to acknowledge that Jesus really is Lord: from the pit of hell, outside the gates.*

374

The Shining City on a Hill

The diagram below is merely a proportional concept to show the incredible magnitude of God's eternal structure. The tallest building in the world, in the year 2014, is the Burj Khalifa, in Dubai, United Arab Emirates, which stands at 2,722 feet. At 1/2 mile high, this building when scaled, looks like a speck of dust on this page. On this side of the new wall of Jerusalem there are three gates. Assuming that millions of people are entering these gates to worship, we have drawn them at 200 miles wide, 250 miles apart and 10 miles high.

1500 Miles

1500 Miles

The Exosphere

The Thermosphere - from 311 to 621 Miles High

The Mesosphere - 53 Miles High

The Stratosphere - 31 Miles High

The Trophisphere - 12 Miles High

JESUS IS COMING QUICKLY.

Rev 22:16 "I, Jesus, have sent My angel to testify to you these things for the churches. I am the root and the descendant of David, **the bright morning star."**

Rev 22:17 The Spirit and the bride say, "Come." And let the one who hears say, "Come." And let the one who is thirsty come; let the one who wishes take the water of life without cost.

Rev 22:18 I testify to everyone who hears the words of the prophecy of this book: **if anyone adds to them**, God will add to him the plagues which are written in this book;

Rev 22:19 **and if anyone takes away** from the words of the book of this prophecy, God will take away his part from the tree of life and from the holy city, which are written in this book.

Rev 22:20 He who testifies to these things says, "Yes, I am coming quickly." Amen. Come, Lord Jesus.

Rev 22:21 The grace of the Lord Jesus be with all. Amen.

> *The bright morning star.* Isaiah 14:12 refers to Lucifer as the "star of the morning", but Revelation 22:16 refers to Jesus as the "bright morning star". Perhaps the clue to understanding the distinction between these two phrases lies in the planet Venus, which is also referred to as the morning star, but should probably, more appropriately be titled the "star of the morning." We understand that Venus can be seen in the early dawn just before the sun rises. It is therefore a precursor, a warm-up act, for the real "daystar" which will soon light up the skies and provide warmth and light to the entire world. In eternity past, Lucifer was a bright light that set the stage for the one and only "daystar", King Jesus. That was not good enough for Lucifer. He had his chance. He will soon be cast into a lake of fire, where he will observe from a distance, the brilliant translucent golden city of Jerusalem, and King Jesus will replace the sun as the light of the world. 2 Peter 1:19 paints a beautiful picture of salvation, when we shall have the morning star. "So we have the prophetic word made more sure, to which you do well to pay attention as to a lamp shining in a dark place, until the day dawns and the morning star arises in your hearts."
>
> *If anyone adds . . . If anyone takes away.* Extra-biblical commentaries such as the Jehovah Witness "New World Translation", the Latter Day Saints "Book of Mormon" and Islam's "Quran" are just a few of the texts that add to and take away from the purity of scripture. It is a woeful thing to take the words of scripture and distort the truth. We must always remember that "all scripture is inspired by God and profitable." Any variation with intent to take the focus off of King Jesus will face condemnation.

THE THIRD HEAVEN

2 Corinthians 12:2 I know a man in Christ who fourteen years ago, whether in the body I do not know, or out of the body I do not know, God knows, such a man was caught up to the third heaven.

THE THIRD HEAVEN, The Spiritual Realm. This is the throne room of God, and it is likely that our eyes cannot take in all the splendor and majesty of the home that God has promised us. I believe that after death or rapture, we Gentiles will live in a garden paradise, until the time that planet earth is newly restored. At that time, we will join our brothers, the Children of Israel, as they inhabit their new home, the City called New Jerusalem.

THE SECOND HEAVEN, THE Cosmic Realm. God created the planetary universe to show man the infinite expanse of God's creative power. The mere idea of traveling light years to reach another galaxy stretches the mind of man. It is not clear whether stars and planets will be part of God's plan for our future universe. But it is clear that God gave us the galaxies: to gaze, to wonder, to imagine, and most of all: to honor Him, the God of glory for the amazing work of His hands.

THE FIRST HEAVEN, The Atmospheric Realm. For the average human, the sky above is all the heaven that our eyes will ever see. Though this pales in comparison to the galaxies and the abode of God, the majesty of a morning sunrise set against a blue sky with fluffy white clouds is a human superlative. To sit on a balcony overlooking a mountaintop with a pink and orange sunset in the background is truly a unique expression of the artwork of God. And each day, God's palette is unique.

THE HEAVENLY CONCEPT OF INNOCENCE

How I long to recover the innocence that was once mine. In Matthew 19:14, Jesus said that the kingdom of heaven would belong to the children. Did Jesus mean that we would literally be children in our eternal state? Or did He mean that we would inherit a new nature, one that was completely void of sinful thoughts and actions? Can you imagine the Garden of Eden filled with ten thousand children, all playing innocently with no hint of pride or jealousy or possessiveness? The culture we live in today robs us of our innocence. At the age of seven, I remember following a young friend of mine as he broke into a church nursery. I watched him destroy the toys that had been lovingly purchased for the children, and I remember having remorse for his actions, but was too ashamed to tell anyone. I lost a touch of innocence that day. I would later learn that my own heart was deceitful (Jeremiah 17:9), and that my own sinful nature would rob me of many beautiful things that God wanted me to enjoy. Perhaps the most heinous crime among men is that of abusing a young child - emotionally, physically or sexually. I have heard testimonies from adults who were abused as children. Many of them fell victim to sexual predators whose aberrant behavior was then transferred to the young child. For years, the young child would suffer an addiction to that very behavior, leading to bondage that is often irreversible. In Matthew 18:6, Jesus had harsh words to say about those who stole the innocence of young children: *"but whoever causes one of these little ones who believe in Me to stumble, it would be better for him to have a heavy millstone hung around his neck, and to be drowned in the depth of the sea."* Woe unto those men and women who traffic in the abuse of young children. Heaven will be a place of innocence and purity that is beyond our very imagination. In this life, God gives us the freedom of private thoughts, and we are so used to <u>thinking</u> bad thoughts that we cannot imagine the joy of living a year, or a month, or even a day, without compromising ourselves. In heaven, there will be no shame or guilt, and every moment will be filled with pure, innocent thoughts. Jesus is always our model for earthly living. In an inexplicable way, Jesus lived a human life that was totally innocent, yet also possessing the wisdom of the ages. In God's future kingdom, the tree of life is mentioned five times in the book of Revelation. There is no hint of the tree of good and evil. Innocence will prevail. Yes, God's future kingdom will be full of children. What age, we do not know. But what we do know is this:

Our eyes will look upon King Jesus with the innocence of a little child.

THE HEAVENLY CONCEPT OF NATURE

Scripture teaches that there will be a tree of life on both sides of the river that flows from the throne of God, and twelve fruits, one for each month, and leaves for the healing of the nations. There are approximately 270,000 plants around the globe; there are 23,000 species of trees, 350,000 species of flowers and 2,000 species of fruit. Within those 2000 varieties of fruit, the apple alone has 7500 different varieties. God's original intent for man in the Garden of Eden was to cultivate and care for this seemingly endless variety of plants. Genesis 3:17 says that God cursed the ground and caused thorns and thistles to grown among the plants. We have never known a world that was not cursed. We have never known what it would be like to walk on a carpet of grass into a pristine garden and choose from a thousand different varieties of fruit - any of which would be so satisfying to the taste that it was as if we had never tasted before. That was God's original intent. Can you imagine walking barefoot out into the field, and gently using your fingers as tongs in the soft soil to plant a rose seed several inches deep. Then you take a cup of water and pour it over the soil, and immediately the plant begins to grow. We're not used to the idea of immediate gratification in the process of plant cultivation, but who knows, maybe that is God's design for the future. Mankind has lived off the earth for thousands of years, and only in this generation has it become more common to be a "consumer" of the ground than a "producer". Could it be satisfying for mankind someday to push back from the technology and superficial entertainment, and simply enjoy cultivating an endless variety of plants in the garden? I thought that's what we called "retirement." Take this test. Find a botanical garden close to home and visit there soon. Sit quietly in the midst of this local paradise and imagine that the entire earth looked like this. Imagine that God has given this garden to you. Don't imagine labor, because you have boundless energy, and it no longer requires "sweat and toil" to tend the garden. We have become so sophisticated in these last days that the simple beauty of a flower no longer captures our attention and fascination. Our future home may well be a personalized "gazebo" in the midst of a vast acreage of trees and shrubs and fruits and flowers. Perhaps God will allow you to create new species not yet thought of. Remember the verse: *"Eyes have not seen, nor ears heard, nor entered into the mind of man, the things that God has prepared for them that love Him."*

THE HEAVENLY CONCEPT OF FOOD

God did good when He made food - but we may as well be eating rocks if not for the amazing creation called taste buds. Science tells us there are 3,000-10,000 tiny receptors called papilllai (puh-pill'-eye) on the tongue and surrounding surfaces of the mouth. Man has identified five known tastes: salty, sweet, sour, bitter and "umami." Maybe you'll remember this last one if I tell you that your first exposure to this one was "you mommy's milk". Fish, meat, cheese, and vegetables like tomatoes, celery and mushrooms are rich with glutamates, which give a pungent taste that can best be described as "savory." Will we eat food in heaven? Absolutely. Will we have to worry about body waste? Not likely. God will have some system (like perspiration) that completely absorbs waste. Revelation 22:2 (like the Millennial verse in Ezekiel 47:12) tells us: *"On either side of the river was the tree of life, bearing twelve kinds of fruit, yielding its fruit every month; and the leaves of the tree were for the healing of the nations."* Twelve "kinds" of fruit probably means 'categories', which might still mean we'll have many of the 2000 fruits in the world today. The 'leaves of the tree" may still mean vegetables, rich in life-giving nutrients that produce perfect health in a perfect world. We'll forget the taste of steak in an environment that no longer kills its food, and even the fish of Ezekiel 47 will probably cease to be eaten in the New Jerusalem - unless, of course, they jump onto your plate already fileted! Remember the marriage supper of the lamb? Yes, God created our present day taste buds to prepare us for an even more savory experience on the new earth. Every taste of every fruit will be exhilarating with every bite. There's just something special about gathering around the table to eat. Food has always been a good excuse for building relationships, and even in tomorrow's Paradise, God will likely use food as a catalyst for fellowship. Yeah, just one big "covered dish dinner" after Church. It's not by accident that the seven appointed times of the Lord are called "feasts." I want to sit at the dinner table while Jesus laughs and eats and tells stories about his three years of teaching kingdom principles to those "keystone cops" we called the apostles. Yes, Paradise will allow us to eat all the food we want without gaining a pound. Now that's what I call heaven.

THE HEAVENLY CONCEPT OF ANIMALS

For anyone who has had a beloved pet, the dominant question is this: Will there be animals in heaven? My theology for years said, "No, heaven is a spiritual place inhabited by only those who acknowledge Jesus as Lord." While that statement is true, I have changed my mind. Heaven will be like Eden, and the Garden of Eden was a zoo, with no restrictions other than: don't eat the apple and don't listen to the serpent. My wife, grandson and I took a trip to Pine Mountain, Georgia to a place called Wild Animal Safari. We hopped in a zebra-colored jeep and rode for an hour through woods filled with buffalo, giraffe, deer, camels and a hundred different varieties of outdoor life. It was hilarious. The animals would come right up to the windshield and eat food pellets right out of our hands. We were even given a "slobber" towel to minimize all the drool coming from the tongues of these domestically hungry animals. Revelation says that Jesus will be riding on a white horse. Isaiah 11:6 and 65:25 tell us that the Millennium will be a tranquil, pristine environment in which wolves and lambs lie down together with the leopards and young goats, and in their midst will be a little boy. Much of our theology has been based on Ecclesiastes 3:21, which says *"Who knows that the breath of man ascends upward and the breath of the beast descends downward to the earth?"* While this is true in THIS life, I believe it has little to do with the restored Paradise, in which man and animals will be in complete and perfect harmony. Numbers 22:28 portrays still another dimension of possibility. Balaam's donkey spoke to him. For those who own a dog that seems to understand your commands, is it possible that God might actually allow animals to obey our commands in Paradise? Remember the song: *"If we could talk to the animals, learn their languages, even take an animal degree. We'd study elephant and eagle, buffalo and beagle, alligator, guinea pig and flea. If people asked us, 'Can you speak rhinoceros, we'd say of courserus.' Imagine talking to a tiger, chatting to a cheetach, what a neat achievement that would be."* Wild animals today are segregated and caged from the civilian world. But IS IT POSSIBLE that God will allow us to enjoy nature, not only with the plants of the field, but also with the birds of the field. What a wonderful thought that I could have a pet lion. Daniel did. What an amazing thought that every neighborhood in Paradise could be a zoo, completely tame and domesticated, allowing you to live out your childhood dreams of having a circus in your back yard.

THE HEAVENLY CONCEPT OF ACTIVITY

There seems to be a consensus among heavenly minded people that we will all be casually walking around at a gentle pace for all eternity. No one runs or jumps, no competition and no passionate exercise that would give evidence of . . . just plain fun. Every sport wants to be represented in heaven. Golfers imagine Eden to be full of fairways. Perhaps this is a good time to talk about age. After all, activity has always been a function of age. In Matthew 19:14, Jesus said, *"Let the children alone, and do not hinder them from coming to Me; for the kingdom of heaven belongs to such as these."* We don't know what this verse means. Is Jesus saying that innocence will be the prevailing lifestyle of heaven's inhabitants? Or, is Jesus saying heaven will literally be occupied by nothing BUT children. I could imagine Jesus walking among the children while they run and play. Is that possible? Perhaps the body of a child and the intellect of a young adult. On the other hand, our presumption is that Adam and Eve were fully grown. Perhaps they were teenagers - full of energy and promise and passion. I could imagine a game of soccer in which guys and gals are playing with innocent passion before the Lord. Or maybe we're 25ish, fully developed, and beginning to embrace a worldview that will shape the rest of our lives. Will we ride horses? Since horses seem to have a place in heaven, maybe this age group could enjoy riding full bore across the plains of Eden without worry of injury. Jesus was 33 when he died. Many people think that this age, more than any other, seems to personify the very prime of life. Though there will be no seas, it's possible that swimming could be a wonderful pastime. We expect to see Noah and Father Abraham as old men, but I would rather see them in their 40's or 50's - looking seasoned and mature and wise for their years. We just don't know, do we? Heaven will not be lacking laughter or energy. On the contrary, God is reserving the best for last. The best of energy and the best of laughter and the best of fun is yet to come. In Matthew 25:21 Jesus says: *"Well done, good and faithful servant. You were faithful with a few things, I will make you ruler of many things; enter into the joy of your master."* Heaven will be full of activity, celebrating the potential of the human life without it's limitations. No, we're not floating on a cloud. We will be busy, working the garden in the morning, a little recreation in the afternoon, and an evening (daylight, of course) in concert with Christ our Conductor. Now that's abundant life.

THE HEAVENLY CONCEPT OF MUSIC

Music has been defined as a complex amalgam of sound and silence which produces melody, harmony, rhythm, and timbre. It is truly amazing that eight simple notes which form an octave could produce such an endless variety of melodies. Music is one of God's most majestic creations, and He still inspires the simplest of humans today to create unique melodies thousands of years after someone whistled the first song, In 2 Chronicles 5:13 it says: *"the trumpeters and the singers were to make themselves heard with one voice to praise and to glorify the LORD, and they lifted up their voices accompanied by trumpets and cymbals and instruments of music, and they praised the LORD saying, 'He indeed is good for His lovingkindness is everlasting.' Then the house of the LORD, was filled with a cloud."* Revelation 15:3 says that the saints will stand on a sea of glass and fire, and sing the Song of Moses and the Song of the Lamb. When I was in band in middle school, I was always amazed at the band leader, who could play every instrument in the room. There is no doubt in my mind that one of the joys of heaven will be my ability - and your ability, to sit down with a violin, or a piano, or a trumpet and effortlessly create timeless music of matchless inspiration. Then imagine on a larger scale that the Master Conductor stands before a throng of thousands of novice musicians, who need no warmup or no practice, and they begin, under His masterful direction, to create symphonic sounds that will echo through the halls of heaven. Perhaps every voice will have the ability to sound like Andrea Bochelli or Celine Dion. Perhaps the best songs haven't yet been written. Music has the unique ability to elevate the soul. In the right environment, a song of inspiration, whether sung in solo or by listening to a vast choir, can create a personal ecstasy that is unmatched in human experience. BUT, unlike the purpose of much music on earth today, this heavenly music will have the express purpose "to praise and glorify the Lord." Yes, music, both personal and corporate, shall be a major occupation in the heavenly schedule. In our quiet time, we shall pick up an instrument and sing songs of solemn worship. And when we assemble with the multitude of saints, as one voice, in the great concert halls of heaven, we will lift up a magnificent sound that thunders throughout the New Jerusalem and echoes throughout the Gardens of Eden, with a simple melodious message: *"For He is good, and His lovingkindness is everlasting."*

THE HEAVENLY CONCEPT OF CULTURE

I t is interesting to note that the word 'nations' did not come into being until after the flood. You would think that God would have done away with the nations in the Millennium and the New Jerusalem. After all, it seems that the nations, with their unique language and culture, have been the trouble all along. But a closer look reveals that God loved the variety of the nations. Just as He created a thousand varieties of flowers, He did the

same with mankind. The real trouble was when Nimrod tried to unify the nations into one language, one government and one culture at the tower of Babel. Revelation 21:24, 26 says: *"The nations will walk by its light, and the kings of the earth will bring their glory into it (the new Jerusalem) . . . and they will bring the glory and the honor of the nations into it."* Yes, our eternal home in glory will have nations, though our imaginations are stretched beyond limit to conceive what this means. Will there still be multiple languages, and dress, and cultural identities? Since scripture says there will be kings, we must conclude that there is some hierarchy that represents the people - each, of course, in total allegiance to King Jesus. The kings will bring 'their' glory, and the nations will bring 'their' glory. God does not want a monolithic realm of mankind that resemble robots. Our personalities will likely have even more uniqueness than we have on earth. You would think that in Heaven there would be NO glory except the glory of the Lord. But God in His sovereignty desires that His crowning act of creation (called mankind) will continue to enjoy a variety that is endless. Most of us have only gotten a taste of cultural variety on planet earth. If we are honest, it is that cultural variety that lures us to foreign lands for vacation. We like God's variety, and God likes watching His children bask in the variegated nature of his creation: the endless variety of plants and animals and foods and colors and styles of living. Yes, God created these for our enjoyment. And He loves to see His children, of all colors and ethnicities, learning from each other and celebrating our differences. Often, when cultures merge, we refer to the 'assimilation' of one culture into another. In Heaven, there will be no assimilation. God's fingerprint will be clearly delineated in every touch of creation. And if languages continue to exist, in Heaven there will be no language barrier. What began at Pentecost, with comprehension of unknown tongues, will be a pleasant part of our dialogue with other nations. Those of us who struggle in one language will someday be fluent in many. And the nations will finally experience Philippians 2:11: *"Every knee shall bow, and every tongue shall confess, that Jesus Christ is Lord, to the glory of God the Father."*

THE HEAVENLY CONCEPT OF WORSHIP

Tozer called worship *"the missing jewel of the evangelical church."* The implication is that we've learned how to study and pray and fellowship, and share our faith. But we have only scratched the surface of knowing how to worship. At Christmas we refer to Jesus as Immanuel, which means "God with us." Perhaps it's noteworthy to say that the word 'enthusiasm' has an old English root which means 'God in us.' Maybe that's the best way to describe worship. God is so much **IN** us that we are bursting with enthusiasm, with passion, and with a zeal that is uninhibited by this world's limitations. Jesus taught us in John 4:24 that we must worship God in spirit and truth. In Heaven we will have a pure knowledge of the *TRUTH* that will cause each *SPIRIT* to bow down in utter humility and astonishment before the God of Shekinah glory. I believe that worship is best understood as a soothing aroma offered up to God. 2 Corinthians 2:14 says *"But thanks be to God, who always leads us in triumph in Christ, and manifests through us the sweet aroma of the knowledge of Him in every place."* In Leviticus, our training manual for Old Testament worship was a soothing aroma (riach) of sacrifice that allowed the children of Israel to experience God's pleasure as He breathed through His anthropomorphic nostrils the sweet aroma of a simple act of worship. Revelation 8:4 records that an exotic fragrance, known as the prayers of the saints, went up before God just AFTER the silence in heaven, and just BEFORE the wrath of God was to be executed on planet earth. God is seeking true worshippers, and it will be the primary occupation of the New Jerusalem to host worship services like we've never known before. Timeless music and testimonies from the saints of all ages will be the warm-up act for Paul and a legion of God's apostles, prophets, evangelists and pastor-teachers. They will stand before a throng of millions to preach the Word once more. And then, at the appointed time, King Jesus will walk through the gates of the New Jerusalem, and the multitudes will burst into a crescendo of praise like the noise of a thousand stadiums. The fragrance of a soothing aroma will permeate the City of Peace, and every knee will bow as King Jesus takes the stage. At that moment, the ecstasy of loud praise will become a soft whisper of humble worship. And God will receive His glory.

THE CITY OF 2 MILLION SQUARE MILES

Revelation 21:16 says that the new Jerusalem will be a city 1500 miles square, which totals 2,250,00 square miles. When adding the countries of Iran, Iraq, Syria, Israel, Jordan, Egypt, Yemen and Oman, the total square mileage is 2,341,784. Gen 15:18 defined the Promised Land as follows: On that day the LORD made a covenant with Abram, saying, "To your descendants I have given this land, From the river of Egypt as far as the great river, the river Euphrates. The implication is this: For thousands of years, the countries of the Middle East have dominated little Israel, and have actively sought to exterminate Israel completely from the face of the earth. The IRONY of all this is that when God re-creates the earth, the new Jerusalem will encompass <u>ALMOST EXACTLY</u> the footprint of <u>ALL</u> the countries that sought for so long to "push Israel into the sea."

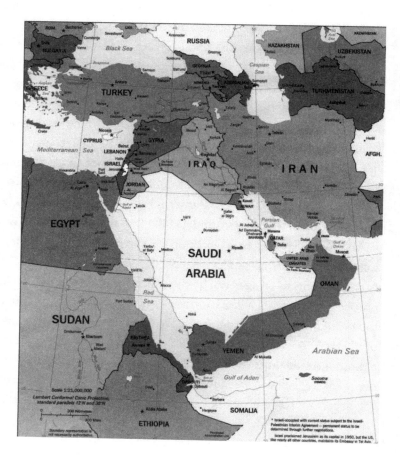

Israel	8,367
Iran	636,372
Iraq	168,753
Syria	71,498
Saudi	756,985
Jordan	35,637
Egypt	386,659
Yemen	203,849
Oman	82,031
TOTAL	**2,341,784**

EVENING AND MORNING, THE FIRST DAY

"And the evening and the morning were the first day."
Genesis 1:5

It has always been a curious thing to wonder why scripture begins the day in the evening and concludes it with the morning . . . until you read Revelation closely and realize that the segregation of the day (the Hebrew word 'yom') has been ordained by God as symbolism for eternity. Now the Jewish people, from time immemorial, have built all of their traditions around the structure of evening and morning: the weekly Sabbath, or Shabbat event, begins with the lighting of the candle, followed by the sacred service, then a night of rest, followed by the dawn of the new day. Shabbat concludes at sunset, after the participant has had a twelve hour period from six am to six pm, to rest from his labor once a week. The annual Passover event, the most sacred tradition, always begins at sunset and concludes at sunset the next day.

For the western mind, this is backwards. You begin the day at dawn and conclude the day at sunset, which is the beginning of night, and then the night climaxes at the dawn of the new day. Seventh Day Adventists even go so far as to say that the day consists of morning (dawn to noon) and evening (noon to sunset). In their mind, the night is evil and is not even part of a day. But when you frame human history in the light of eternity, suddenly the whole imagery of evening and morning takes on a new spectacle of understanding. For you see, we as humans, caught up in the Adamic curse of a life that has been tainted by sin, live our lives as if ***our day begins at sunset***. We live for a short time, we rest for the night, and then we rise to the dawn of a new day.

In other words, the human experience is based on a brief interlude that begins at sunset. We live briefly. We THINK we are living the best part of the day because we just can't see beyond the night. And then comes the dawn of the new day! We are fresh. We are rested. We are full of energy from the evening's fast, and we are ready to experience life in its fullness. ***That is the picture of eternity***. Our brief life begins at sunset. We try to maximize every moment; but alas, our time is short. Death has now become symbolized by sleep, and we lie down for a brief time, only to find that the day actually begins with the dawning of eternity! We thought we were living the full life! We thought we understood the abundant life! But now, Christ has raised us from the dead, and we awaken, full of post-mortal vitality, to experience the "real meaning" of the dawn of a new day. No longer will there be night because God himself will illumine the sky. Our days will now be endless, living in the beauty of the re-created Eden - basking in the magnificence of the new Jerusalem, and dwelling forever in the joy that God intended for the children of Adam and Eve. Yes, live your life to the fullest here on earth, and close your eyes to rest when death briefly has its way. But be assured, that when the 'morning star rises' in your heart, you will experience the true meaning of . . . "the dawn of a new day."

"It is crucial for westerners
to understand
that the fundamental duty of Islam
is to "Arabize" the world -
to unite humanity under one language,
one government and one religion, Islam.
It is an attempt to reverse what God did
at the tower of Babel. "
Walid Shoebat
"God's War on Terror"

CONCLUSION

"Global Persecution is Coming"

Judge Pir-Abassi of the Iranian Revolutionary Court, known as the "hanging judge," sentenced American Pastor Saeed Abedini to eight years in prison for threatening the national security of Iran. He was accused of counter-government activity because of his relationship to Christian house churches. The evidence provided was of Pastor Saeed's Christian activities primarily during the early 2000s, when under President Khatami, house churches were not perceived as a threat to Iran. Here's the troubling reality: A U.S. citizen, who has been beaten and tortured since his imprisonment last fall, is now facing eight years in Evin Prison, one of the most brutal prisons in the world. The 34-year-old father of two denied that he was evangelizing in Iran, and claims he had only returned to his native land to help establish an orphanage. Authorities pulled him off a bus, then threw him into the notorious Evin Prison in Tehran. His wife Naghmeh said "The promise of his release was a lie. We should not trust the empty words or promises put out by the Iranian government. " He was arrested in the summer of 2012, and imprisoned in January of 2013. This former Muslim-turned-Christian pastor has become a symbol throughout the world of the disregard that the Islam religion has for the human rights of the individual. Not only his human rights, but his religious rights have been violated. The Muslim world would have us believe that the word "Islam" means "submission" to God, but it more likely means submission to the totalitarian practices of this oppressive world power.

Dietrich Bonhoeffer was a gifted pianist who earned a doctorate in theology, taught at the University of Berlin, and was a Lutheran pastor. His father was a neurologist/ psychiatrist who had hoped Dietrich would follow in his footsteps. Perhaps that is why he said: "In the presence of a psychiatrist I can only be a sick man; in the presence of a Christian brother, I can dare to be a sinner." When Hitler rose to power, Dietrich voiced opposition and became a key member of the Nazi resistance movement. He was eventually banned from Berlin by the Gestapo in 1939. He was arrested in 1943 for conspiracy against Hitler and was hung in a German concentration camp just four weeks before the end of the war. Days before he died, he was quoted as saying: "This is the end - for me the beginning of life." His book, *The Cost of Discipleship*, has become a classic inspiration, and it begins with the following: "Cheap grace is the mortal enemy of the church." Of prayer he said: "To be silent does not mean to be inactive; rather it means to breathe in the will of God, to listen attentively and be ready to obey." The US Holocaust Memorial Museum honors his memory with his own words: "Only he who believes is obedient, and only he who is obedient believes." Bonhoeffer had this to say about persecution:

"To endure the cross is not tragedy;
it is the suffering which is the fruit
of an exclusive allegiance to Jesus Christ"

The Christian community, especially the West, must wake up to the reality that persecution is at the doorstep. We must begin to preach the message of boldness in the face of persecution, and be reminded daily of Paul's warning to us in 2 Timothy 3:12:

"Indeed, all who desire to live godly in Christ Jesus will be persecuted."

The Promise of Persecution

MATTHEW 5:10-12

Blessed are those who have been persecuted for the sake of righteousness,
for theirs is the kingdom of heaven. Blessed are you when people insult you
and persecute you, and falsely say all kinds of evil against you because of Me.
Rejoice and be glad, for your reward in heaven is great;
for in the same way they persecuted the prophets who were before you.

LUKE 21:12-17

They will lay their hands on you and will persecute you,
delivering you to the synagogues and prisons,
bringing you before kings and governors for My name's sake.
It will lead to an opportunity for your testimony.
So make up your minds not to prepare beforehand to defend yourselves;
for I will give you utterance and wisdom which none of your opponents
will be able to resist or refute.
But you will be betrayed even by parents
and brothers and relatives and friends,
and they will put some of you to death,
and you will be hated by all because of My name.

ROMANS 8:35

Who will separate us from the love of Christ?
Will tribulation, or distress, or persecution, or famine, or nakedness, or peril, or sword?
Just as it is written, "For your sake we are being put to death all day long;
we were considered as sheep to be slaughtered."
But in all these things we overwhelmingly conquer through Him who loved us.
For I am convinced that neither death, nor life, nor angels, nor principalities,
nor things present, nor things to come, nor powers, nor height, nor depth,
nor any other created thing, will be able to separate us from the love of God,
which is in Christ Jesus our Lord.

JOHN 15:20

A slave is not greater than his master.
If they persecuted Me, they will also persecute you;

A SUMMARY OF CHRISTIAN PERSECUTION
Foxes' Book of Martyrs

1. THE DISCIPLES AND APOSTLES.

Stephen - one of the first seven deacons appointed to the church; stoned to death; see Acts 11:19.

James the son of Zebedee - 44 ad. Sentenced to death by Herod Agrippa, his accuser repented of his actions and the two were beheaded together.

Phillip - 54 ad. He was the first of those called a disciple; ministered in Upper Asia; he was scourged, imprisoned and crucified.

Matthew - the tax collector and author of the Gospel; he was killed with a halberd (an axe attached to a long pole) in 60 ad In Ethiopia.

James, the brother of Jesus - author of the book of James, he was beat to death at the age of 94.

Matthias - replaced Judas as a disciple, he was stoned and then beheaded.

Andrew - brother of Simon Peter, he was crucified in Turkey.

Mark - author of the Gospel; he was dragged to death in Alexandria.

Peter - the passionate, impulsive disciple, was crucified in Rome. He asked to be crucified upside down because he was unworthy to die like Jesus did.

Paul - converted on the Damascus Road, Paul became the champion of the gospel to the Gentiles; when he was sentenced, his two executioners asked to be saved and baptized, then they led him out of the city to be beheaded.

Jude - the brother of James and author of the book, was crucified in 72 ad.

Bartholemew - translated the gospel of Matthew in the language of Indian, he was beaten, then crucified.

Thomas - Didymus, called Doubting Thomas, was speared to death in India.

Luke - author of the gospel, he was supposedly hanged on an olive tree in Greece.

Simon - known as the Zealot, this disciple was crucified in 74 ad.

John - the one who Jesus loved, author of John and Revelation, he was placed in a cauldron of hot oil, but he miraculously escaped without injury. Domitian exiled him to Patmos, where he was the only disciple not to be martyred.

2. THE EARLY CHURCH

Nero 67 ad - The first widespread persecution was set in motion when Roman Emperor
Nero ordered Rome burned while he played his harp; After he lamented, he
blamed the Christians and set them on fire at his palace, in order to illuminate
the gardens.

Domitian 81 ad - Nicodemus (of John 3) and Timothy, Paul's disciple, were the best known of
all those believers who were the object of this emperor's savagery.

Trajan 81 ad - Pliny recorded that thousands of Christians were put to death every day.
The best known of these was Ignatius, the bishop of Antioch. Upon being sentenced
to death, he said: *"Let fire and the cross, let the companies of wild beasts, let breaking
of bones and tearing of limbs, let the grinding of the whole body, and all the malice of
the devil, come upon me; be it so, only may I win Christ Jesus!" While being thrown to
wild beasts, he was quoted as saying, "I am the wheat of Christ: I am going to be
ground with the teeth of wild beasts, that I may be found pure bread."*

Marcus Aurelius 162 ad - Though considered a noble philosopher, this emperor was ruthless to
the Christian community.   Polycarp, the bishop of Smyrna, was sentenced to burning
at the stake. He responded as follows: "Eighty and six years have I served him, and he
never once wronged me; how then shall I blaspheme my King, who hath saved me?"
Witnesses said that the flames encircled his body but would not touch him. He was
finally killed with a sword.

Severus 192 ad - Two bishops of Rome, Victor and Calistus were both martyred, as was the
father of Origen, who was beheaded for his faith. A number of women were
mentioned in this time period. Perpetua, Felicitas, Saturninus and Cecilia were named
as victims of either beheading, scalding baths or goring by mad bulls. Tertullian
commented that if all the Christians had evacuated, the Roman population would have
been severely reduced.

Maxiums 235 ad - Multiple bishops of Rome were killed as well as multiple Roman senators.
Hippolitus was tied to a wild horse and dragged till dead.

Decius 249 ad - Fabian, the bishop of Rome as decapitated in 250 ad.   Chysostom was put
into a leather bag full of snakes and scorpions and he was thrown into the sea. Lucian
and Marcian, two former magicians who later preached the gospel, were burned alive.
Denisa, a 16 year old Christian girl, upon observing another execution, reacted, and
was immediately taken out and beheaded. Seven of the emperor's own men stood
firm in their faith, fled to a cave that was sealed up where they died.

Valerian 257 ad - Cyprian, the bishop of Carthage, was considered a hero of the Christian faith. Foxe describes him as follows: "His doctrines were orthodox and pure; his language easy and elegant; and his manners graceful and winning: he was both the pious and polite preacher." The pagans who targeted him for death said: "Cyprian to the lions, Cyprian to the beasts." He was beheaded on September 14, 258 ad.

Maximian 284 ad - With an army of 6,000 troops, all of whom happened to be Christians, they marched into Gaul and were ordered by the new emperor to kill all the Christians. The troops refused, and one of every ten was sentenced to death. They refused again and another 10% were killed. Finally Maximian ordered the entire Theban Legion to be put to death by another legion.

Diocletian 303 ad - Timothy and his new bride Maura lived in Mauritania, where he served as a deacon. The governor of Thebais challenged him to recant or be executed, to which he replied: "Had I children, I would sooner deliver them up to be sacrificed, than part with the Word of God." The governor was incensed, and he ordered Timothy upside-down with a weight on his neck and a gag in his mouth. Timothy and Maura were crucified beside each other in 304 ad.

The list goes on. Throughout the centuries, the followers of Jesus have endured ridicule and discrimination, leading to persecution and death. The modern movement of Islamic jihad is systematically purging the Middle East of any vestige of God's faithful. Churches and synagogues will soon become mosques, and even the cultures and traditions of a humble people group will be eradicated. What is the Church to do? God has not called us to be victorious. He has called us to be faithful. Our test must become our testimony. The battle is not ours. The battle is God's, and He will vindicate Himself in due time.

It is our task to pray for our brothers and sisters in countries where religious freedom has turned into terror. America is safe at the time of this writing, but political correctness will soon level the playing field to allow hostile elements to encroach upon our cultural freedoms. And suddenly one day, you will wake up and discrimination will turn into open violence.

Do not forget that the battle before us is a spiritual war. Our first responsibility is to awaken our churches to the reality of persecution, and to understand that the false security of a wishful theology called Pre-Tribulation Rapturism will steal away our ability to stand strong when the days of Abomination begin. Our hope is grounded in Jesus' words from John 16:33. *"These things I have spoken to you, so that in Me you may have peace. In the world you have tribulation, but take courage; I have overcome the world."*

In the Arms of Jesus

John MacArthur tells the story of a peasant farmer who was going into town for an evening meeting with a shopkeeper. His young son asked if he could join him on the trip and the father gladly consented. The trip was an hour's journey through the woods and across a stream, so the two decided to walk. Unexpected storm clouds began to gather, and then the rain. Father and son were having a good time enjoying nature, and the little boy was having fun jumping from one puddle to the next. The dark clouds continued to roll in, and the earth was now being pounded by the relentless rain. Evening was approaching and the shadow of darkness was close behind. They finally came to the stream crossing, which by now was swollen to the edge of the banks. The son was now frightened by the unpredictable merging of darkness and high waters. The father quickly scooped him up into his arms and carried him across the wide stream. By the time they reached the other side, the little boy was fast asleep. The father conducted his business in town, and then began the journey home. The next morning, the little boy awakened to the warmth of the sunshine. He was in his own home, in his own bed, looking at his father who was standing in the doorway greeting him good morning.

This is the picture of death for the Christian. One moment there is happiness and security. The next moment there seems to be impending doom. What we fear the most we never experience. We go to sleep in the arms of Jesus, and wake up the next morning to find ourselves at home in our own bed, with God the Father standing at the doorway, welcoming us to the dawn of a new day. The end is always good for the believer. Although tragedy befalls us everyday in a life that is surrounded by the Adamic curse, we know that God is in control. And even though "the back of the book" takes us through the darkest days mankind has ever known, we understand that God has NOT destined us for wrath, and we have His assurance that He will never leave us nor forsake us. Be encouraged by the words of Jeremiah, during Israel's dark days of the Babylonian captivity:

Jeremiah 29:11-13
'For I know the plans that I have for you,' declares the LORD,
'plans for welfare and not for calamity to give you a future and a hope.
'Then you will call upon Me and come and pray to Me, and I will listen to you.
'You will seek Me and find Me when you search for Me with all your heart.

IF JESUS WAS STANDING BESIDE YOU . . .

Imagine, if you will, the following possible future scenario:

The world is changing before your very eyes. The national government has finally conceded its power to the GG (Global Government) and announced martial law. There is anarchy in the streets. Food supplies are dwindling. The currency is subject to changing standards and therefore of little value. Gangs of thugs walk the streets while city and county police are being executed.

Two uniformed men approach your door. In the past, when police approached you, there was a sense of order and security and procedure that accompanied them. Now, there was only a sense of fear and intimidation. They are the Government Guard. Every city and township, and every county, is now strictly connected to the national police state. When the US President announces that the Government Guard will soon be approaching you, you know that the first order of business will be to confiscate any weapons that you may have - pistols, rifles, ammo, bb guns, antique swords, etc. The hope of hiding your precious arms is a thing of the past. New infra-red technology can now identify everything in the house.

We have said for years that the more we asked for security, the more we would give up our freedom. That time has finally come. Our government, under the direction of the United Nations, has now implemented a national identification code. Since the borders have been compromised for years, and international thieves are everywhere, a single unified, "one size fits all" system has been enforced.

The two men gather your family together and inform you that a new global system is now in effect. The Global Leader has declared that since all local systems of government have failed, it is necessary for him to step in and take control. Only his immediate intervention will save the world from a global economic collapse. In order to provide you this security, and the prospect of food and water sources, it is imperative that your family prove their loyalty to this new network of government.

Freedom of assembly has now been discontinued. You are informed that the right to assemble for political or religious purpose is forbidden until further notice. It is obvious to you now that the church you have been a member of for years has now been padlocked and faces permanent shutdown. Though you still have the right to communicate by cell phone, the government closely monitors all calls, and any attempt to protest or rally together will be met with punishment.

The two men now state their conditions. In order for your family to sustain itself with food and water and opportunity to work, you will be required to pledge your allegiance to the new world order. All religions have been immediately and officially terminated . . . except one. The new law of the land is Sharia Law. And with that law comes the very necessary requirement to prove your loyalty to this new one world religious system.

The process is very simple. All you are required to do is repeat the "shahadatan." It's a simple oath. Eleven words and you're done. No requirement to give money or attend meetings. Simply say the oath and you will be presented with a national security card that will allow you to buy and sell as you please. *"Repeat after me"*, they say. *"There is no god but Allah, and Mohammed is his prophet."* For the average pagan in the 21st century, that's no problem. But you are a Christian, and you **SUDDENLY** understand that the "mark of the beast" is an ideology. Simply say the slogan, receive your card, and the men will be gone. Your family is waiting. The consequences of refusing are likely to be severe - imprisonment or even death.

Then you remember a verse from Revelation 12:11. ***"They loved not their lives, even when faced with death."*** Suddenly you sense a presence with you. The angel of the Lord appears before you and says,

> *"It's OK. Don't be afraid. This is the moment I have prepared you for. This is your opportunity to show your allegiance to me. The consequences will be brief for you and your family. Your life is a mere vapor. Your body is only a temporary house for your eternal spirit. Stand strong in the face of persecution. I have given you the ultimate test. It is also the ultimate opportunity. Declare your confession of faith, for I will be with you always."*

This is the true test for every believer. It's not how often I go to church or even read my Bible. The true test is this:

> ***"If Jesus is standing right next to me, and he offers me his strength for a momentary threat to my body, will I understand that this test reveals the true motives of my heart?"***

Unfortunately, most of the church members in today's world would rationalize that they must preserve their lives at all cost. Survival is essential! And they will miss the point that what Jesus requires of each of us is an unflinching loyalty that once and for all, proudly and without compromise, says to the world, ***"Jesus is Lord."*** Romans 8:18 says, *"For I consider that the sufferings of this present time are not worthy to be compared with the glory that is yet to be revealed to us."* Some of us may be faced with that opportunity.

I pray that I will be ready if Jesus calls me to that ultimate test of my devotion to Him.

FULL CIRCLE

It is amazing to look at human history and see the parallel between the progression of sin which prompted the need for the cross of Christ, and the parallel sin which finally escalates into a second world judgment and the re-creation of God's intended state of eternal paradise.

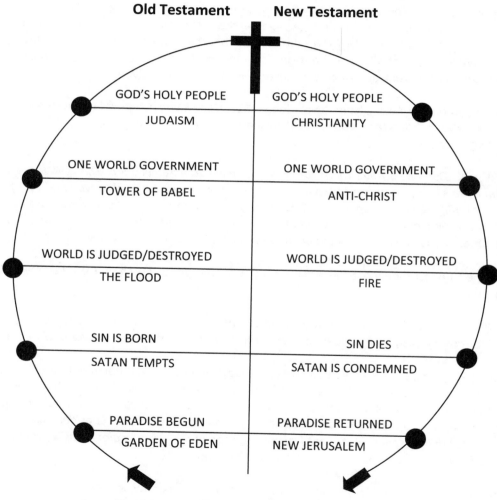

Old Testament   **New Testament**

GOD'S HOLY PEOPLE — GOD'S HOLY PEOPLE

JUDAISM — CHRISTIANITY

ONE WORLD GOVERNMENT — ONE WORLD GOVERNMENT

TOWER OF BABEL — ANTI-CHRIST

WORLD IS JUDGED/DESTROYED — WORLD IS JUDGED/DESTROYED

THE FLOOD — FIRE

SIN IS BORN — SIN DIES

SATAN TEMPTS — SATAN IS CONDEMNED

PARADISE BEGUN — PARADISE RETURNED

GARDEN OF EDEN — NEW JERUSALEM

Jesus Christ is the same yesterday, today and forever.

HEBREWS 13:8

Old Paradigms Die Hard

I have labored many long nights, even long years, in an attempt to understand and to simplify some of the deep and difficult things of God that are written in the book of Revelation. The convictions registered in this book will meet with some criticism. Traditional mainline scholars, who I hold in high esteem, will dismiss the Pre-Wrath Rapture as "misguided."

In his book, "Rapture Under Attack" author Tim LaHaye, the originator (with Jerry Jenkins) of the "Left Behind" series, has this to say about Marv Rosenthal and Robert Van Kampen:

> *"After years of public scrutiny, it looks as if this view is going nowhere. Except for Van Kampen and Rosenthal, I know of no serious prophecy student that has embraced it. I predict that it will prove to be an aberrant brainstorm, and that, despite its deep pocketed promotional campaign, it will fade away before it becomes a fad."*

Quite the contrary, I would suggest to Dr. LaHaye (whom I respect for his longstanding ministry for the cause of Christ) that I have encountered many godly and scholarly men and women across the country who have embraced the Pre-Wrath position. Books now line the shelves providing excellent exposition of scripture that upholds the Pre-Wrath position.

Unfortunately, old paradigms die hard, and it may take a generation of knocking on the closed door of Pre-Tribulation thinking before a new generation of objective students of scripture can see through the rigid ideology of escapism - to embrace the growing sentiment and conviction that persecution among believers will be an end-time reality that cannot be ignored.

Like Cyprian, the bishop of Carthage, who lived from 200 to 258 a.d., and was martyred by the Roman Emperor Valerian, I hope I can stand strong if called on to bear my testimony. The words of Cyprian echo through 16 centuries of time. It is these words that caused Cyprian to face beheading because of his faith in Christ.

"Robbers on the highways, pirates on the sea, armies fighting, cities burning. In the amphi-theaters, men murdered to please applauding crowds. Selfishness and despair and cruelty under all roofs. It is a bad world, my friend - and incredibly bad world. But I have found in the midst of it a quiet and holy people who have learned a great lesson. They have found a joy which is a thousand times better than any pleasures of our sinful lives. They are despised and persecuted, but they care not. They are masters of their souls. They have overcome the world. These people, my friend, are the Christians, and I am one of them."

Revelation 12:11. "They loved not their lives, even when faced with death."

WHERE IS AMERICA IN BIBLE PROPHECY?

On September 11, 2001, the evil forces of Osama Bin Laden descended upon The United States of America with an intended goal of overthrowing the country. Their strategy was to cause destruction and death and panic upon the American public by neutralizing U.S. finances (plane crashes into the World Trade Center) U.S. military (plane crashes into The Pentagon) and our U.S. government (attempted plane crash into the Capitol building, averted by the plane crash in Shanksburg, Pennsylvania.) Had he been successful, the game plan would have looked much like the 2014 movie *"Olympus Has Fallen"*, in which foreign terrorists took control of Washington and its leaders. Two things thwarted his efforts: the resolve of the American people, and . . the sovereignty of Jehovah God.

There is little doubt that America is on a path of national decline. President Barack Obama has succeeded in drawing down our military strength to that of a pre-WWII status. Our three branches of equilateral power have been hijacked by the Executive branch, which now espouses a position more akin to the 'divine right of kings' than a government 'of the people, by the people and for the people.' Proverbs 14:34 summarily defines our problem: "Godliness makes a nation great, but sin is a disgrace to any people." The following are several 'possibilities' for America's place in the Bible:

America as Babylon. Revelation 14:8 says, *'And another angel, a second one, followed, saying, "Fallen, fallen is Babylon the great, she who has made all the nations drink of the wine of the passion of her immorality." '* Jeremiah 51:7 echoes those fateful words: *"Babylon has been a golden cup in the hand of the LORD, intoxicating all the earth. The nations have drunk of her wine; Therefore the nations are going mad."* America's moral decline over each generation has signaled for many that America is actually the great harlot, Babylon. Atheism, Sexual immorality, drugs, abortion and idolatrous materialism have certainly signaled the decline, if not the death toll, of the once proud beacon of world hope. If not Babylon, America may well be the daughter of Babylon. Zechariah 2:7 warns us: *"Ho, Zion! Escape, you who are living with the daughter of Babylon."*

America as a casualty of the Middle East conflict. Rev 6:8 *"I looked, and behold, an ashen horse; and he who sat on it had the name Death; and Hades was following with him. Authority was given to them over a fourth of the earth, to kill with sword and with famine and with pestilence and by the wild beasts of the earth."* Because of America's favored status as a world leader, we Americans tend to think that America can never fall. Like Rome, who shared many similarities with America, each of the world's great nationalities has crumbled before the sovereign eyes of Almighty God. It is possible that the world lens will refocus on the Middle East in the future, and though we can't believe that God wouldn't protect the U.S., we fail to understand that God is not as concerned with our flesh as we are. God is concerned with fulfilling His plan to unite His Church with His Chosen, as they become His Children for eternity. This ashen or pale horse is translated from the Greek text as 'chlorous'. Perhaps chemical warfare will be one of Satan's cruel schemes to dispose of 1/4 of the earth, including America.

America as a casualty of death and martyrdom. Rev 12:17 *"So the dragon was enraged with the woman, and went off to make war with the rest of her children, who keep the commandments of God and hold to the testimony of Jesus."* The 'rest of her children' is an allusion to God's Church throughout the world. We like to think that America, with its churches on every corner, is still the hub of global Christianity. Even if we are no longer the hub, this verse could still refer to the fate of the Church in America. The churches of America would either diminish and dissolve because of their shallowness; or they would be swept away by persecution leading to death and martyrdom.

America as the Guardian of Israel. Revelation 12:14. *"But the two wings of the great eagle were given to the woman, so that she could fly into the wilderness to her place, where she was nourished for a time and times and half a time, from the presence of the serpent."* One interpretation of this verse is that The United States of America, symbolized by the eagle, must be the guardian of Israel in the last 3.5 years, and therefore, uses aviation to carry the saved remnant of Israel (prior to its salvation) into a desert hiding place.

We do not know our fate, and scripture is not explicit in stating our destiny. Perhaps the fate of America is found in the warning to the church in Laodicea in Revelation 3:15-19

'I know your deeds, that you are neither cold nor hot;
I wish that you were cold or hot. So because you are lukewarm,
and neither hot nor cold, I will spit you out of My mouth.
Because you say, "I am rich, and have become wealthy,
and have need of nothing, and you do not know that you are wretched
and miserable and poor and blind and naked,
I advise you to buy from Me gold refined by fire so that you may become rich,
and white garments so that you may clothe yourself,
and that the shame of your nakedness will not be revealed;
and eye salve to anoint your eyes so that you may see.
Those whom I love, I reprove and discipline; therefore be zealous and repent.'

WHERE IS RUSSIA IN BIBLE PROPHECY?

The primary references used to describe what may be Russia in scripture are the phrases: 'the land of the north, the remotest part of the north and the prince of Rosh'. It should first be stated that there is no explicit mention of Russia in scripture. Certainly, however, we cannot imagine how Russia could be exempt from a coming world conflict.

Rosh, Meshech and Tubal.

Eze 38:2 "Son of man, set your face toward Gog of the land of Magog, the prince of Rosh, Meshech and Tubal, and prophesy against him

Eze 38:3 and say, 'Thus says the Lord GOD, "Behold, I am against you, O Gog, prince of Rosh, Meshech and Tubal.

Eze 39:1 "And you, son of man, prophesy against Gog and say, 'Thus says the Lord GOD, "Behold, I am against you, O Gog, prince of **Rosh, Meshech and Tubal;**

> *For a hundred years, commentators have speculated about this phrase. At a glance, it would seem apparent that this passage is a vague reference to Russia, Moscow and Tobolsk (a city and river in Russia). But upon closer examination, (see page 198) we see that Meschech, Tobol and Beth-Togarmah are all located in Turkey, which is north of Israel. Deeper examination into the word 'rosh' indicates that this Hebrew word is used today (Rosh Hashanah) to describe the Jewish civil new year. Scholars in recent years have begun to re-describe this passage as 'head' prince, or the more appropriate term 'chief prince'. Therefore, the verse would read that Gog (of the land of Magog) is the chief prince of Meshech and Tubal. In this author's opinion, this passage is NOT speaking of Russia.*

the land of the north.

Jer 6:22 Thus says the LORD, "Behold, a people is coming from the north land, And a great nation will be aroused from the remote parts of the earth.

Jer 6:23 "They seize bow and spear; They are cruel and have no mercy; Their voice roars like the sea, And they ride on horses, Arrayed as a man for the battle Against you, O daughter of Zion!"

> *It is true that Russian is a land to the north of Israel, and actually, it is the remotest part of the north. It is true that we perceive them to be cruel and have no mercy as a godless nation that is thirsty for world power. The United States has long been in a 'cold war' with Russia, meaning that our two world powers have cautiously held each other*

suspect as contenders for world power. Russia befriended Cuba, and the result was a standoff between President Kennedy and Soviet Premier Krushchev, now referred to as the "Cuban Missile Crisis". President Ronald Reagan succeeded in warming up international relations with Russia by dismantling the Berlin Wall, and the result was glasnost', a time of openness in Russia, led by Premier Gorbachev. Today, once again, our two nations are the godfathers who arm other nations to fight battles and occupy territories. We fully expect Russia, who openly arms Syria and Iran, to be in 'at least', a proxy battle to engage the United States against the protection of Israel.

For the record, the latitude and longitude of Israel is 31 degrees north and 35 degrees west. In that context, Syria is north, Babylon is north, Turkey is north and Iran is north. Perhaps a reminder of world kingdoms is in order at this point. The kingdom of Assyria (to the north) conquered the northern kingdom of Israel in 722 bc. Then Babylon conquered the southern kingdom of Israel in 586 bc. Medo-Persia (Iran) conquered Babylon in 536 bc. Then came the kingdoms of Greece and Rome. The point is that the ancient kingdoms that dominated Israel were all to the north of her.

Notice the following two verses of scripture. One refers to the land of the north as Babylon. The other refers to the remotest parts of the north as Turkey. Both verses provide substance for questioning any reference to Russia as the biblical land of the north.

Jer 46:10 For that day belongs to the Lord GOD of hosts, A day of vengeance, so as to avenge Himself on His foes; And the sword will devour and be satiated And drink its fill of their blood; For there will be a slaughter for the Lord GOD of hosts, In the land of the north by the river Euphrates.

Eze 38:6 Gomer with all its troops; Beth-togarmah *from* the remote parts of the north with all its troops, many peoples with you.

*Does that mean that Russia is not involved in the eschatalogical battles of the future? Not at all. It only means that we need to be careful when we use scripture to define prophetic world places and events. Most likely Russia **WILL BE** the 'enabler' that fuels the war between Anti-Christ and Israel. But, don't overlook the possibility that the ten nation confederacy will be centered around the Middle East only, and perhaps the ancient kingdoms of world domination - Assyria, Babylon and Persia - will in fact be the primary players in this apocalyptic drama . . . while the United States and Russia look on from the sidelines.*

WHERE IS CATHOLICISM IN BIBLE PROPHECY?

Since the Protestant Reformation in the 16th century, the Free Church tradition has pointed to the Roman Catholic Church as an illegitimate system of political and moral abuses. Every Christian denomination is guilty of sinfulness among its members and its leaders, but the Roman system has long been targeted because of papal corruption, immorality among the priesthood and the general nature of systematic rituals that are considered unbiblical and foreign to the simple teaching of scripture. For this reason, the Catholic Church has suffered much from loose interpretations of biblical prophecy. Though this author does not share the sentiment of many prophecy scholars of the 20th century who generally refer to the Catholic system as Babylon, the Great Harlot, the question still remains: "What part does the papal allegiance of 1 billion Catholics play in the drama of apostasy, persecution and martyrdom?

1. The City of Seven Hills.

Revelation 17:9, 10. "Here is the mind which has wisdom. The seven heads are seven mountains on which the woman sits, and they are seven kings; five have fallen, one is, the other has not yet come; and when he comes, he must remain a little while.

> *The seven mountains spoken of in Revelation 17:9 do NOT refer to the Roman Church, but prophecy scholars for the last hundred years have used this as prooftext for their position. Rome has long been called "the city of seven hills", because of the seven hills that form the locus of Rome's political and geographic center. The inference is made that seven hills equal seven mountains. The correct interpretation is that these moun-tains represent ancient kingdoms that have all dominated Israel. The text clearly says that. Sure, Rome was one of those kingdoms, but to allude to the seven mountains as Rome is just not good biblical interpretation.*

2. The Great City of Purple and Scarlet.

Rev 18:16 saying, 'Woe, woe, the great city, she who was clothed in fine linen and purple and scarlet, and adorned with gold and precious stones and pearls;

> *Vatican City in Rome has been called by some interpreters as "the great city", and truly Rome is a great city among the nations of the earth. The official colors of the papal system are purple and scarlet, and it is no secret that the Catholic system worldwide is rich with real estate and vast fortunes, as the result of faithful giving of its members. Yes, this seems to align with Rome, but in the larger context of interpretation, I believe that there is a far more dangerous foe than the RC Church that represents Babylon, the great harlot.*

3. The Golden Cup of Abominations.

Rev 17:4 The woman was clothed in purple and scarlet, and adorned with gold and precious stones and pearls, having in her hand a gold cup full of abominations and of the unclean things of her immorality,

> *It is an unfortunate statistic that approximately 3,000 priests in the past fifty years have been accused or indicted for sexual crimes of pedophilia by the local priesthood (BBC News, June 15, 2015). Whether this tendency has to do with the policy of celibacy among the male priests is not the concern of this author. What is of concern is the sexual abuse of any church leaders, whether Catholic or Protestant, and the indelible stain that this leaves upon the unbeliever in the world, who points to this hypocrisy as one more reason not to associate with the Church. Whether this sin is the cup of abomination and immorality spoken of in Revelation 17:4 is a matter of interpretation. Again, in the larger context, I believe the woman is not the Catholic Church.*

4. The Authority of the Second Beast.

Rev 13:11 Then I saw another beast coming up out of the earth; and he had two horns like a lamb and he spoke as a dragon.

Rev 13:12 He exercises all the authority of the first beast in his presence. And he makes the earth and those who dwell in it to worship the first beast, whose fatal wound was healed.

> *It is generally accepted that the first beast, the Anti-Christ, who rises out of the sea of humanity, embraces a political platform to accomplish his evil agenda. The "other" beast, the False Prophet, rises out of the earth and leverages a religious agenda to influence the masses to worship the first beast.   For decades, interpreters have pointed to the Pope as either the Anti-Christ or the False Prophet. At the time of this writing, I believe the False Prophet is more likely to be the Shi-ite Ayotollah OR a unified leader of the Sunnis and Shi-ites, rising out of the forthcoming Caliphate, whose goal is to govern the Muslims AND the pagans by Sharia Law.*

> *Where does that place the Papal system and the 1 billion adherents to the Catholic system? The easy answer is to place them among the categories of the rest of the Church: one of the Seven Churches. This mean they will either be the Persevering/Persecuted Church, which become the overcomers, the saved remnant at the time of the Rapture. OR, they become one of the five churches that fall victim to the apostasy and deception of the Anti-Christ. The more difficult question is to determine the role of the Pope and the Cardinals, when the mark of the beast is instituted. Will the Pope stand strong in the face of persecution, or will he cut a deal with the Anti-Christ, suggesting that his flock take the mark in order to survive? It is my prayer for the Catholic community that they clearly understand that following King Jesus is the only way to salvation.*

DEATH, SHEOL, HADES, HELL AND PARADISE

The word 'die' is first used in Genesis 2:17, when God warned Adam not to eat of the tree of good and evil, "for you shall surely die." Since that time, death has been a painful reality for mankind. The curse upon man guaranteed that all life processes would eventually cease. One of the great questions of this life is what happens at the time of death. The Hebrew word 'sheol' is used 65 times in the Old Testament to describe the place of the dead. King Hezekiah laments in Isaiah 38:10: *"I said in the middle of my life, I am to enter the gates of **Sheol**; I am to be deprived of the rest of my years."* **Abaddon** is coupled with the word Sheol in Proverbs 15:11, implying that the demon angel Abaddon (in the Greek, Apollyon) is the gatekeeper for the place called Sheol. *"Sheol and Abaddon (the destroyer) lie open before the LORD, how much more the hearts of men!"* Since the word 'sheol' is not used in the New Testament, we have to ask, what word is used to describe this mysterious realm? The Hebrew word 'Sheol' appears to be replaced by the word '**Hades**' in the Greek language of the New Testament. But it also im-portant to understand that Hades was the Greek god of the under-world. Very strange. Why would Jesus, Matthew, Luke, John and Paul refer to a Greek god? There is probably only one explanation. Hades, the Greek god of the underworld must be a real person. This leads us to a stunning conclusion. If Hades was a Greek god who Jesus referred to, and Hades would later be cast into the lake of fire (Revelation 20:13,14), then Hades had to be a demon. And if Hades was a demon, then the entire pantheon of Greek gods must have been . . . demons. No wonder I didn't like Greek mythology in the third grade. It is now very important to understand that Jesus distinguished between Hades and Hell as follows:

The Greek god of the underworld, and his 3 headed dog, Cerberus.

> Matthew 16:18 "I also say to you that you are Peter, and upon this rock I will build My church; and the gates of **Hades** will not overpower it.
> Matthew 10:28 "Do not fear those who kill the body but are unable to kill the soul; but rather fear Him who is able to destroy both soul and body in **Hell.**

How many sermons have you heard that quoted the Bible, stating, *"the gates of Hell will not overpower it"*? The word is Hades, and the pronunciation of this word is actually, 'hah-dace'. Interesting how we have mispronounced this word. Jesus and John used the word 4 times each, and Paul used it twice. So the implication is this:

Death was our first enemy, and the place of the dead, Sheol/Hades, was the temporary resting place of the dead. Since death was a curse, Satan claimed ownership (and victory) over the souls of mankind. Then Jesus came along, and there was a new place called **"Paradise".** Luke 23:43 (This day you shall be with me in Paradise), 2 Cor. 12:4 (Paul was caught up to Paradise) and Revelation 12:7 (you shall eat from the tree of life in Paradise). If Jesus had not conquered death, there would have been no resurrection of the dead, and there would have been no Paradise (another name for the Garden, in Eden). When Paul said, *"Absent from the body is to be present with the Lord"*, the meaning is that we go to Paradise at death to reside in the temporary abode until finally the New Jerusalem and Paradise descend to re-clothe the planet, now becoming the New Earth. I believe that Paradise is the residence on the New Earth for the Gentiles, and the New Jerusalem is the abode of the newly saved Tribes of Israel. The final piece of this puzzle is the place that we call **Hell.** The New Testament Greek word is actually translated 'geh-enna'. This name, Geh-enna, was formally called the Valley of Hinnom, and was located partially surrounding the city of Jerusalem, and intersecting the Kidron Valley, which separated the Mount of Olives from the Temple Mount. See page 329 for a fuller explanation of this place. The Kidron Valley was a common path of travel from the city to the garden, where 150,000 Jewish people have been buried over the centuries. On the other hand, Geh-enna was a desolate place that we might call a 'landfill' today - a place of smoldering ruins of the city. More important, it was a place of child sacrifice by those pagans who worshipped the god Molech. For the Jewish community 2000 years ago, this was the symbol of the lake of fire that Jesus spoke of when he condemned those who worshipped foreign gods. It is not a coincidence that this place, used for the sacrifice and disposal of children, was also a place of fire and torment and eternal condemnation. Is there a parallel in our culture? The abortion industry, sanctioned by the Supreme Court of the United States, is guilty of killing an estimated 50,000 babies, for the purpose of hiding the "inconvenient truth" of sex without the consequence of childbirth. This very selfish and superficial act is encouraged by half of our country, under the guise of protecting a woman's bodily rights, in order to sanction destroying another human being. Watch a commercial on animal rights and you'll be surprised to see the very same liberal activists rallying to protect those little puppies that have been abused. Yes, **Hell** was created for the devil and his angels (2 Peter 2:4), but mankind followed the voice of the Deceiver. Jesus cheated death, and snatched his chosen ones from the jaws of **Hell.** Those who have chosen to reject Jesus, were condemned to join the devil and the Anti-Christ, and the False Prophet, and death and Hades, as they were cast into the eternal lake of fire. Where is this lake of fire? See page 374. God's plan of salvation is complete. He has Gathered His Church, Restored His Chosen and United His Children, while the condemned are watching from a distance the joyful activity of knowing Jesus. John 3:16 was a very simple formula for all to obey:

"that whosoever believes in Him (Jesus) will not PERISH, but have everlasting life."

A Nod FROM God

In the beginning . . . God created, out of nothing - ex nihilo - a universe so vast that 21st century scientists push the limits of their erudite knowledge to understand some of the simplest theories of creation.   I want to pose a very simple idea - something just to get you thinking - not trying to alter your theology or stretch your faith. Just a thought. From Genesis 1:3, it is the voice of God that sets in motion the heavens and the earth. But what if there is a gesture, even more slight than a voice, that is behind the voice. Certainly, we understand that God doesn't need a voice to orbitize the planets or animate the biology of earth. He can merely think the thought and it's done. But I believe that God possesses the very same characteristic that you and I have to show His emotions. For you and I, the slightest, the most insignificant means of communication that God has given us is . . . the NOD. Think about it. Everyday we human creatures express ourselves with the slightest of gestures that we call the NOD. We register satisfaction and dissatisfaction, pain, joy, comfort, approval and disapproval with this minute little motion. Our facial expressions are SO KEEN that a simple nod can bring joy or tears to a child. The raised eyebrows of a father can set in motion guilt or conviction by a son who has just done the wrong thing. The mere glance, and a grin from one friend to another, communicates a world of language. There are a hundred different nods that the human face can register to show joy or pain, and since God has given them all to us, it makes perfect sense to believe that God possesses those very same qualities.

So here's the point of this theological exercise to bring you closer to God. I would suggest to you that there are seven major events in human history in which God has "nodded" (to show facial emotion) that ultimately have affected the destiny of man. This is actually an exercise in systematic theology, because the seven events are as follows:

1)   Creation

2)   Delegation

3)   Inspiration

4)   Salvation

5)   Illumination

6)   Reconciliation

7)   Sanctification

In order for your view of God to be comprehensive, you must understand these monumental elements of the sovereignty and the grace of God. These components are each a gift from God, and each is a progression of His wonderful revelation to us. In this view, God's revelation from man begins with the most distant revelation (Creation) and moves through human history to the closest of revelations (Sanctification), which is the manifestation of Christ's power on earth, through the heart of the individual.

These seven events, in some ways, are the ultimate revelation of God. They begin in a very distant other-time, thousands of years ago, and progressively reveal God's truth to us, until reaching the final and most intimate of all God's revelation: the residing person of the Holy Spirit, indwelling each of us, and providing us with God's gift of sanctification.

1. **Creation.** God's revelation began when he "nodded" the world into being. The mysterious Trinity of Father, Son and Spirit used every facial expression of delight imaginable to craft our majestic universe. Evolution so sadly perverts the beauty and simplicity of a loving Creator who designs a world of untapped mystery for his crowning achievement - man.

2. **Delegation.** After the fall of man in the Garden, God was once again lonely for fellowship with mankind. Because of the curse, which now held man's heart captive, God chose to begin again, and raise up a tribal seed that would love Him. With a squint of the eye, He chose Abraham to father the tribe of Israel which would become the seed of salvation.

3. **Inspiration.** God knew that man needed an objective source of truth. Oral tradition was good, but not enough to provide a trans-generational text that would embody the truth of God as recorded in every language on the planet. With a slight gesture representing incalculable precision, the Word of God became a thought that later became a book.

4. **Salvation.** God knew that man was still bound in sin by the curse. He needed a solution, something to atone for man's sin. With a joyous smile and a wince of pain, God created a plan for His only Son, to become "the way, the truth and the life". Jesus would become the only way to salvation, and would begin incarnate, then crucified, and finally glorified.

5. **Illumination.** Though the Spirit has always existed, and was manifest occasionally through the Old Testament, it was after Jesus ascended to heaven that the Spirit was sent to be "the Comforter", "the Paraclete", who would reside in, and empower every believer. God's Spirit was now resident in man's spirit, and God nodded a sigh of relief.

6. **Reconciliation.** It was not enough that God breathed His spirit individually into those who chose to follow Him. He still needed a people, a vessel of righteous energy, an army of worshippers and servers and ministers and missionaries to perform the all-important ministry of reconciliation to the Gentiles of the world. Since Israel was prodigal, God would shake His head and then nod the Church into his sovereign plan.

7. **Sanctification.** The impartation of the Holy Spirit of God was an act that happened at Pentecost 2000 years ago. Like salvation, it was a down payment of blessings to come. And now, the Spirit not only resides in ME, but He enlightens and empowers ME each day to be consumed by the love and grace of God, to live in victory as a child of the King.
See next page, for the continuation of this message . . . A Nod **FOR** God.

A NOD FOR GOD

On the preceding pages you learned that there are seven major revelations of God, beginning with Creation, and each one getting progressively closer, until finally God's revelation finds its zenith in the life of a believer whose life is sanctified for His purpose. Each revelation was identified as if God had nodded His head to make things happen. Now we turn our attention to the unregenerate heart of man, to the man or woman whose childhood has somehow inoculated them against the love of God. Or, to the young person who is now in the throes of liberalism or atheism or amoralism - determined to live out their lives in defiance of a Creator God, the God who has a plan for their life.

Perhaps this is an oversimplification. Perhaps this sounds too easy or too liberal. But all that God wants from you is a NOD. He'll take care of the rest. You see, God doesn't expect you to be a theologian. He's not trying to drag you off to a foreign country to be a missionary. All He wants from you is that first NOD, a simple gesture that says, "Yes God. In spite of the world's attempts to disprove Your existence, I see the miraculous work of Creation all around me. The Bible says that You have planted eternity in the heart of man. I acknowledge my sinful nature. And I want to know You as I learn to follow Jesus, who gave His life to reveal your love to mankind." That . . . Is a Nod for God. A simple gesture. A step toward God. An indication that you understand, like the message on a t-shirt that said: "There is a God and I am not Him." The world wants you to make it on your own without God. The world will try to convince you that God is a primitive superstition that we have outgrown in this new age. But the message of the Bible is clear. *"The Lord is not slow about His promise, as some count slowness, but is patient toward you, not wishing for any to perish but for all to come to repentance." 2 Peter 3:9*

God has nodded the world into existence. He has revealed Himself through Creation and Israel and Jesus and the Bible and the Holy Spirit and the Church. And finally, He wants to reveal Himself through you. He nodded the world into existence for you. All He wants from you . . . is a NOD - a gesture - an indication that you acknowledge His omnipotent power throughout the earth. He wants you to NOD . . . that you accept the reality of Jesus as the pre-eminent personality in all the universe. He wants you to NOD . . . to allow the Jesus of the Bible to reveal Himself to you. The Bible says, "You have not, because you ask not." This is a good time to ask. This is a good time to NOD your head (maybe even bow your head). More important, bow your heart, in humility before a loving God who wants you to experience fulfillment. God's Bridge of Salvation will further explain this wonderful plan.

GOD'S BRIDGE OF SALVATION

1. GOD'S PLAN *for mankind from the beginning was FELLOWSHIP with Him and FULFILLMENT from Him. God, the creator of the universe, had great plans for man. Jeremiah 29:11-13 says: "For I know the plans I have for you; plans for welfare, not for calamity; to give you a future and a hope; 'Then you will call upon Me and come and pray to Me, and I will listen to you. And you will seek Me and find Me when you search for Me with all your heart."*

MAN	FELLOWSHIP/FULFILLMENT	LOVING GOD

2. MAN'S PROBLEM *throughout all the centuries has been hereditary willful separation from God which began with Adam's first sin in the Garden. Romans 3:23 says: "For all have sinned and fallen short of the glory of God." The separation between God and man could not be spanned by religion or good works or morality or church.*

SINFUL MAN	RELIGION, GOOD WORKS, MORALITY, CHURCH, ETC.	MERCIFUL GOD

3. GOD'S REMEDY *for this unreachable chasm between God and man could only be filled by God's son Jesus. Romans 5:8 says: "God demonstrated His love for us, because while we were still sinners, Christ died for us." Jesus was the only person in human history who could give His life in exchange for our sins. We call His death, burial and resurrection THE GOSPEL, because it is the bridge between heaven and earth.*

COMPETED MAN	Jesus the Messiah	ETERNAL GOD

4. MAN'S RESPONSE *to God's gift is to accept it. Accept the fact that God has a plan for your life. Accept the fact that you have inherited a spiritual problem called sin. Accept the fact that the only remedy for this disease called sin is Jesus, who died on a Roman cross 2000 years ago, and then rose from the dead.*

Romans 10:9,10 says "If you confess with your mouth Jesus as Lord, and believe in your heart that God has raised him from the dead, you will be saved. For with the heart, man believes, resulting in righteousness, and with the mouth, he confesses, resulting in salvation."

Mankind today stands between two great mountaintops which symbolize human history. The first mountaintop is the Incarnation of God in the Person of Jesus 2000 years ago. The second mountaintop represents Jesus' Second Coming to rescue His Church and His beloved Israel, before exacting judgment upon unrepentant man. It is important to acknowledge that these two mountaintops tower far above any other events in human history. As Christians, we understand that the gospel of Jesus is NOT ONLY about Jesus' advent to earth as a humble teacher who shed His blood for the sins of mankind. It is also about the cataclysmic events which signal the end of the age and prepare mankind to worship King Jesus as the Creator and Redeemer God.

Jesus' first advent can be compared to the majestic mountaintop called Ama Dablam, (pictured above) located in the Himalayan range of eastern Nepal, and rising to 22,239 feet. The term 'ama dablam' means 'mother's necklace', as symbolized by the long lower arms of the mountain, which appear to be reaching out or protecting a child. 'Ama' means mother and 'dablam' means necklace. The hanging glacier on the upper peak has traditionally been viewed as a double pendant on the neck of the mountain. In an abstract way, this mountain might personify the first advent of Jesus, the teacher who came in humble fashion to share God's love and convey God's grace to a world that was desperately searching for meaning and hope. His arms reach out to us as a mother hen for her chicks.

412

The second mountain, Everest, (above) the highest mountain peak in the world, symbolizes the majesty and strength of King Jesus as He returns someday to exhibit His power and glory upon planet earth as the King of all Kings and the Lord of all Lords. The first time He came as a lamb, the second time He will come back as a lion. The first time He came in grace, the next time He will return to earth to snatch the Church and Israel away from the jaws of sin and death, and He will pour judgment upon the nations that rejected Him and sought to destroy His people. Everest, standing tall at 29,029 feet, is an ominous mountain, full of danger and power that often consumes the best of men as they seek to conquer the elements and share the glory that is singularly Everest. In much the same way, King Jesus towers above the nations, demanding fear and respect like an ominous mountain, and always testing each man who claims to go after God's glory. In Daniel 9:25, Jesus was likened to a stone that became a great mountain and filled the earth. This mountain demands that you humbly acknowledge its power, and recognize that, like God, it is no respecter of persons. This mountain rises above all others, reminding us all that the sovereignty of God bows before no foreign power. Just as raw nature cannot be harnessed, we are reminded that someday Jesus will return, with eyes of flaming fire and a voice like the sound of many waters. Philippians 2:9 says every knee will someday bow before Him. We must remember that our gospel teaches us to <u>learn</u> from His ministry of grace, but also to <u>look forward</u> to His majesty as El Shaddai, the Rock of all the Ages, the Almighty God.

THE SILENCE IN HEAVEN 'BOOKMARK'

The GRAY Days of Global Birth Pangs. A New World Leader Deals with War and Famine.
The seven year period known as "The Seventieth Week of Daniel" begins with a 3.5 year period of global unrest. Heaven introduces a scroll with seven seals. A global leader (seal one) rises into world power to create a 3 nation confederacy. He then unifies the powers of government and religion, with a faithful prophet at his side. Seals 2 and 3 are peeled off, and the world is thrust into unprecedented war and famine. Israel is threatened and the Global Leader brokers peace with their enemies, luring Israel into a false hope. The global leader will perform miracles, signs and wonders as he mesmerizes the world community into accepting him as the long awaited Messiah.

The Raging RED Days of Tribulation. Anti-Christ and 666 Control the World.
At the beginning of the second 3 and a half year period, the global leader exposes his true nature as the man of lawlessness, better known as the Anti-Christ. The fourth seal, death, is on the mind of every human being. God sends Moses and Elijah to preach redemption to the Jews, but the lawless one requires every person to swear allegiance by taking "the mark of the beast." The consequences of resisting this mark will deny families the normal activity of shopping and employment. Those who try to defend the faith and defy his leadership will face the ultimate persecution - the fifth seal - being martyred and beheaded for their faith in Christ.

The Brilliant LIGHT of the Second Coming: Jesus Gathers the Elect, Raptures the Church.
As the sixth seal is peeled from the scroll, darkness begins to enshroud the earth. The stars fall from the sky and the moon turns red like blood. Suddenly, the sky splits open and light brighter than a nuclear blast bursts through the atmospheric envelope. An angelic voice cries out and a trumpet blast opens the graves, causing the followers of Jesus to rise from the earth. Every eye is upon Jesus the Messiah, and the wicked kings of the earth run in fear, hiding from the presence of Jesus, whom they mocked during their days of arrogance and power upon the earth. In a moment, in the twinkling of an eye, Jesus has raptured the Church, and taken them to be with Him in glory.

The BLACKNESS of God's Wrath Begins. The World is Plunged into Absolute Chaos.
Immediately before Jesus raptures the Church, the Holy Spirit places a protective seal over the 144,000 of God's noblest young men. There is sudden silence in the halls of heaven for 30 long minutes. Then comes the first of six trumpet blasts that announce God's wrath on His loving planet. One third of the earth's vegetation are burned up, then one third of the sea and its creatures are destroyed. Then one third of the sun, moon and stars are struck

down. Then locusts will torment men for 5 long months, before the sixth trumpet, which allows the demon hosts to destroy one third of the defiant population. On the final day of the seven year period, the Two Witnesses are martyred in the streets of Jerusalem, and Satan gloats at the presumed short victory. But the next 75 days will signal the nearing end for the Accuser.

The **BLUE** Sky of Israel's Atonement.   The Nation Finally Receives Salvation.

Christ descends to earth with one foot on land and one foot on sea. He appears to the 144,000 as they march from the desert to collect the remnant of Jews who have endured the Tribulation and the Trumpet judgments. One third of the nation of Israel now looks upon the Messiah as the crucified Christ, and they experience immediate salvation. Jesus ascends with the 144,000 to the top of Mt. Zion as the seventh trumpet sounds, announcing the coronation of the King.   The two witnesses are resurrected, the temple in heaven is opened and the arc of the covenant is revealed. The Mount of Olives splits and the Jews are placed in hiding in the mysterious Azel, while the bowl judgments begin. The cosmic battle of the ages, Armageddon, ends with the Anti-Christ and False Prophet being thrown into the lake of fire.   The remnant Jews, along with submissive Gentiles, will spend the next 45 days preparing the Middle East for Israel's future.

The **GREEN** Rebirth of the Millennial Age. Israel Now Enjoys its Destined Glory.

Earth has just been destroyed by God's wrath. The angel seizes Satan and casts him into a pit of darkness for a thousand years. God then miraculously restores part of planet earth, rebuilding the temple into a common place of worship for all the nations. Three remnants of mankind remain: the Jews, the Gentiles who did not take the mark, and those who were beheaded for their faith in Christ. Jesus now begins His rule over the earth, with David as prince over the land of Israel. The nations will serve Israel, and the earth will flourish once again.   Satan is released from the pit long enough to tempt man into rebellion once more before being cast into the lake of fire. Sin and death are destroyed. The Church and Israel are finally united as God's children.

The **ROYALTY** of KING Jesus is Sovereign Over Heaven and Earth and New Jerusalem.

Sin and death were finally destroyed at the end of the Millennium. God now restores the earth to its original pristine paradise. The holy city Jerusalem comes down from heaven, revealing walls and foundations constructed from the most precious jewels and minerals the world has ever known. Outside the gates of Jerusalem is the lake of fire, a silent memorial to Satan's doom. The Jews will likely inhabit the Golden City, while the Church, the Gentile nations, will likely live in the garden paradise of the restored Eden. Gardening and music may become our new occupations. The nations will enter the city to celebrate the ancient Feasts. And ultimately, God's Church and His Chosen People, will shake the planet with praise and worship as they bow down to King Jesus.

415

BIBLIOGRAPHY

Alcorn, Randy; *Heaven;* Wheaton, Il; Tyndale House Publishers; 2004

Anderson, Sir Robert Anderson. *The Coming Prince.* Grand Rapids, MI; Kregel Pub. 1957

Bussard, Dave; *Who Will Be Left Behind, and When?;* Milesburg, PA; Strong Tower Pub.; 2002

Cooper, Charles. *God's Elect and the Great Tribulation.* Bellefonte, PA: Strong Tower. 2008.

Eddleman, Leo; *The Second Coming*; Nashville, TN; Baptist Press; 1963

Froese, Arno; *Preparing for the Mark of the Beast; Olive Press Publiisher;*

Gariel, Mark A.; *The Unfinished Battle: Islam and the Jews;* Lake Mary, Fl. Front Line; 2003

Gundry, Robert H. *The Church and the Tribulation.* Grand Rapids: Zondervan. 1973.

Hagee, John; *Four Blood Moons; Worthy Publishing, 2013.*

Hindson, Ed; *The Book of Revelation, Unlocking the End Times;* AMG Publishers, 2002.

Hindson, Ed; *The New World Order;* Wheaton, Il; Victor Books; 1991

Hitchcock, Mark; *Breaking the Apocalypse Code; Word for Today Publiishing; 2007*

Hitchcock, Mark; *Blood Moons Rising*; Carol Stream, Il; Tyndale Press; 2014

Jeffrey, Grant; *The New Temple and the Second Coming;*

Jeffrey, Grant; *Countdown to the Apocalypse;* Colorado Springs, Co; Waterbrook Press; 2008

Jeremiah, David; *Agents of the Apocalpyse; Tyndale House Publishers; 2014*

Jeremiah, David; *Escape the Coming Night;* Wheaton, Il; Tyndale House Publishers; 1971

Kahn, Jonathan; *The Harbinger*; Frontline Publishing; 2103

Kath, Jonathan; *The Mystery of Shemitah; Frontline Publishing; 2014.*

Kerschner, Alan; *AntiChrist Before the Day of the Lord. Eschatos Publishing; 2013*

Ladd, George Eldon. *The Last Things.* Grand Rapids: Eerdmans Publishing, 1978.

LaHaye, Tim; *Rapture Under Attack*; Sisters, OR; Multnomah Press; 1998

LaHaye, Tim; *Charting the End Times*; Eugene, OR; Harvest House Publishers; 2013

LaHaye, Tim; *A Quick Look at the Rapture and the Second Coming*; Eugene, OR; Harvest House; 2013

Mayhue, Richard; *Snatched Before the Storm*; The Woodlands, TX; Kress Publications; 2001

MacArthur, John; *The MacArthur Commentary on Revelation 1-11;* Chicago, Moody; 1999

MacArthur, John; *The MacArthur Commentary on Revelation 12-22;* Chicago, Moody, 1999.

MacArthur, John; *Because the Time is Near;* Moody Press; 2007;

Nigro, H.L. *Before God's Wrath*. Bellefonte, PA: Strong Tower. 2004.

Pentecost, Dwight; *Things to Come; Zondervan; 1965*

Renner, Rick; *A Light in the Darkness; Harrison House; 2010*

Richardson, Joel; *Mideast Beast;* Washington, D.C. WND Publications, 2012.

Rhodes, Ron; *The End Times in Chronological Order;* Eugene, OR; Harvest House Publishers; 2012

Rogers, Adrian; *Unlocking the End Times in Our Times; B and H Books; 2013*

Rosenthal, Marvin and Howard, Kevin. *The Feast of the Lord*. Nashville: Thomas Nelson. 1997.

Rosenthal, Marvin. *The Pre-Wrath Rapture of the Church.* Thomas Nelson, 1990;

Salerno Jr., Donald A.; *Revelation Unsealed; Virtural Bookworm.com; 2014*

Shoebat, Whalid and Richardson, Joel. *God's War on Terror.* Top Executive Media. 2010.

Smith, Carol; *Bible Prophecy Handbook; Barbour; 2010*

Stone, Perry; *Unleashing the Beast. Charisma Media; 2012*

Thomas, Major W. Ian, *If I Perish, I Perish;* Grand Rapids, MI; Zondervan; 1967

Vanderlugt, Herbert; *Perhaps Today: The Rapture of the Church*; Grand Rapids, MI; 1984

Van Impe, Jack. *2001: On The Edge of Eternity*. Dallas: Word Publishing. 1996

Van Kampen, Robert; *The Sign*. Wheaton: Crossway Books. 1992.

Van Kampen, Robert; *The Rapture Question Answered;* Grand Rapids, MI; Fleming H. Revell; 1997

Vine, Jerry; *I Shall Return;* Wheaton, Il; Victor Books; 1977

Walvoord, John F. *The Revelation of Jesus Christ;* Wheaton, Il; Moody Press; 1966.

Walvoord, John F. *The Rapture Question*. Grand Rapids: Zondervan. 1979.

Walvoord, John F. *Major Bible Prophecies*. Grand Rapids: Zondervan. 1991.

Walvoord, John F. *Armageddon, Oil and the Middle East Crisis*. Grand Rapids: Zond. 1990.

TOPICAL INDEX

Pictorial Index

Pictorial Index

Scriptural Index

GIVE YOUR HEART A HOME

Don Francisco, songwriter
You'll love this song.
Go to Youtube, Signature Songs, Album Cover version.

I hear your hollow laughter, your sighs of secret pain
Pretending and inventing, just to hide your shame
Plastic smiles and faces, blinkin' back the tears
Empty friends and places, all magnify your fears

If you're tired and weary, weak and heavy laden
I can understand how it feels to be alone
I will take your burden, if you'll let Me love you,
Wrap My arms around you, Give your heart a home

It hurts to watch you struggle, and try so hard to win
But trade your precious birthright, for candy coated sin
Wasting precious moments, restless and confused
Building up defenses, for fear that you'll be used

If you're tired and weary, weak and heavy laden
I can understand how it feels to be alone
I will take your burden, if you'll let Me love you,
Wrap My arms around you, Give your heart a home

Take My yoke upon you, and walk here by My side
Let Me heal your heartaches, dry the tears you've cried
Never will I leave you, never turn away
Keep you through the darkness, lead you through the day

If you're tired and weary, weak and heavy laden
I can understand how it feels to be alone
I will take your burden, if you'll let Me love you,
Wrap My arms around you, Give your heart a home

Thank You

for reading this book.

If you have questions,

or would like to schedule

a conference . . .

gordon@silenceinheaven.org

770-682-8855